IN THE FOOTSTEPS OF VINCENT DE PAUL

VINCENTIAN STUDIES INSTITUTE PUBLICATIONS

# In the Footsteps of Vincent de Paul

## A GUIDE TO VINCENTIAN FRANCE

### BY JOHN E. RYBOLT, C.M.

DePaul University Vincentian Studies Institute

CHICAGO, ILLINOIS

2007

*Edited by* Nathaniel Michaud, Publications Editor, Vincentian Studies Institute
*Designed and produced by* the DePaul Publications Group, DePaul University, Chicago
*Frontispiece:* Engraving of a statue of Saint Vincent de Paul in the Church of Saint Sulpice, Paris.
Vincentian Studies Collection, VSI-271.7702 V768 YL. 1880, page 191

Maps appear courtesy of Michelin Travel Publications, all rights reserved.

DePaul University
Vincentian Studies Institute
2233 North Kenmore Avenue
Chicago, Illinois 60614-3594
773/325-7348

Printed in the United States of America

## 1. PARIS

## 2. ILE-DE-FRANCE

## 3. NORTH

## 4. WEST, CENTER

## 5. SOUTH

## 6. EAST

I AM DELIGHTED TO PRESENT TO YOU this new work written by Fr. John Rybolt. It provides detailed, interesting information about the many places with which Vincent de Paul was associated, as well as about the major sites in the life of Louise de Marillac. The inclusion of illustrations and maps makes it all the more helpful for those who will use this book as a real "Guide to Vincentian France."

The book will be of interest both to those traveling in France and also to those who are unable to wander through the cities and countryside of Vincent and Louise's native land, since it offers valuable historical information related to each of the "Vincentian places" that it describes and that so many of us have read about.

I congratulate the author on the preparation of this guide. It is the latest of many rich contributions that he has made to the study of our Vincentian heritage. I am certain that it will serve not only to inform readers already interested in Vincent de Paul, but will also attract newcomers to the story of this extraordinary man. As the preacher at Vincent's funeral stated, he "just about changed the face of the Church." Beginning in 1617 he organized groups of lay men and women to serve the poor through "Confraternities of Charity." In 1625 he founded the Congregation of the Mission "to preach the gospel to the poor," initially in rural France and eventually throughout the world. He and the members of his Congregation quickly became involved in the reform of the clergy in France, establishing seminaries and giving retreats all over the country. In 1633, with Louise de Marillac, who did so much in organizing service to the poor of her time, he co-founded a new, even revolutionary, type of community, the Daughters of Charity.

Some may be surprised to discover the vast territory that Vincent covered on foot or horseback in the first half of the 17th century. A mere glance at the map of France, on which the localities he visited are highlighted, makes one marvel at his extraordinary energy and zeal. While Louise traveled less, she visited many more places than did most people of her time. And where she herself did not go, she sent her Daughters in the service of the most abandoned.

I encourage those who use this book on pilgrimage to study each location before visiting it, to review the description again on the spot, and then to allow the presence of Vincent or Louise to sink in while picturing all they did in response to the needs of their era.

Finally, I want to express my deepest gratitude to Fr. Rybolt for all that he has done in the service of the Vincentian Family and especially in promoting a love and knowledge of St. Vincent and St. Louise. As the reader of this book will quickly recognize, we all owe him deep appreciation for his careful scholarship and for his commitment to communicating our Vincentian heritage to others.

Robert P. Maloney, C.M.
Former Superior General of the
Congregation of the Mission and
Company of the Daughters of Charity
November 23, 2006

# In the Footsteps of Vincent de Paul

## A GUIDE TO VINCENTIAN FRANCE

THIS WORK IS INTENDED TO GUIDE VISITORS on pilgrimage to the France of Vincent de Paul, Louise de Marillac and the members of their religious families. It arose out of an increasing interest shown by Vincentians, Daughters of Charity and their many coworkers in the places of importance to Vincent de Paul and Louise de Marillac. Although much has been written about some sites, such as Paris and Versailles, other have simply disappeared from view, such as Notre Dame de la Rose. When traveling around France with groups of clerical and lay Vincentians, it became clear to me that a comprehensive guide to Vincentian France, understood in a broad sense, would be of service to others. Before beginning, however, I had to determine what constitutes a Vincentian site. I developed several criteria. First, I have set out to describe all the places where Vincent de Paul lived, worked and visited, from his birth at Pouy near Dax to his death in Paris. Second, I included the religious houses that he founded, even though he may never have visited them. Third, I have included other places that he visited in passing, and about which we know something specific about his presence there. Lastly, I have tried to include those places in which he took an interest, such as Moulins and Bourbon, although he did not found any works there.

Louise de Marillac, a saint in her own right, deserves the same coverage. Consequently, I have included the places where she lived, visited and worked, and the houses and works of the Daughters of Charity that she founded, whether she visited these or not. Since Louise traveled widely, perhaps more than Vincent did at certain periods, I have sought to retrace her steps, at least where there are incidents that were important in her life or in the subsequent life of the Sisters.

I have added some brief historical, cultural and artistic references to help to appreciate these places better, particularly where the Daughters of Charity or the Vincentians, the members of the Congregation of the Mission, carried on their ministries after the death of the two founders. However, I have not described all the houses of the two communities founded in France until the Revolution (such as Auxerre and Bourges), but only those connected with previous history leading back in some way to Vincent and Louise.

I have also given attention to the lives and deaths of the Vincentians or Daughters of Charity martyred during the French Revolution, as well as to Catherine Labouré, Frédéric Ozanam and other significant members of the Double Family of Vincent de Paul and Louise de Marillac in the nineteenth century. Further, I have included references where possible to the founders of other congregations or works associated in some way with the two founders, such as Francis de Sales and Jane Frances de Chantal and other friends and acquaintances in the seventeenth century, and Jeanne Antide Thouret in the nineteenth.

The many works outside the borders of modern France have not been included here, namely the missions founded by members of both communities in Europe and elsewhere. Also, I have included only those works of the Daughters of Charity and the Vincentians in France in the twentieth century that continue previous commitments, such as Arras and Marseilles. Lastly, some other less known places are mentioned in passing, particularly since they lie close, geographically, to more important sites, and could be visited on the same trip with only a small effort.

Vincent originally intended that his band of mission preachers go only to the countryside to evangelize the religiously abandoned there. However, even though he forbade his confreres to give missions in larger cities, they generally lived in the cities. The reason was that, as they became involved in seminary teaching, they had to live where the seminaries were, normally in the cities. This dichotomy between country and city has been an abiding feature of Vincentian life. A glance at the cities where Vincentian houses were founded in the lifetime of Vincent de Paul, such as in Troyes, Annecy, Marseilles, Cahors, Sedan, Le Mans, Périgueux and Montauban, to name only some, will prove the point. Only a few houses (La Rose, Richelieu, Crécy, Montmirail, Saint-Méen), were in smaller towns. The Daughters of Charity, by contrast, had no such restrictions, and lists of their earliest foundations show that they were spread widely in both towns and cities in France, almost exclusively in the northern half of the country. Nevertheless, many Sisters lived in small temporary communities of two or three in country towns and ministered to the poor there, or at least left town to minister to the sick poor in the country.

I have spent many weeks in the last nine years visiting each of the major sites mentioned here. These visits have been preceded or followed by a review of archival and printed materials describing them. Further, local people have helped in the search for obscure sites, once important for the Sisters or for the Priests and Brothers of the Mission. Their charity and welcome of a foreigner has made the task much easier and rewarding. My travels were much easier than those of the sisters, priests and brothers of past centuries. They often traveled with friends or had someone to accompany them in private vehicles. If not, they took public transport by land or water. If they survived the dangerous roads or waterways (by sea, rivers or canals), they might lodge with friends or in religious houses. If not, they found that public inns offered only minimal services. In some cities, permission was needed before they could seek lodging, and once installed, guests often found their rooms noisy and crowded. The situation was the same for both men and women travelers unlucky enough to have to look for public accommodations. Both Louise de Marillac and Vincent de Paul took such occasions to evangelize those they met and urged this practice on others. But Vincent also remarked occasionally that the innkeeper's drunken friends partying below disturbed his sleep. For someone as sensitive to noise as Vincent was, this must have been particularly painful.

Vincent and Louise often wrote about travel by public coach lines linking major cities. They had a further interest in that their missions were supported in some measure by income from these same coaches. An attentive reading of their correspondence will uncover many remarks about travel, such as fatigue, motion sickness, delays and accidents.

It is hoped that those who use this guide will come to appreciate more the breadth of vision of the two founders seen against their geographical and historical background. A traveler could read the book at home or bring it along to serve as a reference while traveling almost anywhere in France, since the country is so full of Vincentian reminiscences.

* * * * *

To facilitate an appreciation of the rich fabric of Vincentian France, I offer the following somewhat technical observations. First, the sources for the lives of Vincent de Paul and Louise de Marillac are principally their own letters. The two main collections are those of *Saint Vincent de Paul. Correspondance, entretiens, documents*, ed. Pierre Coste (Paris, 1920-1925), 14 vols.; *Sainte Louise de Marillac, Écrits Spirituels*, ed. Élisabeth Charpy, (Paris, 1983), and *La Compagnie des Filles de la Charité aux origines. Documents.*, ed. Élisabeth Charpy (Paris, 1989). These excellent sources, both available in English and other languages, in turn made use of the original biographies of the two saints, Louis Abelly, *Vie du vénérable serviteur de Dieu, Vincent de Paul*, (Paris, 1664) and Nicolas Gobillon, *La vie de Mademoiselle Le Gras* (Paris, 1675). Many subsequent biographers, especially in the case of Vincent de Paul, have enlarged and filled out the pictures, and they are rich in geographical details. Such references as there are to any of these works are given here to their English editions. Where an English version does not yet exist, the reference is to the French version.

For Pierre Coste, these are to the volume followed by the page number and include the number of the letter in the English edition.

There are also problems in locating various works. The earliest of Vincent's charitable works, one animated as well by Louise, was the Confraternities of Charity. It has not proven possible to uncover all the sites where a confraternity existed in their lifetimes. Nevertheless, I have mentioned some of the more significant ones, particularly the earliest.

Frustrating research into the history of the early Daughters of Charity is the lack of an accurate and comprehensive list of their establishments. The best one was drawn up in the mid-nineteenth century by Gabriel Perboyre, C.M., a cousin of the martyr. He sought to list all of their foundations until 1792. Gobillon, the first biographer of Louise de Marillac, provided no list. Pierre Collet's revision of Gobillon (Paris, 1769) did include a list of the houses open in his time, but he admitted that it was difficult to be sure about the dates when certain houses began in Paris. Indeed, many houses of the Daughters were temporary since their service was sometimes destined for those in greatest short-term need, such as war refugees, wounded soldiers, or the victims of famine and plague. From another perspective, since the Daughters of Charity were so numerous in France, less so before the Revolution, it might be easier to list where they were not than where they were. Together with their Vincentian brothers and other congregations, they were suppressed in France by the Revolution (18 August 1792), and were dispersed a second time at the beginning of the twentieth century. Lastly, despite the printed and manuscript sources, it has not been possible to determine exactly the length of service of the Daughters at many missions. Those of the Vincentian are, by contrast, better documented.

Besides formal houses, each with a specific contract that Vincent de Paul or his representative, and a local bishop signed, the Congregation of the Mission had many other properties that it was responsible for in a variety of ways. For example, Vincent de Paul inherited numerous farms when he took possession of the priory of Saint Lazare, and he later purchased and managed many others. The Congregation of the Mission continued this practice of purchase or trading properties. The Vincentians also received some country properties as gifts or legacies. Because of the fluid nature of these property holdings, only the most prominent ones have been included here, such as Orsigny and Frenneville. Locations not mentioned here were, for example, Courcelles, a small place, now part of Levallois-Perret, near Clichy; Marly, where Saint Lazare had property; and Le Bourget, where Saint Lazare had property dating back to the twelfth century. The income from these properties went to support the work of the Mission. Since the houses where the Daughters of Charity worked did not generally belong to them, the Sisters were not as involved in the management of extensive properties—a situation that must be understood from the context of France of the Ancien Régime.

Despite the mention of properties (including farms, priories, chapels, bridges, mills and the like, all income producing), it may appear from reading the text that this guide concentrates excessively on church buildings. This observation is justified since these churches or their successor buildings still exist, whereas many others, such as seminaries, hospitals and convents, do not. The ravages of wars and revolutions, in particular, are to blame for much of this.

One issue that is relatively unknown outside of France is what has sometimes been styled the "second act" of the Revolution. This was the mass expulsion of congregations of men and women religious (including Vincentians and Daughters of Charity) from France around the year 1900. Anticlerical governments succeeded in freeing schools (including seminaries), hospitals and other institutions from any control by religious congregations. The result was that, in the case of the Vincentians, they were expelled from their eight French provinces, and forty-one of their houses in France closed. The Daughters suffered a similar diminishment, but both congregations found ways to continue their works in other countries. Only after the first World War was the situation redressed somewhat.

For the purpose of consistency, the metric system has been used here, although it is occasionally impossible to give accurate calculations of the meaning of the *arpent*, a measure of area. This is even truer for modern values of money from past ages.

Also for the purpose of consistency, and to give a certain French flavor to the text, place names and personal names are generally given in their French form, unless an English form is better known (Francis, instead of François, de Sales, for example).

Where significant individuals appear in the text, I have endeavored to give inclusive dates of birth and death the first time they appear. Otherwise, they can be identified from the Index.

To facilitate travel and visits to the various sites, each one has been identified first by its region (which I have further assembled into four different chapters), and then by the name of its *département* (similar to a county or other small jurisdiction). For locations outside of Paris, street names and addresses have been occasionally given to help locate a site. Following a well-known system, I have given values to several sites. Those with three stars (***) are of exceptional importance, not to be missed. Two stars (**) designate important sites, for those with more time for visits. One star (*) sites are worth a detour in a given area.

I wish to acknowledge the quiet and unstinting help and advice given me by Father Paul Henzmann, C.M., archivist of the Maison-Mère. He has helped me in countless ways to avoid the pitfalls that confront a foreigner in France, and to uncover the abundant resources of our Vincentian history. The late Raymond Chalumeau, C.M., was an inspiration because of his brief guide to Vincentian Paris. Thomas Davitt, C.M., a tireless traveler and able researcher, was probably the first Vincentian to retrace many of the journeys to forgotten Vincentian sites. Thanks are also due to many readers and reviewers, particularly Ignatius Melito, C.M., and to my translators, whose practiced eyes caught errors that would have otherwise passed unnoticed. The Vincentians of the ongoing formation program at C.I.F. (International Formation Center) received various early versions of this work. I hope they will overlook the many errors and omissions of earlier efforts and recognize their own contributions here.

Besides archival and library resources, I have also been greatly helped by the Blue Guide to religious sites (*Guide Religieux de la France "Bibliothèque des Guides Bleus."* Paris: Hachette, 1967).

John E. Rybolt, C.M.

# 1

# Paris

# Paris

*The city of Paris with its surrounding villages was the center of Vincent de Paul's life from about 1610 to his death in 1660, and of nearly the entire life of Louise de Marillac. Since the history of their involvement with the city is so complex, the material on Paris has been divided into three major sections, reflecting the three major parts of the city: the Left Bank, the Islands, and the Right Bank. Within each section, the materials are divided by arrondissements, the present-day urban arrangement of Paris districts. The numbering of the arrondissements begins at the center of the city, on the island, Ile de la Cité, and generally spirals outward in a clockwise direction. The city is further divided into smaller traditional neighborhoods, mentioned here only in passing. Many major sites, most of which are still standing, also include references to minor ones near them or to important persons associated with the area. These sites are numbered for convenience in locating them. At the end of this section are some notes on suburban locations. We begin with the Vincentian motherhouse, where the remains of Saint Vincent are exposed above the high altar.*

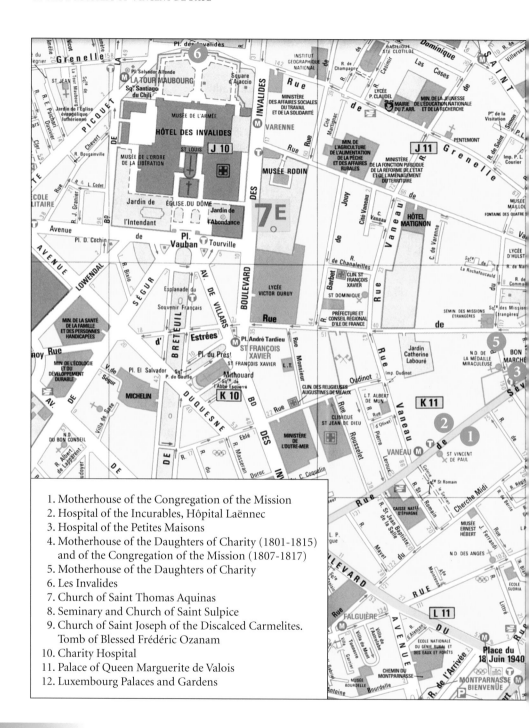

1. Motherhouse of the Congregation of the Mission
2. Hospital of the Incurables, Hôpital Laënnec
3. Hospital of the Petites Maisons
4. Motherhouse of the Daughters of Charity (1801-1815)
   and of the Congregation of the Mission (1807-1817)
5. Motherhouse of the Daughters of Charity
6. Les Invalides
7. Church of Saint Thomas Aquinas
8. Seminary and Church of Saint Sulpice
9. Church of Saint Joseph of the Discalced Carmelites.
   Tomb of Blessed Frédéric Ozanam
10. Charity Hospital
11. Palace of Queen Marguerite de Valois
12. Luxembourg Palaces and Gardens

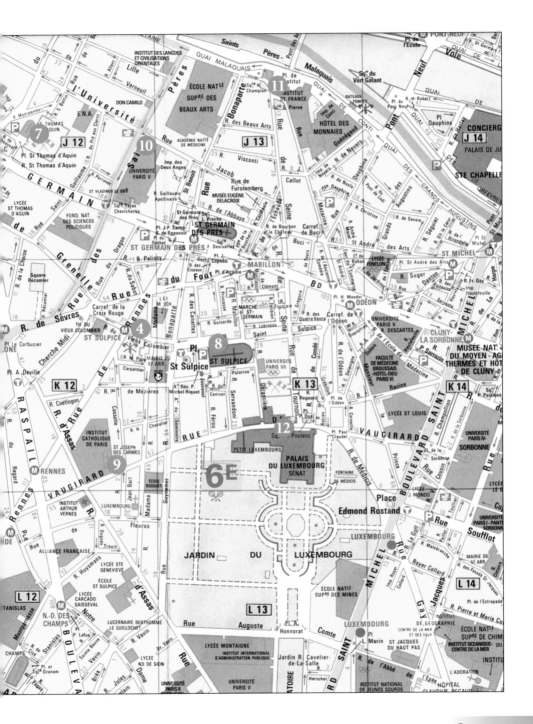

# *Left Bank*

## ARRONDISSEMENTS 6, 7

Motherhouse of the Congregation
of the Mission

### *1. Motherhouse of the Congregation of the Mission (New Saint Lazare)*** (95, rue de Sèvres, Paris 6)

Saint Vincent de Paul, so far as is known, was never on the property of the present motherhouse of the Congregation of the Mission. He may have noticed the grounds, inasmuch as he worked in the area, but the oldest buildings date from 1685-1686. This present large house has sometimes been called the new Saint Lazare. It replaced the old Saint Lazare, ruined by the infamous sack that took place during the night and early morning of 13 July 1789, the eve of the taking of the Bastille. During this disaster, the superior general, Jean Félix Cayla de la Garde (1734-1800), fled for his life by climbing over the garden wall. He later hid out in France and then took refuge in the Palatinate (a region in modern Germany), and later in Rome, where he died. The revolutionary government then abolished all religious congregations in France, declared their vows null and seized their properties.

A decree from Napoleon, dated 24 May 1804, reestablished the Congregation of the Mission. Dominique Hanon (1757-1816), the French vicar general from 1807 to his death, had much to suffer, since Napoleon suppressed the Congregation anew on 26 September 1809. Further, Hanon was jailed in Paris, then under house arrest and finally imprisoned in Italy from May 1811 until 13 April 1814. The Congregation, reestablished 3 February 1816, had to wait until the election of Charles Verbert (1752-1819) as vicar general to get a house from the government of Louis XVIII. To compensate for the loss of the original Saint Lazare, the Vincentians took possession of the former Hôtel (or city residence) of the duke of Lorges. The state had acquired this house for the Congregation's use from the hospital

Chapel of the Motherhouse

across the street, which gained it at the Revolution. The Vincentians became lodgers (the government owns the property, the Congregation has use of it), and the house opened officially on 9 November 1817. At the time, the house, 95, rue de Sèvres, included: (1) a three-story main house, with courtyard and garden; (2) a two-story section looking out on Rue de Sèvres, joined to the main house by two side buildings, one story each, used as stables, storehouse, and hay barn; (3) a one-story wing situated where the present refectory is located. The community moved into cramped quarters as best it could. Jean Baptiste Étienne (1801-1874), a seminarian at the time, recalled: "It was the stable of Bethlehem."

On 17 August 1826, the vicar general, Charles Boujard (1752-1831), laid the cornerstone of the chapel. Previously, there had been only a tiny and unsuitable oratory. To build the chapel, the Congregation acquired adjoining property, 5 July 1826. Next the left wing of the old Hôtel de Lorges and half of the adjoining house were demolished to make way for the chapel. Then, during the generalate of Pierre de Wailly (1827-1828), construction on the chapel continued, and the archbishop of Paris, Hyacinthe de Quélen, blessed it on 1 November 1827. Little by little, the

Reliquary of Saint Vincent de Paul, chapel of the Motherhouse

community acquired adjoining properties: in 1835, numbers 92, 94, and 96, rue
de Cherche Midi, located at the rear of
the present property; and in 1875, number 90. By a strange coincidence, Jean-
Léon Le Prévost (1803-1874), founder of
the Religious of Saint Vincent de Paul,
lived at number 98.

Above the chapel were built the
rooms in Corridor Saint Mathieu and
the dormitory for the novitiate. Father
Étienne , then superior general, undertook the construction of the present
refectory, the prayer hall, a large number
of rooms in Corridor Saint Marc, and an
oratory for the novices. Always careful
about the beauty of the chapel, he had a
new main altar built, with two staircases
leading up to the casket of Saint Vincent.
Then, in 1857, because of the needs of
the ever-increasing community, he
bought the property at 97, rue de Sèvres,
and built another wing on that land.
Next, in 1864, he constructed the right-
hand wing of the main entry courtyard,
and side aisles for the chapel now grown
too small. At that same time, the façade
of the central building was rebuilt, and a
bell tower added, to announce the
Congregation to its neighbors. The last
section bought was 93, rue de Sèvres,
built by the zealous superior general as
lodgings for retreatants and Vincentians
passing through. In forty years, this new
Saint Lazare had become again a "place
of resurrection," as Saint Vincent
described the original Saint Lazare to his
confreres. (Conference 9)

During the celebration of Father
Étienne's jubilee, Eugène Vicart, his first
assistant general for many years, could

say with no little triumphalism: *We love
to look on you as our second founder, and
if this title is ever questioned, if one day
the Company forgets what it owes you,
may the stones themselves cry out and
accuse us of ingratitude.*

The house contains many souvenirs of Vincent de Paul. The most
noteworthy, of course, is the silver casket
containing his remains, and placed over
the main altar in a solemn ceremony in
1830. His body is not incorrupt.
Although the skeleton has been hidden
or transferred several times because of
wars, revolutions, and religious celebra-
tions (the latest in 1960), it has been preserved. Wax covers the face and hands.
The crucifix in his hands is the one he
used when assisting Louis XIII on his
deathbed. This precious souvenir passed
down through the royal family that gave
it to the archdiocese of Paris. At the time
of the translation of the relics in 1830,
the then archbishop of Paris and his
canons gave it to the Congregation to be
used as it is today.

Other items of great importance
are the tombs of Saint John Gabriel
Perboyre (1802-1840), canonized in
1996; Saint Francis Regis Clet (1748-
1820), like Perboyre a martyr in China,
canonized in 2000; and Jean Baptiste
Étienne, superior general from 1843
to 1874. The extraordinary cult of
personality surrounding him led his
confreres to move his body from the
Montparnasse cemetery to a tomb in the
center of the chapel, surrounded by the
remains of the founder and two martyrs,
as well as by his confreres at prayer. The
remains of the two martyrs were trans-

ferred for safekeeping to the Vincentian house in Liège, Belgium, from 1907 to 1919, avoiding complications arising from the anti-clerical laws then in force in France and the first World War.

A major side chapel is dedicated to the Passion of Jesus. Built in the time of Father Étienne, it commemorates two similar devotions: the "Scapular of the Passion of Our Lord and of the Sacred Hearts of Jesus and Mary" (the Red Scapular), and the Archconfraternity of the Holy Agony of Our Lord. The first developed through the experiences of Sister Apolline (Louise Alice) Andriveau (1833-1895), a Daughter of Charity. The second was popularized through the devotion of a Vincentian, Antoine Nicolle (1817-1890). Shrines to honor the suffering of Jesus in the Garden of Olives characterize many older Vincentian churches.

The tribune of the chapel, reached from inside the building, features some side altars and confessionals, but the main items of interest are the eight large canvases painted by Brother François Carbonnier (1787-1873). He was a trained artist at the time of his entry into the Congregation in 1839, having studied at the studio of the painter Ingres. His paintings hang in several other places in the building. The small organ, built by the renowned Cavaillé-Coll, was completed in 1864 and is a registered historical object. Power used to be supplied by manual pumping, but the instrument is now electrified.

The Salle des Reliques (Musée Vincentien) displays many items used by Vincent de Paul, Louise de Marillac

(1591-1660), and the saints and some of the blesseds and other members of the Congregation of the Mission and the Daughters of Charity. Most noteworthy is a miniature painting of Vincent, one of the few authentic likenesses of him painted during his life. Another original, or perhaps an early copy, is found in the sacristy of the main chapel. This is believed to have been in the possession of Anne of Austria, Queen of France (1601-1666) who gave it to the Vincentians, who then brought it to the Invalides (1675), where it remained until after the Revolution. A former chaplain restored it to the Congregation in 1809. Today, it is the first in a series of portraits of the superiors general that Brother Carbonnier and others have painted.

**1.a.** The long narrow building at the rear of the property began as the *Seminary of Saint Vincent de Paul* in 1899, an annex of the Institut Catholique for young priests. Its first superior was the remarkable *Fernand Portal* (1855-1926). He had entered the Vincentians in Paris, hoping to go to China as a missionary. During his studies, his health deteriorated, so after his ordination in 1880, his career turned to seminary teaching. He met Charles Lindley Wood, Lord Halifax (1839-1934), an Anglican, on the island of Madeira where Portal had gone for his health, and Halifax accompanied his daughter, also seeking recovery. The two worked to increase contact and understanding between Anglicans and Roman Catholics, and pursued the historical issues separating them. He made this

9

seminary a center for contacts among Catholics, Anglicans and Protestants. He was silenced by Rome in 1908 and left his post. His interests continued and he and Halifax planned ecumenical dialogues on a more official level. With Rome's permission, Cardinal Mercier of Malines, Belgium, sponsored these "Malines Conversations" from 1921 to 1925. Both Portal and the cardinal died in 1926, and such conversations were put on hold until the era of Vatican II. The seminary buildings are divided between provincial offices and a hotel. *(88, rue du Cherche Midi, Paris 6)*

**1.b.** The motherhouse falls within the boundaries of the parish of *Saint François Xavier.*
This diocesan parish recognizes the work of Vincent de Paul through a modern window featuring Vincentians, Daughters of Charity, poor children and a galley. *(12, place du Président Mithouard, Paris 7)*

## 2. Hospital of the Incurables (Hôpital Laënnec)*
### (42, rue de Sèvres, Paris 7)

Across the street from the motherhouse is the Hospital of the Incurables, to use its original name. Cardinal François de La Rochefoucauld (1558-1645) endowed it in 1633 to care for incurables—a name that included those suffering from syphilis, tuberculosis and epilepsy. Its chapel was dedicated in 1640. Vincent had considered sending Daughters of Charity here but never carried out this plan. Jean-Pierre Camus

(1583-1652), bishop of Belley (1609-1629), spent his retirement years here in the exercise of charity. He had been close to Francis de Sales, who had ordained him a bishop. He was also loosely related to Louise de Marillac and was her spiritual director before she met Vincent de Paul and he went to live in his diocese, 1623. He was buried in the cemetery but in 1855 his coffin was removed to the center of the chapel transept. His tombstone recounts that, among other things, "he lived the life of a poor man but was rich toward the poor. He wanted to live, die and be buried among the poor." His coat-of-arms was deliberately effaced at some point.

Daughters of Charity came here in 1690 and served until the Revolution. A future saint, *Jeanne Antide Thouret*

Chapel entry,
Hospital of the Incurables

Tombstone, Bishop Camus,
Hospital of the Incurables

(1765-1826, canonized 1934) entered the Daughters of Charity in 1787 and was sent here in 1791 to serve the sick poor. Along with 44 other sisters, she was sent away and returned in 1793 to her family home. She later founded a community, now the Sisters of Charity Under the Protection of Saint Vincent de Paul.

After the Revolution, the hospital stood empty for some time before being set aside exclusively for women. The Daughters of Charity resumed their work here in 1810. They also cared for Dominique Hanon and Charles Verbert, consecutive vicars general of the Congregation, who had come here in their last months. The sisters also helped their Vincentian confreres become estab-

lished across the street when they moved in to the dilapidated Hôtel de Lorges in 1817. Some elderly Vincentians lived here until 1823 since their house was still unfit.

In the nineteenth century, another future saint came here to discern a possible vocation. *Micaela Desmaisières*, viscountess of Jorbalán (1809-1865, canonized 1934), had been influenced by the Ladies of Charity in Paris. She joined them, the first Spanish woman to do so, and was influenced by the charity of Sister Rosalie Rendu. Attracted to the Daughters of Charity by the accounts of the Miraculous Medal, she became a postulant here in 1848, but her family and her director dissuaded her from continuing, so she returned to Madrid, her home. There, with the religious name of María Micaela del Santísimo Sacramento, she founded the Sisters Adorers of the Blessed Sacrament and of Charity.

In 1878 the hospital was named to honor Doctor René Laënnec (1781-1826), the inventor of the stethoscope. He lived nearby. The hospital continued to use some buildings from Vincent's time. The spire on the chapel is one of only two in Paris to survive the Revolution. The Incurables was a general hospital until 1999.

**2.a.** The sisters also served in the nearby *Necker Hospital* from its opening in 1778 through the Revolution and even afterwards. *(149, rue de Sèvres, Paris 15)*

### 3. Hospital of the Petites Maisons (or: Petites Ménages)
### (21, rue de Sèvres, Paris 7)

This hospital, dating from perhaps the twelfth century, was founded to care for lepers. After 1557 it received the mentally afflicted and the impoverished, especially children with skin diseases. It consisted of cottages for the patients and could shelter 400 patients of both sexes. In addition, it had two prisons. This institution fell under the responsibility of the Office of the Poor, which worked in individual sections of the city. The hospital was located on the site of Square Boucicaut, north of the Bon Marché, claimed to be the oldest (1852) example of a modern department store. Even before the foundation of the Congregation, Vincent went to this hospital to preach one or more missions, and he continued to take an interest in it during his life (in 1643, for example). He sent members of the Tuesday Conferences to visit the elderly here. He also sent Daughters of Charity to work here beginning in 1655, where they remained until the Revolution. During the revolutionary period, some Daughters were able to remain to care for the poor, although the sisters had to lay aside their habit to do so. They returned after the Revolution and remained until the hospital closed.

It has been suggested that the shop in this hospital, which sold goods made by the patients cheaply (*à bon marché* in French), was an ancestor of today's large department store. More likely, the name comes from another shop on the site with the same name. When the building east of their motherhouse burned down in November 1915, the Daughters of Charity could have bought the property to build a basilica in honor of the Miraculous Medal. They turned down the offer, and the present annex to the Bon Marché was built in 1924.

One of the last chaplains of the hospital before the Revolution was *Jean Dubois* (1764-1842), a Sulpician. He left France for America and, after various missionary journeys, became the superior of the Sisters of Charity founded by Saint Elizabeth Ann Seton. His previous service of the Daughters of Charity in Paris undoubtedly influenced his approach to Mother Seton's Daughters in America. With the foundress, he translated and adopted Saint Vincent's rule for the new American community.

Of the ancient hospital, whose main entry was on Rue de Sèvres, and its cemeteries (located under the department store), nothing remains. They were demolished in 1868.

3.a. Just a few doors east along rue de Sèvres was another small convent that continues to exercise a large influence on the Daughters of Charity. The *Sisters of the Annunciation* of the Ten Virtues (*Annonciades des Dix Vertus*) were founded by Saint Jeanne de France (1464-1505). They came here in 1638 and remained until 1654 when they moved to a quieter area in the northern suburbs of Paris. On one of his visits in the district around Saint Sulpice Vincent must have visited here. He said to the Daughters of Charity: *I noticed that their*

*Mother Superior was called* Ancelle. *The word* ancelle, *my dear sisters, comes from the Latin word* ancilla, *which means 'handmaid,' and that is what the Blessed Virgin called herself. . . . This led me to think, my dear sisters, that, in future, instead of calling the Sister in charge by the title of 'Superior,' we should use the expression 'Sister Servant.'* (Conference 11, 1642) Nothing is left of the old building, demolished in 1907. *(16, rue de Sèvres, Paris 6)*

Motherhouse of the Daughters of Charity, rue du Vieux Colombier

### 4. Motherhouse of the Daughters of Charity (1801-1815), and of the Congregation of the Mission (1807-1817)*
### (11, rue du Vieux Colombier, Paris 6)

This motherhouse of the Daughters in the parish of Saint Sulpice succeeded a parish orphanage for girls,

*(de la Mère de Dieu)*, begun in 1680. The former motherhouse of the Daughters of Charity, located across the street from Saint Lazare, was confiscated at the time of the Revolution and soon became uninhabitable. From 1793 to 1797, "Citizeness" Marie Antoinette Deleau (1728-1804), the mother general, lived in her native town, Bray-sur-Somme, but kept in contact with as many sisters as possible. From 1797 to 1801 she assembled a few postulants and other sisters in a small lodging on a narrow street near the Sorbonne. In 1797, she was able to buy back the coffin and remains of Louise de Marillac, which she then hid for a few weeks in the basement of a house not far from the pre-Revolutionary motherhouse. After an official ecclesiastical recognition of the remains, she had them brought to her temporary quarters. *(15, rue des Maçons Sorbonne, now Rue Champollion, Paris 6)* When in 1800 Napoleon allowed her to prepare candidates to serve in hospitals, she began to reassemble sisters here and to admit postulants. Later, in 1801, the state recompensed the Daughters of Charity for the loss of their traditional house by assigning them this establishment on Rue du Vieux Colombier.

The building has been a firehouse since 1823. Inside is an old courtyard (visible from a side street) next to which is the former chapel.

In a small house on the same property, but with an entrance at the back *(Rue Pape Carpentier)*, the first two Vincentian vicars-general (Fathers Brunet and Placiard) were able to live informally from about 1804. Since this building was soon taken for use as a primary school, Dominique Hanon, at the time the vicar general of the Congregation in France had to move close by. *(5, rue de Vaugirard)* He was arrested suddenly on 29 October 1809 following Napoleon's decree suppressing the Congregation for the second time. Hanon regained his liberty only in 1814. After his release, he returned to this provisional motherhouse until his last years.

Former chapel, Motherhouse of the Daughters of Charity, rue du Vieux Colombier

## Important dates in its history

*1801:* The statue of Our Lady of the Mission, hidden with a family near the old motherhouse, is brought here and erected in the garden.

*1802:* The body of Louise de Marillac is transferred here, 4 March. Rosalie Rendu enters, 25 May.

*1804:* Pope Pius VII comes to the chapel for Benediction, 23 December, accompanied by archbishops, prelates and princes, after visiting the church of Saint Sulpice.

*1805:* The sisters are permitted to resume wearing the habit. The color was black, since blue was not available. To mark this occasion, Cardinal Fesch, Napoleon's uncle, celebrates mass here, attended by Napoleon's mother.

*1806:* François Brunet (1731-1806), vicar general of the Congregation (there was no superi-

or general at the time), retires here. He entrusts the body of Vincent de Paul to the sisters, 18 July.

*1807:* The French government assigns this house to the Congregation of the Mission as its motherhouse. (Napoleon suppressed the congregation for a second time, however, 26 September 1809, and it was reestablished only 3 February 1816.)

*1813:* The decree giving the sisters their present house on the Rue du Bac is signed; construction begins on a chapel and main building.

*1815:* On 25 March, Napoleon signs the act officially granting the sisters the Hôtel de Châtillon, their present motherhouse. The chapel is finished and the sisters move in on 29 June, bringing with them Our Lady of the Missions and the remains of Vincent and Louise.

### 5. *Motherhouse of the Daughters of Charity*\*\*\*
### (140, rue du Bac, Paris 7)

The present motherhouse is located at 140 (formerly 132), rue du Bac. This street was laid out in 1563 and took its name from the ferry *(bac)* that brought stones quarried in the village of Vaugirard on the left bank to be moved across the river to build the Tuileries Palace, now destroyed.

When the temporary motherhouse on Rue du Vieux Colombier became too cramped for the Daughters of Charity and had been given to the Congregation of the Mission, the state chose the former Hôtel de la Vallière (later called Hôtel de Châtillon) to replace it. The earliest buildings (now the refectory and offices above) had been built after 1681 by the marquis of Lassay on property formerly belonging to the Hospital of

Staircase, Motherhouse of the Daughters of Charity, rue du Vieux Colombier

the Incurables. The duke of La Vallière acquired the property in 1766 and moved its main entrance from Rue de Sèvres to Rue du Bac. His daughter, the duchess of Châtillon, inherited it, but the state seized it at the Revolution. Since 1815, it has become the nucleus of a large institution. The chapel was blessed on 6 August 1816. The remains of Louise de Marillac had been transferred on 29 June 1815 and were placed in the floor of the new chapel in 1824. The novice sister, Catherine Labouré (1806-1876), had visionary experiences here (1830). As a result, the chapel was enlarged (1849, 1930), and it has become the center of devotion to Our Lady of the Miraculous Medal. Other buildings were added in the nineteenth century. Another sister, Justine Bisqueyburu (1817-1903), experienced visions during her novitiate here. These eventually led to the devotion of the Green Scapular honoring the Immaculate Heart of Mary. She had these visions in front of the altar where the medieval statue, Our Lady of the Missions, was placed.

In the main chapel are kept the bodies of Louise de Marillac and Catherine Labouré, as well as the heart of Vincent de Paul enclosed in a reliquary above the right side altar. The previous reliquary, made at the initiative of the duchess of Aiguillon, one of his most important benefactors, has been removed because of its fragile state. The body of Saint Vincent was kept in this chapel from 1815 until its solemn transfer ("Translation"), via the cathedral, to the Vincentian motherhouse, 25 April 1830. His body, however, was secretly returned to the motherhouse of the Daughters and kept hidden in a cellar during the 1830 revolution and the Franco-Prussian war of 1870. It was next placed discretely under the protection of the American embassy, which declared it the property of an American Daughter of Charity. She kept it from April to July 1871, but then restored it again to its rightful place. His body last traveled in 1960, visiting Notre Dame cathedral once more to mark the tercentenary of his death.

There are several special features of this chapel:

(1) The *fresco* over the main altar, recalling the first vision of Catherine Labouré, 18-19 July 1830; below is the text: "Come to the foot of this altar where graces will be showered on all."

(2) The statue, *Virgo Potens*, coming from the visions of 27 September. The Blessed Virgin holds a globe surmounted by a small cross. Inside the globe are kept the names of the provinces of the Company. Below lies the body of *Saint Catherine Labouré* clothed in the habit used by the Daughters of Charity until 1964. Her remains were brought here in 1933. Besides various other bones, her hands have been removed, replaced by wax models. Her face, also in wax, depicts her as a mature woman.

(3) The *main altar*, with another large statue of Mary based on the Edme Bouchardon statue predating the medal. It was used as the model for the medal, on the orders of the archbishop of Paris. Above is the text: "O Mary, conceived without sin, pray for us who have recourse to you." The tabernacle, brought from the house on Vieux Colombier, was here in Catherine Labouré's time.

(4) The body of *Saint Louise de Marillac* exposed in a glass casket over a side altar. Below the body is a mosaic demonstrating her devotion to the Holy Spirit and the Passion of Christ. The text in gold letters is her spiritual testament to the Daughters of Charity: "Take good care of the service of the poor. Above all, live together in great union and cordiality, loving one another in imitation of the union and life of Our Lord. Pray earnestly to the Blessed Virgin, that she may be your only Mother." Her body is not incorrupt; her face and hands are modeled in wax to give a lifelike appearance. A stone inscription in the center aisle marks where her body had been interred until 1920, its last transfer. Nearby is a *plaque* commemorating the visit of Pope John Paul II, 31 May 1980, after a renovation of the chapel.

(5) The *heart of Saint Vincent de Paul* is kept in a large reliquary above the side altar to the right of the chapel. Behind it is a large white marble statue of the saint. Surrounding it are two angels in mosaics bearing copies of the seals of the two communities, the Daughters of Charity and the Congregation of the Mission. Above is a famous Vincentian text: *Let us love God, but*

*at the expense of our arms and the sweat of our brows.* To each side are other texts relating to the lives of the Sisters. In front of the altar is kept the famous director's armchair, upholstered in dark blue velvet. It is here that Catherine reported seeing the Blessed Virgin seated and conversing with her.

(6) On both sides of the sanctuary are circular stone *medallions* recalling the martyrdom of Daughters of Charity at Cambrai and Angers during the French Revolution.

(7) *Paintings* from the chapel in Catherine's time now hang in the tribunes and organ loft. A painting of the Holy Family attributed to Louise de Marillac also hangs in one of the tribunes. It appears to be the original of an engraving used by Vincent in his *Common Rules.*

Within the large property are other buildings that served at one point in the nineteenth century as the seminary (novitiate, built 1843-1845) for more than 600 sisters at a time. The record was 686 novices for 1856. The superioress general and her council live here. Part of the property has been given to the city of Paris for a park, entered from Rue de Babylone. It is named in honor of Catherine Labouré. The original property reached further south to the present Rue Vaneau.

In 1879, it became known that the Daughters of Charity were not the property owners but had received the grounds from the State. In the anti-reli-

gious spirit of the time, some wanted to expel them. The case dragged on until the end of the century, when the sisters were finally left in peaceful possession of the property.

5.a. Behind the house is a former Daughter of Charity house opened in 1816, the Maison de la Providence, now used by others. Adjacent at number 1 was the sisters' chapel built in 1842 by *Alphonse Marie Ratisbonne* (1814-1884), to commemorate his conversion to Roman Catholicism, due in part to the Miraculous Medal. He had a large painting made of the Virgin, which is now found on the stairway of the sacristy of the motherhouse of the Daughters of Charity. To make room for an expanded school, this chapel has now been demolished, although the two faces of the Miraculous Medal appear over the two main doors of the Sisters' house. *(3, rue Oudinot, Paris 7)*

5.b. The *Rue de Babylone* recalls an event in Vincent's life. The Carmelite Bernard of Sainte Thérèse (Jean Duval, d. 1669) had been named titular bishop of Babylon in 1638, with residence in modern Iran. He returned shortly to France in hopes of securing another diocese or an abbey. His missionary diocese was offered to the Congregation of the Mission, but Vincent was unable to accept it. Vincent's refusal caused some problems with the bishop and accusations at the Holy See. The bishop founded the seminary for Foreign Missions (Missions Etrangères) in 1663, still standing. The present chapel began in

1683 and was completed in 1691. One of its organists was the composer Charles Gounod. Nationalized and sold at the Revolution, it became a parish chapel whose place was taken in 1874 by the church of Saint François Xavier, "of the Foreign Missions," to use its formal title. (128, rue du Bac, Paris 7)

5.c. Down the Rue du Bac stood the third *Visitation Convent*. Although this foundation dated only from 1675, Vincent de Paul authorized its foundation in 1659 elsewhere in the city at a temporary location, which has now disappeared. (35-37, rue des Petits Carreaux, formerly rue Montorgueil, Paris 2) This was the first daughter-house of the second Visitation convent, but Vincent agreed to it only with great reluctance. It was perhaps the bowling alleys in the house, which the sisters were to make into living quarters, that put him off. The Impasse de la Visitation, at Rue de Saint Simon, recalls the presence of the nuns. (68-76, rue du Bac, Paris 7)

## 6. The Invalides*
### (Place des Invalides, Paris 7)

Although the work of the Vincentians at the Invalides does not date from the time of Vincent de Paul, their ministry at this prominent military hospital should not be overlooked.

Louis XIV founded this hospital for sick and wounded soldiers in 1670. The soldiers' church, dedicated to Saint Louis, was and is part of it. Adjoining it is a second church, called the Dome, built for royal visits. Later it was set aside for the tomb of Napoleon Bonaparte, as well as for others.

Vincentians were chaplains at the Invalides, from the beginning, at the king's express order. They remained, therefore, from 1671 to 1791. In 1676, the Daughters of Charity, likewise, received responsibility for the physical care of the patients and for the pharmacy. The work of the chaplains was more like seminary formation than modern hospital ministry, in that it followed set hours for mass, prayers, catechism lessons and devotions, such as a general confession. They regarded it as a kind of permanent mission. The priests and brothers lived on four floors in a section of the buildings divided off from the officers and patients. Their residence was located to the west of the soldiers' chapel, between the present Nîmes and Toulon courtyards, in a section now closed to the public. Some of the museum galleries illustrate weapons, armor and military paraphernalia dating from the seventeenth century. Following the anticlerical legislation at the beginning of the century, the Daughters were forced to leave definitively in 1904. A painting of Saint Vincent watching over the work of the sisters with the old soldiers was given to the Daughters at that time, and it now hangs in the Vincentian motherhouse.

## 7. Church of Saint Thomas Aquinas
### (Place Saint Thomas d'Aquin, Paris 7)

The nearby parish church of *Saint Thomas Aquinas* replaces an earlier chapel of Saint Dominic, founded here in 1631. The present church, dating from 1682, became a parish in 1791 according to the decision of the National Assembly. Restored to Catholic worship in 1803, it received a visit of the peripatetic Pius VII on 26 December 1804. The right transept displays a signed plaster statue of Vincent de Paul made in 1817 by Jean Baptiste Stouf (1742-1826), above a side altar (erected in 1851) decorated with symbols and the names of four of his great works: the priests of the Mission, Daughters of Charity, foundlings and hospitals. Two paintings recall his work with the orphans and for the poor; each has an unusual biblical citation: "Of the fatherless you are the helper" (Ps 9:28 = 10:14), and "He gathered together those who were perishing" (1 Macc 3:9). The statue copies another placed at the former Saint Lazare in 1787. This original was smashed during the events of 13 July

Fountain, Place Saint Sulpice

1789. The saint is further represented in the decoration surrounding the dome, in company with Francis de Sales, Thomas Aquinas and Dominic.

**7.a.** The present Rue de Gribeauval, entering the square in front of the church, bore the name *Rue Saint Vincent de Paul* from 1790 to 1847. This name probably attests to the saint's residence in this district (as chaplain for Queen Marguerite), as well as to his surprising popularity during the revolutionary period.

### 8. Seminary and Church of Saint Sulpice*
### (Place Saint Sulpice, Paris 6)

Relationships between Vincent de Paul and Jean Jacques Olier (1608-1657), the pastor of the parish from 1642, were cordial. Parisian-born Olier, who prepared for his ordination in 1633 at Saint Lazare, had, among other things, given missions with the Lazarists. So deep was their friendship that Vincent assisted Olier on his deathbed (1657) and presided at the election of the founder's successor. Olier built a *seminary* here, completed in 1651 and destined to become one of the major establishments of the French Church. He was interred in its chapel. The seminary continued until the Revolution and was demolished from 1802 to 1808. Its only visible remains are a colonnade, the Allée du Séminaire, located on the corner of Rue Bonaparte and Rue de Vaugirard.

Like the Vincentians, the Sulpicians returned after the Revolution and built another seminary next to the same property. They moved in during 1826 and remained here until 1906 when forced to leave by anti-clerical laws. Their building then became state property and remains so today, housing some offices of the ministry of finance, the Hôtel des Finances. Among others, Saint Jean Baptiste de la Salle (1651-1719), founder

Church of Saint Sulpice

of the Brothers of the Christian Schools, attended this seminary. Later, at the invitation of the Sulpicians, he founded three schools in this parish. A side chapel in the church recalls his memory.

The square in front of the large church, the *Place Saint Sulpice*, is where

the original seminary stood. Construction of the square dragged on from 1757 to 1838. In the middle is a large fountain. Built in 1844, it features four celebrated preachers: Bishops Bossuet, Fénelon, Fléchier and Massillon. They are placed seated in niches, and above their heads are their episcopal coats of arms. (Some jokingly

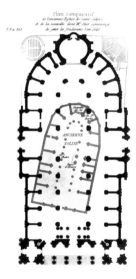

Historical plans of
Church of Saint Sulpice

call it the "Fountain of the Four Non-Cardinal Directions," since none of these famous bishops ever became a cardinal. Its official name is the Fountain of the Sacred Orators.)

The current *church*, dedicated to the holy bishop of Bourges (d. 621), replaced an earlier church begun in 1211, the one in which Vincent de Paul often preached. Lower walls of that earlier church can be seen in the crypt of the present church. Also visible there is the well, which at the time served the people of the neighborhood. In February 1646, Anne of Austria laid the cornerstone of

Church of Saint Sulpice,
17th century engraving

the present church, an edifice more than four times the size of its predecessor. Construction continued until interrupted in 1678. Work resumed in 1718 and finished in 1736. The classical façade designed by Servandoni—the right tower is still unfinished—differs from the Gothic interior. Saint Sulpice is one of the largest churches in Paris. Its main pipe organ is world famous, and its elaborate woodwork dates from 1781. There is also, in a side chapel, a small organ built for the father of Louis XVI. Queen Marie Antoinette (1755-1793) played it at the Trianon palace at Versailles. During the revolutionary period, a grateful nation gave a banquet here for 750 guests to honor Generals Napoleon and Moreau (6 November 1799). The church underwent several transformations in this period, lastly the Temple of Victory of the Theophilanthropists (1797-1801), but it was restored to Catholic worship in 1802. John Gabriel

Perboyre was ordained deacon here in May 1825, and the funeral of Frédéric Ozanam was celebrated here 24 September 1853.

In the chapel dedicated to Saint Vincent, on the left side of the nave, are some monuments to his presence and work in the parish, as well as that of Saint Louise. The first foundation of the Ladies of Charity in Paris took place in this parish. Vincent had founded this organization of lay women to work for the poor in local parishes, and gradually the Daughters of Charity took a leading role in this work, also in this parish, arriving first in 1641. Although expelled at the Revolution, the Daughters stayed in the parish in rented quarters and nine years later returned to the parish school.

Statue of Saint Vincent de Paul,
Church of Saint Sulpice

For many years the duchess of Aiguillon, who lived in the parish, was the president of its Confraternity of Charity. There are two large frescoes of the saint, painted by Alexandre-Charles Guillemot (1786-1831) in 1825, among the earliest in the church. The painting on the left depicts Saint Vincent speaking to the Ladies of Charity of the Hôtel Dieu about the foundlings; that on the right shows the saint assisting Louis XIII in his last moments. An unusual feature is Vincent's elaborate Parisian-style surplice, with the long flowing appendages on each shoulder. The ceiling, also by Guillemot, shows Vincent entering heaven, accompanied by angels. At the four corners of the ceiling painting are other paintings of the saint: rejecting the offer of a bribe to present to the king a friend's proposal, singing the psalms during his captivity, distributing food to the poor and offering aid to convicts. These paintings are in need of restoration. The seated statue of Vincent (1857) is the work of Emilien Cabuchet (1819-1902), a marble copy of a bronze original in Châtillon-les-Dombes.

An elaborate astronomical clock graces the left transept. Finished in 1744, it marks the passage of the sun throughout the year by a small opening high on the right apse window. Sunlight streams in at different angles along a meridian line, traced in bronze on the floor, depending on the time of year. At its north end is a curious obelisk (the "gnomon") of white marble. Another plaque nearby recalls the visit to the church of Pius VII, present for the coronation of Napoleon, three weeks previously. He

celebrated mass here 23 December 1804, the first of his parish visits in Paris, where he lived from 28 November 1804 until 4 April 1805. (He returned to Saint Sulpice 2 February 1805, to consecrate a bishop.) Like the Vincentians, the Sulpicians lost some members in the infamous September massacres of 1792. A plaque in a side chapel lists them and celebrates their beatification. By a strange coincidence, a meeting held to plan the massacres had been held in the church.

"Jacob wrestling with the angel,"
Delacroix (detail), Church of Saint Sulpice

In 1735, a life-size silver statue of the Virgin Mary was enshrined in the Mary chapel here. The work of the sculptor Edme Bouchardon (1698-1762), who designed the other large statues in the sanctuary, it became the model for subsequent representations of the Immaculate Conception. Copies and paintings of the statue were widely available in the years following. Its Vincentian importance is that it became the model for the Miraculous Medal, on orders of the archbishop of Paris. The revolutionaries, of course, melted down the original, made from silverware collected from the parishioners. This statue depicted a buxom young woman, whose arms extend downward, with her hands open. The connection of this statue, if any, with the emblem of the Congregation of the Mission, which has the same gestures, is an open question, but the similarities are striking. The parish has a nineteenth-century copy, also in silver, but the place of the original has been taken by another work in white marble.

The chapel of the Holy Angels features paintings by Eugène Delacroix (1798-1863), who worked here from 1853 to 1861. These frescoes are regarded as among his finest works, and the political message of the triumph of good over evil is striking.

**8.a.** The *Sulpician motherhouse* contains several important souvenirs of Vincent de Paul and Jean Jacques Olier, founder of the Society of Saint Sulpice. The Sulpicians came here in 1906 when forced to leave their previous home near the church of Saint Sulpice. In a meeting room is one of the original canvases painted for Vincent's canonization, depicting him presiding at the Tuesday Conferences. The artist was Jean François de Troy (1679-1742), who painted four others in this series.

"Descent of the Holy Spirit," Le Brun, Sulpician motherhouse chapel

Unfortunately, the canvas has been cut down, perhaps during the Revolution to remove the group of bishops sitting at Vincent's side. This had the effect of placing Olier instead of Vincent in the center of the painting, surrounded by other priests of the time. An engraving of the original painting placed at the side shows its original features. The chapel contains the painting of the "Descent of the Holy Spirit," emphasizing the Virgin Mary at Pentecost, a work of Charles Le Brun, 1655. Vincent might have seen this painting, since it (or an artist's copy) had been placed in the seminary chapel. (*6, rue du Regard, Paris 6*)

**8.b.** The first meeting of the "Conference

of Charity," the immediate predecessor of the *Society of Saint Vincent de Paul*, took place near Saint Sulpice. A wall plaque has been placed on the first floor of what were the offices of a Catholic newspaper, *La Tribune Catholique*. It reads: "Here, on 23 April 1833, Emmanuel Bailly, Frédéric Ozanam and his five student friends founded the Society of Saint Vincent de Paul." It was Ozanam's twentieth birthday. *(38, rue Saint Sulpice, formerly 18, rue du Petit Bourbon, Paris 6)*

**8.c.** While Francis de Sales was in Paris, 1618-1619, he was the guest of Louis XIII, who lodged him in one of his residences, the *Hôtel du Maréchal d'Ancre*, in the parish of Saint Sulpice. As with so many other properties, this one has a long history. After the Revolution, it was the seat of the archdiocese of Paris for a time. In 1819, it became a military barracks, a role it still fulfills. Since Vincent de Paul had to visit the famous bishop of Geneva concerning the Sisters of the Visitation, it is quite probable that he came here on various occasions. *(10, rue de Tournon, Paris 6)*

### 9. Church of Saint Joseph of the Discalced Carmelites (Carmes), Tomb of Blessed Frédéric Ozanam** (70, rue de Vaugirard, Paris 6)

Discalced Carmelite priests came from Italy in 1611 and, following the renewal of life begun by Saint Teresa of Avila, began to build on Rue de Vaugirard. The church was built during Vincent's life; he several times men-

tioned Carmelites in his letters. This was the first Parisian church in the new Italian Baroque style, and some of its original decoration has been preserved, particularly in the side chapels.

On 11 August 1792, the revolutionary government turned the monastery into a prison for the priests and bishops who refused to take the constitutional oath. The notorious massacres of clergy erupted on 2, 3, 4 September 1792, and three bishops and 115 priests perished at

---

### The September Massacres

*The September Massacres marked a violent turning point in the Revolution. Fearful of domestic enemies, the crowds turned their fury on prisoners, mainly clergy, during three days in September 1792. The principal events took place on the dates and at the places as follows:*

*2 September - Prisons of Rue de Vaugirard, the Carmelite convent, the abbey of Saint Germain des Prés, the Châtelet, the Conciergerie*

*3 September - Prisons of La Force, the Bernardin convent, and Saint Firmin (the former Bons-Enfants)*

*4 September - Hospitals of la Salpêtrière and Bicêtre*
*In imitation of their Parisian leaders, other revolutionaries massacred prisoners elsewhere in France shortly after that date, notably in Versailles.*

---

Church of Discalced Carmelites,
17th century engraving

Tomb of Frederick Ozanam,
Church of Discalced Carmelites

the Carmelites. On the same occasion, Vincentian confreres were murdered at the Saint Firmin seminary (the former Bons-Enfants). The remains of some of those martyred here have been preserved in the crypt of the church, alongside those of the Carmelites.

Since 1876, the Carmelite church and monastery grounds have served as the site of the Catholic Institute, a private Catholic university. The prominent Dominican preacher Henri Lacordaire (1802-1861) lived here from 1849 to 1853. He was a friend and admirer of Blessed *Frédéric Ozanam* (1813-1853), whose tomb is in the crypt of the church. Ozanam had lived close by with a former Vincentian seminarian, Emmanuel Joseph Bailly (1794-1861) at the "Pension Bailly," still standing, *(7, rue Cassette, Paris 6)*. After his wedding, Ozanam had two consecutive homes in Paris. The first *(31-33, rue Fleurus, Paris 6)* is now demolished; the second *(7, rue Garancière, Paris 6)* remains, directly behind the church of Saint Sulpice. Ozanam, however, died in Marseilles,

after returning from a trip to Italy to recover his health. The members of the Society of Saint Vincent de Paul often come to visit his grave. A fine fresco of the Good Samaritan adorns the small chapel, completed in 1953, the centenary of Ozanam's death. The crypt also contains relics and memorials to the many clergy murdered during the September massacres. It is said that Ozanam was buried here at the request of students who wished him in their midst. His wife, in fact, had wanted him interred in a church, but such an honor was not granted to laity. She secured permission for his remains to lie in the crypt. In 1913 a new tomb was designed, and it was opened again in 1929 for the process of his beatification. Since the crypt chapel was located within the men's cloister, neither Ozanam's wife nor daughter could visit it.

**9.a.** A few blocks away, next to the church of *Notre Dame des Champs* (Our Lady in the Fields) is the Square Frédéric Ozanam, a public park. Besides his university duties, Ozanam also taught at the Collège Stanislas, near the church. The park, named in 1933, perpetuates his memory. A marble plaque with his name, dates, and a bronze portrait medallion of him is attached to the church walls facing the park.

### 10. Charity Hospital
### (39-45, rue des Saints-Pères, and rue Jacob, Paris 6)

The modern Faculty of Medicine stands on the spot where the Charity Hospital for men (more properly the Hospital of Saint John the Baptist) opened here in 1608. Brought in 1602 by Marie de Médicis from her native Florence, four Brothers of Saint John of God directed it. Vincent de Paul came here to visit the sick poor, at least in 1611, and made a gift of money to the brothers to help finish the hospital. He came here as an almoner of Queen Marguerite, the first wife of Henri IV. A visit from Queen Anne of Austria (about 1640) demonstrates the interest taken in this institution by the rich and powerful, following in the tradition of the saintly Louis IX. Apart from a façade, now in an inner courtyard, nothing remains of the old building. It had been rebuilt in 1841 but was demolished in 1935-1937. At 49, rue des Saints-Pères, stood the chapel of Saint Peter, the chapel of the hospital, and Monsieur Vincent must have visited it. Its name, Saint Pierre, was corrupted to Saint Père and later to Saints Pères, the name of the main street in the area. At number 51 is now the Cathedral of Saint Vladimir the Great for Ukrainian Catholics, a church building constructed on the still-visible foundations of the original hospital chapel. South of it, where a park now stands, was the cemetery. It is often said that Vincent's awareness of the poor took on new urgency as he worked for them in this hospital. He was about 30 years old. After the Revolution, Daughters of Charity staffed the hospital and remained until it was put under secular management in 1900.

**10.a.** One street to the east is the location of the headquarters of the *Society of Saint Vincent de Paul*, carrying on his charitable works all around the world. It also contains several belongings of Blessed Frédéric Ozanam. *(5, rue du Pré aux Clercs, Paris 7)*

**10.b.** All this area stands on the site belonging formerly to the great abbey of *Saint Germain des Prés*, a rival to Saint Lazare and Saint Victor as a dominant ecclesiastical landowner in Vincent's day. Vincent did not speak of Saint Germain

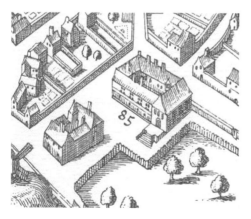

Charity Hospital, 17th century engraving

des Prés, but at least one letter to him, written by its commendatory abbot, has been preserved. This man, Henri de Bourbon Verneuil, an illegitimate son of Henri IV, became bishop of Metz at age twelve, and abbot of Saint Germain at age 23—all the while remaining a layman. He held these positions and received the income attached, until his marriage late in life. The abbey was also the scene of some of the frightful massacres of some 300 refractory priests in September 1792, the same time as those at the Carmelite convent and the seminary of Saint Firmin (Bons Enfants). The ancient abbey church has some claim to be the oldest church building in Paris. Today, however, it has been much restricted in size and setting and is far from its former glory. Another Vincentian connection is that Jan Casimir, former Jesuit and cardinal, then king of Poland from 1648 to 1668, and husband of Queen Louise Marie de Gonzague (d. 1667), became commendatory abbot here after his wife's death and his subsequent abdication. He died in Nevers in 1672 but is buried here. A large correspondence between Vincent de Paul and the queen exists. (*Place Saint Germain des Prés, Paris 6*)

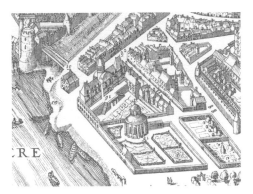

Palace of Queen Marguerite,
17th century engraving

## 11. *Palace of Queen Marguerite de Valois*
### (2-10, rue de Seine, Paris 6)

After the annulment in 1599 of her marriage to her Protestant cousin, Henri IV, Queen Marguerite (nicknamed Margot) bought property for a palace and immense gardens facing on the Rue de Seine. She sought to fulfill a dream she had of the ladder of the patriarch Jacob in the Old Testament, who had vowed to build an altar in praise of God. (Rue Jacob recalls this connection.) To accomplish this, in 1602 the queen secured monks to sing the praises of God day and night. She wanted them to sing, in fact, melodies she herself had prescribed. Unfortunately for the monks, the queen did not like the results and began looking elsewhere. Fourteen Augustinians (*Petits Augustins*) tried it beginning in 1607. The queen had a round chapel built (1608), the chapel of Praises (*Louanges*) in the middle of the garden for them, but they too failed to satisfy her. (*Entry, 14, rue Bonaparte, Paris 6*) She found other Augustinians, but the queen soon died and left her singers with many debts. Nevertheless, they remained until the Revolution. Born in 1553, Marguerite lived here from 1606 to her death in 1615. Her stepson and heir, Louis XIII, who had no great love for her, sold her palace and grounds to satisfy his debts. The palace was soon demolished and its gardens subdivided. The garden walks became various streets of the modern city (Rues de Lille, Verneuil, Bonaparte, Saints Pères, Beaune). The national college of fine arts occupies the site of the palace and monastery and preserves some of its buildings (the round chapel and a larger one to which it was attached). The façade of the old chapel, however, has been covered over by another, brought from a chateau in the nineteenth century.

**11.a.** Young Father De Paul became one of the queen's chaplains on 17 May 1610. He probably secured this position through the influence of his bishop, the bishop of Dax, who himself had been one of her many chaplains. Vincent had his *residence* across the street from the palace from 1610 to 7 December 1612. His lodging was probably across from the palace on the east side of the street, between the buildings of the Institut de France and the first houses on the Rue de Seine. He came here after the disastrous accusation of theft leveled against him by a relative, later to become the judge of Sore. This man, Bertrand Dulou, his contemporary in age, accused him of theft, a charge later proven false. During this period, too, Vincent underwent trials against his faith, not surprising considering the dissolute court to which he was attached, even peripherally. His length of service with the queen is unknown, but he probably remained until his appointment to Clichy in 1612. He never mentioned his service in his extant writings.

**11.b.** Near her palace on the river stands the ***Institut de France***. Cardinal Jules Mazarin (1602-1661) had it built as the Collège des Quatre Nations, that is, for students from Spain, Italy, Germany and Flanders, parts of whose territories had been added to France in his time. Since 1806 it has been used for meetings of the French Academy and other organizations. It also houses the Bibliothèque Mazarine, France's oldest public library. During the revolutionary period, this library received books and other items confiscated from religious houses (including Saint Lazare) and from persons guillotined, such as the king and queen. Cardinal Mazarin is buried in an elaborate marble tomb in the former chapel, and his name figures prominently on its façade. *(21-25, quai de Conti, Paris 6)*

## 12. Luxembourg Palaces and Gardens* (15, rue de Vaugirard, Paris 6)

The senate of the French Republic has been housed in the Luxembourg Palace since 1852. Beginning in 1615 the widowed queen Marie de Médicis, second wife of Henri IV and regent for her son, Louis XIII, had a palace built here for herself. She called it the Medici Palace, after her Florentine family, but the name of the previous owners, the Luxembourg family, has remained. An old fountain in the garden, in pure Italian Renaissance style, is a prominent reminder of her. It was built in 1620 and moved here and rebuilt in 1862-1863 from another section of the garden. The fountain depicts an ancient grotto peopled with figures in Greco-Roman style, representing the Seine and the Marne rivers, which meet just east of Paris. The painter Peter Paul Rubens decorated the apartments; these paintings, glorifying Marie, are now in the Louvre. During the Revolution, the palace became a prison, housing some of the most famous and influential revolutionaries, including Danton and the painter David.

**12.a.** Adjoining on the west is the *Petit Luxembourg,* now the residence of the president of the senate (at number 17). Marie de Médicis purchased it in 1612 for her residence, and in 1627 placed it at the disposition of Cardinal Richelieu (1585-1642), her son's principal minister. Her new palace adjoining it on the east was by then ready for her to live in. The cardinal left in 1631 and, in 1638, deeded it to his niece, Marie de Wignerod (1604-1675), marquise of Combalet (in 1638 she became officially the duchess of Aiguillon). Two years before, she had insisted that Monsieur Vincent send a Daughter of Charity to live with her here. He asked one, but she refused, saying that she could not serve a great lady when her vocation was to serve the poor. He asked another, "Big Barbe" Angiboust, who at first agreed because she supposed she would also be able to work for the poor of the parish. She quickly realized she did not belong in Madame's household and left shortly after. Vincent recounted this in Letter 224, and later recalled her good example in a conference on this sister's virtues. (Conference 109, 1659) The duchess inherited the Petit Luxembourg, and

Entry, Petit Luxembourg palace

Vincent de Paul came often to this residence, whether on legal matters (signing contracts for foundations, for example) or on the business of the Ladies of Charity, who met here while the duchess was their president (1652-1675).

**12.b.** Adjoining the Petit Luxembourg to the west, at number 19, is the important façade of the convent of the *Daughters of Calvary* (Dominicans). Above the door is an inscription mentioning Marie de Médicis, with the date 1625. Above that is a portrait bust of the queen. Likewise the two doors present her and her husband, Henri IV, carved in profile. The chapel behind these doors was rebuilt in 1842 on its old plans but was closed in 1905. The convent was destroyed in the mid-nineteenth century, except for the nuns' cloister, which was converted into a glass-covered winter garden.

**12.c.** Behind the Luxembourg Palace are the *Luxembourg Gardens*, begun in 1613. They covered about the same area as today and were much visited by the upper classes.

**12.d.** After the Revolution, the gardens expanded up to the Observatory, thanks to the seizure of the property of the *Carthusian* monks of Vauvert, situated directly south of the palace. These hermit monks arrived in 1257 to lodge in a former country residence of King Robert II, surnamed the Pious (996-1031); they left only in 1790. This is a classic French garden, with its symmetrical terraces, fountains, basins, flowerbeds and statues of historical and allegorical figures. They follow to some extent the lines given them by the Carthusians. Vincent often spoke of these religious, and it may be supposed that he visited this monastery. The monks offered Friday meals to as many poor as arrived to eat. Once he said to his confreres: *Someone said to me one day: Look at the Carthusians. They are like oxen. They all walk alike. When you see one, you have seen them all.* He did not disagree with this observation, calling them solid and firm. (Conference 206) Louis Abelly, (1604-1691), Vincent's first biographer, reported that Vincent also commonly said that genuine missionary confreres *should be like the Carthusians at home and like the Apostles elsewhere.* (Bk. I, ch. 22) Perhaps Vincent got this insight after visiting the hermits here. The Rue des Chartreux, a short street built on their old property, recalls their presence. *(64, boulevard Saint Michel, Paris 6)* One reason that brought Vincent here was to visit his friend, the abbé of Saint Cyran. He had rented quarters close to the monastery during the time of his troubles at the end of 1637. Today the faculty of Pharmacy occupies the site of the monastery, perhaps recalling medical services given by the monks.

**12.e.** North of the Luxembourg palace, on the Rue de l'École de Médecine and Rue Antoine Dubois, stood the *Franciscan convent*, founded about 1230. The large monastic refectory and some other small traces remain of the buildings, which included a school and church. Despite some early years spent with the Franciscans, Vincent de Paul had little to say about them in his letters or conferences. He seems to have attended the funeral services here (11 March 1654) of Antoine François Frassella de San Felice, archbishop of Myra, and administrator of the church in both Japan and China. Vincent had assisted him in various ways. This convent became the site of an influential political club during the Revolution, taking its name, *Cordeliers,* from the former Franciscan inhabitants, whose cords attracted popular attention. Under the leadership of Danton and Marat, the club met in their former chapel and planned, in all their rigor, various revolutionary schemes, including the constitution of 1793. Today, a section of the University of Paris, called Cordeliers, occupies the site. *(4-6, rue Antoine Dubois, Paris 5)*

**12.f.** An old church, *Saint André des Arts*, lives on in the Place Saint André des Arts, which stands on the site of the church, destroyed following the Revolution. *(Paris 6)* Francis de Sales (1567-1622) preached the Advent sermons there in 1618, the year he met Vincent. Later, charitable women of this parish requested sisters from Louise de Marillac and Vincent de Paul, but they were unable to accommodate them.

Near the church, on Rue de l'Épernon, which abuts Rue Saint André des Arts, lived **Madame Des Essarts**. As the representative of the queen of Poland in Paris, she received and sent letters between Vincent and his confreres in Poland. He often referred to her in his correspondence, and either he or one of his confreres often stopped there to get mail. Daughters of Charity worked in this parish from 1722 to 1794.

18. Saint Vincent de Paul Hospital
19. Saint Joseph Hospital

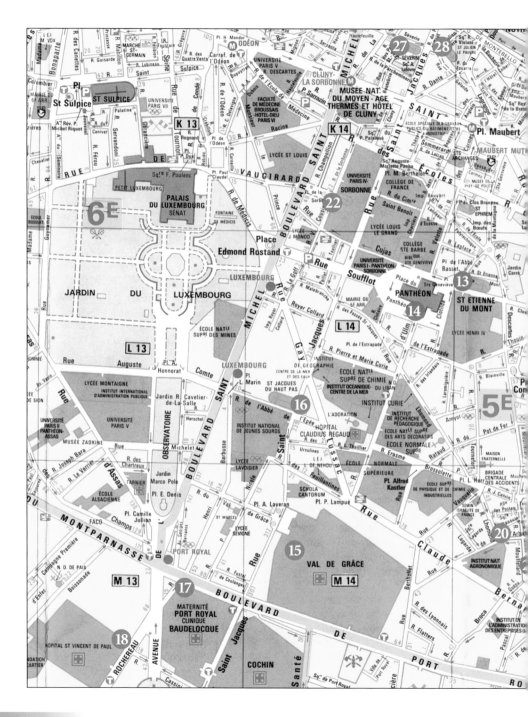

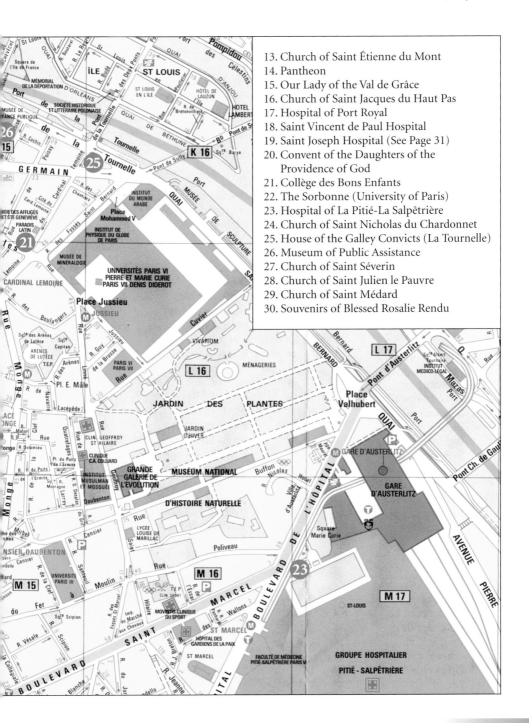

# ARRONDISSEMENTS 5, 13, 14

## 13. *Church of Saint Étienne du Mont*\*\* (Place Sainte Geneviève, Paris 5)

Many important events are gathered around Saint Geneviève, the patron saint of Paris. She was born about 420 in Nanterre, became a consecrated virgin and, at the death of her parents, lived on the hill that now bears her name. The people attributed the safety of the city to her prayers during a siege by Attila in 451. She died about 496. The abbey of Saint Geneviève, located on the Saint Geneviève Hill, kept alive her memory. This abbey, dating from the sixth century, was founded under King Clovis. He wished to be buried here with his queen and near Geneviève, who had been his friend and advisor. In later centuries, it

Churches of Saint Étienne du Mont and Sainte Geneviève, 17th century engraving

was an abbey not of monks but of canons regular. Although demolished at various times, some remaining parts have been incorporated into a school, the Lycée Henri IV. The most visible element is its imposing tower. The contents of its ancient library were transferred to the nearby Saint Geneviève Library.

The church of Saint Étienne du Mont was built for abbey servants and for others living nearby, but it was independent of the abbey. The current building and bell tower were begun in 1492 but were consecrated only in 1626 by Jean François de Gondi. The style is Flamboyant Gothic, richly decorated but already old fashioned when completed. It also includes many Renaissance elements, mainly its decoration. The hanging keystones are noteworthy. The beautiful façade is unique in Paris. The church was restored in 1862 after the madness of the Revolution. Next to the church, which served university students in particular, was a cemetery, but the remains have been moved to the Paris catacombs. Inside the church are buried some important figures, particularly Cardinal François de La Rochefoucauld

Bust of Cardinal de la Rochefoucauld, Library of Sainte Geneviève

Procession with relics of Saint Geneviève, stained glass, Church of Saint Étienne du Mont

the civil war known as the Fronde, on 11 June 1652, when Louise de Marillac probably took part. The stained glass windows recount some of this history. Geneviève's remains were destroyed in the Revolution.

(2) The **jubé** *(altar screen on rood loft)*, called after the Latin liturgical formula: *Jube, Domine, benedicere* (Give, Lord, a blessing). In early times, the scripture lessons were read and sermons were preached from this structure separating the sanctuary and choir from the faithful. Pulpits systematically replaced *jubés* in the sixteenth and seventeenth centuries. This altar screen, finished in 1545, is

(1585-1645), whom Vincent assisted on his deathbed in the abbey itself, the philosopher-scientist-theologian Blaise Pascal (1623-1662), and the dramatist Jean Racine (1639-1699). During his extended stay, Pius VII made one of his visits here for mass on 10 January 1805. On 3 January 1857, an apostate priest stabbed Archbishop Marie Dominique August Sibourd (b. 1792) here. Like his predecessor, Denys Affre, he died in the line of duty. The priest was guillotined before the end of the month.

The church, one of the most beautiful in Paris, contains several elements of great interest:

(1) The *reliquary* of Saint Geneviève. Her relics were often removed from the church to be carried in procession around the city, particularly in time of plague or war, such as during

"Nine Choirs of Angels," Church of Saint Étienne du Mont

the only *jubé* remaining in Paris, and one of the few in France.

(3) The **woodwork**, particularly the 1630 organ case, and the pulpit, dating from 1650.

(4) The **memorials** to the founders of the Society of Saint Vincent de Paul (1914) in the Saint Vincent chapel. The Society was founded in this parish (as noted below, although the first regular meeting was held in the parish of Saint Sulpice). The painting of Saint Vincent is said to be by Simon François, and possibly painted from life, depicting Vincent at age 68.

(5) Another **painting**, that of the nine choirs of angels, by Louis Licherie came from the chapel of the original Saint Lazare. Louis Abelly commissioned it in 1679, and it conforms to his theological writing on the subject. Abelly himself was buried in the Holy Angels chapel at Saint Lazare.

(6) The first **stained glass window** of the former cloister, reached from behind the main altar, depicts a well-known legend with serious anti-Semitic overtones. In 1290, a woman is supposed to have been accused of having received Communion at the church of Saint Merry and then selling the host to a Jew, Jonathan. He then defiled it by piercing it with a knife, nailing it to his hearth, piercing it with a lance, and boiling it. Each time the host began to bleed, and an image of the crucified Savior appeared over it. Another woman returned the host to the bishop, who kept it in a reliquary at another church in Paris. Jonathan was supposedly burned at the stake. The relic disappeared after the Revolution, along with the shovel used to recover the host from the blood-red water. The account is universally regarded as apocryphal. The other windows in this old cloister date from the sixteenth and seventeenth centuries, and continue the rich theological symbolism of the Middle Ages. These windows are the finest in Paris after those of the Sainte Chapelle.

Both Vincent de Paul and Louise de Marillac lived near here for some ten years, and certainly came here to pray, as had Francis de Sales during his student days in this area of the University of Paris, called the Latin Quarter. A Confraternity of Charity existed here from an early date (late 1636 or early 1637), and the Daughters of Charity worked for it beginning about 1640. Vincent called Saint Geneviève a model for the Daughters, inasmuch as both she and they were good country girls. (Conference 13, 25 January 1643)

The monks of the adjacent Saint Geneviève abbey did not favor Vincent's being at Saint Lazare. In 1658, one of them let it slip to a Vincentian relative that the monastery would wait until Vincent's death to try to resume control of the valuable Saint Lazare properties. Vincent felt some anxiety about securing his title to them. (Letter 2650) At the same period he related, in a conference to his confreres, that two monks of this abbey had been killed in a conflict with the public authorities who had tried to

Pantheon

He secured the land, raised the funds, and began to build in 1755. Unfinished at his death in 1780, the church was completed at the beginning of the Revolution. The National Assembly decided to turn it into a mausoleum for French persons noteworthy for their talents, virtues and services to the nation. The term pantheon ("of all the gods" in Greek) echoes the name of a similar building in Rome.

Napoleon had the Pantheon changed back into a church, but it was switched again to its present usage—not a church but a mausoleum. In its crypt are buried a few heroes, such as François Marie Voltaire, Jean Jacques Rousseau, Victor Hugo, Emile Zola, Jean Jaurès, Pierre and Marie Curie and André Malraux. Its dome, one of several in Paris, dominates the skyline. Interior decoration features paintings of French heroes.

**14.a.** The road leading up to the Pantheon, Rue Soufflot, between Boulevard Saint Michel and Rue Saint Jacques, marks the site of an ancient *Roman forum*. This complex contained a temple, public spaces and shops. It was first discovered in the nineteenth century; more excavation was done in 1971. Nothing can be seen of it above ground, however.

**14.b.** Although it is difficult to locate them precisely, two *homes of Louise de Marillac* stood nearby. Probably after her husband's death she moved to Rue Saint Victor (1626-1631, now at 43, rue du Cardinal Lemoine), and then to Rue

gain entrance to put an end to some disorders within. Vincent drew the conclusion that if the monks had kept religious silence and not become involved with secular affairs, their scandalous deaths would never have occurred. (Conference 190)

## 14. Pantheon
### (8, place du Panthéon, Paris 5)

At one side of the great square in front of the former abbey and the present church stood the *Collège de Montaigu*. Such luminaries as Ignatius Loyola, John Calvin and Desiderius Erasmus studied here. Today, in its place, stands the Sainte Genevieve Library. It faces the *Pantheon*, which Louis XV decided to build to replace the dilapidated church of Saint Étienne du Mont as a votive offering for his recovery to health.

de Versailles (1632-1636), in the parish of Saint Nicolas du Chardonnet. It was here (now 21, rue Monge) that she brought together four or five young village girls for the first time on 29 November 1633—thus founding the Daughters of Charity. It is clear that Marguerite Naseau, the first Daughter of Charity, served in the parish of Saint Étienne du Mont. It was from these residences that Vincent sent out Louise to visit the Confraternities of Charity.

**14.c.** Down the Rue Clovis, east of the Pantheon, at number 3, can be seen some parts of the **wall of Philippe Auguste** (dating from the twelfth century). This same wall formed the boundary of the property of the Collège des Bons Enfants in Vincent's time. Recent excavations have uncovered at least one arch of this wall below the Bons Enfants. The arch covered a channel of the river Bièvre, which emptied into the Seine nearby. *(30 bis, rue du Cardinal Lemoine, Paris 5)*

**14.d.** Down the Rue Clotilde, south of the Pantheon, begins the Rue des Irlandais. This is named for the Irish students who for centuries came to study in Paris. Vincent de Paul was among the benefactors of Irish clergy, particularly since they were living in times of persecution in Ireland. Several Irishmen joined the Congregation in Vincent's time, and he sent Irish missioners back to their homeland, and elsewhere in the British Isles. Vincentian priests came to staff the *Irish College* in 1858 and continued for more than a century.

Memorials to them and to Saint Vincent are to be seen in the college chapel. *(5, rue des Irlandais, Paris 5)*

**14.e.** The Irish College previously was located at the **Lombard College**. Its chapel is now the parish church of Saint Ephrem of the Syrians, for the use of Catholics of the Syrian rite. Although the present church dates only from 1733, earlier ones occupied the same site. The effects of revolutionary destruction can be seen on its façade, where in 1794 its coat of arms was chipped away. The Irish returned in 1815 but by 1825 ceased using the chapel. A painting of Saint Vincent at the deathbed of Louis XIII, based on the standard engraving, still hangs in this church amid the decora-

Chapel, Notre Dame du Val de Grâce

tions and icons of a Syrian church. *(15, rue des Carmes, Paris 5)*

**14.f.** Also south of the Pantheon, *(11-13, rue des Fossés Saint Jacques, formerly Place de l'Estrapade)*, was the second location of the Pension Bailly, which moved here in 1825. The Society of Good Studies *(Société des Bonnes Etudes)* met here under the direction of Emmanuel Bailly. Frédéric Ozanam was a member, and out of this organization grew the Society of Saint Vincent de Paul. The related Conference of History met at the parish church of Saint Étienne du Mont. The site of the Pension Bailly now forms part of the mayor's office of the fifth arrondissement. It was here that on 8 December 1835 the first meeting of the **Society of Saint Vincent de Paul**, with its new rule and name, took place.

**14.g.** North of the Pantheon was yet another seminary in Vincent's time, the ***Collège des Trente-Trois*** ("thirty-three," after the number of poor seminarians admitted). Its founder was Claude Bernard, known as the "Poor Priest" (1588-1641). Although given to embarrassing ecstasies during the celebration of mass, Bernard enjoyed the favor of Queen Anne of Austria. He was, together with Vincent de Paul, one of the founders of the charitable movement of the seventeenth century, although he is not mentioned in Vincent's extant correspondence. He died 23 March 1641 and was buried in the Charity Hospital where he had so zealously worked. His successor as head of the seminary was Jacques Charton (d. 1684), a member with Vincent de Paul of the prestigious Council of Conscience. The buildings to be seen today were built in the eighteenth century. The seminary lasted until 1790. *(34, rue de la Montagne Sainte Geneviève, Paris 5)*

### 15. Our Lady of the Val de Grâce (Notre Dame du Val de Grâce)*
**(1, place Alphonse Laveran, Paris 5)**

Queen Anne of Austria enjoyed the company of nuns. She frequently visited the Visitation nuns, as well as the Benedictine nuns at the monastery of Val de Grâce. She had these Benedictines brought to this old royal fief in 1621 from their former property in Clamart, then falling into ruins and, in 1624 laid the cornerstone of their cloister, partially in hopes of living here herself. Richelieu suspected the queen of corresponding with foreign powers from the supposed security of the monastery—she was—and in 1637 he ruthlessly put a stop to the practice.

At age 37, the childless queen vowed to build a magnificent church if her prayers for a child were answered. Louis XIV was born 5 September 1638, thus assuring the royal succession. Queen Anne then had the architect Mansart draw up plans for the church in Baroque style. The king himself, age seven, laid its cornerstone. This abbey and its church honored "Our Lady of the Cradle," and bears a large dedication on its façade "to the new-born Jesus and his Virgin Mother," transparent allusions to the queen's vow. The three figures above the tabernacle show Mary, Jesus in the crib and Saint Joseph, also clearly symbolic of Anne, Louis XIV, and Louis XIII. Napoleon III, however, replaced the main altar, since the original had been destroyed in 1793. Anne and Louis's monogram (AL) is found in several places on the building. The chapel was completed in 1667 and consecrated in 1710. In the chapel of Saint Vincent is a late portrait showing Vincent upheld by angels. He visited this monastery at least once (in 1643) to see the queen. It became the custom for the hearts of the monarchs to be preserved here in the crypt below the Saint Anne chapel, to the left of the main altar, but these were all destroyed at the Revolution. The queen's private apartments have been restored and can be visited as part of an interesting museum. The church was restored in the mid-nineteenth century. Daughters of Charity served the military hospital here from 1855 until it was put into lay hands in 1904.

**15.a.** Closer in to the center of the city was the *second Visitation monastery*, founded in 1626. Vincent de Paul came here often in his role as the ecclesiastical superior of the Visitation nuns. This meant that he was their extraordinary confessor and exercised other functions as well. Nothing visible remains of the original buildings, sometimes known as "Saint Marie in the suburbs" *(faubourgs)*. During the Revolution, the Theophilanthropes held their secular worship in the nuns' chapel. After the dispersal of congregations in France in the early twentieth century, the convent buildings were taken down. *(187-193, rue Saint Jacques, Paris 5)*

**15.b.** Another monastery, one among more than a dozen along the Rue Saint Jacques, was the *Carmelite monastery of the Incarnation*, on the other side of the street from the Val de Grâce. Built in 1604-1605, this was the motherhouse of the reformed Carmelite nuns, whom Pierre de Bérulle (1575-1629) introduced into France. Vincent de Paul stayed near here perhaps at several different times with Bérulle, "that great servant of God," as Vincent called him, as he was ascertaining his vocation. Because of his connection with Bérulle, Vincent certainly came to the monastery. Marie-Madeleine de Wignerod, Madame de Combalet, the widowed niece of Cardinal Richelieu, entered this monastery. Only eighteen years old, she received the habit from Bérulle, but Richelieu had the pope annul her vows. The noble Michel de Marillac (1563-1632), Louise's uncle, was buried here after his death in prison. It was perhaps here that Vincent came to visit him and noticed something that struck him as curious. He glimpsed a spider's web on the crucifix and deduced that Marillac was so recollected that he never saw it. He drew lessons about this for his confreres. (Conference 133, 16 August 1655) One famous Carmelite was the beautiful Louise Françoise de la Baume le Blanc, duchess of La Vallière (1644-1710). She was Louis XIV's first official mistress and mother of several of his children. After he rejected her, she entered this Carmel at age 31 and spent the rest of her life here in great austerity. The king came to visit, according to the stories. None of the old buildings are extant, although some fragments are visible inside other buildings. The chapel's rose window, for example, can be seen from the garden of a new building on the back street. *(25, rue Henri Barbusse)* A notable funerary monument of Bérulle, marking the place where his heart was buried, was erected here in 1657, decades after his death. This monument is now in the Louvre. *(284, rue Saint Jacques, Paris 5)*

**15.c.** Since the *Hôtel de Bérulle (15, rue de Grenelle, Paris 7)* dates from 1766, it has no direct connection with the cardinal, only with his family. Nevertheless, they brought his body here in 1793, where it remained hidden until 1840. Vincent learned much from Bérulle and adopted some of his practices, such as the style of his conferences, the chapter of faults and many other points of the rule. Many years later, in 1658, he recalled to his confreres how, for example, the Oratorians dealt with salads: *It's*

Port Royal des Champs, Chevreuse

*true that they serve salad at the Oratory, but how much do you suppose they give each one? Very little, in fact. I wish you could have seen what is served. You would realize the difference between them and us.* (Conference 187)

### 16. Church of Saint Jacques du Haut Pas (252, rue Saint Jacques, Paris 5)

Because of Vincent de Paul's struggles against the Jansenist movement, two other sites are also worthy of note near the Val de Grâce. The first is the parish of *Saint Jacques du Haut Pas*, named after an Italian religious order founded at Alto Pascio, near Lucca, to care for pilgrims. These religious established a hospital in Paris on this site, the first of many lining the pilgrim route to Saint Jacques (James) of Compostela, Spain. The present church began in 1630, and became a Jansenist stronghold. The abbé of Saint Cyran (1581-1643) is buried in the church. His modern tombstone reads: "Jean Duvergier de Hauranne, abbé of Saint Cyran, died 11 October 1643 in the unity of the one Church that he wanted to serve and love completely with his brilliant intellect." Daughters of Charity worked in the parish from about 1640. Vincent de Paul himself established the Charity here, 2 May 1646. The church was closed briefly at the Revolution.

**16.a.** Part of the parish property became a retirement home and seminary for the Oratorians, founded in France by Pierre de Bérulle. Philippe Emmanuel de Gondi was buried in the chapel of *Saint*

**41**

*Magloire*, the chapel of this home. He entered this community here and often lived here in later years, usually in a small building in the gardens. Bérulle himself was also buried here, but his body has been moved. The seminary remained here only until 1650. The chapel has been demolished, but the other buildings now serve as an institution for the deaf. (*254, rue Saint Jacques, Paris 5*)

### 17. Hospital of Port Royal (121-125, boulevard de Port Royal, Paris 14)

The second Jansenist site is *Port Royal*. The Cistercian monastery of Our Lady in the Fields (Notre Dame des Champs) is at Port Royal in Chevreuse, some distance southwest of Paris. It was one of the main sites of the Jansenist movement. In 1625 its Paris headquarters, likewise called Port Royal, began because the nuns had to leave the humid and unhealthy location in Chevreuse. This suburban location gradually attracted a large number of vocations under the guidance of Mother Angélique Arnauld (1592-1633), who had the abbé of Saint Cyran form them in Jansenist teachings. Its chapel, begun only in 1646, remains. The choir of the nuns housed an important relic, the Holy Thorn, at whose touch at least three nuns were cured. The most celebrated of these was Blaise Pascal's niece, Marguerite Périer, reported in 1656. As part of his anti-Jansenist campaign Vincent referred to this event in Letters 2238 and 2242a.

Many of the old buildings are still standing and now form part of the Maternity Hospital. These austere buildings were either never finished, for financial reasons, or despoiled at the Revolution. Vincent visited this Port Royal several times, particularly to see the abbé after his release from prison in 1643. Mother Angélique is buried in the chapel, which is still used for mass. The choir, much larger than the chapel, adjoins it and its old grille is still in place. As the tide turned against Jansenism, this independent monastery was suppressed, and the nuns were dispersed among other houses. The Visitation nuns replaced them until the Revolution, when they were expelled.

### 18. Saint Vincent de Paul Hospital (72-74, avenue Denfert Rochereau, Paris 14)

Vincent's memory is also kept alive at the Saint Vincent de Paul Hospital, near Port Royal on avenue Denfert Rochereau. This institution earlier housed the Oratorian seminary (1650 to 1790) after it moved from Saint Magloire. Following a distinctive Oratorian spirituality, the original chapel was dedicated, as the inscription on the façade indicates, both to the Trinity and to the Infant Jesus. This present hospital succeeds the one for the Foundlings built facing Notre Dame de Paris in 1748. Daughters of Charity served there, and sisters were able to remain to care for newborns all through the Revolution. That hospital was taken down in 1877. The elaborate paintings in the chapel by Paul-Antoine Brunetti

(1723-1783) and Charles-Joseph Natoire (1700-1777), preserved only in copies, depict works of the Daughters of Charity. They are important for the details of their habit, among other things.

The façade of the present chapel dates from 1655-1657. On it is a carving of the child Jesus wrapped in swaddling clothes, attended by several cherubs, a design Bérulle gave to the Oratory. This became the symbol of the Foundlings (the Enfants Trouvés) and, with its gesture of the arms extended downward, recalls the Lord of Charity, which became the emblem of the Congregation of the Mission. An inscription below the carving and over the main doorway quotes Luke 2:12 in Latin: "You will find a baby wrapped in swaddling clothes." The peripatetic body of Cardinal Pierre de Bérulle was moved here from the Oratorian seminary for a time before the Revolution.

In the courtyard adjoining the chapel is the marble original of the renowned *statue of Saint Vincent* by Jean Baptiste Stouf, completed by 1798. Its design, however, was finished before 1787. A plaster model of the final marble version was at Saint Lazare but did not survive the sack of 1789. The mob smashed the statue and someone carried its head in triumph to the Royal Palace and unceremoniously threw it into the pool of a fountain. The members of a revolutionary cult (the Theophilanthropes) so admired the finished version that they had it erected in Saint Jacques du Haut Pas, their temple of Well-being *(Bienfaisance)*.

Afterwards, the statue was moved several times, the last move being to the chapel of the present hospital. At some point it was moved outdoors. A signed plaster version is in Saint Thomas Aquinas church, one among a few others in Parisian churches. The statue is the likely ancestor of all others depicting kindly Father Vincent with infants or young children in his arms or at his feet—a staple of French ecclesiastical design.

The interior of the chapel has been much reduced. The present oratory occupies less than one-quarter of the original space. A large seated statue, an original design, of Saint Vincent with two children occupies the back of the chapel, and an old statue depicting him standing in an attitude of blessing is near the altar. The rest of the original chapel is used as hospital offices.

**18.a.** Adjoining the hospital property is the current **Visitation convent**, the post-Revolutionary successor of those presided over by Saint Vincent. One of those whose remains were transferred here from the first chapel of the Visitation, rue Saint Antoine, is the

Commemorative plaque,
Saint Joseph Hospital

Site of Bons Enfants, Rue des Écoles

Commander, Noël Brûlart de Sillery, one of Vincent's friends and benefactors.

### 19. Saint Joseph Hospital
### (7, rue Pierre Larousse, Paris 14)

Less historically important than the Saint Vincent de Paul Hospital, Saint Joseph Hospital was at one time a Daughter of Charity institution. The large chapel, built in 1900, is still in use, and its modern stained glass windows are its most interesting Vincentian feature. Especially noteworthy are the windows of Saint Louise de Marillac on the right and, facing her on the left, Saint Vincent de Paul. In the transepts are earlier windows with traditional Vincentian themes, including Saint Catherine Labouré's visions at the Rue du Bac. A large plaque on a side wall commemorates Mère Marie Sophie Mathilde Inchelin (1861-1940), onetime superioress general of the Daughters of Charity. She was the sister servant of this hospital before and after her election. A bronze bas-relief plaque depicting Saints Vincent and Louise adorns the entry gates to the chapel itself. It is one of several portraying various religious scenes.

### 20. Convent of the Daughters of the Providence of God
### (28-40, rue de l'Arbalète, Paris 5)

Marie de Lumague, Mademoiselle de Pollalion (1599-1657), was one of Vincent's spiritual directees. She had married François de Pollalion and, after his early death, adopted a simple life style, dedicating herself to works of charity. One of the most active of the Ladies of Charity, she dressed in peasant clothing and helped Louise de Marillac to serve the poor country people. With Vincent's encouragement she founded a congregation to take care of wayward girls and to provide a refuge for women whose virtue was threatened.

The convent buildings were completed in 1652, and Vincent de Paul is said to have celebrated the first mass in

Bons Enfants, 17th century engraving

their chapel. He undoubtedly visited her at her home and, after her death, 5 September 1657, looked after the affairs of her congregation. Both Anne of Austria and the duchess of Aiguillon were major benefactors of this work. These buildings were closed in 1790 and demolished in 1859. The cause for the beatification of Mademoiselle de Pollalion has been introduced in Rome.

### 21. Collège des Bons Enfants*
### (2-4, 4 bis, rue des Écoles, and 28-30, rue du Cardinal Lemoine, Paris 5)

The Collège des Bons Enfants takes its title from the term for proper young men attending the University of Paris, but which came to designate poverty-stricken scholars as well. It dates from about 1250. Its previous principal vacated this dilapidated and nearly deserted property of about eight hectares on 1 March 1624, and Vincent de Paul, already chaplain general of the galleys, succeeded him. The college was located next to the city walls near the corner of Rue du Cardinal Lemoine and Rue des Écoles, adjoining the much grander college of Cardinal Lemoine. A branch of the Bièvre river ran through both colleges. Vincent continued to live with the Gondi family until after the death of Madame (in 1625), as he had promised, and until the departure of Monsieur (in 1626) to join the Oratorians. The Gondis had assured his ownership of the property, so that Vincent could use it as the headquarters of projected groups of mission priests which, in 1624, did not yet exist. He recalled that, in the earliest

days, he and his confreres would commonly leave the keys with a neighbor while they were away giving missions. One of these neighbors could well have been a certain Madame Guérin, wife of a royal counselor, who kept up her association with Vincent as well as with Louis. (Letter 1438) While returning from a mission, Vincent sometimes reflected that he had not done enough, and that, in punishment, the gates of the city—the Saint Victor gate, located next to the College—might fall on him. *I remember that formerly when I returned from a mis-*

Saint Victor Gate outside Bons Enfants, 18th century engraving

*sion, it seemed to me that when I got back to Paris the gates of the city would fall and crush me; seldom did I return from a mission without that idea coming into my mind.* (Conference 177) Part of the Rue des Écoles runs over the site of the college chapel. The saint's room was at about number 4. The present Rue du Cardinal Lemoine, laid out in 1852, runs through the college garden.

Vincent made the Bons Enfants his headquarters until 1632, at which time he moved the Congregation's motherhouse to the priory of Saint Lazare. Despite his departure, he retained the title of "Principal" of the college and managed its lands and other income. Saint Louise, who lived nearby toward the end of Rue Saint Victor, often came to pray in the poor chapel of the house. Vincent often returned and probably stayed here when business kept him on the Left Bank of the city. Nothing remains of the old buildings, demolished between 1844 and 1920. Their place has been taken over by a post office and other buildings. The condition of the buildings of the old College of Cardinal Lemoine gives some idea of the Bons Enfants. Another of the "neighbors," to whom the first missionaries gave the key to the house when they left on mission, could possibly have been the doorkeeper or someone else living in the College of Cardinal Lemoine.

In 1707, the college became a diocesan seminary, called Saint Firmin after the bishop of Amiens, already the titular patron of the chapel. It remained under Vincentian direction until 1791. It was here too that two Vincentian priests, *Louis Joseph François* (1751-1792), the superior, and *Jean Henri Gruyer* (1734-1792), were massacred, 3 September 1792, along with 74 other priests and religious imprisoned here. The bodies of the two Vincentians were never recovered, since they had been brutally beaten and their corpses tossed into a common grave along with those of the other victims. These martyrs were beatified in 1926. Two of the other priests killed that day were diocesan priests who had been Vincentians: Jean Charles Caron and Nicolas Colin. They were beatified with the others.

**21.a.** Near the old Bons Enfants stands the *Scots College.* The rector of the college at Vincent's time kept him abreast of such news as could be had concerning the progress of two missioners Vincent had sent to Scotland, Fathers Francis White and Thomas Lumsden. The present buildings, however, date from after Vincent's death. The chapel contains, in the fashion typical of the time, the brain of the deposed James II, king of

Chapel, Sorbonne

England, who spent the last years of his life in France. The urn containing this relic was stolen at the Revolution. The king was much attached to the Vincentians. It is said that many of the books from the old Saint Lazare were deposited in the library of this college, but this cannot be proven at present. If so, they have been moved to the Bibliothèque Sainte Geneviève. (*65, rue du Cardinal Lemoine, Paris 5*) A few are also in the Irish College.

## 22. The Sorbonne (University of Paris) (Place de la Sorbonne, Paris 5)

As noted above, the students of the Bons Enfants before the time of Vincent attended one of the colleges of the University of Paris, the most ancient of which was the *Sorbonne* (founded in 1257 by Robert of Sorbon, the name of his native place in the Ardennes). The signatures of some noteworthy graduates are reproduced in the Cluny La Sorbonne metro station, such as Bossuet, Richelieu, Henri III, Henri IV, and Francis de Sales. That of Vincent de Paul could be added, since he received a licentiate in canon law from the university by early 1624. The details of his studies are unclear (that is: did he really study for it, or was it an honorary degree?) but his competence in the law is not.

The *chapel* of the Sorbonne, now used for exhibitions, contains the tomb of Cardinal Richelieu (violated and defaced in 1793). His cardinal's hat hangs from the ceiling and his coat of arms is everywhere evident. Another tomb is that of André Duval (1554-1638). The latter, dean of the theological faculty, was a close collaborator of Vincent de Paul and his confessor after about 1618. In the south transept of the chapel is a large fresco, dated 1875, by the artist Louise-Charles Timbal (1821-1880). In the lower register is "Theology, or the Dispute about the Blessed Sacrament." The artist depicts several theologians, among whom is Vincent de Paul, shown in green vestments and kneeling before the Blessed Sacrament. He alone among them is at prayer; the others, such as Bérulle and Francis de Sales, are in discussion. The university granted Frédéric Ozanam his first doctorate, in law, in 1836. In 1840, he was awarded the chair of foreign literature here, the year after receiving his second doctorate, in literature.

**22.a.** Facing Rue Saint Jacques, at number 46, on the northeast corner of the Sorbonne, was the church of *Saint Benoît*. This parish, home of the third Confraternity of Charity founded in Paris, was served by Daughters of Charity in the year of their foundation, 1633. Its name appears across the street on a small private passageway, the Rue du Cimetière Saint Benoît, at about 50 bis, rue Saint Jacques. The parish was suppressed in 1790 and its buildings demolished in 1854. Its main entry has been reerected in the gardens of the Cluny museum.

**22.b.** Next to the Saint Benoît site stands the former Jesuit college. Called the *Collège de Clermont* in Vincent's time, it became known in 1682 as Louis le Grand, now the Lycée Général Louis le Grand. Among its students was the unhappy Michel Antoine Le Gras, (1613-1696), son of Louise de Marillac. Vincent de Paul arranged for his studies here. A more successful graduate was Francis de Sales, a student here from 1580 to 1586. *(123, rue Saint Jacques, Paris 5)*

**22.c.** Also facing Rue Saint Jacques, at number 143, stood the church of *Saint Étienne des Grès*. An ancient black madonna, the statue of Notre Dame de Bonne Délivrance, was venerated here. Francis de Sales received comfort here during a time of spiritual despair. Vincent and Jean Jacques Olier are said

Chapel dome, La Salpêtrière

to have prayed here also. The church was closed in 1790 and torn down two years later. After the Revolution, the statue was given to the Sisters of Saint Thomas of Villanova, *(27, rue de Sèvres)*, one of the stopping places during the translation of the relics of Saint Vincent. When their convent was demolished in 1907 to make way for Boulevard Raspail, the sisters moved the statue again, this time to their new convent. *(52, boulevard d'Argenson, Neuilly-sur-Seine)*

### 23. Hospital of La Pitié-La Salpêtrière (47, boulevard de l'Hôpital, Paris 13)

To avoid accidental gunpowder explosions, Louis XIII moved the arsenal from inside the city to new buildings in a country area to the southeast. The hospital took its name, Salpêtrière, from the saltpeter used in the manufacture of gunpowder. Later, the buildings were rehabilitated to make room for the crowds of the indigent whom the king had planned to enclose here. Vincent hesitated in his support but managed to have his friend and biographer, Louis Abelly, appointed the first superintend-

ent of the new General Hospital in 1657, a post he held only from May to October. Louis XIV had the entire complex rebuilt, including the large chapel of Saint Louis, which dates from 1670 to 1679. One of its four naves is now dedicated to Saint Vincent de Paul, as is one of the other buildings. Vincent probably visited the hospital, although his advanced age and precarious health in 1657 would have precluded a lengthy engagement. Daughters of Charity worked here beginning that same year. The hospital gradually shifted its attention to housing the mentally ill, and the government used its inmates, including prostitutes arrested in the city, to populate its American colonies. It has been suggested, based on local tradition, that some of the Daughters accompanied these women as far as Mobile, now in the state of Alabama, before the Revolution. If so, these were the first Daughters of Charity to land in the Americas, however briefly.

23.a. The present name of the hospital includes the title *La Pitié*, after another old hospital, demolished in 1912. It was located where the Paris mosque now stands. *(2, place du Puits de l'Ermite, Paris 5)* La Pitié had been founded in 1612 as a refuge for beggars and the homeless. Mademoiselle de Pollalion had placed in this institution her young women snatched from a life of prostitution and crime. Vincent visited it occasionally and oversaw the missions given here by the priests of the Tuesday Conferences. In 1657, La Pitié was joined administratively to the General Hospital, destined for the enclosure of poor and sick beggars. Following the Revolution, it continued from 1809 to 1912 as a general hospital. After that date La Pitié was moved near the hospital of La Salpêtrière. Their names are now joined, and they form one institution. *(1, rue Lacépède, Paris 5)*

**23.b.** Practically contiguous with the hospital is the site of the ancient *Abbey of Saint Victor*. Founded in 1108, its members excelled in academic achievements and reform of priestly life. The abbey became the head of a powerful congregation of abbeys, whose monks were called Victorines. Several attempts to reform the life of the monks failed and, by the time of Vincent de Paul, the common life of these canons regular had deteriorated.

These monks of Augustinian lineage were associated with those of the old Saint Lazare priory, and so pressed their confreres not to give up that valuable property to Vincent and his young congregation. Even after he moved into the priory, the Victorines pursued their cause in court. It was only on 7 August 1659 that Vincent finally achieved the unchallenged union of Saint Lazare with the Congregation of the Mission. He visited the abbey at least once, with the archbishop (between 1632 and 1636), but the purpose is unknown. The monks tried again in 1670 to get the property, also to no avail. At the Revolution, the monastery was demolished. On its property now is a unit of the University of Paris (Jussieu), the Jardin des Plantes, and the Austerlitz train station.

## 24. Church of Saint Nicolas du Chardonnet*
### (23, rue des Bernardins, and 24, rue Saint Victor, Paris 5)

A chapel was constructed in a *chardonnet*, an area of thistles *(chardons)* in the thirteenth century and was rebuilt in the last half of the 1600s. The modern porch and façade dates from the 1930s, and incorporates thistles around the top of the columns. Of the old chapel where Monsieur Vincent celebrated mass and gave communion to Saint Louise and the earliest Daughters of Charity, only the bell tower remains (rebuilt in 1625). This old chapel was oriented traditionally, east-west, and lay below the present side altar of the right transept. Francis

Statue of Saint Vincent de Paul by Stouf, copy in Church of Saint Nicolas du Chardonnet

de Sales preached here. The board of overseers of the parish decided to expand the church beginning in 1656 but chose a north-south orientation. In any case, this was Vincent's parish from 1625 to 1632, and Louise's from 1626 to 1636. At Louise's home in this parish, Vincent gave his first conferences to the Daughters, and a plaque in the Saint Vincent side chapel commemorates his work. This chapel also features a copy of the Stouf statue of Saint Vincent, modeled on the one in Saint Thomas Aquinas church in Paris. Louise paid her first visit to a Charity in this parish, the second such confraternity established in Paris. Marguerite Naseau also worked and prayed here, as other Daughters of Charity would do, since their house did not have a chapel. Lastly, the Ladies of Charity of the parish served the galley convicts in the nearby tower, La Tournelle.

Monsieur Vincent greatly venerated its pastor, *Adrien Bourdoise* (1584-1665). This zealous priest founded a community, the "Nicolaites," who ran the seminary of Saint Nicolas du Chardonnet beginning in 1631. He is buried under the choir, but the exact location is unknown. Since 1977, the church building, property of the French state, has been in the hands of the traditionalist followers of Archbishop Marcel Lefebvre.

Next door to the church, where the Palais de la Mutualité stands, was Bourdoise's *seminary*, begun in 1620. The hapless Michel Le Gras, Louise's son, attended here for a time. The seminary of Saint Nicolas du Chardonnet continued until the Revolution and produced numerous priests and prelates for the Church. Some of them were among those massacred in 1792 at nearby Saint Firmin (formerly the College des Bons Enfants). The seminary reopened in 1815 and lasted until its suppression in 1906. A prominent graduate was the future Vincentian superior general, Charles Léon Souvay (1870-1939). The building was demolished in 1911. *(14, rue Saint Victor)*

**24.a.** A few steps to the left of the church is the *Place Maubert*. In the early thirteenth century, no less a person than Albert the Great preached in the square to the university students congregated here—a practice that students continue today. In later years, one of the gallows of the city was located here as well. The seven laymen who witnessed Vincent's will, drawn up in 1630, all lived on this square.

**24.b.** Beginning in 1638 the Daughters of Charity had a home for foundlings

La Tournelle, 17th century engraving

*(Maison de la Couche)* somewhere on the Rue des Boulangers near Louise's home. She took a close personal interest in this work. In keeping with ancient tradition, on Sundays and feast days the sisters often took the children to Notre Dame cathedral to encourage the faithful to give alms for the children's upkeep. The location of the home, however, is unknown. It ceased to function in 1645, when the Daughters of Charity opened the Thirteen Houses *(Treize Maisons)* near Saint Lazare.

### 25. House of the Galley Convicts (La Tournelle, Tour Saint Bernard) (1, quai de la Tournelle, Paris 5)

Vincent de Paul had been appointed royal chaplain of the galleys 8 February 1619. Previously, he had seen the degrading conditions in which the prisoners lived before being marched off in the twice-yearly chain gangs to Marseilles. One of his first tasks was to procure more humane lodgings. The first was near the Royal Palace *(Palais Royal)*, as noted below, used from 1618 to 1632. The second was the square tower *(La Tournelle)* of a castle that guarded the eastern entry to the city on the Seine. This tower was also near his parish church, Saint Nicolas du Chardonnet. The early Vincentians took care of the convicts in both locations from 1625 to 1634; the Ladies of Charity of Saint Nicolas du Chardonnet began in 1632, and the Daughters of Charity in 1640. This tower was situated at the time between the Saint Bernard gate and the river, now the Quai de la Tournelle,

between the La Tournelle bridge and the Sully bridge. Nothing remains of the old tower and castle, demolished at the Revolution. In its place stands a large statue of Saint Geneviève, remembering her charity towards the people of Paris. During the September massacres (2-4 September 1792), the mob killed the galley convicts here, thinking they were religious in disguise. Seventy died in this senseless slaughter.

Louise de Marillac and Vincent de Paul had to face a difficult situation in 1655: a Daughter serving the prisoners fell in love with one of them and arranged to marry him. Their marriage contract was being arranged when the two founders became aware of the impending scandal. Vincent received the young sister courteously, but it appears that their "mutual affection," as Louise styled it, had gone on too long for them to turn back.

### 26. Museum of Public Assistance* (47, quai de la Tournelle, Paris 5)

On the same Quai de la Tournelle stands the well-preserved city home of Marie Bonneau, Madame de Beauharnais de Miramion (1629-1696). Widowed at sixteen, she turned to works of charity, particularly in her parish of Saint Nicolas du Chardonnet and at the Hôtel Dieu. She also founded a congregation of sisters, the Daughters of Saint Geneviève, whose rule Vincent de Paul helped write. The sisters, popularly known as the Miramiones, lived at her home from 1691 to 1792. The building then became a pharmacy for the hospi-

Saint Julien le Pauvre, postcard

tals of Paris. Today it houses the **Museum of Public Assistance**, interesting for its exhibits on the foundlings, Saint Vincent and Sister Rosalie Rendu. During Madame Miramion's earlier life, as wife and then widow, she lived on the other side of the river. She developed her plans for her congregation, and Vincent must have visited her there more than once. Unlike many others from this period of his life, this building still stands. *(15, rue Michel le Comte, Paris 3)*

Entry, Saint Julien le Pauvre

### 27. Church of Saint Séverin
### (1, rue des Prêtres Saint Séverin, Paris 5)

According to legend, Vincent found an abandoned baby in the Rue de la Huchette, in the heart of the Latin Quarter. He brought the child to the thirteenth century church of Saint Séverin for baptism, before confiding it to the care of the Daughters of Charity. A side chapel dedicated to the saint has stained glass windows depicting the sisters and scenes from Vincent's life. He also preached in this church. The parish had a Confraternity of Charity in his time, and Daughters of Charity worked with its members. This vast building dates from the thirteenth and the fifteenth centuries and has excellent examples of stained glass dating from the fifteenth century.

27.a. To the right of the church, at the corner of Rue de la Parcheminerie and Rue Boutebrie stands an **Office of Public Assistance**. This organization takes its inspiration from Vincent de Paul and looks to him in some way as its founder. A statue of the saint graces the corner of the building, built in 1861. Vincent is not otherwise identified, but his statue recalls the legend of the abandoned baby and Saint Séverin. The pose of the statue is unique.

### 28. Church of Saint Julien le Pauvre
### (1, rue Saint Julien le Pauvre, Paris 5)

The ancient church of *Saint Julien le Pauvre*, dating from about 1170, is one of the oldest churches in Paris. (It has been, since 1889, the parish church of

Melkite Catholics, Byzantine rite.) Its patron was the charitable Julian, bishop of Le Mans, whose name was often attached to churches located near hospices for poor pilgrims journeying to Compostela. In 1655, after a period of decline, this church was given to the Hôtel Dieu of Paris. It is possible that the two founders, Vincent and Louise, the Ladies of Charity and many of the early Daughters of Charity came here to pray as they went to serve the poor in the hospital. However, it had its own chapel, Saint Agnès, which burned in 1772. In the park to the side of the church stands one of the oldest trees in Paris, dating from the time of the founders. *(Square R. Viviani)*

Churchyard, Church of Saint Médard

Oldest tree, Square R. Viviani

### 29. *Church of Saint Médard* (141, rue Mouffetard, Paris 5)

The church of Saint Médard replaces one built in the seventh or eighth centuries, destroyed by the Normans. The present twelfth-century building was originally a chapel in the small market town of Saint Médard on the river Bièvre, now mostly covered over. It became a parish church only in 1655, and the Daughters of Charity were established in this parish in the lifetime of Vincent and Louise. There are, however, no monuments to them or to the founders. The sisters remained until the revolution. It was in this rough neighborhood that Sister Rosalie Rendu, Daughter of Charity, brought the young Frédéric Ozanam and his companions to meet and aid poor families in their homes.

In 1727, a Jansenist deacon of saintly reputation, François de Pâris, died at the age of 36, having killed himself through his excessive austerities. The sick came to pray at his tomb in the churchyard, and their presence led to a belief in miraculous cures and eventually to massive scenes of collective hysteria. Those afflicted became known as the Convulsionaries of Saint Médard. It was at this time that Vincent was being considered for canonization, and deacon François offered a tempting alternative candidate for the Jansenists to espouse. In 1732, Louis XV decreed an end to the events. A joking inscription was posted: "By order of the king, in this vicinity / no more miracles by the Divinity." (*De par le Roi, défense à Dieu / De faire miracle en ce lieu.*)

**29.a.** Near Saint Médard, the church of *Saint Martin* stood from 1158 to 1790. (*1-4, rue de la Collégiale, Paris 5*) Daughters of Charity worked in this parish in their earliest days, as they did in the neighboring parish—actually built on the same property—the church of *Saint Marcel* (or Marceau). This latter parish (*53-57, boulevard Saint Marcel, Paris 13*) took its name from the ninth bishop of Paris (d. 436). He is said to have delivered Paris from a monstrous dragon, the way he is pictured on the Saint Anne door of Notre Dame de Paris. Peter Lombard, the renowned medieval theologian regarded as the founder of the theological faculty of the Sorbonne, was buried here (d. 1164). The parish was in a very poor area. A "Court of Miracles" was located here,

that is, one of several places in Paris where seemingly crippled beggars were miraculously cured at the end of each day's work. Vincent visited this parish to support the work of the Ladies of Charity in the Confraternity of Charity erected here. The building was demolished in 1806 under Napoleon. The modern successor, church of Saint Marcel, keeps the name of this ancient sanctuary.

### 30. Souvenirs of Blessed Sister Rosalie Rendu (1786-1856)*
### (Paris 5, 13, 14)

In the same neighborhood, called the Gobelins after the Gobelins tapestry factory, are found souvenirs of an extraordinary sister beatified by Pope John Paul II, 9 November 2003.

This Daughter of Charity came to the Mouffetard Quarter of Paris—at the time very poor and crowded—to complete her novitiate. From that time, with some slight absences, until her death, 7 February 1856, Sister Rosalie Rendu lived and worked for the poor of Paris. She was named superior of a social welfare office and succeeded in opening and managing a school, workshop, home for the aged, orphanage, etc. In her office she also received the founders of the Society of Saint Vincent de Paul, a relationship she continued throughout her life. The house has largely disappeared. A large white marble plaque on a wall in the yard in front of the kindergarten recalls the old-age home she founded in 1850, transferred here in 1858. The plaque also mentions her office where she received many rich and poor persons. This office has now been removed, but some of its furnishings are found in the mother-house of the Daughters of Charity. *(3-5, rue de l'Epée de Bois, Paris 5)*

**30.a.** A *school* named in her honor, the "Groupe Scolaire Soeur Rosalie," is located in the Maison Soeur Rosalie. In the front reception area is the original large portrait of this sister. Furnishings from her time, and engravings of her heroic efforts to stop revolutionary bloodshed in 1848, are also kept in the mother-house. *(32, rue Geoffroy Saint Hilaire, Paris 5)*

**30.b.** Sister Rosalie is buried in a special tomb in the **Montparnasse Cemetery**. It can be visited by entering from Boulevard Edgar Quinet. Enter some seven or eight meters and on the right at the corner is a series of monuments. Behind this and in the fourth row to the south of the *Allée principale* is the large white cross marking her tomb. The inscription reads, in part: "To good mother ROSALIE [from] Her Grateful Friends, the Poor and the Rich." Some 70,000 people attended her funeral and the lengthy procession to the cemetery. Since then, her tomb has regularly been adorned with flowers. Since she had some years before incurred the disfavor of Jean Baptiste Étienne, the Vincentian superior general, he forbade his confreres from having anything to do with her, not even to take part in her funeral. *(3, boulevard Edgar Quinet, Paris 14)*

Near her tomb, to the right of the Edgar Quinet entry, also four rows to the south, is the monument of the Congregation of the Mission, which holds the remains of former superiors general and others. Tombs for the Daughters of Charity, including the mothers general, are also found in this same cemetery.

**30.c.** Close by Place d'Italie is the parish church of **Saint Rosalie**. It was founded as a chapel in 1861 as part of a "patronage," that is, a shelter and workshop for young apprentices and others. Sister Rosalie was its inspiration and driving force, and an admiring and wealthy layman, a member of the Society of Saint Vincent de Paul, established a foundation for its upkeep. When a new road was put through, the chapel was torn down. A new chapel replaced it, built between 1867 and 1869. Vincentians of the Paris province cared for this institution from 1862 to 1903, and again from 1922 to 1971. Inside the church are notable windows, dated 1871, depicting Saint Vincent de Paul and Sister Rosalie Rendu. Four women killed in the Charity Bazaar fire (4 May 1897) are commemorated in two plaques in the church. *(50, boulevard Auguste Blanqui, Paris 13)* A small street in the neighborhood, opened in 1868 is named **Avenue de la Soeur Rosalie**. It runs northwest from Place d'Italie for one block, originally part of the property of the "patronage."

**30.d.** Not far away from the church of Saint Rosalie is the parish church of Saint Albert the Great. Opened in 1969, this modern church marks the site of the former "Symbolic Monument," the chapel of the Holy Agony. It is the Paris house of the Sisters of the *Holy Agony*, now the Sisters of Christ at Gethsemane, founded by a Vincentian, Antoine Nicolle. To emphasize the devotion to the Holy Agony, Nicolle's successor Léon Bernard found the former chapel and convent of the Franciscan Missionaries of Mary to be suitable for the Holy Agony Sisters. The chapel, closed in 1896, was refurbished and opened in 1898. *(122, rue de la Glacière, Paris 13)*

Statue of Saint Vincent de Paul,
Church of Saint Sulpice

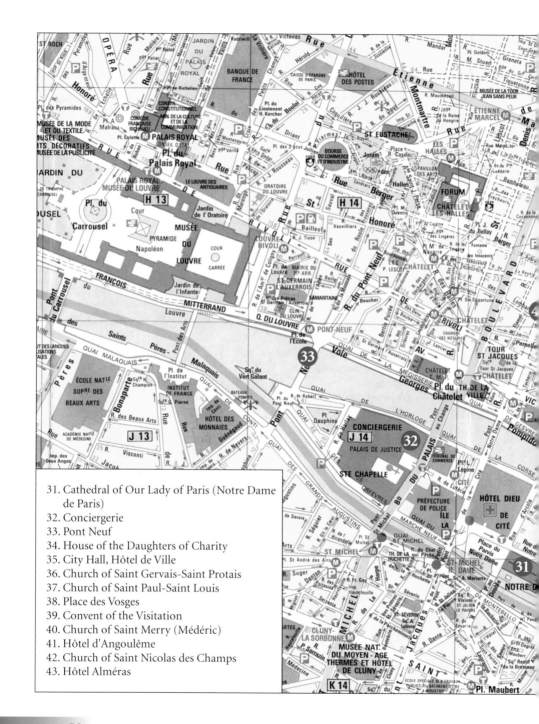

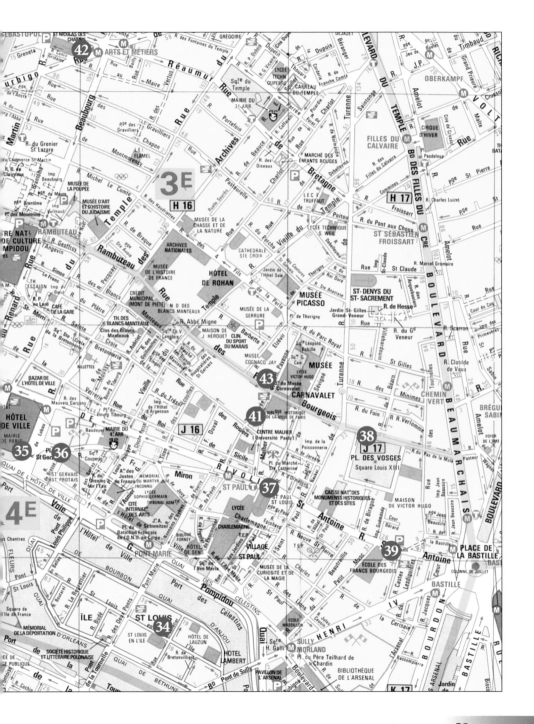

# Ile-de-la-Cité & Ile-Saint-Louis

## ARRONDISSMENTS 1, 4

Notre Dame de Paris,
17th century engraving

### 31. Cathedral of Our Lady of Paris
### (Notre Dame de Paris)***
### (6, place du Parvis Notre Dame, Paris 4)

The Cathedral of Our Lady of Paris stands on the site of a Gallo-Roman temple and two earlier Christian churches. The main façade was completed in 1250 but was heavily restored in the nineteenth century to repair the ravages of time and revolutionaries. A dark side chapel is dedicated to Saint Vincent ("Apostle of Charity," a marble statue by Adolphe-Victor Geoffroy, 1816-1880, which depicts him holding a cross and book, not the infants characteristic of most French statues). At the back of the apse are monuments to the Gondi family, four of whose members were bishops and archbishops of Paris in the days of Saint Vincent: Pierre (1533-1616), his nephew Henri (1572-1622), Henri's brother Jean François (1584-1654) and Jean François's nephew Jean François

Paul (1613-1679). Both Henri and Jean François Paul were cardinals, called the Cardinals de Retz, after a place in southern Brittany erected as a duchy-peerage in 1581.

**31.a.** Of special interest is that Vincent visited here often between 1636 and 1658. One reason was because of the hospital, the *Hôtel Dieu*, situated until 1878 to the south of the cathedral, where today there is an open space, and also across the river on the left bank. Two small bridges joined its two sections. (The present hospital, built 1867-1877 and also called the Hôtel Dieu, is situated to the north of the cathedral.) The hospital is among the oldest in Europe, a foundation of Saint Louis IX, king of France. Its foundations can be seen in the archaeological exposition under the cathedral square, and the statue of Charlemagne stands where the hospital once was.

A second reason for Vincent's presence was that the Ladies of Charity of the Hôtel Dieu used to assemble at the cathedral. Here they would attend mass and receive communion from the hands of Vincent de Paul, notably on the day of the election of officers. He did this since he oversaw in some manner their voluntary service of the sick. This group of Ladies of Charity differed from others, who were parish-based, since these members specialized in only one work,

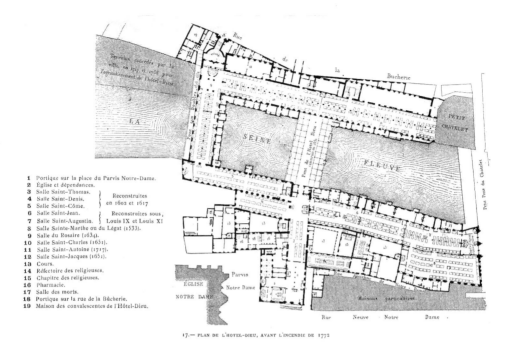

1 Portique sur la place du Parvis Notre-Dame.
2 Église et dépendances.
3 Salle Saint-Thomas.
4 Salle Saint-Denis. } Reconstruites
5 Salle Saint-Côme. } en 1602 et 1617
6 Salle Saint-Jean. } Reconstruites sous,
7 Salle Saint-Augustin. } Louis IX et Louis XI
8 Salle Sainte-Marthe ou du Légat (1533).
9 Salle du Rosaire (1634).
10 Salle Saint-Charles (1651).
11 Salle Saint-Antoine (1717).
12 Salle Saint-Jacques (1651).
13 Cours.
14 Réfectoire des religieuses.
15 Chapitre des religieuses.
16 Pharmacie.
17 Salle des morts.
18 Portique sur la rue de la Bûcherie.
19 Maison des convalescentes de l'Hôtel-Dieu.

17.— PLAN DE L'HÔTEL-DIEU, AVANT L'INCENDIE DE 1772

Floor plan, Hôtel Dieu,
18th century engraving

that of care of the sick at this hospital. The members, most of noble families, gradually extended their interests to other kinds of specialized assistance that, because of their wealth and influence, they could assume. During the Fronde, a series of civil wars, he used to assemble the Ladies and celebrate mass for them here once a month. From 1634, the Ladies of Charity and, from 1634 or 1635, the Daughters of Charity worked here. The Parisian-born Louise de Marillac must have come here often, of course.

A third reason for Vincent's presence was that in July 1637 he, one of the members of the Company of the Blessed Sacrament, had remarked on the "large number of bad priests who were celebrating mass with great lack of propriety," especially at Notre Dame. Vincent eventually agreed to the confinement of these "vagabond and beggar priests" at Saint Lazare for a year, during which time they undoubtedly learned how to improve as priests.

Vincent certainly would also have had questions about *Antoine Adrien Lamourette* (1742-1794). This celebrated ex-Vincentian took the constitutional oath at the time of the Revolution, and was ordained in Notre Dame as the constitutional bishop of the civil diocese of Rhône and Loire (Lyons), 27 March 1791. Lamourette reconsidered his

Pont Neuf, 17th century painting, detail

Pont Neuf, 17th century painting

choices nearly three years later and publicly retracted his oath. The government responded by beheading him within four days.

In the post revolutionary period, the enthusiasm of *Frédéric Ozanam* and his friends for the Catholic faith led to the foundation of the "Conferences of Notre Dame." This series of conferences on the faith was confided to the cathedral. Its most famous preacher at the beginning was the Dominican, Lacordaire. These conferences have continued until the present, particularly during Lent. It was here that Pope John Paul II beatified Ozanam in 1997.

**31.b.** Near the hospital was the building used for the foundlings before Vincent's day. They were brought first to the Hôtel Dieu and then farmed out to others, who often mistreated them. Vincent and Louise remedied the situation with the help of the Ladies of Charity. This building *(Maison de la Couche)* was at the corner of the Pont d'Arcole and the Quai de la Corse. It has been taken over by the maternity hospital on the same spot.

## 32. Conciergerie
### (1, quai de l'Horloge, Paris 1)

The *Conciergerie* is a section of the old royal palace last used in the fourteenth century, but in Vincent's time it housed the galley convicts. He visited them often here, and their frightful conditions led him to move them first to a building near the Royal Palace, and then to the Tower *(La Tournelle)* mentioned above. During the Revolution, Queen Marie Antoinette was confined here before her execution; and during sixteen months, from 1793 to 1794, some 2600 prisoners left here for the guillotine. Adjacent to the Conciergerie are the law courts, as they were in the saint's time. He spent countless hours here in the company of judges, notaries and attorneys.

**32.a.** Also part of the law courts is the *Sainte Chapelle*, built in the thirteenth century to house relics of the Passion, particularly part of the Crown of Thorns. Today the chapel is a museum, featuring astonishing and original stained glass. In Vincent's day, it was still

Pont Neuf, 17th century engraving

in use as a chapel. One day, while receiving an important letter in the Palace of Justice, he climbed the staircase to the upper section of the chapel to open the letter before the tabernacle. The door was locked, so he simply knelt down on the spot to read the letter.

**32.b.** Nearby, across the Boulevard du Palais, is the Tribunal de Commerce. On this site stood the church of *Saint Barthélemy*. Ladies of Charity worked in this parish, and Daughters of Charity worked with them. This royal parish, with the oldest church building in Paris after Notre Dame, was closed in 1790, and demolished in 1858. Across the

street is the medieval public clock, known to the founders.

### 33. Pont Neuf
(Paris 1)

At the western end of the island is the *Pont Neuf*, the New Bridge. Despite its name, it is the oldest standing bridge in Paris, dating from 1578, and finished in 1604 under Henri IV. Vincent and the early missionaries and sisters must have passed over it countless times. It features a statue of Henri IV, restored after the Revolution. His was the first statue erected on a public roadway in France. In Vincent's day, the bridge was full of activity: markets, entertainments (licit

63

Statue of Henry IV, Pont Neuf

Name plate, Daughters of Charity school,
Ile Saint Louis

Samaritaine. Facing the statue was the entry to the elegant Place Dauphine, built in 1607, and similar to the Place des Vosges, then under construction. Perhaps in reference to this bridge, Vincent once recalled for his confreres that he had seen a performer. *[He had] a pointed awl that, in proportion as one wished to drive it in, collapsed back into itself. This man placed it as his throat, and when the people saw him forcing it into his throat they used to shout: Take it out, take it out.* (Conference 214) Vincent used this as an example of false illusions. There was no illusion, however, in another experience. *You...know that many persons learn what impurity is by seeing and listening to those mountebanks, those buffoons who depict immodest actions and indulge in evil talk.* (Conference 221)

Saint Vincent de Paul with priests and sisters,
Church of Saint Louis en l'Ile

and illicit), and traffic but, unlike most other bridges in Paris, had no houses built on it. Beneath the bridge was a sculpture of the Samaritan woman giving a drink to Jesus; it marked the spot of an old pump used to bring water to the Louvre. This sculpture gave its name to the pump, then to the area, then to the large department store, La

### 34. *House of the Daughters of Charity* (5 bis and 7, rue Poulletier, Paris 4)

On the Ile Saint Louis, the small island east of the Ile de la Cité, stands a house where Vincent is said to have installed the Daughters of Charity in 1658. They have used it for a school almost continuously from that time, although it became the property of the Daughters only in 1728. During the Revolution, the neighborhood committees let them remain in peace but without their customary dress. In 1853, the first Paris association of the Children of Mary began in this house. A plaque outside recalls the presence of the Daughters.

**34.a.** The *parish church*, Saint Louis en l'Ile, recalls that Vincent explained to them that they should have *for a chapel their parish church, for a cloister the streets of the city.* (Conference 111) Francis de Sales preached in the original chapel. Vincent presided there over meetings leading to the founding of the Daughters' school. (The present church, however, began only in 1664.) A side chapel, with three nineteenth-century paintings, is dedicated to him. Pius VII visited here 10 March 1805. The building contains a small plaque, dated 1926, recalling the relationship of Ile Saint Louis with the city of Saint Louis, Missouri. *(19 bis, rue Saint Louis en l'Ile, Paris 4)*

**34.b.** Many of the exclusive houses on the island date from the seventeenth century. Among these was the home, practically a château, of the *Bretonvilliers* family. This elegant construction, the largest on the island, opened in 1637. It was demolished in 1866, and only a few traces remain. Madame de Bretonvilliers, a Lady of Charity, opened some storerooms on this property for clothing and other items destined for the relief of the war-torn Ile de France. It is likely that, beginning in 1658, Vincent came here in his work of supervising this charitable undertaking. *(Main entry: 4, rue de Bretonvilliers, Paris 4)*

**34.c.** The old bridge leading from the island to the right bank is the *Pont Marie*, named after Jean-Christophe Marie, the businessman who built it beginning in 1614. Vincent mentioned its disastrous collapse in spring floods on 1 March 1658. Those same floods, he reported to one of his correspondents, caused water from the river to come into the enclosure of Saint Lazare. *It is so bad that in many of the streets of Paris we see more boats than carriages go by.* (Letter 2541)

# *Right Bank*

## ARRONDISSEMENTS 2, 3, 4

Church of Saint Gervais-Saint Protais

### 35. City Hall (Hôtel de Ville)
### (Place de l'Hôtel de Ville, Paris 4)

This grandiose building succeeded several previous public buildings devoted to city government. Begun in the sixteenth century, and completed in the early seventeenth century, it was completely renovated between 1874 and 1882. On the square in front, formerly called the Place de Grève (Square of the Foreshore) public executions were commonly held. Among those executed was the marshal Louis de Marillac (b. 1572), one of Louise's uncles. He died on the orders of Richelieu, 10 May 1632. Vincent wrote to Louise: *The way our* relatives go to God is of no importance to us, provided they go to Him. . . . Let us not feel sorry for him then, but let us accept the adorable will of God. (Letter 105) It was here, too, that the guillotine was first erected, 25 April 1792.

### 36. Church of Saint Gervais-Saint Protais*
### (Place Saint Gervais, Paris 4)

This church, located on a small mound, commemorates two Roman officers martyred by Nero. A church has been here since the sixth century. The main part of the present church, in Flamboyant Gothic style, was completed in 1657.

Inside, there are sixteenth-century windows and choir stalls. The organ is the oldest in Paris. Eight members of the Couperin family were organists here (1656-1826). In this elegant church Louise de Marillac married Antoine Le Gras (d. 1625), 5 February 1613. In

Church of Saint Gervais-Saint Protais,
17th century engraving

keeping with custom, Louise was henceforth addressed as Mademoiselle Le Gras, although she referred to herself by her maiden name. By a strange coincidence, René Alméras (1613-1672), the second superior general of the Congregation of the Mission, was baptized here in his family's parish church on the same day. In this church, too, is the tomb of Geneviève Fayet, Madame Goussault (d. 1639), president of the Ladies of Charity at the Hôtel Dieu, one of Vincent's closest collaborators in the work of the Charities and the Daughters of Charity, and Alméras' aunt by marriage. She had lived nearby, rue Roi-de-Sicile, until her death, assisted by her friend Vincent de Paul. Her death touched him, and he often referred to her dying words of commendation of the Daughters of Charity. (Conference 70, for example) Daughters of Charity worked in this parish beginning about 1640. A group of monks (founded 1975) and nuns (1984) living and working in the world, combine work and contemplation, and make up the Monastic Fraternities of Jerusalem centered at this parish.

**36.a.** Facing the front of the church was the apse of the church of *Saint Jean en Grève*. The Daughters of Charity worked in this parish in the time of Vincent and Louise. It was demolished after the Revolution, and the modern city hall (Hôtel de Ville) is built over part of it. Bishop Camus, the spiritual director of Louise de Marillac, was baptized here.

**36.b.** On Rue des Archives, north of Saint Gervais is the *Billettes*, in Vincent's time a Carmelite monastery. The "miracles of the Billettes" was a popular expression of anti-Semitism in the Middle Ages. The story of the profanation of the consecrated host, its bleeding, etc., and its recovery is referred to above concerning the church of Saint Étienne du Mont. To expiate the supposed sacrilege, a church was built here in 1295. In 1633, Discalced (reformed) Carmelites took over the monastery. Vincent came here in October 1651 on the orders of the papal nuncio to look into possible candidates for the episcopacy. After the Revolution, the church was given to Lutherans, who still maintain it. North of the church the old monastic cloister walk can be seen, the only one remaining intact in Paris after the Revolution. *(22-24, rue des Archives, Paris 3)*

**36.c.** Close by is the Tour Saint Jacques, the bell tower of the former church of *Saint Jacques de la Boucherie*, built in 1509-1523 for the butchers' guild *(Avenue Victoria)*. It was a meeting place for pilgrims on their way to Compostela, Spain, to venerate the memory of the apostle Saint James (or Jacques). Daughters of Charity worked in this parish in the lifetime of the two founders. The rest of the church was demolished in the nineteenth century. *(Square de la Tour Saint Jacques)*

**36.d.** The *Hôtel Acarie* was the home of Pierre Acarie and Barbe Avrillot (1566-1618), later known as Marie of the Incarnation (and subsequently beatified). After her husband's death,

Jesuit house, now Lycée Charlemagne,
adjoining Church of Saint Louis

Madame Acarie developed a large circle of followers who met at this house. Regarded as the foremost founder of the French school of spirituality, she numbered among her friends and admirers Pierre de Bérulle and Vincent de Paul. The latter possibly attended gatherings here at her home. *(11, rue Ferdinand Duval, Paris 4)*

### 37. Church of Saint Paul-Saint Louis* (99, rue Saint Antoine, Paris 4)

In 1582, the new Society of Jesus built a small chapel in honor of Saint Louis in the district of Paris called the Marais ("marsh"), since the district was once the bed of the Seine and later became swampland. The Jesuits returned to their chapel in 1603 after being expelled from France in 1595. As the population of the Marais was growing, particularly in wealthy and influential people, the Jesuits began a large and sumptuous church decorated in what then was modern art, now called Baroque. Louis XIII, who had a Jesuit confessor, laid the corner stone in 1627. Cardinal Richelieu laid the first stone of the façade in 1634 and, in 1641, celebrated the first mass here (something he rarely did). Vincent himself commented that his confreres should learn from this Jesuit house, where *persons are not brought inside, they are made to wait under the portico or perhaps brought into a corridor. . . . Therefore, I request the porters, whenever anyone calls on one of us, to ask them to wait under the portico, or bring them into a room, but not into the cloister.* (Conference 124) Louis Abelly, Vincent's first biographer, was ordained bishop here in 1664. At the

Fig. 19. — L'église Saint-Paul, avant la Révolution.

Church of Saint Paul,
19th century engraving

Statue of Louis XIII,
Place des Vosges

royal residence, the Hôtel Saint Pol, 1361-1543, which surrounded the church on three sides.

Vincent founded a Confraternity of Charity in this parish. To commemorate this event, a statue of him was erected in the nineteenth century in the Saint Louis church, now found in a side alcove on the right. Daughters of Charity came to work for the Confraternity of Charity in the Saint Paul parish in 1634, the year after their foundation. Several years of faithful work increased their outreach to a daily service of 5000 poor persons during the lifetime of the founder.

**37.b.** The Marais district is filled with elegant seventeenth-century homes, and Vincent would have visited many of them. One in particular, the *Hôtel de Sully*, renowned for its splendor, has been restored to its seventeenth-century condition. *(62, rue Saint Antoine, Paris 4)* Directly across from its entrance is the Rue de l'Hôtel Saint Paul, which led in former times to the Saint Paul parish cemetery.

### 38. Place des Vosges*
**(Paris 4)**

The Place Royale, now the *Place des Vosges*, is Paris's oldest public square and one of its most elegant. Cardinal Richelieu was one of its inhabitants, at number 21. His niece, the duchess of Aiguillon, held her salon here as well. This vast square was built in 1605-1612. In that final year, 1612, the first carousel was held in Paris to inaugurate the square, and to celebrate the planned

time of the Revolution, the church was turned into a Temple of Reason—perhaps a backhanded compliment to the Jesuits who had a house for their professed members on the property. In August 1804, the emperor Napoleon gave Saint Louis to the Vincentians as their motherhouse—a decision never implemented, perhaps because of the small number of available members.

**37.a.** The old parish church of *Saint Paul (des Champs)*, facing Rue Saint Paul only one block away, was the one which Vincent de Paul and Louise de Marillac knew. Her husband, Antoine Le Gras, was buried in a side chapel in this church. Destroyed in the Revolution, its name was joined to that of the newer Saint Louis church in 1802. Only a tower remains, built into a later house. *(30-32, rue Saint Paul)* The parish has given its name to streets and passageways in the neighborhood, known principally for a marriage of Louis XIII and Anne of Austria. A carousel combined parades and old-fashioned sporting events, in which knights and their horses played prominent roles. Philippe Emmanuel de Gondi had the honor of being one of the costumed knights at this or another such event. Cardinal Richelieu was among its inhabitants, at number 21. His niece, the duchess of Aiguillon, held her salon here as well, and it could easily be supposed that Vincent came to see her here.

**38.a.** Adjoining the Place des Vosges lived Marie Lhuillier, Madame de Villeneuve d'Interville (1597-1650). She was one of the many noble Ladies of Charity of the Hôtel Dieu. She founded

Chapel, Visitation Convent,
rue Saint Antoine

the *Daughters of the Cross*, a congregation of religious devoted to the education of young poor girls. Vincent de Paul was her spiritual director and took an active interest in her community, particularly after her death on 15 January 1650. She and the sisters lived in the convent at this location beginning in 1643, and Vincent probably visited here on several occasions. *(4-6, impasse Guémenée, Paris 4)* The duchess of Aiguillon was one of their major benefactors. Following the Revolution, the property was sold (1797). At the end of the street *(26, rue Saint Antoine)* are found some vestiges of the old convent, notably the novitiate (located in an inner courtyard). Vincent occasionally referred in his conferences to these charitable nuns.

**38.b.** Vincent de Paul often remarked on the charitable sisters of the Place Royale. He was referring to a convent of the hospital sisters of Our Lady (*Hospitalières de la Charité Notre Dame*). With the help of Anne of Austria, this community undertook the care of poor girls and women, beginning in 1629, or perhaps earlier. Vincent compared them to the Daughters of Charity: *they are both nuns and Daughters of Charity at the same time, because they devote themselves to the service of the sick, but with this difference, however, that they nurse the sick poor in their own house and only look after those who are brought to them.* (Conference 50) The nuns left in 1791 and the buildings were demolished in 1828. *(35, rue des Tournelles, Paris 4)* Close by was the church of the Minims, where, on 19 July 1797, the feast of Saint Vincent was first publicly celebrated since the Revolution began. Some 200 priests attended—a proof, if any were needed, of Saint Vincent's continuing importance in Catholic life. *(37, rue des Minimes, Paris 3)*

### 39. Convent of the Visitation*
### (17, rue Saint Antoine, Paris 4)

The first monastery of the Visitation, founded by Francis de Sales, began in 1621 in a small house on Rue du Petit Musc. It was enlarged in 1628 and opened on to the Rue Saint Antoine, the main east-west street of the ancient Romans *(decumanus)*. Its chapel, the only remaining building, was built between 1632 and 1634. It is one of the early buildings in French Baroque style designed by the famed architect François Mansart and is his only intact building in Paris. During the construction, in 1633, Vincent arranged that certain priests who had recently made the ordination exercises give a mission to the workers. Their success here led in some way to the foundation of the Tuesday Conferences.

Jane Frances de Chantal (1572-1641) lived at this convent during her stay in Paris. As ecclesiastical superior of the Visitation convent in Paris, Vincent de Paul often came here to give conferences, preside at meetings, etc., from 1622 until his resignation, 18 March 1660, shortly before his death. He gave canonical testimony here (17 April 1628) concerning the cause of beatification of Francis de Sales. As their "spiritual

Saint Vincent in captivity,
Church of Saint Merry

father," as he described himself (Letter 2054), Vincent sometimes refused permission to princesses to visit the nuns, an indication of his care for their spiritual well-being. Louis XIII, however, had the right to visit and did so often, as did his queen, Anne of Austria. Vincent also received regular financial reports but generally left the management of the monastery to others.

At the convent school, many prominent girls attended, such as the nieces of Cardinal Mazarin. Their prank, emptying their inkwells into the holy water fonts in the chapel, is still recalled. Many noteworthy persons were buried here, including the brother of Jane

"Saint Vincent taking the chains of a galley prisoner," Leon Bonnat, Church of Saint Nicolas des Champs, 19th century engraving

Frances, André Frémiot, archbishop of Bourges. In 1737, at the time of Vincent's canonization, the first side chapel at the right of the entry was dedicated in his honor. The convent remained open until 1790. A Protestant church since 1802, it has been nearly stripped of its former interior adornment. Its exterior remains virtually unchanged, however, and clearly points to its former use, with the AM monogram *(Ave Maria)* on the doors, and a heart pierced with arrows above the main door.

**39.a.** On the Rue du Petit Musc, on the west side of the convent, lived *Noël Brûlart de Sillery* (1577-1641). This wealthy knight and former Keeper of the Seals gradually gave up his former life. Under Vincent's direction, he began to live a charitable life and was finally to be

ordained a priest. A commander of the Knights of Malta, he was involved in many religious enterprises, among which was the building of the present chapel of the Visitation. He gave large gifts to the Congregation of the Mission and was instrumental in the foundation of the house at Troyes. Vincent assisted at his deathbed and presided at his funeral in the Visitation chapel. He recalled the commander's extraordinary meekness in a conference to his confreres: *He had an extreme affection for the virtue of meekness on account of an incident he witnessed when he was counsel to the parlement. He saw two of his brother lawyers fall to words and insults; and, seeing that their countenance was deformed, pale and frightful, he made this reflection: What! Those whom I saw with the faces of men I now behold transformed into beasts! They snarl, they foam, they treat each other like brutes!* (Conference 202)

### 40. Church of Saint Merry (Médéric) (78, rue Saint Martin, Paris 4)

The church of *Saint Merry*, named after Medericus, who died here in the

Church of Saint Nicolas des Champs

Main altar, Church of
Saint Nicolas des Champs

seventh century, was completed in 1612 in Flamboyant Gothic style. It was the parish church of Louise de Marillac from 1613 until about 1620. Her son, Michel Antoine Le Gras, was baptized here, 19 October 1613. Noteworthy are the sixteenth-century windows, the nineteenth-century fresco (1840) of Saint Vincent in the side chapel on the left, and the painting of him singing the psalms, bare-chested, during his captivity. Another important personality baptized here was Barbe Avrillot, Madame Acarie. Her portrait can be seen in the baptistery. With Bérulle, she helped to found the Carmelite nuns in France. She was beatified in 1791. The Daughters of Charity were established in this parish during the lifetime of the two founders

and they worked with the Confraternity of Charity.

During the Revolution, the church was used simultaneously by Constitutional clergy from 1795 and by the Theophilanthropes, 1797-1801, who called it a Temple of Commerce. One of the organists in the restored church was the renowned composer Camille Saint-Saëns.

**40.a.** The church of *Saint Josse* was originally a chapel of ease for the parish of Saint Laurent. It fell under the responsibility of Saint Lazare, and for this reason Vincent de Paul inaugurated the young Louis Abelly as its pastor here, 20 September 1643. During the nearly eight years of his pastorate in this small parish, Abelly formed a community of clergy to serve the parishioners. He also began his prolific career as a writer here, culminating in his biography of his friend and mentor Vincent de Paul. The church was closed in 1790 and later demolished. (*18, rue Aubry le Boucher, Paris 4*)

### 41. Hôtel d'Angoulême (later: de Lamoignon)
### (24, rue Pavée, Paris 4)

Meetings of the Company of the Blessed Sacrament took place in this elegant home in the Marais. Its members included some of the most highly placed and influential persons, lay and clerical, in France. Among them was Vincent de Paul. He undoubtedly influenced the members in their works of charity as much as they influenced him in the choice of certain works that he undertook. Although Chrétien François de Lamoignon gave his name to this home, he did so only in 1688. We do not know, therefore, where Marie Des Landes, Madame de Lamoignon, lived. She was the superioress or president of the Ladies of Charity from 1643 to 1651. In a letter of 24 January 1648 Vincent mentions a meeting at her home that he planned to attend. Today, the building contains the Historical Library of the City of Paris.

Church of Saint Sauveur,
17th century engraving

## 42. Church of Saint Nicolas des Champs**
### (252 bis, rue Saint Martin, Paris 3)

The church of *Saint Nicolas des Champs* is Flamboyant Gothic, with five naves and about 100 columns, all numbered, and in many different styles. The altarpiece in the rear chapel behind the sanctuary, dating from the seventeenth century, is the only one in Paris left in its original location after the Revolution. It was completed in 1629. Many paintings decorate the side chapels. The organ dates from the eighteenth century; one famous organist was Louis Braille, who founded the system of reading for the

blind. During the Revolution the church became the Temple of Marriage and Fidelity. It was restored to Catholic worship in 1802. A community of priests and lay members, the Community of Emmanuel, staffs the church today. The Daughters of Charity lived in the parish nearly continuously from Vincent's time until 1825. During the Revolution, Daughters of Charity from other Paris communities assembled here and were left in peace.

During mass on Pentecost, on 4 June 1623, a full ten years before the foundation of the Daughters of Charity, Louise had a spiritual experience that resolved doubts about her vocation, her new spiritual director, and the immortality of the soul. A plaque, blessed in 1952 and placed in a chapel on the left side, recalls this grace, called in later years the "Light of Pentecost." Louise kept an account of this on her person and read it often. The original is in the Archives of the Mission, Paris.

In the chapel of Saint Anne is the original large painting by Léon Bonnat (1833-1922) of Vincent taking the chains of the galley convict (1865). In the chapel of the Holy Family is the original easily recognized painting by Pierre-Nicolas Brisset (1810-1890) of Vincent helping a beggar to get into his carriage (1858).

42.a. This church is located here because of the traditional north gate of the city, which lay on the ancient north-south Roman road *(cardo)*. Near it was the ancient abbey of *Saint Martin des Champs* (in the Fields), which succeeded a chapel dating from the fourth century. The eleventh-century chapel, a Gothic marvel, is now part of the National Technical Museum. A small chapel was built for the monastery servants and neighboring peasants, dedicated to Saint Nicholas. It was enlarged in the sixteenth and seventeenth centuries and is the church described above. From 1642 or 1643 until 1659, Vincent was the vicar general of the abbots of this monastery, the two nephews of the duchess of Aiguillon—another of the many coincidences linking him with the lives of so many persons. As such, he was responsible for overseeing their administration and for providing pastors and priors for the institutions dependent on the abbey, undoubtedly burdensome work.

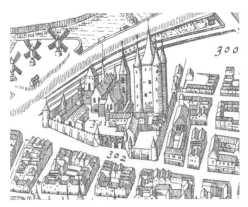

The Temple,
17th century engraving

**42.b.** However, another church, **Saint Sauveur** (Holy Savior), was the local parish. Holy Savior was Louise's parish church on three occasions: from 1604 to 1613 while she was living under the guidance of her uncle Michel de Marillac; in 1619 when she lived with her husband and son on Rue Courteau Vilain (Rue Montmorency); and lastly from 1623 to 1626 *(corner of Rue du Temple and Rue Rambuteau)*. Vincent lived near them in the Gondi residence on the Rue Pavée from 1616 to 1625 or 1626 and, by 1623, had met Louise de Marillac. Madame de Miramion (see above) also lived in the parish. Louise's son, Michel, was married here to Gabrielle Le Clerc (18 January 1650). Although ultimately unsuccessful, the first group of Ladies of Charity in Paris also began in this parish (1629), and the pioneer Daughter of Charity, Marguerite Naseau, served it briefly in 1631. The second house of the Daughters of Charity (1633) was founded in this parish. Holy Savior church stood until 1787 when it was demolished to make way for a larger replacement. The Revolution, however, put an end to those plans. *(183, rue Saint Denis, and 2, 4 and 4 bis, rue Saint Sauveur, Paris 1)* Its baptismal font, however, was relocated to the church of **Saint Elisabeth**. *(195, rue du Temple, Paris 3)* Nothing remains of the homes of the Marillacs, the Gondis or Madame de Miramion.

**42.c.** Behind the church of Saint Elizabeth stood the monastery of **Saint Madeleine**. Charlotte Marguerite de Gondi (1570?-1650), the marquise of Maignelay and sister of Philippe Emmanuel de Gondi, bought the building in 1620 to house women converted from prostitution to a religious life. The nuns of the Visitation supervised their formation from 1629 to 1671. Vincent supervised the spiritual care of the "Madelonnettes" and the governance of this institution. At Louise's suggestion, the Daughters planned a pilgrimage to honor Our Lady of Loretto here, where a replica of the chapel at Loreto had been built around 1645. During the Revolution, in 1793, it continued its role as a women's prison and was then demolished in 1868. A small part of a wall remains today, and a plaque high on the wall records its history. *(6, rue des Fontaines du Temple, Paris 3)*

**42.d.** One of the great sights in Paris, visible on old maps, was the *Temple*, the headquarters of the Knights Templar, later the Knights of Malta. Vincent de Paul and his directee Noël Brûlart de Sillery had worked on a plan to establish a seminary at the Temple. They formu-

Hôtel de Bourgogne,
wooden model

lated their plans hastily and did not succeed. At the Revolution, some of its buildings were turned into a prison, and the royal family was imprisoned there. Because the Temple symbolized great power, wealth and secrecy, and to keep it from becoming a royalist shrine, it was demolished beginning in 1808. Its name continues in the Rue du Temple, the Square du Temple, etc. *(Rue de Bretagne, Paris 3)*

**42.e.** Near Saint Nicolas des Champs stands what is claimed to be the *oldest house* in Paris. It dates from the end of the thirteenth century and was a combination of workshop, store and dwelling. The ground floor was developed before the use of windows set into stone frames—something that occurred in the fifteenth century. Vincent could well have seen it, although in his day it was only one among many old houses. It is not otherwise marked. *(3, rue Volta, Paris 3)*

**42.f.** Another nearby institution was the *second Carmelite monastery*, (de la Sainte-Mère de Dieu), parts of which (a courtyard and a balcony) are visible, but not from the street. The nuns welcomed Madame Acarie and Saint Jane Frances de Chantal at various times. The chapel was dedicated in 1625, the year of Madame de Gondi's death. She was buried in the side chapel that her family had endowed. The chapel was demolished in 1796, and most of the buildings were taken down in 1914. *(13, rue Chapon, Paris 3)*

**42.g.** Near the church of Saint Nicolas is the old parish church of *Saint Leu-Saint Gilles*. Daughters of Charity worked in the parish beginning about 1640 with a Confraternity of Charity. The pastor of Saint Leu, as vicar general of Paris, presided over the commission for the canonical investigations leading to the beatification of Vincent de Paul. Its meetings took place during 1705 and 1706 in one of the chapels of the church, probably in that confided to the Lamoignon family since 1623. Madame de Lamoignon, mentioned above, is buried here. *(92, rue Saint Denis, Paris 1)*

### 43. Hôtel Alméras
### (30, rue des Francs Bourgeois, Paris 3)

This fine home was built in 1598, in the style of Henri IV. From 1632, it became the home of Pierre Alméras, probably the brother of *René Alméras*, who succeeded Vincent de Paul as superior general. His father, also René (1575-1658), joined him at Saint Lazare, living as a simple novice.

**43.a.** Nearby is the *Musée Carnavalet, the museum of the city of Paris*. Interesting exhibits concerning the Paris of Vincent's time can be viewed here. *(14-16, rue des Francs Bourgeois, Paris 3)*

**43.b.** *Rue du Grenier Saint Lazare*, located nearby, perhaps took its name in the fourteenth century from a resident (Guernier), whose property perhaps was sold or given to Saint Lazare. Indeed, this entire area was covered with houses and properties to which the priory had feudal rights. When Vincent de Paul took over that ancient institution, he also inherited its vast properties in the country as well as in the city of Paris.

**43.c.** A few blocks to the west of this street stood the *Hôtel de Bourgogne*, of which only the tower now remains. The *Tour Jean Sans Peur,* named after Jean the Fearless, duke of Burgundy (1371-1419) protected the duke and his family after he had his rival, Louis, duke of Orleans, assassinated. During the Fronde, Vincent was able to install one of his charitable shops in that part of the Hôtel de Bourgogne known then as the Hôtel de Mendosse. The poor received clothing and supplies here. *(20, rue Étienne Marcel, Paris 2)*

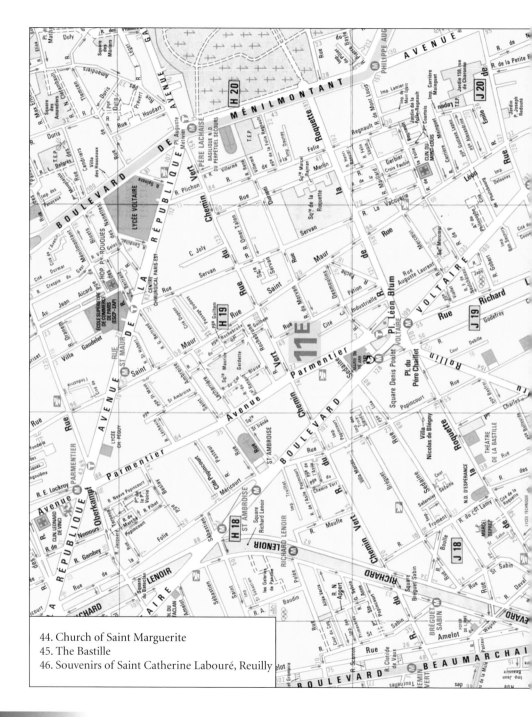

44. Church of Saint Marguerite
45. The Bastille
46. Souvenirs of Saint Catherine Labouré, Reuilly

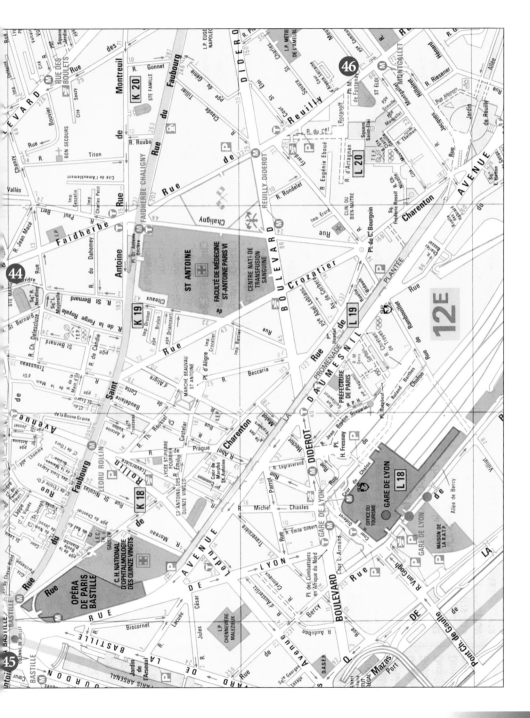

# ARRONDISSMENTS 11, 12

### 44. Church of Saint Marguerite**
### (36, rue Saint Bernard, Paris 11)

This parish church began as a chapel of ease under the leadership of a secular priest, Antoine Fayet, who oversaw its construction in 1624-1626. It became an independent parish in 1712. This parish church remained more or less open during the Revolution, since its clergy took the constitutional oath. Because it was near the Place de la Bastille and other prisons, many of those guillotined there were brought to the church cemetery for burial. Among them was a mysterious figure that some have claimed was Louis XVII, the Dauphin or crown prince. Recent research, however, suggests that the child was not murdered but died of tuberculosis in prison, 8 June

Commemorative plaque, Jean-Jacques Dubois, Church of Saint Marguerite

1795. A small monument in the old cemetery recalls this murky event. After the restoration, Pope Pius VII, who must have visited nearly every parish in the city, came here to celebrate mass on 11 February 1805.

Of Vincentian interest are the five important paintings of the life of Saint Vincent brought from the chapel of Saint Lazare. The first pastor after the restoration (1802) was Jean Jacques Dubois (1750-1817), a Vincentian. He agreed to accept from François Brunet, Vincentian vicar general, four of these five from the larger collection of eleven originals, painted for Vincent's canonization; one painting is later. These had been kept briefly (1802-1805) in Saint Nicolas du Chardonnet. Brunet had no place to put them so, according to the story, he sold them to Dubois until the Congregation could buy them back. Three are found in the Blessed Sacrament Chapel (Preaching for the Foundlings, 1732; Preaching to the elderly at the Name of Jesus hospice; Presenting the founders of the Daughters of Saint Geneviève for approbation to the queen—this painting is later than the others and did not form part of the original series). Two are in the chapel of Saint Marguerite (Saint Vincent with Saints Francis de Sales and Jane Frances de Chantal, before Queen Anne of Austria, 1732; Vincent sending the Missionaries and sisters to help wounded soldiers, 1731). The Vincentians can be easily recognized from their distinctive white collar. The young women in the light blue dresses are not Daughters of Charity—whose habit at the time was gray or gray-blue—but are either Daughters of Providence or orphans in uniform. In addition, there is a copy of the renowned statue by Stouf over the altar dedicated to Saint Vincent. On the right side of the church, near the entry, is a modern stained glass window of him. Daughters of Charity work in the parish, continuing a mission dating from before the Revolution. During that revolutionary period, three sisters died here from injuries sustained when hostile crowds attacked them.

The effigy of the founding pastor is instructive. He died in 1634 and has the same style beard and wears the same skullcap and ample surplice that Vincent is depicted as wearing.

Of further Vincentian interest is the fact that the parish residence served as an unofficial motherhouse of the Congregation of the Mission for a time in 1816. Charles Verbert, the first assistant after the death of the previous vicar general, Dominique Hanon, should have been living in the building assigned to the Daughters of Charity on Rue du Vieux Colombier. However, Verbert had nowhere to live since the sisters were unable to leave pending the completion of repairs at the Rue du Bac. Dubois welcomed Verbert as his guest and also invited him to hold the assembly of 12 August 1816 in his house. At this assembly, Verbert was elected vicar general. Dubois' name appears on a plaque with the list of other pastors, and a plaque in his memory was erected in the garden near the supposed tomb of Louis XVII.

## 45. *The Bastille*
### (Place de la Bastille, Paris 12)

Whether Vincent ever entered the *Bastille* fortress or ministered to those imprisoned here is unknown. He mentioned it occasionally, however, according to his biographers, and took care that a chaplain be appointed from among the members of the Tuesday Conferences. Although they thoroughly despised the fortress for the royal power it represented, the revolutionaries did not completely demolish it. Part of its stones can be seen in the Bastille metro station (line 5), and also in Square Henri Galli. (*Pont de Sully and Boulevard Henri IV, Paris 4*) Here, the foundation of one of its towers, discovered in 1899, was reerected.

Tomb effigy of Antoine Fayet,
Church of Saint Marguerite

45.a. Behind the Bastille is the *Quinze Vingts* Hospital. This institution for the blind was located originally near the Louvre (now with an historical marker on Place André Malraux). In Vincent's time, its administrators asked that a

Confraternity of Charity be established there. This he did (1633), and in later years members of the Tuesday Conferences for clergy preached a mission there. Vincent probably visited the original site, but no proof exists. Daughters of Charity worked here until about 1905. *(28, rue de Charenton, Paris 12)*

**45.b.** Near the hospital *Archbishop Denys Auguste Affre* (1795-1848) was wounded during the 1848 revolution on 25 June. He had been trying to arrange a truce but was felled by a bullet in the back. He died two days later at his home. His murder in the pursuit of peace deeply affected Sister Rosalie Rendu and

Desk and chair of
Saint Catherine Labouré, Reuilly

Frédéric Ozanam, along with many others. *(4, rue du Faubourg Saint Antoine, Paris 12)* His assassin, never discovered by the police, confessed his deed on his deathbed to the Daughters of Charity from Saint Paul-Saint Louis parish. He attributed his reconciliation to the effects of the Green Scapular placed in his room.

### 46. Souvenirs of Saint Catherine Labouré, Reuilly**
### (77, rue de Reuilly, Paris 12)

"Sister Catherine Labouré, Daughter of Charity, the Saint of Reuilly, lived here 1831-1876, 46 years of a life completely given to God for the service of the poor." This plaque announces the importance of this retirement home for elderly sisters and lay persons. The present buildings, except for the much-renovated chapel, are modern. In the nineteenth century, far to the back of the present garden, was the Enghien hospice. Members of the Bourbon family built it to care for their aged retainers and named it for Henri de Bourbon, duke of Enghien (1772-1804), executed on Napoleon's orders after the Revolution. Sister Catherine worked in that hospice which was administratively attached to the main house on Rue de Reuilly. The institution, open from 1828 to 1904, was entered from the back street. *(42, rue de Picpus, Paris 12)*

A plaque in the crypt of the chapel reads: "Here rested the body of Zoe Catherine Labouré, known in the community as Sister Catherine, Daughter of Charity. She died at the hospice of

Enghien, 31 December 1876 in the 71st year of her life, and the 46th of her vocation. The body of Sister Labouré was exhumed on 1 March 1933 and brought to the motherhouse, 140, rue du Bac. His Holiness Pius XI beatified Sister Catherine Labouré, 28 May 1933, and she was canonized by His Holiness Pius XII on 27 July 1947." The local physician removed her heart from her corpse, found to be still intact in 1933, and promptly placed it in a reliquary. Exposed at first in the chapel, this reliquary now rests in the crypt.

In addition to her heart, other items of clothing, personal effects and furniture are also on view in this crypt, along with photos and explanations of her experiences of the Miraculous Medal as well as images of the Virgin Mary. An early statue of Mary, where the saint prayed, is found in the garden behind the house.

Chapel, Hospice of Reuilly

**46.a.** Across from the main entrance on Rue de Reuilly is one of only a handful of modern parish churches in Paris, the church of *Saint Eloi*. The patron of goldsmiths and metal workers, Eloi lived in the area in the seventh century. In his day, a royal hunting lodge had been built here, and around it the hamlet of Reuilly developed.

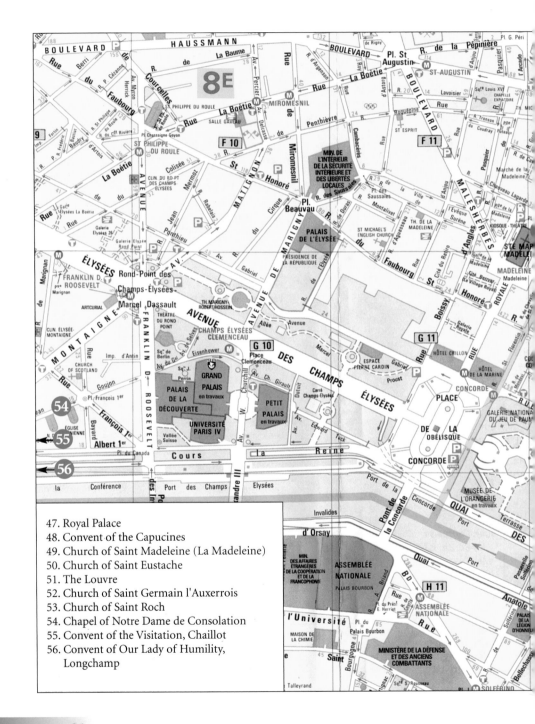

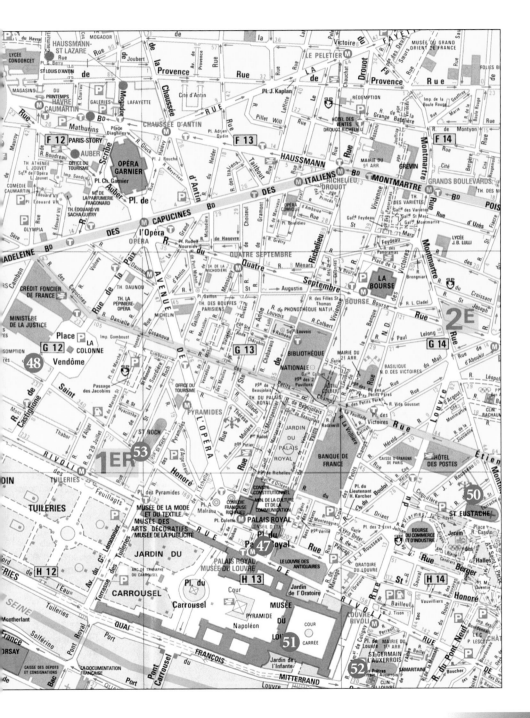

## ARRONDISSMENTS 1, 8, 16

### 47. Royal Palace (Palais Royal)
### (Place du Palais Royal, Paris 1)

This building was originally named the Cardinal's Palace, since Armand Jean Du Plessis, Cardinal Richelieu, built it. He became the principal minister of Louis XIII in 1624, and gave up his diocese of Luçon to devote himself to state matters. He bought this property in an area north of the royal palace of the Louvre and, at his death, 4 December 1642, bequeathed it to the king or his heirs. Then the royal family lived here, that is, Queen Anne of Austria, the regent, and her young son, Louis XIV. Cardinal Jules Mazarin, her chief minister, lived nearby at the site of the future Bibliothèque Nationale.

Vincent often came here to see Cardinal Richelieu in the years 1635-1642 and Queen Anne from 1643 to 1652. These meetings dealt particularly with the affairs of the Council of Conscience (for religious affairs), to which Vincent belonged from June 1643 until the end of September 1652. It was here that the cardinal, who rarely celebrated mass himself, attended daily mass celebrated by one of his chaplains. During mass, he often spent the time being shaved, having his hair combed, and dictating important letters. The royal family chose to flee Paris during the Fronde and, when they returned, they moved to the Louvre, more a fortress than a palace at that time. Today, the Royal Palace has been much restored, and its interior courtyard (the Garden of the Royal Palace) is a pleasant place to stroll.

### 48. Convent of the Capucines
### (Capuchin Nuns)
### (360-364, rue Saint Honoré, Paris 1)

This convent opened with great fanfare in 1608. The Daughters of the Passion, as they were also known, enjoyed for their foundation the support of Henri IV, a duchess and several princesses. Michel de Marillac, Louise's uncle, was a Third Order Franciscan, and his son became a Capuchin. Michel naturally attended the opening ceremony. Louise did not, but attracted by the penitential life of the sisters and various family connections, the seventeen-year-old Louise spent time with the nuns in their garden, refectory and chapel. Her spiritual director at the time was the Capuchin provincial. When she asked about entering the convent, he refused. The convent she wanted to enter lasted only until 1685, when Louis XIV had need of it. He had the nuns moved to another location and built the magnificent Place Vendôme on the convent property. Marguerite de Gondi, marquise of Maignelay, the sister of Monsieur de Gondi, was buried in their chapel—another bond linking Vincent (through the Gondis) with Louise (through the Capucines). Although nothing remains of the buildings (now at the Cour Vendôme), the Rue des Capucines (Paris 1) and the Boulevard des Capucines (Paris 1, 9) recall their presence, since the boulevard ran along the front of their convent at the north end of the Vendôme.

### 49. Church of Saint Madeleine (La Madeleine)
### (Place de la Madeleine, Paris 8)

This lavish and beautifully situated parish church, successor of earlier buildings, began as a Temple to Glory, part of the revolutionary cult. It was turned over to Catholic worship, and then consecrated in 1845 in honor of Saint Mary Magdalene. The Madeleine has a Saint Vincent chapel, with an imposing statue of him designed by Nicolo Raggi (1791-1862). The style (Vincent and two infants) is familiar, but the execution is not. Other than this, the Madeleine has no connection with Vincent de Paul.

Bust of Cardinal Pierre de Bérulle, Church of Saint Eustache

### 50. Church of Saint Eustache
### (Place du Jour, Paris 1)

This parish began in the fourteenth century in the district of the public markets of Paris *(Les Halles)*. The present Gothic church was begun in 1532 but was consecrated only in 1637 by Jean François de Gondi. It has, however, never been finished. The future Cardinal Richelieu was baptized here, and Louis XIV made his first communion here. In Vincent's time, in 1630 or 1631, a Confraternity of Charity was established here, but it did not work out well. Perhaps the reason was lack of support from the pastor, Etienne Le Tonnelier. In that same year, representing the other pastors of Paris, he had led an attempt against the approval of the Congregation of the Mission. During the period of the Revolution, Saint Eustache was named a temple of Agriculture. Afterwards, the building was restored to the Church and it has been often renovated. The third side chapel on the north is dedicated to Vincent de Paul, who lived in this parish in the Gondi household (somewhere on rue des Petits-Champs). A plaque notes that he lived here from 1613 to 1623. A small portrait of him and of Francis de Sales are just above the small chapel altar. Behind the main altar is a small monument to Cardinal Pierre de Bérulle, founder of the French Oratory, the community that serves the parish today. This monument is all that remains from Berulle's original tomb in the Oratorian seminary.

**50.a.** Adjoining Saint Eustache stood the

*Hôtel de Soissons*, built on a large property dating from at least the twelfth century. Here took place one of the most curious incidents reported about Vincent. Its source is Gédéon Tallemant des Réaux (1619-1692), whose anecdotes illuminate upper-class life in Vincent's time. Jean-Baptiste Crosilles (d. 1651), a young and corrupt diocesan priest, decided to secretly marry the young object of his affections. He and his valet changed identities to hide the truth, but after some time the girl's mother realized that something was amiss. Since she knew the duchess of Aiguillon, the latter referred the case to Vincent de Paul. He, in turn, summoned to Paris the priest who had unwittingly married Croseilles and the young woman. Then, on 20 August 1634, Vincent established a stakeout: the priest and two other witnesses would try to catch sight of the unfortunate priest as he left the Hôtel de Soissons. His red hair gave him away, and he was apprehended, judged and imprisoned. The magnificent building and gardens where he was visiting, now destroyed, were on the site of Les Halles and the Bourse de Commerce. *(1-7, rue Coquillière, Paris 1)*

### 51. The Louvre***
### (Quai du Louvre, Paris 1)

The Louvre—the meaning of this name is unknown—was the world's largest royal palace and is now one of the world's great art museums. Originally a fortress built to protect the city from the west, it often served as a royal residence. Vincent came here several times for royal functions before 1643 (when Louis XIII moved to Saint-Germain-en-Laye) and after 1652 (when the court returned). In Vincent's time, however, the palace was much smaller than it is now, missing most of the side wings. At the western end was the Tuileries Palace, built by Queen Catherine de Médicis, wife of Henri II. The Louvre began to be a museum with the private collections of Francis I and subsequent kings. The section dating from the saint's time is the western end of the Cour Carré, the enclosed square courtyard on the eastern end of the museum, built 1546-1570, and the Pavillon de Flore, built under Henry IV. It was probably at the Louvre that Mazarin made his insulting remark about Vincent's clothing which Abelly reported: *Look how Monsieur Vincent comes dressed for the court, and look at the beautiful cincture he wears!* (Book III, ch. 18)

Among the paintings in the museum from the time of Vincent, those by the Le Nain brothers are noteworthy because of their subject. They depicted the life of contemporary peasants, a life familiar to Vincent de Paul and Louise de Marillac and to the members of their communities.

51.a. At the end of the gardens of the former Tuileries Palace stands the vast *Place de la Concorde*. More than 1100 persons were executed here during the revolution, including Louis XVI, his wife, and eventually the major figures of the revolution, Danton, Hébert and Robespierre. No Vincentians or Daughters of Charity died here, however.

### 52. *Church of Saint Germain l'Auxerrois (of Auxerre)* (2, Place du Louvre, Paris 1)

This church was the royal parish from the fourteenth century, although the original church began in the eighth century. The present church includes elements from many centuries and styles, and, like other churches, was restored after the Revolution. Gravely damaged during the revolution of 1831, it was again restored and opened in 1837. Still, Saint Germain is one of the most important examples of the Flamboyant Gothic style in Paris, and the transept has preserved its late fifteenth-century windows. Of Vincentian interest is the presence of a Confraternity of Charity and Daughters of Charity in the parish. Also, Henri de Maupas Du Tour (1600-1680), bishop of Le Puy and a cousin of the Gondi family, gave a two-hour *funeral oration* here for Vincent de Paul. Members of the Tuesday Conferences, eager to honor their founder, had commissioned the bishop for the purpose. The resulting text was published in 1661. Although not a biography, it presents the main lines of Vincent's life and spirituality. The Saint Vincent chapel features two important paintings: a large canvas of Vincent searching for abandoned children in the snow, and a smaller portrait, both of nineteenth century origin. The window in the chapel is modern.

**52.a.** Near the church is the former church of the *Oratory*, a royal chapel under kings Louis XIII, Louis XIV and Louis XV. It was here, though in an earlier building, that on Sunday, 11 November 1618, Francis de Sales preached a simple sermon on Martin of Tours in the presence of the king and his court. It greatly affected Vincent de Paul, who was not present, but who referred to it as an exemplary act of humility. He quoted one young woman's sour comment: *Look at this country bumpkin, this mountaineer; how vilely he preaches! What good was it for him to come from such a distance to tell us what he said and to try the patience of so many people.* (Letter 1965) Despite her reaction, she later entered the visitation. The present building began in 1621. The right arm of Cardinal Pierre de Bérulle was buried here but was later transferred elsewhere. The funeral services of Louis XIII and his wife Anne of Austria were held here.

It was here, as well, that the first of three Vincentian constitutional bishops was ordained to the episcopacy. *Nicolas Philbert* (1724-1797), the pastor of the house in Sedan, took the constitutional oath. He then became bishop of the short-lived diocese of the Ardennes (Sedan) on 13 March 1791. The Reformed Church has used the Oratory since 1811. *(145, rue Saint Honoré, Paris 1)*

### 53. *Church of Saint Roch* (296, rue Saint Honoré, Paris 1)

Although this parish began in the fifteenth century, the young Louis XIV laid the foundation stone of the present church in 1653. It was mainly completed in the early eighteenth century, but subsequent additions have made it nearly as large as Notre Dame de Paris. Because of its many burials and funerary monuments, it resembles a pantheon. In this parish, the Daughters of Charity served in the time of Vincent and Louise. Their service often proved difficult, however, since the pastors created problems. After a battle in August 1792, the sisters demonstrated great charity to the wounded. In gratitude for their good example, the government allowed them to remain in the parish despite a general ban forbidding them. In front of this church on 5 October 1795, the young Napoleon Bonaparte won an important street battle that helped to solidify his rise to power. One of the side chapels is dedicated to Saint Vincent and has two large nineteenth-century paintings.

53.a. Across from the church of Saint Roch stood a house rented by Vincent to house the *galley convicts* (1618-1632). Nothing visible remains of this house, and its exact site is unknown.

53.b. Just to the west of Saint Roch is the Rue du Marché Saint Honoré. This street was opened in 1807 over the site of the church of the convent of the Annunciation, of the reformed Dominicans. Founded in 1612 by their confreres from the Rue Saint Jacques, they too were called Jacobins. At the Revolution, the "Friends of the Constitution" began to meet in the monastic dining room, later in the library. Quickly called the *Jacobin Club*, this political group grew very radical and severe. Its public meetings were a source of much revolutionary activity. Because

of the evils that resulted from them, the old monastery was demolished. A large modern market has replaced it.

### 54. Chapel of Notre Dame de Consolation
### (23, rue Jean Goujon, Paris 8)

For many years, a bazaar was held to help various works of charity in the city. The 1897 bazaar opened on 4 May. Flimsy wooden booths and flammable cloth to represent medieval Paris streets provided the decoration. A moving-picture projector bulb exploded, according to witnesses, and flames quickly engulfed the crowds. One hundred thirty-five people died, many of them of the upper classes, such as the duchess of Alençon, sister of the empress of Austria. Among the dead were three Daughters of Charity: Marie Sabatier, Vincent Dehondt and Anna Ginoux de Fermon. A solemn ceremony of remembrance was held at Notre Dame a few days later, and within a year a plan developed to build a commemorative chapel. Our Lady of Consolation was completed in 1900. Among others, Vincent de Paul is depicted inside as a saint known for his charity. The vault of the dome shows Jesus receiving the victims of the fire in heaven. A sign outside reads simply "Memorial of the Charity Bazaar." The building now serves as a chapel for Italian Catholics.

### 55. Convent of the Visitation, Chaillot
### (54, avenue de New York, Paris 16)

Another convent of the Visitation, a daughter-house of the first convent, was founded in 1651 in Chaillot, at the time a quiet Paris suburb. Whether Vincent came here is unknown but, as the ecclesiastical superior of the Visitation convents of Paris, he was involved in the founding of this new work. The convent closed in 1790 and its buildings were demolished in 1794. Since then the area has been spectacularly developed into the gardens of the Trocadero on the banks of the Seine, below the Palace of Chaillot.

### 56. Convent of Our Lady of Humility, Longchamp
### (Allée du Bord de l'Eau, Bois de Boulogne, Paris 16)

Decidedly less austere than the Visitation convent was the notorious convent of Longchamp. Level ground on the banks of the Seine offered a secure and peaceful terrain for this monastery, dating from 1225. Over the years, however, it became extremely lax. Henri IV, in fact, took a mistress from among the nuns—the abbess herself, Catherine de Verdun, aged 22. Vincent de Paul visited here, and his reports (one in French, the other in Latin) detail some of the problems he met. *It is certain that for two hundred years the good odor of Christ in this monastery has been turning into the offensive odor of the corruption of flagging discipline and morals…The parlors are not closed but open to anyone, even to young men who are not relatives…Some nuns wear indecent and immodest clothing; in the parlors they wear flame-colored headbands and gold watches. They also put on special gloves they call Spanish gloves.* (Letter 1564, Latin text) Despite reforming efforts, the convent continued its lax ways until 1792 and was demolished in 1795. One or two place names recall its presence here, and a tower from the old abbey has been preserved. Today, the property is the site of the renowned Longchamp racetrack, at the north side of which the picturesque tower of the abbey mill can be seen.

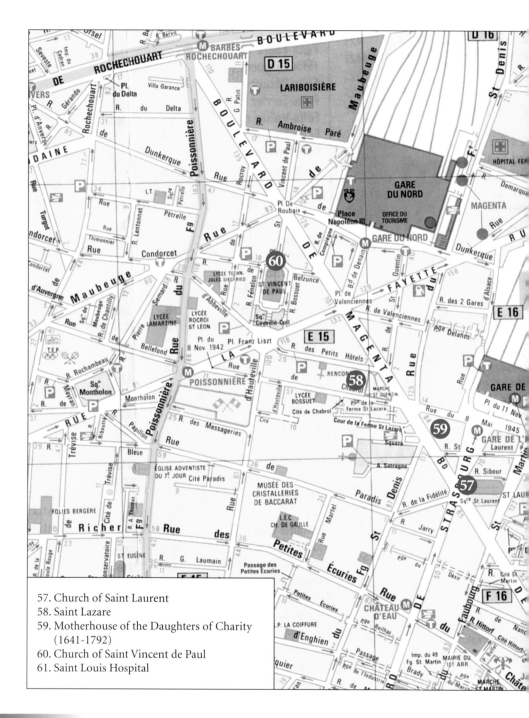

57. Church of Saint Laurent
58. Saint Lazare
59. Motherhouse of the Daughters of Charity
    (1641-1792)
60. Church of Saint Vincent de Paul
61. Saint Louis Hospital

# ARRONDISSMENTS 9, 10

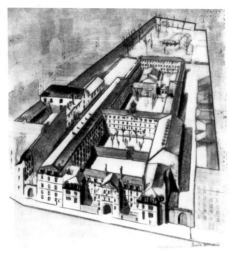

Saint Lazare as a prison,
20th century drawing

### 57. Church of Saint Laurent**
### (68, boulevard Magenta, and 119, rue du Faubourg Saint Martin, Paris 10)

In 583, Gregory of Tours mentioned this monastic church, begun as a chapel. It overlooked a Roman road, now the Rue du Faubourg Saint Denis. The present church, whose choir was dedicated in 1429, replaces an earlier one. Only the old tower remains from the twelfth-century church. The fifteenth-century church has been enlarged and reconstructed several times. During the revolutionary period, it was used as a Temple of Reason, then a Temple of Old Age (1798). It was restored to the Catholic Church in 1802. The monastic enclosure was removed when the Boulevard Magenta was put through in the nineteenth century, and its neo-Gothic façade dates only from 1865,

built to fit the building to the new street.

Saint Laurent was the parish church of Vincent de Paul from 1632 to 1660, and of Louise de Marillac from 1641 to 1660. Although she had requested burial at Saint Lazare, the pastor overrode Louise's wishes, and she was buried in the chapel of the Visitation in this church where she came to pray and to make her Easter Communion with the other sisters. Her remains lay here for 95 years, until 1755, when her body was transferred to the motherhouse. Marking the spot is the simple wooden

Church of Saint Laurent, postcard

cross with the words *Spes Unica*, ["(Hail, O Cross, our) Only Hope"], from the hymn *Vexilla Regis*, the monument she requested in her will.

Several modern paintings and stained glass windows show Saint Vincent blessing Saint Louise and the first Daughters of Charity, and Saint Vincent performing works of mercy (galley convicts, slaves in Algiers, etc.). A small plaque also reads: "1660. Saint Vincent de Paul, founder of the priests of the Mission and of the Sisters of Charity, often visited the Church of Saint Laurent, his parish church." On one of his many visits to Parisian churches during his long stay, Pius VII came to Saint Laurent in 1804.

Guillaume de Lestocq (d. 1661), pastor of Saint Laurent from 1627 to 1661, came with Adrien Le Bon (1577?-1651), the prior of Saint Lazare, to offer the property of Saint Lazare to Monsieur Vincent. After repeated and lengthy discussion and discernment, they succeeded. Lestocq assisted Louise on her deathbed and celebrated her funeral, since Vincent de Paul was ill and confined to his room. Lestocq would also send confessors from the parish to the Daughters' motherhouse. A later pastor, Nicholas Gobillon (1626-1706), revered Louise de Marillac and wrote her first biography. To the right of the church is a small park, the Square Saint Laurent, which marks the site of one section of the parish cemetery. Many of the earliest Daughters of Charity were buried, however, on the north side in another section opened in 1662, adjacent to the chapel where Louise herself was interred.

Their remains were removed beginning in 1804 and placed in the catacombs of Paris. This removal was occasioned by public health concerns all through the city in the late eighteenth and early nineteenth centuries.

During the sack of Saint Lazare, revolutionaries burst into its house chapel. Finding a reliquary of Saint Vincent, four of them brought it reverently to Saint Laurent for safekeeping. Others took the Blessed Sacrament from the chapel to the nearby chapel of the Augustinian Recollects. They then returned to the task at hand—looting and pillaging.

Church of Saint Laurent, interior

Vincent de Paul, stained glass window,
Church of Saint Laurent

### 58. Saint Lazare***
### (107, rue du Faubourg Saint Denis, Paris 10)

The motherhouse of the Congregation of the Mission, which gave the name Lazarists to the members, takes it title from Saint Lazare or Lazarus, its patron. The gospels portray two men named Lazarus. One was the leper in the parable (Luke 16). He accounts for the original purpose of this vast property, the care of lepers. The other Lazarus, the brother of Martha and Mary, Jesus raised from the dead (John 11-12). Vincent was likely referring to this person when he said that Saint Lazare should be a place of resurrection. This Lazarus is the figure on the coat of arms of Saint Lazare.

This ancient property was men-

tioned as early as the sixth century. At Vincent's time, it housed no lepers, or one at the most, and only a few other patients and prisoners. Although it had enjoyed royal support for centuries, the monks who lived here had lost their original mission, were growing old and were looking for someone to take the property. The prior, Adrien Le Bon, offered it to Vincent, who hesitated long before accepting it. In its day Saint Lazare was the largest ecclesiastical property in Paris. Besides its contiguous land north of the city, the priory also owned extensive property and houses elsewhere,

Saint Vincent de Paul altar, Saint Lazare
chapel, 18th century engraving

mainly in the Paris suburbs. It was also responsible for the Saint Laurent Fair (held across the street), and for the exercise of justice nearby. Many years later he reflected on the gift of this huge property: *I was dumbfounded, like a man surprised by the report of cannon fired close to him when he was not thinking of it; he is dazed by such an unexpected noise...I was speechless.* (Letter 2001, 30 January 1656)

During Vincent's lifetime, the house undertook the formation of the missionaries, retreats for ordinands (13,000+ between 1628 and 1660), Tuesday Conferences for clergy, retreats for clergy and lay people (20,000 in 20 years), missions for the poor in the neighborhood, care for refugees in times of war, and feeding the hungry. A relic from its past as a medieval fief was the lunatic asylum and prison located on its vast grounds. A law court also met here, and one day Vincent reported to the Daughters of Charity: *When I was passing through the courtyard of Saint Lazare on my way here, I heard that the Court of Justice had met to condemn a man. I was touched to the heart, and yet what is temporal condemnation compared with spiritual? The state of that poor sufferer seemed most pitiable because he was waiting to be condemned.* (Conference 23) On a happier note, many bishops and religious founders were among the clergy who made their retreats here, such as Bossuet, bishop of Meaux, and Rancé, the founder of the Trappists.

Vincent de Paul lived here from 1632 until his death on 27 September 1660. Saint Lazare was the motherhouse for the Congregation of the Mission until the beginning of August 1792, and received clerical and lay guests from all over France and elsewhere as well during those years. Mobs sacked it in the early morning of 13 July 1789. Originally in search of weapons to defend the city, which they did not find, they began to look for grain and wine, which they did find. This turned into a riot, which succeeded in despoiling the house of its doors, windows, paintings, books, papers, relics, medicines, money, etc. They did not harm the crucifixes in its more than 600 rooms, however. The

Saint Lazare, diorama,
DePaul University, Chicago

Entry, Saint Lazare, postcard

97

Monument, Square Alban Satrange

inhabitants fled as best they could. Some 100 Vincentians returned but had to leave at last by 1 September 1792. Saint Vincent's skeleton had been removed from its gilded reliquary and placed in a small box for safekeeping. The old prison on the grounds then expanded to fill the rest of the buildings. A general prison from 18 January 1794, and later restricted to women until 1932 (among its famous inmates was the convicted spy Mata Hari, executed in 1917), Saint Lazare was partly taken down in 1824, closed in 1932, and mostly demolished the following year. Further changes to the property took place in 1941, at which time some tombs of the early Vincentians were identified, and their remains removed (the original tomb of

Vincent, bones of Fathers Alméras, Jolly and other superiors general, all of whom were buried there).

Of the old buildings, regarded as the headquarters of charity, little remains. The following, however, can be seen.

(1) *Chapel*: Two old walls are still visible in front of the post office. Although not part of the old chapel, they give some idea of the former buildings. The walls today enclose some shops and a small hotel. In the founder's time, the public entered the property from the south side where the old apartment buildings were built. They then went along the walls and entered the chapel on the west. In this chapel, Vincent de Paul was buried. Beginning in 1730, after his beatification, his body was presented more or less as it is today: in a glass-fronted gilt casket above the side altar dedicated to Saint Lazarus. In this chapel were hung eleven large canvases painted for his canonization, although the chapel was too small even for the local community. Out of respect for him, the chapel was not damaged during the sack, but it was briefly used as a hay barn before being restored to public worship. It was demolished in 1823 and covered by a new wing of the prison that had taken the place of the old priory. Many bishops received their episcopal ordination in this chapel, both in Vincent's day and later.

(2) ***Main buildings***: The buildings used by Vincent and his confreres were situated on what is now the public park (Square Alban Satragne, set up in 1964), and the Saint Lazare Hospital. Nothing else remains, however, except the walls mentioned above, and these were probably part of an inside courtyard of the larger building. After Vincent's death, the coat of arms of Saint Lazare, the design for which dates to the thirteenth century, were placed above the main entry. These have been transferred to the hospital building and are visible from the park adjoining the post office and hospital. The "king's residence" *(logis du Roi)* was located among the other buildings. While entering Paris after their coronation, the kings of France customarily stopped at Reims to receive the oath of fealty from the representatives of the city. Royal remains also were brought here after their funeral

Windmill, Saint Lazare,
17th century drawing

mass at the cathedral while on the way for burial at the abbey of Saint Denis.

(3) ***Passageways***: To the north of these old walls is a narrow street, Cour de la Ferme Saint Lazare. This marked the entry to the farm. Leading off from Cour de la Ferme Saint Lazare is the Passage de la Ferme Saint Lazare. At ground level is an old well, now mostly blocked up, which served the old buildings. The sisters came here at times to fetch water for their motherhouse.

(4) ***Apartment buildings***: South of the entry *(99-105, rue du Faubourg Saint Denis)* are two parallel apartment buildings, built in the time of Father Jean Bonnet (from 1719 to 1720) as rental property to help support the establishment. In 1724 the Vincentians advertised for tenants and promised a safe and religious environment, but mainly retired military and police officials lived there. While the crowd of revolutionaries was sacking the building, some of the Vincentians succeeded in crawling along the chapel gutters to safety in these buildings.

(5) ***Mural*** to Saint Vincent on the north end of the apartment buildings, executed in 1988. This work of the artist Yvaral (Jean-Pierre Vasarely, 1934-2002) was sponsored by the 10th arrondissement.

(6) ***Monument*** to Saint Vincent, a gray marble plinth with a bronze medallion based on the one struck in 1960 for the Tercentenary of his

death. The text, *"Que j'ai peine de votre peine"* ["How sorry I am about your suffering"] expresses, in a humanistic way, the saint's compassion, although he addressed it to Louise pestered by a man who claimed she had promised to marry him. (Letter 92) The monument stands in the park. Representatives of the city inaugurated the monument, originally planned as a statue, on 20 June 1974.

(7) *Plaque* on the *Saint Lazare* hospital chapel (later an amphitheater) recalling Vincent's presence and his social activities but not his sanctity. The hospital was built in 1874. The rest of the hospital, built 1935-1940, continues the name and the hospital tradition of the old priory. It was largely remodeled in 1971-1972.

(8) *Gare du Nord* (North railway station): This station stands on the property that ran north to Boulevard Rochechouart/La Chapelle. (However, neither Gare de l'Est nor Gare Saint Lazare stands on former Saint Lazare property. Gare Saint Lazare was named after Boulevard Saint Lazare running in front of it, and which led, in turn, toward the original Saint Lazare.)

(9) *Saint Charles Seminary*: This seminary, originally called Little Saint Lazare, was located north on the same property, today the corner of Boulevard de La Chapelle and Rue du Faubourg Saint Denis. Founded as a minor seminary, it became a retirement home for priests. Property

surrounding it had one or more windmills and houses that Vincent de Paul leased out to others. Somewhere here, at the rear of the property, stood a small hermitage. Louise reported that Antoine Portail (1590-1660), Vincent's first companion, lived in it during his last years. (Letter 650) *(203, rue du Faubourg Saint Denis)*

(10) *Hospice of the Thirteen Houses*: This work for the foundlings, begun in 1645 was confided to the Daughters, and they remained here until 1670, when they began the Foundling Hospital. All the houses have disappeared. For reasons unknown, a rumor circulated that sisters who did not work out elsewhere were missioned here, "as if it were a prison." Vincent squelched the rumor as best he could. (Conference 78) *(132-148, rue du Faubourg Saint Denis)*

(11) *Hospice of the Holy Name of Jesus*: This home for elderly men and women opened in 1653. Although near by, on the site of the Gare de l'Est, it was not on the original Saint Lazare property. The hospice continued at this location until 1790 but was later transformed and moved to suburban Ivry, where it remains. The buildings became in later years the motherhouse of the Brothers of the Christian Schools. Some of Vincent's confreres became unhappy with their service here. He quoted their concerns. *Why burden ourselves with a hospital? Look at the poor people in the*

*Hospital of the Name of Jesus who interfere with our work. Is it necessary to go there to say mass, to instruct them, to administer the Sacraments and at the same time to provide them with the necessities of life?* (Conference 195) *(165, rue du Faubourg Saint Martin)*

(12) **Saint Laurent Fair**: A public summer market of great antiquity took place across the street from Saint Lazare, which oversaw its operation from the twelfth century. In Vincent's time, the fair was located at the north end of the property, near La Chapelle. Early theatrical performances were also held here, as well as games and sports. Vincent commented on the *silly tricks and games* played there, and how they tempted a sister serving in the parish. (Conference 5) In 1663, the Vincentians spent a large amount of money to move the fair closer to its ancient location. Some speculate that the location of the elegant porcelain and crystal shops on the Rue de Paradis began with sales at the Saint Laurent Fair. Several receipts exist signed by Vincent, renting space to exhibitors. The fair remained under Vincentian control until the Revolution. The successor to the fair is the public market, Marché Saint Quentin, built in 1866, located on the west side of Boulevard Magenta.

The enormous Saint Lazare property ran from Rue du Faubourg Saint Denis south to Rue du Paradis, west to Rue du Faubourg Poissonnière, north to Boulevard de La Chapelle, and then again to Rue du Faubourg Saint Denis. An inner section was enclosed, which with the buildings and adjacent land amounted, in Vincent's estimation, to about 80 arpents (equivalent to 32 hectares). Father Jolly later bought a smaller section of about 50 arpents (20 hectares) on the north side. The whole covered the equivalent of about 52 hectares or 128 acres. A map of the eighteenth century noted with amazement that the property was larger even than the Tuileries Gardens, at that time about 35 hectares. Various walls surrounded the entire property at different periods. An important battle was fought on the grounds during the revolution of 1848. The *Lariboisière* Hospital was built on the north side of this property after 1818. Despite its connections with Vincent de Paul, the Italianate hospital chapel contains no mention of him.

58.a. To the south of Saint Lazare is the church of **Notre Dame de Bonne Nouvelle**. Anne of Austria often came to pray here during the years before the birth of Louis XIV. The present church, dating from the nineteenth century, contains many fine paintings. Among them is one of Saint Vincent preaching on behalf of the foundlings (modeled on a painting by Paul Delaroche). *(19 bis, rue Beauregard, Paris 2)* Daughters of Charity worked here at the time of the Revolution and suffered much ill treatment from revolutionaries. Kindly neighbors helped them to survive during a period of house arrest in their convent. The church takes the name Bonne

Nouvelle from the hill on which it is built, called various names over the ages. This hill is actually an artificial mound of debris and garbage in place since the tenth century. In Vincent's time, it was called Ville-Neuve-sur-Gravois, *gravois* being debris. Because the priory of Saint Lazare had feudal rights to legal jurisdiction, its magistrates could pronounce sentences. One of the prisons was on the grounds of the priory, and the other was somewhere here, where stakes and iron collars were set up in the square in front of Vincent's prison.

### 59. Motherhouse of the Daughters of Charity (1641-1792)
**(94-114, rue du Faubourg Saint Denis, Paris 10)**

Directly across the street from Saint Lazare was the motherhouse of the Daughters of Charity. When purchased, it consisted of two joined houses, each with a ground floor and two upper floors, as well as large grounds, next to Saint Laurent church. The sisters at first rented it from Vincent de Paul but after 1 April 1653 owned it outright. It was here that the famous incident of the collapsed ceiling took place, 7 June 1642. Louise and the sisters escaped unharmed, a result that symbolized for her God's providential care of the Company. Since for years the sisters had no water piped directly into their property, they had to go daily to the public Saint Lazare fountain, built in the thirteenth century, to fetch water in buckets for the house. (*116, rue du Faubourg Saint Denis*) However, since the women often had to endure many lewd remarks made by male water-carriers, they were then instructed to go inside Saint Lazare to fetch water in safety. According to testimony given to prepare for Vincent's beatification, the saint one day had met a sister weeping at the main door over these insults. He then filled her buckets himself and brought them across the street to the convent. Fortunately, the sisters were able to have water piped in by 1659. Vincent gave many of his conferences to the Daughters here, and meetings of the Ladies of Charity were likewise held in this house. Louise died here, 15 March 1660. The Daughters of Charity treasure her last words: *My dear sisters, I continue to ask God for His blessings for you and pray that He will grant you the grace to persevere in your vocation in order to serve Him in the manner He asks of you. Take good care of the service of the poor. Above all, live together in great union and cordiality, loving one another in imitation of the union and life of Our Lord. Pray earnestly to the Blessed Virgin, that she may be your only Mother.*

The statue known as **Our Lady of the Mission** stood in their garden until the Revolution. This fourteenth-century statue was originally on one of the gates of Paris. When the gate was demolished, the statue was moved and, in 1681, given to the Daughters of Charity. This statue is today in the present motherhouse, Rue du Bac.

During the attack on Saint Lazare in 1789, some revolutionaries visited the sisters who treated them kindly and got them to leave. One of the Vincentians, the Italian assistant general, Domenico

Sicardi, spent that morning hiding in the confessional. Other revolutionaries came during the evening, but the sight of the sisters, especially of some novices who had fainted in the chapel, caused the leaders of the mob to leave. The sisters were dispersed finally in 1792, although not being nuns, strictly speaking, they were not bound by all the revolutionary decrees concerning nuns. When the building was sold in 1794 as property of the state, the body of Louise was left in the chapel, but in 1797, a new owner decided to demolish the chapel. He sold Louise's remains to Sister Deleau, the superioress general, who had them transferred for a few weeks to a nearby house *(91, rue du Faubourg Saint Martin)*, where two sisters were hiding. On 10 October of the same year the relics were authenticated and brought to the provisional residence on Rue des Maçons Sorbonne (now Rue Champollion). The rest of the buildings remained until 1889 when they were torn down to make way for the new Boulevards de Strasbourg and Magenta. The latter cut in two the site of the old buildings and grounds.

### 60. Church of Saint Vincent de Paul*
### (Place Franz Liszt, Paris 10)

On top of a small hill within the property of Saint Lazare used to be a small shelter that the seminarians and others used for recreation. On that site now stands a parish church of the archdiocese of Paris in honor of Saint Vincent. It replaced a smaller one *(6, rue de Montholon, Paris 9)*, which in turn

replaced the public chapel at Saint Lazare. The present church of this influential parish was built, with interruptions, from 1824 to 1844 in the style of early Christian basilicas. The principal architect, Jacques Ignace Hittorff (1792-1867), one of the leading architects of his day, also designed the neighboring Gare du Nord, completed the presentation of the Place de la Concorde and many other public and private buildings. He adorned the pediment of this church with the imposing, but un-Vincentian, "Glorification of Saint Vincent de Paul" (1848). The work of Charles-François Leboeuf (1792-1865), this sculpture imitates those adorning pagan Greek temples, but depicts Daughters of Charity, a Vincentian, galley convicts, foundlings and a recent convert. The twelve columns are said to represent the twelve apostles. The porch was originally decorated with large paintings of Old and New Testament scenes, done in a new technique using enamel over lava blocks. The scandal caused by the lightly clad figures of Adam and Eve and of Jesus at his baptism caused their removal.

Inside, between two rows of

Church of Saint Vincent de Paul, postcard

Corinthian columns, is a frieze of 205 saints, men on one side, women on the other, moving in procession towards Christ in Majesty. The Lord is depicted on the inside of the half-dome in the apse (1849-1853), surrounded by prophets, kings and apostles, and blessing the children brought him by Vincent de Paul. Strangely, Vincent's face does not show, as he turns toward the Lord. The inlaid floor is noteworthy, as is the fine organ by Cavaillé-Coll, recently restored. A plaque also commemorates Saint Louise de Marillac, co-foundress of the Daughters of Charity. A typical statue of the charitable Saint Vincent with children, the work of Casciani, became the subject of meditation by the actor Pierre Fresnay while preparing to make his award-winning film *Monsieur Vincent*. In the sacristy are, or were kept, some items from the chapel of the former Saint Lazare.

**60.a.** In front of the church is a small park, the *Square Saint Vincent de Paul,* and behind it is a small street bearing his name. The main square takes its name from the composer *Franz Liszt*, who lived nearby. It was once claimed that Liszt either was a Vincentian or wanted to be. This arose from a misunderstanding: the artist had gone to the Vincentian house in Rome, Montecitorio, to make a retreat before his admission to tonsure. Liszt was neither a priest nor a Vincentian.

**60.b.** To the east of the church is a youth center named in honor of the saint *(12, rue Bossuet)*, and to the west *(6, rue de*

Street signs, Rue St. Vincent de Paul

*Rocroy)* is a Catholic school named in his honor. The front of the building has a typical Parisian statue of the saint with a child in his arms and at his side. Both of these institutions keep alive the memory of the saint who made the Saint Lazare property, on which they now stand, so famous.

**60.c.** A church similar in size and age is the church of *Sainte Trinité* (the Holy Trinity). Built between 1861 and 1867, it dominates its district. In a side chapel are two paintings of Saint Vincent, extraordinary for their subjects: Saint Vincent leading the galley convicts to the faith (1876), and Saint Vincent aiding Alsace and Lorraine (1879). Both are the work of Jean-Jules-Antoine Lecomte de Nouÿ (1842-1923). *(3, rue de la Trinité, Paris 9)*

### 61. Saint Louis Hospital
### (1, avenue Claude Vellefaux, Paris 10)

This is the oldest standing hospital in Paris, built by order of Henri IV (from 1607 to 1613) to house the plague-stricken. This order followed the grave epidemics of the two previous years, which filled the Hôtel Dieu to overflowing. Henri IV named this new foundation after his predecessor Louis IX, who died of the plague in 1270. When built, the hospital was outside the city, and presumably ideal for contagious patients, since the building plan kept them isolated behind double walls. The hospital also housed wounded soldiers at various times.

Vincent and Louise did not have priests or sisters working here, although it was close to their respective motherhouses. Instead, seriously ill members of the two congregations were occasionally sent here for care. The best known of these is *Marguerite Naseau*, or more properly Nezot (1594-1632), traditionally regarded as the first Daughter of Charity, although she died one year before the Company's official foundation. Marguerite contracted the plague while ministering to the sick poor and died at this hospital. Vincent described Marguerite's death for the other sisters: *Her charity was so great that she died from sharing her bed with a poor plague-stricken girl. When she was attacked by the fever, she bade good-bye to the sister who was with her, as if she had foreseen that she was about to die, and went to the hospital of Saint Louis, her heart filled with joy and conformity to God's will.* (Conference 12, July 1642)

The hospital's freestanding *chapel* dates from the period of the hospital's construction, opening in 1609. By coincidence, the first religious ceremony held in the chapel was a memorial service in honor of the assassinated king Henri IV.

A statue of Saint Vincent (on the Stouf design) is prominent. The seventeenth-century pulpit is said to have come from the chapel of the Foundling Hospital *(Enfants Trouvés)*, where the Daughters of Charity served. The pulpit is decorated with symbols of charity and of Saint Augustine, noted for his charity. At the Revolution, the chapel windows were destroyed and the furnishings dispersed, but it has been restored to Catholic worship. *(12, rue de la Grange Aux Belles, Paris 10)*

**61.a.** In the same district was the notorious gibbet of *Montfaucon*, where the bodies of as many as 30 or 40 executed criminals were hung to terrify and warn the people. Built in the thirteenth century on a small rise along main roads, the gibbet continued in use until 1627. It came to have a symbolic meaning as can be seen from a conference during which Vincent exclaimed to his confreres: *Sometimes in the evening, when I consider what my mind has been occupied with, a thousand useless things, and I know not how many silly trifles, so that I find it hard to stand myself, I think I deserve to be hung at Montfaucon.* (Conference 185, 5 July 1658) It was torn down finally in 1760. Remains of several bodies and of the gibbet itself were discovered in recent years. With the building of new apartments and recreation facilities, and its old pathways named after poets and composers, Montfaucon has lost its grim character. *(53-61, rue Grange aux Belles and Place Robert Desnos, Paris 10)*

62. Montmartre (the "Butte")
63. La Chapelle
64. La Villette

## ARRONDISSMENTS 18, 19

### 62. Montmartre (The "Butte") (Paris 18)

The Mount of the Martyrs commemorates Saints Denis (the first bishop of Paris), Rusticus and Eleutherius, martyred about the year 250. A large Benedictine abbey was built here, lasting to the Revolution. The only remaining building of the abbey is the church of Saint Peter, perhaps the oldest church in Paris, and its first Gothic church. Its marble columns are believed to have come from a Roman temple on the hill. The tomb of Queen Adelaide, wife of Louis VI, "the Fat," is in a side aisle. She had founded the abbey in 1133. Such saints as Bernard and Joan of Arc came here to pray. In addition, one of the witnesses for his canonization proceedings said that Vincent had given a mission to the poor workers in the stone quarries of Montmartre. Daughters of Charity often asked permission to come here on pilgrimage. *(2, rue du Mont Cenis, Paris 18)*

62.a. Down the hill is the small chapel where Ignatius Loyola and his first followers came to pray. This chapel, the *Martyrium*, marks the site of the martyrdom of Saint Denis and his companions. Vincent is presumed to have come here often, since it was on the way between Paris and Clichy. Many others in his period also did the same, such as Pierre de Bérulle, Francis de Sales, and Madame Acarie. It was probably here, too, that Vincent's early confreres, fewer than twelve at the time, came to pray and commit themselves to the practice of poverty. Because of the founder's illness, he was unable to accompany them. The date is unknown, but it must have been before 1630. The present chapel, built in 1887, replaces the one destroyed at the Revolution. *(11, rue Yvonne-Le-Tac, Paris 18)*

62.b. After the Franco-Prussian war (1870-1871), some Catholics undertook the construction of a shrine on the top of Montmartre. Its purpose was to honor the Sacred Heart *(Sacré Coeur)*, to fulfill a national vow to obtain the deliverance of the nation. The building, in Roman-Byzantine style, was completed in 1910, consecrated in 1919. Its dome dominates the skyline. An important chapel is dedicated to Saint Vincent; the Vincentians and the Daughters of Charity, who paid for the chapel and its furnishings, were in the habit of yearly renewing a consecration to the Sacred Heart in this chapel. The mosaic on the left side of the chapel illustrates the devotion of Saint Louise to the Sacred Heart, depicting the Lord of Charity, with the sacred heart painted by Louise herself. (The original of this canvas belonged to the cathedral of Cahors, which later gave it to the motherhouse of the Daughters of Charity.) Vincent is also represented in the large mosaic in the apse, among the group of saints approaching the figure of Christ in Majesty.

Perpetual adoration has been held in the basilica since 1885, and many thousands have come to pray. It narrowly escaped destruction during the second World War as bombs dropped near the front of the building. A marble plaque records the places where the bombs fell. Pope John Paul II came here in 1980. The building has been designated a minor basilica.

**62.c.** Behind the Butte is the parish of *Notre Dame du Bon Conseil* (Our Lady of Good Counsel). It is under the administration of the Religious of Saint Vincent de Paul. This congregation was founded in 1845 by Jean Léon Le Prévost and others, former laymen active in the Society of Saint Vincent de Paul. Le Prévost's cause for canonization has been introduced. This modern church has a window depicting Saint Vincent exhorting the Ladies of Charity. *(140, rue de Clignancourt, Paris 18)*

### 63. *La Chapelle** (Paris 18)

This village north of Paris, but now a part of the city, inhabited by wine-growers, market gardeners and innkeepers, adjoined the north end of the property of Saint Lazare. The village took its name from a small chapel dedicated to Saint Geneviève, who is said to have stopped here on her way to Saint Denis, farther north. Joan of Arc, on her way to liberate Paris from the English in 1429, stayed in La Chapelle and prayed in the old chapel, now called *Saint Denys de La Chapelle*. Vincent de Paul held missions here (1641, 1642) for war refugees from Lorraine, and erected a Confraternity of Charity. With the passage of troops during the Fronde, many inhabitants were slaughtered at the doors of the church, where they had hoped to receive sanctuary. The parish church has a side altar dedicated to Saint Vincent, with nineteenth-century paintings and a stained glass window depicting the founding of the Daughters of Charity. *(96, rue de La Chapelle, Paris 18)*

**63.a.** *Louise de Marillac* moved to La Chapelle in 1636 from the parish of Saint Nicolas du Chardonnet to be close, but not too close, to Vincent de Paul. She remained here until about 1641. During that time, she formed the sisters and occasionally received Ladies of Charity who arrived to make a retreat. Years later, a grateful sister recalled that Antoine Portail exercised great charity toward the sisters, coming to see them here in the winter, through the mud, even to hear the confession of just one sister—perhaps herself. (Conference 118) After 1641, Louise and the others left here to move to buildings across the street from Saint Lazare. A plaque today marks the site in La Chapelle, and a small park bears Louise's name (*Square Louise de Marillac*). The building where Louise and the first sisters lived was demolished about 1885. *(2, rue Marx Dormoy, Paris 18)*

**63.b.** The other parish church in the village, *Saint Bernard de La Chapelle*, began in 1858. It contains a small chapel dedicated to Saint Vincent. Its most notable feature is two paintings of the saint (exhorting a prisoner, finding an abandoned child) dated 1867. They depict an aged saint. *(11, rue Affre, Paris 18)*

**63.c.** The archdiocese of Paris honored Louise de Marillac by dedicating a new church in her honor in the suburban town of **Drancy**, not far from La Chapelle. Daughters of Charity served in this working-class suburb, now in the new diocese of Saint Denis, in Louise's lifetime. Saint Lazare had property in the area as well. Louise's work is summarized in a large painting in the apse as well as in others around the church. *(1-3, rue Anatole France, Drancy)* Daughters of Charity returned to Drancy about 1862, and the Vincentians briefly had the original parish (1872-1875).

### 64. La Villette
### (Paris 19)

In Vincent's day, the Saint Lazare priory also possessed property in *La Villette Saint Lazare*, now called simply La Villette. The name was known as early as the twelfth century. When Vincent took over the old priory, he also received its 57 houses and gardens, the church and presbytery of La Villette Saint Lazare, as well as the convent of Saint Périne. Vincent looked here at property for a motherhouse for Louise de Marillac. Not finding any, he settled on La Chapelle.

The present church is called **Saint Jacques-Saint Christophe de La Villette.** The first church, *(132, rue de Flandre)*, depended on the Saint Laurent parish but was under the jurisdiction of Saint Lazare. Across from the church was another of Saint Lazare's jails. As La Villette grew, it was decided to relocate the church. The present church has a façade from the nineteenth century, but the interior construction and design dates from the 1930s. *(Place de Bitche, Paris 19)*

**64.a.** The convent, named **Saint Périne** after Saint Petronilla, dated from the twelfth century. It changed its affiliation several times over the centuries. After the first nuns left or died out, some Canonesses Regular of Saint Augustine, founded in Compiègne, took it over in Vincent's time. These nuns suffered financial and disciplinary problems, and merged with another group in Chaillot in the eighteenth century. They took the old name with them, which accounts for the convent of Saint Périne of Chaillot. The property in La Villette was sold in 1748, and in a few years was purchased to house a new community founded by Sister Marie Ignace Malo (1701-1761), a former Daughter of Charity. She sought to help the poor and sick children of the district, and gradually gathered some other women. They formed the community of the Holy Family of the Sacred Heart of Jesus of La Villette, nicknamed the Malottes. The community was suppressed at the Revolution.

**64.b.** On the property today is **Notre Dame des Foyers**, a small parish church. The entrance to the old convent in La Villette was on rue de Flandre, and the property continued west to Rue de Tanger. *(61-65, rue de Flandre, Paris 19)*

# Suburbs

*These near suburbs of Paris are listed below in alphabetical order. In the seventeenth century they were villages surrounding Paris. Today, they form part of greater Paris, located in three départements: Hauts-de-Seine, Val-de-Marne and Seine-Saint-Denis. Vincent de Paul and Louise de Marillac had many connections with these villages.*

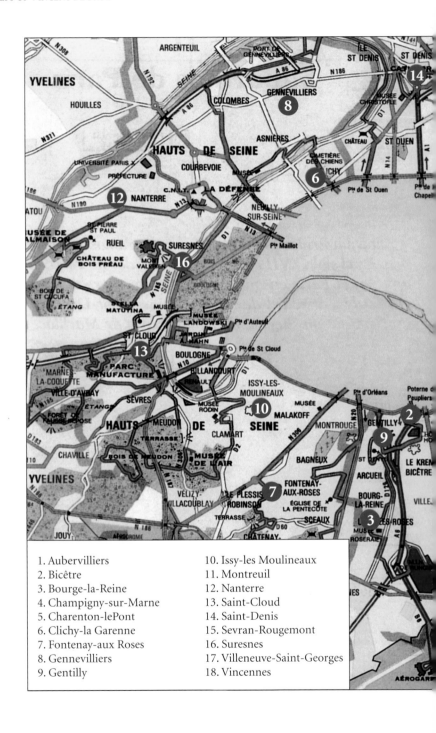

1. Aubervilliers
2. Bicêtre
3. Bourge-la-Reine
4. Champigny-sur-Marne
5. Charenton-lePont
6. Clichy-la Garenne
7. Fontenay-aux Roses
8. Gennevilliers
9. Gentilly
10. Issy-les Moulineaux
11. Montreuil
12. Nanterre
13. Saint-Cloud
14. Saint-Denis
15. Sevran-Rougemont
16. Suresnes
17. Villeneuve-Saint-Georges
18. Vincennes

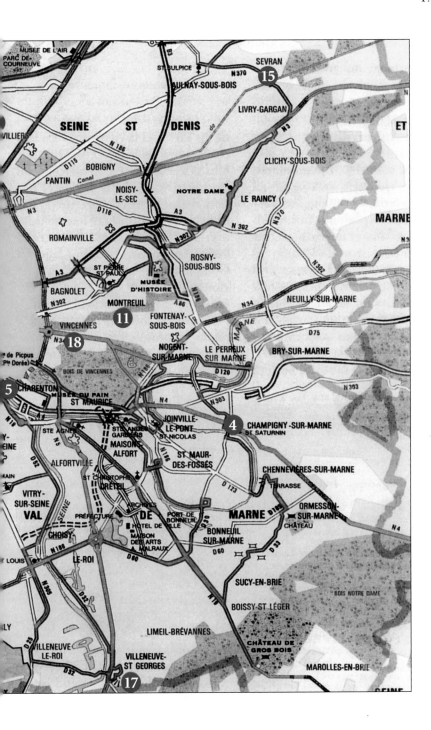

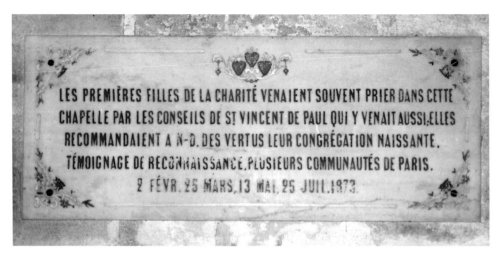

LES PREMIÈRES FILLES DE LA CHARITÉ VENAIENT SOUVENT PRIER DANS CETTE CHAPELLE PAR LES CONSEILS DE ST VINCENT DE PAUL QUI Y VENAIT AUSSI, ELLES RECOMMANDAIENT A N-D. DES VERTUS LEUR CONGRÉGATION NAISSANTE. TÉMOIGNAGE DE RECONNAISSANCE, PLUSIEURS COMMUNAUTÉS DE PARIS. 2 FÉVR. 25 MARS, 13 MAI, 25 JUIL. 1873

Commemorative plaque, Aubervilliers

## AUBERVILLIERS*

In this suburb directly northeast of Paris, is the parish church of *Notre Dame des Vertus* (Our Lady of the Powers, or, Miracles). It is located on a large square behind the city hall. *(1, rue de la Commune de Paris)* Its fame began in 1336, when, after the fervent prayers of a young woman, rain arrived at the end of a punishing drought. Its renown drew many notables, such as Ignatius Loyola and Louis XIII. This king attributed his victory over the Huguenots at La Rochelle to Notre Dame des Vertus, and had yet another church built in Paris, Notre Dame des Victoires (Our Lady of Victories). Vincent encouraged the early Daughters of Charity to come to pray here (in 1638, for example), as he did himself. The sisters prayed for their young congregation here. It appears, too, that they continued to come to Aubervilliers on pilgrimage. (Confer-ences 63, 73) His confreres also came to celebrate mass and pray for Mary's protection. The Oratorians assumed responsibility for this shrine in 1622.

The key statue of Mary is located to the left of the main altar, and is surrounded by many plaques given in answer to prayers. As expected, the original statue has been destroyed, but a new one has taken its place. In 1873 several communities of Parisian Daughters of Charity erected a large plaque: "The first Daughters of Charity often used to come to pray in this chapel, at the advice of Saint Vincent de Paul, who also came here. They recommended their infant congregation to Our Lady of the Powers. In thankful testimony, several communities in Paris [erected this]. 2 February, 25 March, 13 May, 25 July, 1873." Daughters of Charity opened a house in Aubervilliers in 1858 and continue to work in the parish.

## BICÊTRE

This old *chateau*, built under Louis XIII to house sick and wounded soldiers, had fallen into disuse when the Ladies of Charity of Paris had the idea of placing the foundlings here. After some four years of discussion, and against the wishes of Louise de Marillac, the transfer of the orphaned boys and girls to Bicêtre took place in 1647. Saint Louise believed it too far south of Paris, too dangerous to reach (because of the vagabonds and old soldiers), and too difficult to support financially. Nevertheless, she visited the hospice often and organized its works. Eventually Vincent wanted to find other solutions for the Daughters of Charity who worked here, and a return to the city took place in 1649. In 1656-1657, the chateau of Bicêtre became part of the General Hospital of Paris. Its new role was to lock up those homeless beggars who could not otherwise find useful employment. Vincent de Paul did not support the concept, at least in this form. At the Revolution, 166 inmates were slaughtered in the courtyard as part of the September massacres (4 September 1792). Today, a large hospital occupies the same property in the town called Le Kremlin Bicêtre, but nothing remains of the original chateau.

## BOURG-LA-REINE

In the *parish church* of Bourg-la-Reine, Saint Leu-Saint Gilles, directly south of Paris, is one of the original paintings commissioned for the canonization of Vincent de Paul. Its subject is the glorification of Saint Vincent, a work of Brother André Jean, O.P. This huge canvas was the main one of the series originally hung in the center of the sanctuary at Saint Lazare. After being dispersed at the time of the Revolution, these canvases were made available to various churches. This painting was cut down, and then moved here from the original Saint Vincent de Paul church in Paris, in 1845. It has been hung in the right transept of this nineteenth-century church, which otherwise has no known connection with Vincent de Paul. (*Saint Gilles, 8, boulevard Carnot*)

## CHAMPIGNY-SUR-MARNE

On the banks of the Marne southeast of Paris is Champigny, site of an

Saint Saturnin church,
Champigny-sur-Marne

115

early Confraternity of Charity. Vincent came here in 1632, and reported to Louise that the women of the Charity needed her help in getting organized. In 1642, a small group of Daughters of Charity was here to serve, but after that period nothing more is heard about it. The parish church, Saint Saturnin, dating from the twelfth and thirteenth centuries, is still standing, although it suffered considerable damage during a battle with the Prussians in 1870. Nothing remains in the church to recall the ministry of the two saints or the Sisters here. (*Place de l'Eglise*)

## CHARENTON-LE-PONT

Charenton-le-Pont is a suburb southeast of Paris. The ***parish church***, Saint Pierre, was the site of a mission in May 1654. Vincent de Paul preached some or all of the time. (Letter 1744) The church, however, has nothing to recall his presence, a condition repeated in many others. He would have preferred it that way. Instead, the building has a sign stating that it is the property of the people and not of the Church, an issue concretized because of the Revolution. (*1, rue Alfred Savouré*)

## CLICHY-LA-GARENNE***

Clichy is a Suburb west of Paris, now part of the new diocese of Nanterre. "Garenne," an old term, refers to a restricted forest area that in feudal times was located here. Vincent de Paul was the resident pastor of the parish dedicated at that time to the Holy Savior and Saint Médard. The parish, located on the

Church of Saint Médard,
Clichy, interior

plain of the river Seine, was much larger in his day than today, reaching, for example, into the Batignolles district, now a part of Paris north of Montmartre. Clichy itself was mentioned in the seventh century and in the saint's day, the Catholic inhabitants numbered about 600, mainly poor devout peasants. He served here as pastor only from 2 May 1612 (living, however, in Paris at least until December) to 1613. Vincent was nominated for Clichy through the support of Pierre de Bérulle, founder of the Oratory in France. Vincent succeeded François Bourgoing (1585-1662), who left to become one of the first French Oratorians. Bourgoing then went to Lyons, and assisted the archbishop in his visitation of Châtillon in 1614. Through his own funds and those from others, Vincent oversaw the reconstruction of the church building, an undertaking lasting until 1630. The transepts and the bell tower date from his time.

Vincent learned something from the good people of Clichy, as he related to his confreres in 1659: *I will confess, to my shame, that when I found myself in my parish, I did not know how to set about chanting the Office. I listened with admiration to peasants intoning the Psalms, and not missing a single note. Hereupon I said to myself: "you who are their spiritual father are ignorant of all that!" I was deeply distressed.* (Conference 213) Although the saint did not mention Clichy by name, it is presumed that he was referring to this parish and not to Châtillon, where he remained only a few months.

Church of Saint Médard, Clichy

Church of Saint Médard, Clichy, 19th century engraving

Church of Saint Médard, Clichy, 17th century drawing

Vincent left Clichy in 1613 to become tutor and chaplain of the Gondi family in Paris. From that date, he followed the custom of the time and continued as nominal pastor until 1626, after the foundation of the Congregation of the Mission. During those thirteen years, he often returned to his parish to preach and administer the sacraments,

LES SEPT FONDATEURS
DES CONFÉRENCES
DE St VINCENT DE PAUL
OZANAM.BAILLY.LALLIER
LAMACHE.LE TAILLANDIER
DEVAUX ET CLAVÉ
SONT VENUS EN PÉLERINAGE
DANS CETTE ÉGLISE
AU DÉBUT DE LEUR ŒUVRE
LE 20 JUILLET 1834

Commemorative plaque, Society of Saint Vincent de Paul, Church of Saint Médard, Clichy

The following are noteworthy in or near the old church:

(1) The **baptismal font** at which the saint presided at baptisms. Since the date 1612 is visible on the side, Vincent certainly commissioned it for the parish.

(2) The **pulpit**, regarded as the one where he preached, although it is probably later.

(3) A **crucifix** said to have belonged to him is preserved at the left of the main altar in an alcove.

(4) A **statue** of the saint in white

as was his right. He also received financial reports and a little income from Grégoire le Coust, his vicar since he was still pastor. Even afterwards, he had a mission given here (1642) and paid other visits. It should be recalled that Vincent retained the pastorate of Clichy while he was pastor of Châtillon-les-Dombes.

The present parish church, the parish of *Saint Vincent de Paul*, adjoins the old church that the saint knew. The apse of the old church joins the left aisle of the modern church. The parish is now in a "missionary" situation, since many of the people here are either not practicing Catholics or are not Christians. *(99, Boulevard Jean Jaurès)*

Saint Vincent's door, Church of Saint Médard, Clichy

Saint Vincent in Clichy, stained glass window, Church of Saint Vincent de Paul, Clichy

Saint Vincent baptizing, stained glass window, Church of Saint Vincent de Paul, Clichy

marble, a signed work of the noted sculptor Alexandre Falguière (1831-1900). This statue was brought here from the Pantheon.

(5) A *plaque* with the names of the founders of the Society of Saint Vincent de Paul, who came to the parish church to dedicate their work to the saint on 20 July 1834.

(6) A *Judas tree* (now dead) in the garden, supposedly planted by the saint.

(7) A *mural painting* of the saint in front of the church, to the left of the entry.

(8) The *stained glass* in the old

church was destroyed in a hailstorm on 11 July 1823, and modern windows have replaced it.

(9) A *reliquary* that used to contain a bone from the saint's right arm. It has been stolen.

(10) *Two doors* from the main entry. Too weak to continue in use, these doors, probably from the saint's time, have been added as decoration in the sanctuary.

The new church, too, has interesting features:

(1) The *stained glass windows*, some

Saint Vincent planting, stained glass window,
Church of Saint Vincent de Paul, Clichy

Saint Vincent preaching, stained glass window,
Church of Saint Vincent de Paul, Clichy

of which depict scenes from his life not pictured elsewhere, such as his help during the 1615 flood of the Seine. It was particularly severe at Gennevilliers, down river from Clichy. The depiction, however, is more symbolic than real, since Vincent did not actually come in a boat to distribute food in person. He sent his colleagues from Clichy instead. Another window depicts the first meeting of Vincent de Paul and Louise de Marillac at the chateau of Clichy. Although hard to imagine, this meeting was possible since Louise was related to Alexandre Hennequin (b. 1583), the lord of

Clichy. Alexandre's son Antoine, Monsieur de Vincy, became a close friend of Vincent and joined the Congregation on his deathbed. Alexandre's daughter Isabelle, Mademoiselle Du Fay, was a lifelong friend and supporter of her cousin Louise and of Vincent. Yet another shows Vincent's arrival on horseback, 14 January 1649, on his way to Saint Germain. These windows, dating from 1908-1910, were made from glass given by the Clichy glassworks.

(2) The modern *picture* of the saint, depicted seated. His large charitable hands are a main feature of this canvas. The artist was Robert Falucci

(1900-1989), a well-known painter and designer of popular posters.

(3) A modern *statue* of the saint, outside facing the street.

Of Vincent's parochial residence, it is said that nothing remains. However, an old engraving shows it on the same site as the present one. In it, Vincent gathered about a dozen young clerics around him to help them in their formation. Among those was young Antoine Portail, about twenty years old, and destined to be the saint's earliest follower and pioneer member of the Congregation of the Mission. Vincent

Baptismal font, Church of Saint Médard, Clichy

Saint Vincent's Crucifix, Church of Saint Médard, Clichy

once rescued his young companion from the attacks of a violent character whose release from jail in Clichy Vincent had just arranged. Another old building behind the church, now part of another property, probably dates from Vincent's time.

Vincent recalled his time in Clichy in a conference given to the Daughters of Charity (Conference 55, 27 July 1653): *I was once a country parish priest. (Poor parish priest.) I had such good people who were so obedient in carrying out all that I asked them to do that when I told them that they should go to Confession on the first Sunday of the month, they never failed to go. They came to me and went to Confession and I saw from day to day how it profited these souls. This afforded me so much consolation and I was so happy about it that I used to say to myself: "How happy you are to have such good people!"*

Saint Vincent in Clichy, mural painting,
Church of Saint Médard, Clichy

*And I used to add: "I think that the Pope himself is not as happy as a parish priest in the midst of such kind-hearted folk." And one day His Eminence Cardinal de Retz asked me: "Well, Father, how are you?" I said to him: "I am so happy, my lord, that I cannot express it." "Why?" "It is because I have such good people, so obedient to all that I tell them that I think to myself that neither the Holy Father nor you, My Lord, are as happy as I am."* To further their piety, he also established a confraternity of the Rosary here, perhaps a presage of his interest in confraternities of charity.

The Daughters of Charity opened a house here in 1839. The sisters conducted a school and were engaged in various social works.

The chapel of the hamlet of *Monceaux* depended on the parish of Clichy, and it is likely that their zealous pastor would have visited his parishioners there. Generally poor farmers,

they had their own chapel from 1529, located in the chateau, near the present parish, Saint-Charles de Monceau. It remained dependant on Clinchy until its demolition in 1828. Monceaux was annexed to the city of Paris in 1860. *(22 bis, rue Legendre, Paris 17)*

Directly across the river from Clichy is *Asnières-sur-Seine*, site of another Confraternity of Charity. Louise came to visit here in February 1630 and returned about 1632. Her first visit was made while in poor health. She prayed during her trip here that she would be given strength and the faith to continue, as Peter had when the Lord called him to walk on the waters.

## FONTENAY-AUX-ROSES

Marie de Lumague, Mademoiselle de Pollalion (whom Vincent always called Poulaillon), had a house here. Since she was so supportive of both Vincent de Paul and Louise de Marillac, it is highly likely that both of them visited her here. Vincent, in particular, was involved with the community that she founded, the *Daughters of Providence*. They lived with the foundress at the beginnings here. The Daughters of Charity also had a foundation here, beginning in 1641 or 1642. After the Revolution, they returned to this site of their former apostolate.

## GENNEVILLIERS

Located on the flood plain of the Seine, not far from Clichy, Gennevilliers profited from the ministry of Vincent de Paul, at least indirectly. He saw to it that the villagers, suffering from one of their frequent floods, received food and other material assistance from his missionaries—an event depicted symbolically in a window in the Clichy church. The present parish church of Saint Mary Magdalene was built only after Vincent's time. Previous buildings suffered from the wet soils. Nothing in the church at present recalls Vincent's work on behalf of the parish except for one of the stained glass windows. He is depicted only in the form of a bust, but no inscription alludes to his efforts here. Further help came from the superior general, Edme Jolly, after the great flood of 1690, but this too is unremembered. Nevertheless, Daughters of Charity are at work here.

## GENTILLY

A chasuble in the Vincentian Museum of the Motherhouse is identified as belonging to Vincent de Paul and coming from Gentilly. His connection with this suburban village is unknown, apart from a Confraternity of Charity here from 1627 that he might have founded. Other connections date from after the Revolution. The Daughters of Charity had a school here from 1874 in a country house formerly belonging to the seminary of Saint Nicolas du Chardonnet, noted above. Next door to this house, the Vincentians had property from 1824 to the 1930s, purchased, it is said, with funds saved by a Vincentian after the Revolution. The Community used it in various ways, such as for a country house for the motherhouse, and as a minor seminary. The property was sold for development, and the house was taken in 1959-1960 to make way for new highway construction. In compensation, the Vincentians acquired a property in *Villebon-sur-Yvette*, not far away, to use in much the same way as the Gentilly property. The sisters, however, continue their work in Gentilly.

## ISSY-LES-MOULINEAUX

It is uncertain whether Vincent de Paul visited Issy, but it appears likely. His onetime employer, Queen Marguerite de Valois, had a chateau here, and he could well have accompanied her court here. Beginning in 1642, Vincent's friend Jean Jacques Olier began building the seminary of Saint Sulpice here. Olier placed students from the French provinces or from other countries here. In 1695, important meetings were held at the seminary concerning Quietism, a movement that involved some Vincentians because of their influence in French seminaries. *(33, rue du Général Leclerc)*

A Confraternity of Charity existed here from at least 1643 as well, although the parish church from his day no longer stands. To aid this Charity, the Daughters of Charity had a house here, 1642-1649. Because of financial and other problems, they were withdrawn, although they returned after the Revolution. Since the parish church of Saint Étienne dates from 1634, the early sisters knew it.

## MONTREUIL

This village, also called Montreuil-sous-Bois, had a *parish church* from at least the eighth century. The present church of Saint Peter and Saint Paul is early Gothic, one of the earliest in the entire region of the Ile de France. It had something of the character of a royal parish, since the royal family lived for a period at Vincennes, located close by. Louis XV, for example, lived there from 1715 to 1722. Vincent founded a Confraternity here for men and women on 11 April 1627, and he returned at least once (1631) to supervise it. Later, he sent Louise de Marillac here to oversee its reorganization. Despite these connections, the church does not display any reminiscences of the presence of the two founders. *(2, rue de Romainville)* Saint Lazare also owned farmland in the Montreuil area. Daughters of Charity opened a school here beginning in 1712. Following the Revolution, they remained until 1903 and have since returned. In Vincent's lifetime, his confreres gave missions in this district east of the city. One extant document mentions *Pantin, Belleville-sur-Sablon* (now a district of Paris), *Romainville* and **Livry** (now Livry-Gargan) as parishes they had evangelized in 1659. (Doc. 119) They must have given missions in the majority of these rural parishes in the Paris suburbs.

## NANTERRE

In letter 533, 7 August 1641, Vincent de Paul mentions that he would be going to Nanterre, an ancient town northwest of Paris. He did not say why he was going, but perhaps it was because of his work in inaugurating the Confraternities of Charity. Nanterre itself had become a place of pilgrimage, since Saint Geneviève (420-496), the patroness of Paris, was born here. For example, Saint Louis, Anne of Austria and thousands of others came here to pray. The basilica, now the *cathedral* of Saint Geneviève and Saint Maurice, has a fourteenth-century bell tower. The present cathedral building, however, dates only from the twentieth century. Its last sections were finished in 1973. This reconstruction became necessary, since the older building, the one Vincent de Paul and Anne of Austria knew, had become decrepit and most of it could not be saved. In any case, Nanterre had grown tremendously and became a diocese in 1966.

There is only one significant memorial of Saint Vincent de Paul inside, one of the ceiling paintings illustrating the beatitude "Blessed are the merciful." It dates most likely to the late 1920s or early 1930s.

Outside the cathedral is an ancient well associated with Geneviève, with whose miraculous waters she cured her blind mother. Below the church is a crypt chapel said to have been her family home in the fifth century. *(24, rue de l'Eglise, Nanterre)*

## SAINT-CLOUD*

The ancient village of Saint-Cloud, situated across the Seine west of Paris, takes its name from Saint Clodoald, a grandson of Clovis and abbot of a monastery founded in the sixth century. Because of the terrible devastation suffered by the village, particularly in 1870-1871 and during the first World War, much of the old village was destroyed, including the *parish church*. Louise de Marillac informs us that in February

Gardens of palace of Saint-Cloud,
Saint-Cloud

1630, she came to this parish to visit the Confraternity of Charity founded here. On 5 February, a special day for her, she left for her visitation. It was the anniversary of her marriage to Antoine Le Gras but, out of concern for poverty, she did not ask that mass be said for her intention, to save the stipend. Nevertheless, Vincent de Paul celebrated the mass and did not ask for an offering from her for it. The mass formulary he chose was for betrothals (engagements). During communion, Louise had the inspiration of being betrothed to Jesus, and needing to leave all and follow him. After that experience, she came to Saint-Cloud and remained there at least until the nineteenth of the month. During the same year, the Vincentians gave a mission in the parish, most likely in November. There are no memorials to the presence of Louise de Marillac in the present nineteenth-century church. *(14, place Charles de Gaulle)*

The Vincentians staffed the *royal hospital* and the small *royal chapel* of the chateau from 1688 to 1790. A hospice had existed here since 1208, but Philippe, duke of Orleans and brother of Louis XIV, had a new one built. Its charter, dated June 1698 and displayed in the city museum, shows that Louis XIV approved the granting of funds for the poor sick of Saint-Cloud. Vincentian service here was in keeping with other royal assignments, such as Fontainebleau, Versailles, Saint Cyr and the Invalides in Paris. The duke invited the Congregation and the Daughters of Charity here. Since the chateau was primarily a summer palace (Philippe normally lived at the Palais Royal in Paris), the work of the Vincentians here must have concentrated on the small hospital. The sisters were responsible for the physical care of the sick, while the Vincentians celebrated mass daily in the hospital chapel and provided spiritual care for the sick. They also agreed to educate six young altar servers for the royal chapel.

The present hospital building preserves some aspects of the one known in the seventeenth and eighteenth centuries. Its chapel, however, was completed only in 1787 under the patronage of Marie Antoinette. It is no longer in use as a chapel. The last superior at Saint-Cloud, Jean Joseph Avril, was executed in Versailles along with other Vincentians. After the Revolution, the Daughters of Charity returned (1803), but the Vincentians did not. *(Centre Hospitalier de Saint-Cloud, Place Silly)*

In contrast to the hospital, the chateau of Saint-Cloud has disappeared. It burned down in 1870 and its ruins were removed in 1891. Only its extensive gardens and fountains remain. The sumptuous palace with its gardens and vistas overlooking Paris would not qualify as the preferred setting for present-day Vincentian ministry.

Another Vincentian connection with Saint-Cloud is that Napoleon, who lived here for a time, signed the decree here reestablishing the Congregation of the Mission on 27 May 1804. Its peculiar stipulations, making the Congregation of the Mission a community for foreign missions only, were never effectively put into practice. Then, in a fit of pique because of Vincentian refusal to sanction the removal of the Daughters of Charity from their care, the emperor, saying that he had no need of missions, revoked the decree of 1804 on 26 September 1809, thus banning the Congregation for the second time.

## SAINT-DENIS*

Besides exercising responsibility for two other Visitation convents in Paris, Vincent was instrumental in founding in the town of Saint-Denis the first daughter-house of the first *monastery of the Visitation*. The date of its foundation is 29 June 1639. He remarked on the holiness of life of the sisters here. *I [thank God] with all my heart, for the grace He bestowed on me of seeing the union of hearts, the simplicity, the humility, the obedience and the exactitude in the observance of the Rules, in a state of remarkable perfection.* (Letter 679) The sisters had an abridged collection of his remarks made during his canonical visitations of their house (such as 7 November 1648), and these were produced for Abelly, who quoted them for his biography of Vincent de Paul, and for the founder's

beatification. The monastery is now the site of the main post office, and its grounds are used for childcare. As its superior, Vincent came here often to see the nuns, perhaps as late as June 1658. (*59, rue de la République*)

Daughters of Charity began to serve the poor in the *Hôtel Dieu* of Saint-Denis on 2 August 1645, and they also had a school. Louise came here to visit at least once. The buildings, located on the current Rue de la Légion d'Honneur, are no longer in existence. Vincent also founded a Confraternity of Charity here. Over the years, it lost its fervor and the people of Saint-Denis complained that they were not receiving enough help in the spirit of Vincent de Paul. The bishop suppressed the Charity in 1679 and founded a new one in its place. The Daughters of Charity returned in 1849. The work of the sisters continues in a school named after Saint Vincent de Paul. (*27, rue Albert Walter*)

Around the year of their foundation, Vincent was terrorized by some of the great men of the period, all young and hot blooded. One of them, Antoine de Gramont, related the event to Antoine Durand, Vincentian pastor at Fontainebleau many years later. He and his friends chased Vincent, riding a white horse, from Saint-Denis to Paris, shooting their pistols and shouting after him. They were apparently betting that he would stop in the first church he saw to thank God for his miraculous escape. The saint probably did so. If nothing else, this incident shows Vincent to be an accomplished rider.

The main reason for going to

Saint-Denis, of course, is to visit the great *abbey church*, since 1966 the cathedral of the diocese of Saint-Denis. It is named after the first bishop of Paris, who, after being executed, picked up his head and continued on his way. Where he finally expired an abbey was built. The earliest large church dates from 475. The present basilica is France's first great Gothic building, begun about 1140, and became the prototype for many others. In addition, for twelve centuries it was the burial place of the kings of France. On their final trip to Saint-Denis, the funeral procession traditionally stopped at Saint Lazare. At the Revolution, the royal coffins were opened and the remains scattered into unmarked graves. Their tombs, however, were saved and may be seen in the basilica.

## SEVRAN - ROUGEMONT

In Vincent's time, the Congregation had a farm at Rougemont. It had been part of the property of the monks at Saint Lazare when Vincent acquired it. The prior, Adrien Le Bon, kept the property for his own support until he granted it to the Congregation, 11 February 1645. Besides providing food for the priory, this farm gave the Vincentians a good place in the country to stay or rest on their journeys. It was perhaps here that Vincent once allowed the students to go to spend a few days. He wrote: *they behaved so badly there that I did not want to allow them to return. Even when I was pressured to do so just recently, I did not give in, by the grace of God. (Letter 2963, 1659)* Today the Rougement farm has disappeared, its place taken by an exten-

sive apartment development. A small modern chapel, *Saint Vincent de Paul de Rougement*, is on the old property, and thereby preserves some connection with him. (Rue Commandant Charcot, Sevran) Daughters of Charity worked in this neighborhood beginning in 1653. In May of that year, the saint also gave a mission at Sevran to celebrate a jubilee. This was one of his last missions. His friend, the duchess of Aiguillon, complained that the exertion would be too much for a man of his age, given that summer's heat.

Saint Lazare also had lands close by in *Gonesse*, and at least one mission was given there (1638). Income to support the work of the Foundlings came from royal lands here as well. Perhaps in recognition of all of this, a modern parish church is named in Vincent's honor in *Villepinte. (1, avenue Auguste Blanqui, Villepinte)* The old parish church, Saints Peter and Paul, has nothing to recall the saint's presence, apart from a statue of Vincent preaching.

## SURESNES

*Marguerite Naseau*, regarded as the first Daughter of Charity, came from the village of Suresnes, on the slopes of the hills overlooking the Seine, just west of Paris. The parish church where she was baptized no longer stands, but its successor contains two windows depicting episodes in her life. A small square is also named for her: Place Marguerite Naseau. While Louise was visiting the Charity here in 1629 she seems to have met Marguerite and then sent her to Vincent in Villepreux. As often happens, a chance

Street sign, Place Marguerite
Naseau, Suresnes

encounter has great consequences: in this case, the foundation of the Daughters of Charity.

## VILLENEUVE-SAINT-GEORGES

On the slopes overlooking the Seine south of Paris is *Villeneuve-Saint-Georges*. Louise came here in 1632, and stayed with a certain Mademoiselle Tranchot, who lived here. She was also a Lady of Charity, active in the works of charity in Paris. Her name and that of her husband occur in Louise's correspondence with Vincent from 1631 to 1645. Nothing in the Gothic church recalls her presence here, however. *(9, rue de la Bretonnierie)* Besides Villeneuve, Vincent also asked her to visit the Charity of *Crosnes*, the adjoining village. As with so many other sites, we have only place names and little else to tell the story of charity in the earliest days of the confraternities.

## VINCENNES

Located on the eastern side of Paris is the former *royal palace* of Vincennes, surrounded by its magnificent park, zoo, and other attractions. Vincent came

here, and he asked Louise de Marillac to do so to care for the Charities. The chateau, the "medieval Versailles," dates from the fourteenth century. After it ceased being a royal residence, it became a prison. Here were confined supporters of Jansenism (such as the abbé of Saint Cyran), and Jean François Paul de Gondi, then coadjutor archbishop of Paris and future cardinal. The archbishop's crime was that he was an enemy of Mazarin, who imprisoned him. After his escape, he seized the archbishopric but quickly had to flee into exile. Contrary to Mazarin's orders, this future cardinal received hospitality from the Vincentians in Rome, thus alienating Mazarin further from the Congregation. During his time as archbishop, he approved the rules of the Congregation of the Mission and of the Daughters of Charity, although he was living in exile.

The Congregation of the Mission began in 1753 to provide chaplains for the royal military school established there. These Vincentian chaplains were, for legal purposes, attached to the community of Saint Cyr. Not much is known of this undertaking, and the Vincentians had left within nine months. Daughters of Charity came here in 1696, and stayed for nearly a century. They returned to work in the military hospital beginning in 1858.

The castle is one of the great examples of French military buildings. It includes a Sainte Chapelle, or royal chapel, similar to that of Paris.

Monument, Square Alban Satrange

# 2

# Ile-de-France

Saint Vincent with begging bag,
parish church, Fontainebleau

# Ile-de-France

*Once Vincent de Paul began supervising the development of the Congregation of the Mission and the Daughters of Charity, he rarely left Paris. His concern was worldwide, but the references in his writings show that he focused largely on the capital and the region around it, the Ile de France. Similarly, Louise de Marillac, in her younger years, visited and encouraged the Confraternities of Charity and her Daughters but gradually restricted her work to supervision from Paris. The significant places described here are listed simply in alphabetical order, while other sites are described in geographical relationship to the principal ones. Their Vincentian history is rich and complex.*

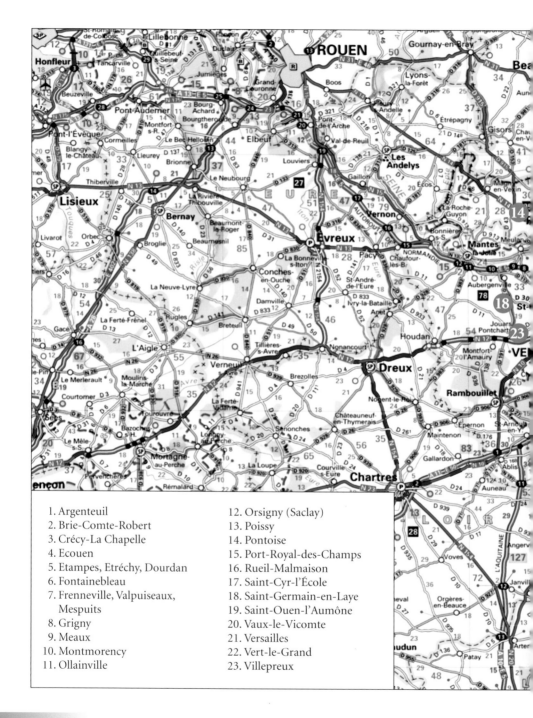

1. Argenteuil
2. Brie-Comte-Robert
3. Crécy-La Chapelle
4. Ecouen
5. Etampes, Etréchy, Dourdan
6. Fontainebleau
7. Frenneville, Valpuiseaux, Mespuits
8. Grigny
9. Meaux
10. Montmorency
11. Ollainville

12. Orsigny (Saclay)
13. Poissy
14. Pontoise
15. Port-Royal-des-Champs
16. Rueil-Malmaison
17. Saint-Cyr-l'École
18. Saint-Germain-en-Laye
19. Saint-Ouen-l'Aumône
20. Vaux-le-Vicomte
21. Versailles
22. Vert-le-Grand
23. Villepreux

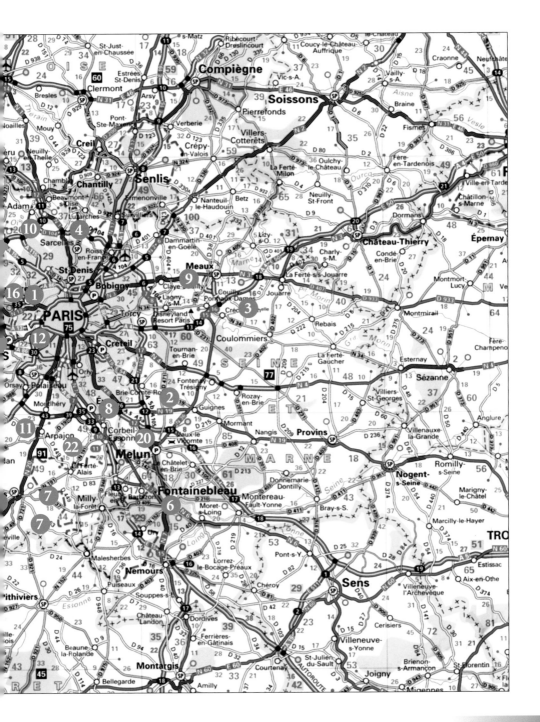

Parish church, Sartrouville

## ARGENTEUIL

When Vincent received the property of Saint Lazare, he also received most of the properties elsewhere that belonged to the ancient priory. Among those properties was land at Argenteuil. As part of his missionary work, he was present for the foundation of the Confraternity of Charity (for women) at the parish of Argenteuil, 24 August 1634. Louise came here to visit the confraternity in 1639. The old church that he knew is no longer standing, but in its place is the basilica of Saint Denis, finished under Napoleon III in 1864. A large modern window of Saint Vincent de Paul recalls, perhaps unconsciously, his presence in the parish.

The present parish church also contains an important relic, the *Holy Tunic*. It is said that the empress Irene gave this relic of the passion of Jesus, the "seamless garment," to Charlemagne in Constantinople in the year 800. He in turn gave it to one of his daughters, Theodrade, a nun in the abbey of Argenteuil. It remained in the abbey until the Revolution, and was later restored to the Church and placed in the new parish church, since the abbey had been destroyed. No record mentions that Vincent came here to venerate it, but it is highly probable, given its proximity to Saint Lazare and the founder's presence in the parish. *(Basilica of Saint Denis, 17, rue des Ouches, Argenteuil)* The city of Argenteuil today numbers around 95,000 inhabitants.

West of Argenteuil is the old town of *Houilles*, today a thriving city of some 30,000. Daughters of Charity came here to work for the poor beginning in 1655. As with most of their early foundations, it is difficult to locate their home, since these were often rented, a common practice even in the upper levels of contemporary society, and there were only two or three Sisters living there.

Farther west is *Sartrouville*. We are better informed here about the work of the Daughters. Vincent wrote: *I am going to Pontoise at the first opportunity. I have heard about a young woman there. I shall hire her for Sartrouville where Madame de Villeneuve wishes someone.* (Letter 86, 17 October 1631) Oral tradition says that the founder himself inaugurated the work of the Daughters at the Charity here. They were certainly here from 1728, maintained their service here even after the Revolution and continue this old mission.

North of Argenteuil are four other towns which Louise visited during her inspection and encouragement of the Confraternities of Charity. The date of her visit is unknown, but she left interesting comments about the Charities in Conflans (now *Conflans-Sainte-Honorine*), *Herblay*, *Franconville*, and *Sannois*. The proximity of these places to each other demonstrates how developed the Charities must have been, even from an early date.

## BRIE-COMTE-ROBERT

This town is the former capital of Brie-en-France, an area east of Paris in the Ile de France. It is still an agricultural market, and its restored street signs show the many streets and lanes devoted to various products. Today, the town has a population of about 11,000.

The town takes its name from Robert, count of Dreux, lord of Brie, and brother of Louis VII. The town has borne his name since the twelfth century when Robert had the castle built. This building is now gone, and all that remains above ground are its walls and corner towers, somewhat restored. Archaeological work has taken place to learn more about the ancient castle. A water-filled moat surrounds the site.

The *parish church* of Saint Étienne is of Vincentian interest since Vincent lived here for a time and certainly prayed and celebrated the eucharist in the church. A Confraternity of Charity had existed from 1628, and it appears likely that Vincent himself was present for its inauguration, since he signed the document establishing it. It seems that Antoine Portail (1590-1660), Vincent's

Lord of Charity painting,
Brie-Comte-Robert

first companion in the Congregation had given a mission in this town in 1635, since Vincent replies to one of Portail's letters written from here. Perhaps Vincent himself gave a mission in 1638, the occasion for his only extant letter written from this town, dated 8 May of that year. In the terrible period of civil wars in 1649, many churches were despoiled, among which was this one. As a mission was already being given, Vincent decided to add public acts of reparation for sacrileges. In this, he was following the lead of the Company of the Blessed Sacrament, to which he belonged. The parish church at Férolles-Attilly joined with Brie-Comte-Robert in this effort.

The church of Brie-Comte-Robert

is Gothic in style, begun in the thirteenth century. Its patron, Saint Étienne (Stephen) is represented in a sculpted and gilded wooden statue and in a large painting over the main altar. The pulpit might be original, coming into use, as other pulpits did, in the early seventeenth century. If so, Vincent probably preached from it. Only a small picture of him recalls his ministry in this church.

In the first chapel to the right is a life-sized canvas of the Lord of Charity. It depicts, in an original style, the standing resurrected Lord of Charity, arms outstretched downward, with the marks of the nails evident in his hands and feet. Louise probably sent this painting, and several others like it elsewhere, from Paris to the Confraternities of Charity. The purpose was to help the members realize that the service rendered to the poor was rendered to the risen Jesus. The two biblical texts in French on the top reinforce this. Left: "Come, beloved of my Father, to take possession of the kingdom prepared for you since the beginning of the world." Right: "Because I was hungry, you gave me something to eat; I was thirsty, and you gave me something to drink; I was sick and you visited me." At the bottom is this text: "The Charity of Jesus Christ urges us on. Cor 25." (The correct reference is 2 Cor 5:14.) This Charity began in April 1631.

Beginning after 1641, Vincentians preached missions in and around Brie Comte Robert. They assumed this obligation as part of the contract for the house in Annecy, signed in 1639. It is unknown how long this obligation continued to be fulfilled.

Daughters of Charity came to Brie, called in those days Brie-en-Beauce, to serve the poor. They began in 1664 and probably remained until the Revolution.

## CRÉCY-LA-CHAPELLE

The present town of Crécy-La-Chapelle was formed administratively from two others. The main one, Crécy-en-Brie, was the site of a foundation in Vincent's time. The former community house is now a poor place on Rue des Caves. At first, the Vincentians had to lodge in a tumbledown chateau and relied on five large farms to support their works. Nothing remains of the chateau today, however. Vincentians had come here to work in the rural missions in the diocese of Meaux. As usual with other early foundations, the priests also conducted ordination retreats and helped in rural parish churches as needed.

In the old town of Crécy Vincentians occasionally served the parish church of Saint Georges. The only reminder of their presence is the ever-present statue of Saint Vincent de Paul. Remains of the Vincentian church, dating at least from the thirteenth century, can be detected in some bits of stone carving put up on the walls. The present church was built between 1779 and 1781. Vincentians remained here until the Revolution.

Jean Le Vacher plaque, Ecouen

Existing documents show that the founder encountered various problems with the Crécy foundation. In particular, the bishop of Meaux, Dominique Séguier (1593-1659), supported the Congregation when its funding evaporated and in 1654 Vincent had to withdraw several of his confreres. Ladies of Charity were also active here in Vincent's time. Daughters of Charity served in the hospital and ran a school from 1757. They returned in 1856 to the hospital.

The other original town was La Chapelle, called after the still-standing Gothic chapel. Crécy-La-Chapelle today has a population of about 3300 inhabitants.

## ECOUEN*

Ecouen is the birthplace of Jean and Philippe Le Vacher, priests of the Congregation of the Mission, and both missionaries in Algiers. Jean, the more famous, was born 15 March 1619 and baptized in the parish church (Saint Acceul or Achuel) on the same day. Perhaps because Jean and Philippe's uncle was André Duval (1564-1638), Vincent's one-time spiritual director and counselor, *Jean* attended the Bons Enfants in Paris. He came to know Vincent personally during the latter's visits there from 1640 to 1643. He was also sent to Ireland in 1646 while still a student. By 1652, he was in Algiers. A plaque in the baptistery recounts the main events of his life: "Here on the 15

Baptismal font, Ecouen

Street sign, Ecouen

The stained-glass windows come from the Renaissance period and are contemporary with the older section of the church, dating from 1536. The newer section dates from the early years of the eighteenth century, and the façade is from the mid-nineteenth century.

The Le Vacher *family home* is on the re-named Place Jean Le Vacher, a few steps behind the church, at number 2. A plaque above the main door of the house reads: "In this house was born, on 15 March 1619, Jean Le Vacher, missionary of Saint Vincent de Paul, French consul at Algiers, put to death at the mouth of a cannon for his country by order of the Dey, on the breakwater of Algiers. 26 July 1683. This memorial was offered by the Historical Society of Pontoise, 1927." Vincent sent him to Algiers to help care for enslaved Christians. Many letters between him and the founder still exist. They offer an extraordinary witness to the trials of their fellow-Christians in Algiers.

Exactly how Jean died depends on who is recounting it. Some have him seated, tied to a chair, and facing the can-

March 1619 was baptized, by Jean Baroche, pastor of the parish and canon of the collegiate church of Montmorency, Jean Le Vacher son of Philippe [Le Vacher] and Catherine Butefer. A very worthy son of Saint Vincent de Paul, he was consul of France and Vicar Apostolic, defender and confessor of the faith. He died at the mouth of a cannon on the breakwater at Algiers, on 26 July 1683. The Sons of Saint Vincent de Paul [erected this on 17 July] 1927." Jean had been seized by rioters and killed in revenge for his alleged complicity in the French bombardment of Algiers.

The *church* building clearly has two parts, the older being the choir and sanctuary, familiar to the Le Vacher family.

non that eventually fired into him. Others have him facing out to the harbor. Others have him tied to the mouth of the cannon or even stuffed inside it— the most romantic version and the least likely. It seems more probable that he was tied to a plank across the mouth of the cannon and then shot out to sea, partly to terrify the attacking navy in the harbor. The cannon itself, renamed "La Consulaire" by the French, had been cast in 1542. Some say it exploded. Others assert that the French brought it to **Brest** in 1830, where it was reerected at the military harbor (not in Jean Le Vacher's honor but as an item of war booty). Some interest was shown in his cause for beatification and canonization as a martyr but it has not progressed.

Jean's younger brother, *Philippe*, also joined the Congregation. Born in 1622, he joined on the same day as his brother, 5 October 1643. Before his ordination in Marseilles in 1650, he worked as a missionary in Algiers. Afterwards, he returned to Tunis to a rough missionary life. After twelve years he left in the company of 70 slaves he had ransomed, and then spent the rest of his years in the Vincentian house at Fontainebleau. Catherine Butefer, their mother, was, like her two sons, very devoted to Vincent. At her death, she was buried at Saint Lazare, and Vincent called her this good mother of such worthy children. (Conference 178)

Ecouen is also the site of the *National Museum of the Renaissance.*

Château, Villeconin

Despite its out-of-the-way location, it is worth a visit since it contains art and artifacts from the period of Vincent and Louise. Ecouen today numbers about 5000 people.

## ETAMPES, ETRÉCHY, DOURDAN

Another site of works of charity by the Vincentians and the Daughters of Charity is **Etampes**, a large town of about 22,000 people, west of Valpuiseaux. Next to the imposing colle-

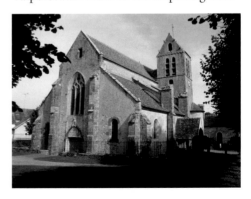

Parish church, Villeconin

Death of Vincent de Paul,
hospital chapel, Dourdan

establishment of this service in the courtyard of the castle facing it. Probably because of the dedication of these priests, brothers and sisters, testimony preparing for Vincent's beatification was taken during 1705 in the chapel of the Etampes Hôtel Dieu. Although this hospital is partly abandoned and in ruins, the chapel (dated 1559) is a registered historical building. In gratitude for the work of the Daughters of Charity and the Vincentians, the people erected a large iron cross near the twelfth-century church of Saint Basile. It was still standing about 1860, but has disappeared. During the Fronde, the Vincentians lodged as the guests of Guillaume de Lamoignon at his imposing chateau of Bâville, above Saint-Chéron. He was the son of the pious Chrétien François de Lamoignon and Marie Des Landes, supporters of the charitable endeavors of Vincent and Louise. The exhausting work of the Vincentians for the poor had ruined the health of several of them, with one dying at the chateau. Daughters of Charity worked here from 1689.

In the parish church of Saint Étienne at **Etréchy**, a traditional window of Saint Vincent and the foundlings (which Vincentians installed in 1898) recalls the tradition that Vincent had ministered here. Behind the church used to be a small priory established to look after the sick. Vincent is said to have come here to minister during a plague, but no record exists. Today, the town numbers about 6000 persons.

giate church of Notre Dame is the Hôtel Dieu. The Daughters and Vincentians came here to help in 1652, during the Fronde, and saw to the establishment of soup kitchens serving hundreds in several surrounding villages: Guillerval, Saint-Arnoult-en-Yvelines, Villeconin and Etréchy. The parish church of Villeconin keeps alive the memory of Vincent's

Not far from Etampes is **Dourdan**, another site of the charitable work of the Daughters of Charity in the lifetime of the founders. As elsewhere, they worked for the sick poor and cared for young children, imparting the rudiments of an education. Their service in the hospital, however, may have begun only in 1663. It is known that Vincent visited the area in 1637. Why he came here to this area on the way to Chartres, and where he went exactly, are unknown. (Letter 268) It is likely, however, that he was on some business concerning property. The Daughters continued here at the Hôtel Dieu after the Revolution, probably until about 1904. Shortly before they left, the hospital chapel was adorned with stained glass windows in honor of Saints Louise and Vincent, and John Gabriel Perboyre. Over the altar is the large painting depicting the death of Saint Vincent, the work of M.L. Roux, dated 1877.

Another Vincentian connection is Blessed *Marie Poussepin* (1653-1744). Following her mother's example, Marie became a Lady of Charity at the Hôtel Dieu of Dourdan. She founded the Dominican Sisters of Charity. Pope John Paul II beatified her in 1994.

## FONTAINEBLEAU**

The hamlet of *Fontainebleau* had been one of the preferred hunting lodges of the French kings at least since the twelfth century. Under François I, the old buildings began to disappear, and the present somewhat haphazard chateau began to take shape. Louis XIII, in fact, was born at Fontainebleau and made it one of his favorite residences.

René Alméras, Vincent's successor as superior general, presided at the establishment of a Confraternity of Charity here, 26 November 1644. This led eventually to the foundation of a Charity hospital, where Vincent installed the first Daughters of Charity in August 1646. He came here also because of his royal duties, especially for the Council of Conscience meeting in July 1646. Other visits may be reasonably supposed.

Anne of Austria wanted to further the moral development of her son, Louis XIV, especially after the death of Cardinal Mazarin and the king's accession that same year, 1661. Consequently, she considered replacing the Mathurins (the Trinitarians, founded by John of Matha) as the pastors of Avon (the main town near the hamlet of Fontainebleau). In her estimation, these priests were

Parish church, Fontainebleau

unfit to be the royal chaplains. Because of her interest in Vincent and his priests and, out of esteem for their piety and dedication, the queen arranged for the king to invite them to Fontainebleau. They would have charge of the royal parish in a town already influenced by the Confraternity and the work of the Daughters of Charity at the "Royal Charity for Women," now the site of the city library. The same Alméras who had begun the Confraternity here tentatively accepted the king's offer.

List of pastors, Fontainebleau

Saint Vincent with begging bag,
parish church, Fontainebleau

After much discussion, Alméras concluded an agreement, and the king assigned the town chapel of Saint Louis, built under Louis XIII, to the Congregation of the Mission. The Mathurins raised several objections. In 1667-1668, after difficult negotiations between the two congregations over matters such as precedence at royal occasions and loss of income, the former Trinitarian chapel was erected as an independent parish.

Ten Vincentians were assigned to Fontainebleau. Along with fulfilling their parish duties, they also gave parish missions and were the chaplains for the royal palace. This was of particular importance, of course, while the court was present. The former *Vincentian residence*, at the side of the parish church, no longer stands, a city building having replaced it. It had been the former Hôtel de Martigues and opened out on a public market, still in use. Vincentian presence is remembered in the "Cour de la Mission," the name given to the site of the residence.

The main doors of the *parish church* have carved high relief figures of Saint Louis on one door, and Saint Vincent de Paul on the other. He is carrying a scroll in one hand and a begging bag in the other, an unusual depiction. His statue also adorns the façade, dated in its present condition to 1868. In the interior of the church two windows depict Saint Vincent. The principal one, above the main altar, shows him celebrating mass. The image itself comes from the engraving of his vision of the "Three Globes," which took place as he celebrated the eucharist one day. These globes represented for him the souls of his friends Jane Frances de Chantal and Francis de Sales. As a subject for a full window, it is probably unique.

The other window, in poor condition, shows Saint Vincent giving the rules to the Daughters of Charity. These sisters remained here, with some gaps, until recent years. Shortly after their arrival, they discovered that it would be difficult to secure enough funds for their living expenses. Louise told them to not be ashamed to beg from the rich, even from the stingy queen herself. On their

departure, the Daughters presented the church with a medieval statue of Mary, kept in their convent for over a century. It is above the main altar of the Mary Chapel. A modern sculptor, Heidi Story, has also depicted him helping a foundling child. Her statue dates from 1984.

A wall plaque records the names of the pastors, the first dozen of whom were Vincentians. They remained here from 1691 until the Revolution. A great Vincentian missionary, *Philippe Le Vacher* (1622-1679), returned to France after years of work in North Africa. He was assigned to Fontainebleau until his

"Vincent de Paul," by Heidi Story, parish church, Fontainebleau

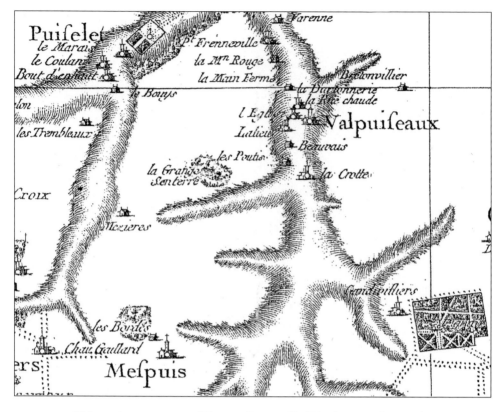

Eighteenth century map of Varenne, Frenneville, Valpuiseaux and Mespuits

death. He was buried in the choir of the church, but his tomb is no longer visible. Another pastor was *Antoine Durand* (1629-1708), whose valuable memoirs of Fontainebleau were published in 1900.

In the *palace* itself are two chapels, of which one, the Trinity Chapel, is open to the public. Louis XIII dedicated it in 1633, and the Mathurins (or Trinitarians) staffed it at the time—hence its name. In the chapel, several significant events took place, including the marriage of Louis XV to Marie Leczinska

Farm house, Frenneville

Parish church, Valpuiseaux

palace. It had the distinction of being the chapel where, in 1162, Thomas Becket was ordained a bishop.

It is also noteworthy that Pius VII, who had visited the parish church in 1805, remained in Fontainebleau as Napoleon's prisoner from June 1812 to 21 January 1814. A plaque in the parish church records these sad events. Today, Fontainebleau numbers around 16,000 residents.

The Vincentians briefly had a house in **Avon**. The minor seminary of Meaux transferred here in 1882 but remained only until 1890, when it moved again.

Notre Dame de Varennes, Frenneville

(1725). Although the Mathurins retained the title of "perpetual preachers" at the chateau, the Vincentians alone were responsible for this chapel and for the celebration of the sacraments. It is unknown what, if any, advice the Vincentians gave to Louis XIV on the occasion of the revocation of the Edict of Nantes, 18 October 1685, which took place in the palace, and which caused harsh reactions in France and elsewhere in Europe. The other chapel, called after Saint Saturnin, was reserved in the seventeenth century for the servants of the

## FRENNEVILLE,* VALPUISEAUX, MESPUITS

In the countryside southeast of Paris is the small hamlet of Frenneville, located in the commune of Valpuiseaux. Charlotte de Ligny, the marquise of Herse (d. 1662), gave Vincent two farms, at Frenneville and Mespuits (23 July 1635), and he went to visit the property at that time. He came on his own several times, for example, in 1636, 1638 (for his health) and 1644. He also came to Valpuiseaux to visit the Daughters whom he sent there to work among the rural poor in 1647. Their work was to visit them in their homes and to teach their young girls. Vincent fled here in early 1649 to escape the wrath of leaders of the Fronde. Valpuiseaux felt the effects of this civil war terribly, with starving soldiers, desperate refugees, and ravenous animals terrorizing the inhabitants. Vincent wrote several letters at the farm, and he used his time here also to give a mission in the region. The Vincentian farm and its buildings were seized 19 November 1792 and sold to benefit the State.

At Frenneville, in a small field adjacent to D837, stands the tiny chapel (only six by six meters), Notre Dame de Varennes. This stone building dates from 1313. Vincent certainly celebrated mass here, and its old altar stone is preserved in the Vincentian museum at the Paris motherhouse. At the Revolution, the chapel was sold, but the bishop of Versailles reconsecrated it in 1872. It was restored to its present condition beginning in 1972.

Vincent's farmhouse still stands. The window next to the faded sundial is pointed out as the room he used. The property and buildings are in private hands. (26, rue de Petit Frenneville)

A witness for Vincent's beatification, Pierre Gâtineau, a farmer in Valpuiseaux, testified that Vincent cared for the poor, giving them seed, tools, and clothing in their time of great need. Others testified at the same time to his good reputation in the area. Today, Valpuiseaux and Frenneville number around 600 people.

The property at Mespuits is less well known. Vincent had others run it for him, but he regularly received income from it. As a prominent landholder, he also was able to increase and centralize his property in Mespuits, a policy followed by his confreres after his death. Many contracts attest to his intense management of his property, and it is still productive and beautiful land. He was also in contact with the local pastor, whom he gifted, at least once (1644) with some vestments for the parish. The parish church boasts one large stained glass window of the saint, a nineteenth-century window of him with foundlings. It recalls his presence in Mespuits, today a village of perhaps 200 people.

## GRIGNY

On 21 January 1635, Nicolas Le Camus and his wife gave Vincent an important farm in this suburban location near Evry. This property, now completely urbanized, is in the town of Ris-Orangis, just on the border of Grigny. This industrial zone is called the Lands of Saint Lazare *(Terres de Saint Lazare)*, undoubtedly keeping the name of its famous proprietor. Otherwise, there is nothing to distinguish this property as Vincentian. The whole area of Grigny numbers nearly 25,000 persons, testimony to its recent growth. *(Route D310, and Route de Grigny)*

It appears that Vincent came here to visit Geneviève Fayet, **Madame Goussault** (d. 1639), who had her country home in Grigny. Widowed at a young age, she gave herself unstintingly to works of charity and was the first to have the idea of an association of ladies to serve the sick poor in the Hôtel Dieu in Paris. It is certain that Vincent came to visit her in Grigny in 1636, and he probably returned later in 1638 or 1639, the year of her death. He also sent Louise here at various times.

## MEAUX

Throughout his episcopate, Dominique Séguier (1593-1659), bishop of Meaux, had experienced the works of Vincent in his diocese. The Vincentian house at Crécy-en-Brie, for example, although it had faced difficulties, was in

Former seminary chapel, Meaux

his diocese. Louise visited the Confraternities of Charity in the diocese, as well. In 1645, this bishop founded a seminary in Meaux, staffed by diocesan clergy. It was not well run and, in 1658, he invited the Congregation of the Mission to assume its direction. A few Vincentians went there but, because of financial problems caused by bad management by the diocese, the Community chose to leave in 1661. One reason may have been the recollection of the sordid story of the seminary at Saint-Méen in Brittany. The seminary buildings at Meaux no longer exist, apart from the chapel. This building, originally part of the Jean Rose Hospital, is located at the end of Rue Saint Rémy. It now forms part of the Lycée Henri Moissan. There is no indication that Vincent visited this foundation. Its work was complicated by the fact that the superior was at the same time the head of the seminary and the head of the hospital, which in some way continued to function. The chapel is not open to the public.

Neither is there any indication that Vincent ever visited the **Convent of the Visitation**, founded in Meaux in 1631. Nevertheless, since he was the ecclesiastical superior of the Visitation in Paris, he might have gone there, particularly since the convent opened in his younger years when he traveled more regularly. The Rue de la Visitation and the chapel of the Sacred Heart mark its location.

Daughters of Charity worked in the hospital in Meaux beginning in 1700. They had a school and other works from 1695 and returned in 1833 after the Revolution.

The dominant figure in Meaux during Vincent's period was its bishop, *Jacques Benigne Bossuet* (1627-1704), known as the Eagle of Meaux because of his eloquence. Bossuet had been the tutor of the Dauphin, the future king Louis XIV, before acceding to the see of Meaux. While here, he combated the considerable Huguenot influence in the city. A model and studious bishop, Bossuet had been formed in Vincent's image and was a member of the Tuesday Conferences. His private study retreat, a small building situated on the city walls behind the gardens of his episcopal palace, attests to many long hours of research and writing. Noteworthy guests at the palace included Louis XVI and Queen Marie Antoinette, as they were being returned under revolutionary guard from Varennes to Paris in June 1791 after attempting to escape to the Austrians.

The exterior of the *cathedral* of Saint Étienne remains in poor condition, and certain details were never finished. The interior was restored in the eighteenth century, but not much renovation has been done since then. Bossuet is buried in the sanctuary, and two large statues of him are found in the side aisles of the church.

The Vincentians took up the Meaux seminary again from 1862 to the general expulsion of congregations in 1903. Meaux today numbers about 50,000 people.

## MONTMORENCY

Montmorency is renowned for its beautiful chateau, formerly the seat of an important family. Vincent undoubtedly visited here on various missionary trips. In a letter written about 1634, he described for Louise at least one visit: Since my slight fever goes on, I decided to go on with your advice which is to do as I did in the past for it, enjoy some country air. I am going to try, therefore, to visit a few Charities and perhaps, if I feel well, I shall go as far as Liancourt and Montmorency to begin what you will be able to complete later. (Letter 198a) Daughters of Charity were also established here in the earliest days of their foundation, but it is unknown how

Staircase, Brothers' house,
Orsigny farm, Saclay

long they remained. Montmorency has a population today of around 20,000.

## OLLAINVILLE

Although the identity of Louise's mother may never be discovered, she was a Marillac, a member of one of the most distinguished families of the kingdom. She naturally remained close to her one son, Michel, his wife Gabrielle and daughter, known affectionately as Little Louise. She also took an interest in the affairs of various relatives. Some of them had country estates in Ollainville near Champlan, south of Paris. In one

Former entry, Orsigny farm, Saclay

letter (2667, dated September 1658), Louise consulted Vincent about the obligation she felt, even in her old age, of visiting Michel de Marillac, lord of Ollainville, and his wife Jeanne. Another letter in her correspondence (L. 594, 29 September 1658) suggests that she made the journey. Vincent's coachman and horses brought her here and back.

## ORSIGNY (SACLAY)*

In 1644, a childless couple, Jacques and Elisabeth Norais, donated to Vincent their large farm, called Orsigny. In return for this land, today located in the town of Saclay, he assigned them a life annuity. Adrien Le Bon (1577?-1651), Vincent's predecessor as prior of Saint Lazare, first proposed the idea of acquiring this land, but Vincent was not keen on it. He signed the contract, however, 22 December 1644. Work began on the buildings and he eventually placed brothers here and hired other farm hands and women servants. Within a year of acquiring the land, Vincent, with his solid peasant background, purchased other properties in the area. For some years, he continued to increase his holdings, nearly doubling the original property by 1660. For example, some property was purchased in Villiers-le-Bacle, but the old buildings on this property have long since disappeared. Other property names listed in the records are Belleville, Villedombe and Toussus-le-Noble.

Because the farm was important— it provided at one point nearly one-sixth

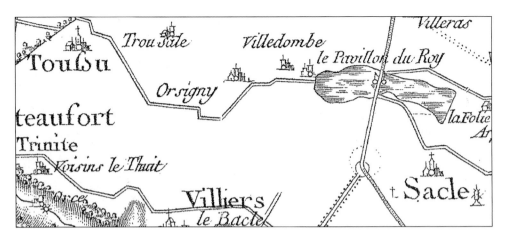

Eighteenth century map of Orsigny and neighborhood

of the needs of Saint Lazare—it was an attractive target. Marauding troops pillaged it during the Fronde in February of 1649. To help save the property, Vincent himself led away 240 sheep and two horses toward Valpuiseaux to the hamlet at Frenneville. Since there was also a problem in Frenneville, he then led them to a fortified town near Etampes (otherwise not identified). Some think that this town was **Itteville**, although nothing in Itteville confirms this suggestion.

After the death of the Norais couple, the two brothers of Madame Norais asserted that the farm had been illegally given to the Congregation and that it should revert to them. They went to court and won. In September 1658, Vincent had to withdraw his confreres from this farm that had been so important for the maintenance of Saint Lazare. He refused, as well, to appeal the verdict. Nevertheless, he was able to hold on to

other nearby properties, since they had not been part of the original Norais farm. In 1663, the Congregation was able to return to part of the Orsigny property and, in 1684, regained the rest. Vincentians continued here until 1792. The saint apparently felt some guilt over his attachment to this farm, since he said once to his confreres:...*God has taken away from us, with this farm, the satisfaction we had in possessing it and the pleasure we used to take in visiting it from time to time. As this recreation was pleasant to the senses, it might have been for us a sweet poison that slays, a knife that wounds, and a fire that burns and destroys.* (Conference 189)

The farm still exists but is private property. The old entry gates lead in to the courtyard. Of primary interest is the oldest building. On its first floor is a series of rooms commonly referred to as the brothers' rooms. The main staircase is old and well constructed, as is the carpentry work in the old loft adjoining their rooms. A separate chapel building has disappeared. The garden contains an icehouse (*glacière*), to contain ice gathered in the winter from the ponds adjoining the property and stored in the icehouse for use all through the year. The age of other outbuildings and walls is open to discussion, but at least the early appearance of this prominent farm can be appreciated from what remains. The farm used to have bells dated 1663 or 1665, belonging to the Vincentian chapel. Their whereabouts today are unknown. (*Country road west of Le Christ de Saclay*)

During a particularly terrible period in the neighboring town of **Palaiseau**, on 5 June 1652, Vincent sent several of his confreres and a surgeon to offer spiritual and corporal help to the sick and starving. The lengthy presence of troops had reduced the inhabitants to misery. Nothing is known of any further ministry here. (Doc. 108)

## POISSY*

Poissy, a royal residence as early as the fifth century, became particularly famous with the birth and baptism in 1214 of Louis IX, Saint Louis, king of France. He sometimes signed his name Louis of Poissy because of the fond recollection he had of this place. The men's abbey in the town has become a prison. The women's abbey, formerly Dominican, was closed at the Revolution. On the same spot, however, some of its works continue, notably the Institut Notre Dame, a school. A portion of the monastery grounds has been set aside as a public park. Louise, perhaps as young as three years old, was sent here under the care of her aunt, Catherine Louise de Marillac, a nun in this abbey. Jeanne de Gondi, aunt of Philippe Emmanuel de Gondi, was prioress in Louise's day—another of the strange coincidences that bound her and Vincent together.

This abbey was founded to honor Louis IX, whose birthplace is located where the convent chapel was built. Although many of the nuns were of the

Monastery buildings, Poissy

Monastery entry, Poissy

highest nobility and adorned the buildings beautifully, they emphasized both piety and learning for the girls sent here for an education. It was probably here that Louise received her training in the classical Latin, philosophy and theology so apparent in her writings.

Some of the former abbey walls and buildings are still standing, mainly a part of the perimeter wall and gate towers, as well as the tithe barn. Nothing directly recalls the presence of Louise here, however. There is no record that she ever mentioned this part of her history in her later life.

The young Louise probably made her first communion in Poissy, most likely in the parish church. Vincent gave a mission in Poissy in February 1634. In 1636, he also worked to reestablish harmony among the Dominican nuns here. The parish church of Notre Dame, in which he preached, dates from the eleventh and twelfth centuries and preserves the baptismal font where Louis IX was baptized. However, it has no memorials to either Saint Vincent or Saint Louise. The modern town of Poissy has about 38,000 inhabitants.

## PONTOISE

Pontoise has a rich ecclesiastical history, perhaps because it has a privileged geographical position, dominating from its heights the valley of the Oise. Saint Louis the king (Louis IX, 1214-1270) founded the Hôtel Dieu here, as he did in Paris, and he lived here for some time. After falling ill here in 1244, he vowed to go on crusade to the Holy Land if he recovered. Unfortunately, the crusaders were routed and the king taken prisoner. He returned to France, resumed the crusade in 1270 but died in Tunis. The church of Saint Maclou, a *cathedral* since the erection of the diocese in 1966, is renowned for its Renaissance art and architecture. The city today has a population of around 28,000.

The *parish church* of Notre Dame (sixteenth century) preserves the statues of Our Lady of Pontoise and Our Lady of Health, for which the first church was built in 1177. Within the parish is the Carmel of Pontoise, where Marie of the Incarnation, Madame Acarie, died in 1618. She had been influential in the development of the French school of spirituality and undoubtedly had an influence on Vincent.

Vincent's connection with Pontoise is not known. It is clear, however, that he visited several times (in 1631, yearly from 1636 to 1639, and probably in 1651), and personally knew the town magistrates. He may have gone through Pontoise on the way to Beauvais to conduct a formal visitation of the Ursulines there. His 1638 visit may have been occasioned by the plague of Pontoise in that year, but the details are unknown. The members of the ecclesiastical conference (the Tuesday Conferences) asked him to send them some help in developing their own conference. It seems quite possible that his friend Michel Alix, pastor of Saint-Ouen-l'Aumône, was a member, although

Pontoise was not in the diocese of Paris, to which Alix belonged.

A few kilometers down the river Seine from Pontoise is **La Roche-Guyon**, site of a work of the Daughters of Charity begun in 1654. They came here at the invitation of the powerful dukes of Liancourt, whose chateau still stands on the heights overlooking the Seine. The original work of the Daughters here was for the sick poor and in the school. It resumed in 1853 as a retirement home, probably lasting until about 1904 when sisters were routinely expelled from their works in France. The hospice, now a children's hospital, still exists on rue de l'Hospice.

Another work founded by a wealthy benefactress was the house at **Chars**, a few kilometers northwest of Pontoise. It opened in 1647 for the service of the poor and the education of children. The foundress, Charlotte de Ligny Madame de Herse (d. 1662), was very devoted to works of charity and to Vincent's two communities. She called for Daughters of Charity in various places besides here. Unfortunately, the Jansenist tendencies of the sisters' pastor and his associate caused them many problems, and they were obliged to leave Chars in 1657.

## PORT-ROYAL-DES-CHAMPS*

The ancient Cistercian monastery for women at Port Royal near Chevreuse had, by the seventeenth century, become very lax. *Angélique Arnauld* (1591-1661), daughter of a powerful noble family, became abbess in 1602, at age eleven. She acceded, since the abbey was something of a family responsibility and she could earn a living as abbess. Following an illness, she began in 1609 to take religious life seriously—very seriously. One of the results of her reforming spirit was that novices flocked to Port Royal, despite its damp and otherwise unhealthy location. She also attracted *Jean Duvergier de Hauranne* (1581-1643), better known from his title as the abbé of Saint Cyran. He was a leader of the Jansenist movement, emphasizing religious conversion in a somewhat Calvinist fashion: austerity, detachment from pleasure, admission of total personal corruption.

As the monastery grew, expansion became necessary. For this reason, in 1625 Mother Angélique led all her nuns to a new house in Paris, also called Port Royal, near the Val de Grâce. Her reforming personality, joined with the power of her family and pushed by Saint

Memorial chapel, Port-Royal, Chevreuse

Cyran, led to an ever-increasing popularity of the Jansenist movement. One of her brothers, *Antoine* (1612-1694), returned to the country location and attracted other men of like temperament. They lived on the hill above the old abbey in refurbished barns. One of their works was primary education. They became known as the "Solitaries" of Port Royal. A group of nuns from the city house who wanted to resume living at the abandoned abbey joined them in 1648.

The theologians of Port Royal found in the work of Jansenius, late bishop of Ypres, a good statement of their convictions. Gradually, Vincent became involved. He had been a friend of Saint Cyran's and continued to visit him (probably at Port Royal in the city). Vincent eventually found himself as one of the leaders of the opposition against the Jansenist movement and promoted multiple papal condemnations. Louis XIV, as a loyal son of the Church, also became involved. He finally forbade the nuns to receive novices, dispersed the Solitaries and, when the nuns were mostly aged, had them removed and leveled their old monastery beginning in about 1710.

Today, the privately owned ruins of the old *abbey* may be visited. Only two original buildings are left: the tithe barn and the pigeon coop. A small memorial chapel (1891) has been erected on the site of the old abbey church. The "canal" or narrow waterway used by the nuns remains, as does their outdoor recreation area, tucked into a fold of the rocks along a creek. They read, sang, prayed, and conversed here.

To reach the residence of the Solitaries from the abbey, the traditional route follows the Hundred Steps cut into the hillside. The school that the Solitaries built in 1651-1652 has been turned into a *museum*. Many of the rooms are maintained as they were originally. Intriguingly, few references to Vincent's work are to be found among the museum exhibits. It appears that the saint visited here at least once, in 1653. His purpose was to try to persuade the Solitaries to submit to the papal condemnation. He was not successful. Louise also visited, in 1649, concerning one of her relatives, a nun of this abbey. (*Route D91, near Chevreuse*)

### RUEIL-MALMAISON

Although most French people know of Rueil (now called Rueil-Malmaison) because the emperor Napoleon and his first wife Josephine de Beauharnais lived here, the town also has Vincentian connections. Cardinal Richelieu made Rueil one of his official residences, perhaps to be close to Louis XIII, who lived at Saint-Germain-en-Laye. Vincent came here to visit the cardinal minister in 1638, to sign the foundation contract for Richelieu, and then again in 1640. He certainly came here after the cardinal's death, 4 December 1642. One reason was that the cardinal's niece, the duchess of Aiguillon, inherited his chateau, and Vincent had many dealings with this pious and charitable woman. Her castle, the *Chateau du Val*, no longer exists, but some of its grounds and artificial ponds remain where the Sandoz chemical company has its headquarters. *(Rue de Zurich, Rue du Lac)*

Vincent also probably came here to give a mission in 1637 (or at least a mission was given here that year). The *parish church* of Saint Peter and Saint Paul, visible today, had been completed just two years before. The architect of the façade, Lemercier, also designed the façade of the church at Richelieu, which it resembles. The present church also contains the tombs of the empress Josephine (1763-1814) and her daughter, Hortense (1783-1837). Hortense married Napoleon's brother Louis and was briefly queen of Holland. She died at Malmaison. Rueil-Malmaison is today a city of some 67,000 people.

## SAINT-CYR-L'ÉCOLE

Saint-Cyr-L'ÉCole, with a population of about 15,000, is best known in France for the military academy Napoleon founded in this city in 1808. He lodged his young officers in a school with unusual Vincentian connections.

Françoise d'Aubigné, Madame de Maintenon (1635-1719), Louis XIV's second wife, but not his queen, founded a school for the daughters of impoverished rural nobility at Saint Cyr. This opened in 1686 and enjoyed the king's support. Her Maison Royale de Saint Louis gradually grew in fame but lacked discipline. Order was restored by turning the school increasingly into a convent and by inviting the Vincentians to provide its chaplains. After much hesitation, the superior general, Edme Jolly (1622-1697), agreed. Vincentians took up residence in August 1691. They had their own section of the building near the chapel with their own courtyard and garden. Their obligation was to staff the chapel and give religious instruction to the nuns, the girls and all the others associated with the institution. At the same time, the Vincentians, who numbered approximately six priests and three brothers, were free to give missions. They remained for 100 years, until the Revolution. Daughters of Charity came to work in the infirmary beginning in 1704 and remained until the Revolution. **Louis Joseph François** was one of the featured preachers for its centenary, July 1786. His printed eulogy of the foundress ran to 78 pages. The last religious left the school in 1793, and mobs pillaged the buildings, but the institution was later reconstructed and repaired, and the Daughters resumed their work in 1802.

Cookery formed a part of the training given the girls. It became so famous that it gave its name to the Cordon Bleu *(blue cord)* style, from the cord or perhaps the blue ribbon worn at ceremonies by the young women in their final year. Equally famous in the beginning were two plays written by Jean Racine (1639-1699) for the girls to perform—a scandalous occasion in the opinion of some, including François Hébert, the influential Vincentian pastor at Versailles.

The chapel was heavily damaged in the bombing of 1944. After thorough restoration, it now forms part of the military academy and can be visited with special permission. It was noted as being especially bereft of decoration. The foundress, Madame de Maintenon, was buried here.

## SAINT-GERMAIN-EN-LAYE*

A royal chateau on the heights of Saint Germain can be dated to sometime in the twelfth century. The old buildings were dilapidated by the time of François I (1494-1547), married in the chapel built by Saint Louis, which still stands. He then built what is substantially the present "old" chateau. Another much smaller building, the "new" chateau, stands on a marvelous height overlooking the plains and the city of Paris. Louis XIV was born in this new chateau on 5 September 1638.

Vincent had many connections with this royal residence. He is said to have given a mission here to the court in 1638, and his pulpit can be seen in the chapel of the former Daughters of Charity hospital. The Vincentians and the members of the Tuesday Conferences joined in the mission, and spoke, patiently, against the low-cut dresses of

Pulpit, hospital chapel, Saint-Germain-en-Laye

the ladies of the court. (Letter 307) Neither Vincent's presence here nor the authenticity of the pulpit can be completely assured, however. The saint often visited the palace, particularly during the last days of Louis XIII, who died here 14 May 1643. The crucifix that Vincent used to comfort the monarch passed down through the royal family and is now to be seen in the hands of the saint's effigy at the Vincentian motherhouse. Vincent, however, was only one among several persons at the monarch's deathbed. Nevertheless, he retained a vivid memory of the king's saintly death, as he recounted to the Daughters of Charity: *God gave me the grace to assist at the deathbed of the late king. He refused food. . . . He then did me the honor of summoning me and said: 'Father Vincent, the doctor has urged me to take some food and I refused him. . . . What do you advise me to do?'* Vincent recommended that he take something and follow the doctors' advice, and so the king had some soup brought. (Conference 85)

A Confraternity of Charity began here in January 1638, perhaps because of Vincent's mission. Its members included ladies-in-waiting to the queen and wealthy ladies of the town. Daughters of Charity, too, arrived shortly afterwards in the same year to help the sick poor and to keep a school. The Ladies bought a hospice for the Daughters, 20 April 1649. This work continued only to 1655—since the work of caring for the sick proved too great for the elegant women of society.

Vincent came here also in 1648, during the difficult days of the civil war (the Fronde) to try to get Cardinal Mazarin to resign and thus restore peace to France. Vincent's brave and selfless appeal, however, came to nothing. He also came here on 13 February 1649 to discuss issues with Anne of Austria, who was battling the Fronde in self-imposed exile away from the Parisian mobs. Unable to return to Paris because of those mobs, Vincent went instead to Orsigny and Frenneville, and then extended his journey to the Community houses in Brittany.

The present **parish church** of Saint Germain is the fourth one erected on this spot since 1028. It was finished in 1827, although Louis XV had laid the cornerstone some sixty years before. It was in Saint Germain that Louis XIII had made his solemn vow dedicating his kingdom to the Virgin Mary, a theme often seen in paintings in French churches, and in one modern window here. The church has a small chapel in honor of Saint Vincent de Paul. The major commemorative work is a painting showing the charitable priest surrounded by his confreres, Daughters of Charity, Ladies of Charity and others. Vincent, however, was not pleased with the way the clergy celebrated mass here. He recalled one day: *I was once at Saint-Germain-en-Laye, where I remarked seven or eight priests, all of whom said mass differently; one did it in one manner, another in another, it was a diversity worthy of tears.* (Conference 206)

The church also contains the tomb of *James II*, king of England (1633-1701). He must have had some contact with French Vincentians while in exile during the Cromwell period (1653-1658). After succeeding his brother Charles as king in 1685, he invited and received four Vincentians to serve as his royal chaplains in London. After James was deposed in 1688, the Vincentians left England, the last Catholic chaplains at the English court. Louis XIV provided the English king and his wife hospitality at the old chateau of Saint Germain, and the royal couple often attended Sunday and feast day vespers at Saint Lazare. James II died in 1701 and requested burial here. George IV had the present monument built, and Victoria came in 1855 to visit the last home of her ill-starred predecessor.

The hospital used to contain one (or perhaps two) of the paintings of the "Lord of Charity." They must be quite old, dating perhaps to shortly after 1638 when they arrived, inasmuch as the serving women depicted there are most likely Daughters of Charity, but they are not wearing the cornette. Its generalized use began only in 1685. The reasons given for this change of headgear were the usefulness of a head covering in summer and winter while serving the poor in their homes, and the uniformity sought among the sisters. It had been worn up to that time only when needed. The sisters began their hospital work in 1692. During the Revolution, a priest of the Constitutional Church replaced their legitimate chaplain, but the sisters refused to attend his masses or go to him for confession. Another priest, sometimes disguised as a soldier or a gardener, would come for the sacraments secretly.

Other hospitals followed, and the present one is certainly the successor of those earlier institutions. The modern city of Saint Germain has a population of about 40,000.

## SAINT-OUEN-L'AUMÔNE

Across the river Oise from Pontoise is Saint-Ouen-l'Aumône, a town of about 19,000 people. The parish church, although dating from the twelfth century, was dedicated to this saint in 1499. One of its treasures is a thirteenth-century statue of the Virgin and Child, previously located in the neighboring abbey. In Vincent's day, its pastor, Michel Alix became his friend and was a member of the Tuesday Conferences (probably the one founded in Pontoise). As a token of his friendship, he dedicated a book to Vincent. Alix edited and, in 1651, republished this volume, the Hortus Pastorum by Jacques Marchant. The founder sought to discourage him from including his laudatory introduction.

Alix probably also had a Confraternity of Charity in his parish, although records are lacking. The only indication in the church is a copy of the Lord of Charity, a painting that Vincent and Louise had copied and sent to the various Charities. It depicts the risen Lord standing on a globe, arms outstretched downward, hands empty in a gesture of charity. To either side of him are groups of people engaged in corporal and spiritual works of mercy. Below is the Latin text "The charity of Christ urges us on." Besides this rare painting, there is no other reminiscence of Vincent here.

Within the parish is the royal abbey of Notre Dame La Royale, called Maubuisson. Mostly destroyed during the Revolution and later reconstructed, this abbey had been founded in 1236 by Blanche of Castile, queen of France,

Château and fountain, Vaux-le-Vicomte

mother of Louis IX. In Vincent's day, it became very important. One letter from him, dated 1630, mentions a trip to this abbey, perhaps during a visit to his friend Michel Alix. The purpose of his visit here is unknown. However, the abbé of Saint Cyran had once gone to Maubuisson to preach and had some connection with the nuns here. Angélique Arnauld, one of the great Jansenist figures, was sent here as abbess in 1619 to introduce reforms.

Also in the same town is property called Saint Lazare, now the site of a public park and a railway station. Perhaps this recalls property owned by the Saint Lazare of Paris, used here to support the Hôtel Dieu.

## VAUX-LE-VICOMTE

The chateau at Vaux-le-Vicomte is one of the masterpieces of seventeenth-century French architecture. It was the creation of Nicolas Fouquet (1615-1680), superintendent (or minister) of finances under Mazarin. His taste was excellent and his funds apparently inexhaustible. When he imprudently invited the young Louis XIV and his mother to the midsummer party to dedicate his new chateau and its sumptuous grounds, the king felt humiliated by his own relative poverty. Nineteen days later, the finance minister was arrested and spent the rest of his life in prison, ostensibly for embezzlement or misappropriation of state funds.

Of Vincentian interest is the invitation from Nicolas to send Daughters of Charity to the adjoining village to work for the poor. They arrived in 1659. The Fouquet family had many dealings with Vincent and Louise. Marie de Maupeou, mother of Nicolas, was a Lady of Charity. Four of her daughters and one sister were Visitation nuns. A brother,

Fountain, Vaux-le-Vicomte

François, was bishop of Bayonne, then of Agde, and lastly archbishop of Narbonne. He invited Vincent to send missionaries and Daughters to Agde and Narbonne. Another brother, Louis, succeeded François as bishop of Agde and had further dealings with Vincent. Louise visited Nicolas in his capacity as attorney general *(procureur)* concerning the contract of foundation of the Daughters of Charity. He lost or misplaced the document, and Louise was forced to begin again.

## VERSAILLES***

Vincentians are often surprised to learn that the royal family (first Anne of Austria, then her son Louis XIV) engaged their confreres as parish priests and chaplains for the royal establishments at Fontainebleau, Versailles, Saint Cyr, and Saint Cloud. Service in these exalted surroundings, amid luxury, power and intrigue, seems to contrast markedly with Vincent's spirit. The queen, however, had maintained close contacts with the founder and, after his death, summoned his confreres. Vincentians assumed control of the Fontainebleau church in 1661. Nearly eleven years later, in 1672, the king summoned the Congregation for the pastoral care of his intended residence, the old town of Versailles. Since the property had belonged to Albert de Gondi and later to Pierre de Gondi, brother of Philippe Emmanuel, on whose lands Vincent was obliged to give missions, he may have done so even here. In any case, Louis XIII purchased its lands and chateau from Pierre de Gondi, a relative, for use as a hunting lodge. Louis XIV transformed it and Versailles completely. By the time of the Revolution, the Vincentians were pastors of its two most important parishes, as well as chaplains of the royal palace.

Versailles had an ancient parish church dedicated to *Saint Julien*. It was located in front and to the left of the present chateau, along Rue Saint Julien. Louis XIV wanted to replace it with a royal parish worthy of his new residence. He had another church built, also called Saint Julien, and the former one demol-

ished. The second Saint Julien was to the west of the present Notre Dame parish. The Vincentians inaugurated their new house there, a royal foundation, on 6 October 1674. A mission preached in that church preceded their arrival. Then, after the funeral of Queen Marie Therese in 1683, it became clear that Versailles would need an even larger church to satisfy parish needs, since in 1682 the king, a parishioner, had moved to the unfinished chateau and transferred the seat of government here.

The king intended that all parochial ceremonies (baptisms, marriages, burials and processions) be held in the new church, *Notre Dame de*

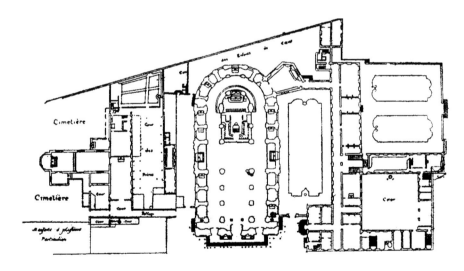

*Saint-Julien, Notre-Dame et la Maison des Missionnaires.*

Floor plans, Saint Julien, Notre Dame and Vincentian house, Versailles

Jean Restout, Vincent preaching,
Notre Dame church, Versailles

**Versailles.** He presided over laying the cornerstone of the new church, 10 March 1684, dedicated 30 October 1686. He reserved a special place for himself in the sanctuary on the epistle side. His new wife, Madame de Maintenon had a prominent place for herself and the numerous royal children, outside the grille enclosing the sanctuary, on the gospel side. The Vincentian parish clergy occupied the choir stalls, but all this has now been removed. The royal ritual continued during the two following reigns, Louis XV and Louis XVI. The old

church, Saint Julien, became a chapel used until 1797 in various ways: for catechism, then for a seminary, later for a Revolutionary political club. It has completely disappeared, although its name is kept for a side altar in the new church.

The work of the architect Jules Hardouin Mansart, Notre Dame church today preserves much of its original appearance. It is well situated at the end of a street. Its height is somewhat restricted, since the king wanted his palace to dominate the town. The whole building is in the classical style favored in that period.

The interior has a wide nave and a barrel vault. Its decoration has always been solemn. The original furniture disappeared during the Revolution, except for the pulpit, some paneling and the organ case. Ten paintings also date to the time of the Sun King. Of Vincentian interest is the painting of Saint Vincent preaching to Emmanuel de Gondi and his family, the work of Jean Restout (1692-1768). The artist modestly included himself at the left, and on the right painted in two Vincentians—known from their high collars and distinctive beards—and two Daughters of Charity in the habits of the period. This canvas, exhibited in the 1739 salon, was painted for this church to mark Saint Vincent's canonization in 1737. Although this painting is found above the altar in a side chapel dedicated to the saint, the altar has no other decoration commemorating him. Vincent was somewhat con-

Joseph Baret portrait,
Notre Dame church, Versailles

cerned about his preaching, as the artist seems to imply, and admitted to his confreres during a conference on preaching: *[do] not do as I do: crying aloud, clapping my hands and leaning far too much over the pulpit.* (Conference 136, 1655) In the nineteenth century, the church was refurbished, and the Blessed Sacrament chapel added.

The Vincentians had a large *community house* situated beside Saint Julien church. Like the church, the house has long since disappeared. In 1686, the king authorized a new and much larger house next to the present church. In 1710, for example, it held the extraordinary total of twenty-six priests, eight seminarians and six brothers. This house befitted one of the most splendid parishes of France,

with its extensive gardens, large library, and gracious rooms for parish functions. This building still stands. *(37-41, rue de la Paroisse)*

The Vincentian pastors of Notre Dame and Saint Louis were both entitled to attend the formal morning rising of the king (the *lever*), held at the palace. Their presence allowed them to petition alms or other favors from the king. On one such occasion, Louis XV asked about the sick and the poor. "Do you have a lot of poor?" "Too many, Sire," replied Joseph Baret (1703-1778), the pastor of Saint Louis, and known for being outspoken. "The numbers of the unfortunates are growing, too?" Yes, Sire. We even have valets from the palace looking for help." To this, the king reportedly sighed, "I really think that we will have to pay dearly for this." Whether the king was moved to help the pastor alleviate their poverty is unknown. The pastors were also entitled to bring the holy oils and Viaticum for the sick and dying to the palace, but the various royal chaplains had the responsibility to give the king communion (done rarely), distribute ashes for Lent, pray at formal meals, etc. In addition, under Marie Antoinette, the pastor of Notre Dame could take up a collection at the queen's weekly gambling parties. She herself would pass among the guests to ask for money.

An event of significance for the Vincentian community was the episcopal ordination of one of its members in this church. On 6 April 1704, the archbishop of Paris ordained *François Hébert* (1651-1728), the superior of the house, as bishop of Agen. Hébert had been the choice of the court for superior general in 1703. When this did not happen, Hébert became the first Vincentian bishop.

The Vincentians also bought property to house the **Charity of the Poor.** Beginning in 1670, Daughters of Charity served the poor here through their school and shelter. These latter two buildings are still standing, although somewhat remodeled. The Congregation also worked with the Ladies of Charity at this location. The king paid for the services of a physician to serve the poor here. *(12-14, rue de la Paroisse)* By the Revolution, the Daughters of Charity had several houses, but they were forcibly expelled by mobs that beat and whipped them. The sisters returned beginning in 1801.

From Notre Dame, the inaugural procession of the **Estates General** began, 4 May 1789, on the eve of the Revolution. Various plaques on the exterior of the building recount the history of this consultative body representing the three estates (clergy, nobility, commoners). The Vincentians remained until March 1791, by which date all religious congregations had been disbanded. The last pastor, André Aphrodise Jacob (1729-1792), was forced out by a constitutional bishop, who chose Notre Dame as his cathedral. This poor bishop

lasted only from 1791 to 1793. The parish church was then adapted for use as a Temple of Reason but after the Concordat of 1801, it returned to Catholic worship. The Vincentians did not return, probably because they were too few in France at that period.

The second Vincentian commitment was to the *royal chapel* of the palace. Louis XIV summoned the Congregation to dedicate 14 of their confreres for this new service after about ten years at Saint Julien (1672-1682). In these capacities, the six priests, six seminarians and two brothers were responsible for the pastoral care of the court and prayers for the king. Their ministry included daily low masses and prayers, with a solemn mass at 10:00 when the king was present, and solemn benediction with the Blessed Sacrament on Sundays, Thursdays and feasts. When the king, the queen and the Dauphin received communion, they did so under both species, an ancient usage which the royal ritual maintained. Although the

Vincent de Paul defaced,
Saint Louis church, Versailles

Vincentians did not hold the position of King's Confessor, they provided an opportunity for confessions by others. In the licentious atmosphere of the court, it was necessary. A special case concerned Louis XIV's mistress, Madame de Montespan (1641-1707). To receive absolution from her Vincentian confessor, the marquise had to leave court. Absence did make their hearts grow fonder, and her repentance was not total. Nevertheless, the king began to nourish an interest in other women. Amid all this, the Vincentians tried to maintain their usual simplicity and devotion. The palace had a succession of five small chapels, the most important being the third one, the guardroom, currently dedicated to Napoleon's coronation, used for worship from 1676 to 1684. The fifth and current one, begun in 1689, was consecrated in 1710 and can be visited in the palace. During weekdays, the king attended mass and vespers from the tribune; on Sundays and feasts, however, he assisted in the nave, probably from a throne in the sanctuary. The Vincentians, in keeping with their lowly station, were constantly in conflict with the principal royal chaplain, with various other chaplains of the king and queen, all diocesan bishops, and with chaplains to the children of the blood royal, also bishops. To assure constant service, two Vincentians were on call day and night from their small apartments in the palace.

As a part of their duties, the

Historical plaque,
Queen's stables, Versailles

Historical plaque, Saint Louis
church and square, Versailles

Vincentians were also chaplains of the *royal infirmary*. This hospital and retirement home for the poor and the domestics of the palace was built between 1693 and 1699, located west of the Vincentian house at Notre Dame. The Ladies of Charity, whose president was by tradition the queen of France, supported it. Marie Leczinska, wife of Louis XV, and Marie Antoinette, wife of Louis XVI, both provided liberally for the hospital. Daughters of Charity also served in this infirmary until the Revolution, and occasionally were seen entering the queen's quarters of the palace to pick up discarded items to serve the poor. Today the old royal establishment, with its prominent chapel, is called the Richaud Hospital. *(78, boulevard de la Reine)*

The third Vincentian site was the parish of **Saint Louis**. Louis XV ordered the construction of this new church, since he wanted the southern quarter of the town furnished with something more imposing than the small chapel formerly here. He asked his architect Mansart to draw up the plans, and construction took twelve years (1742-1754). Although other clergy worked in Versailles, the king summoned the Vincentians to serve this new parish. A portrait of one of the pastors, Joseph Baret, hangs in the sacristy, where it was moved from the chateau. The Vincentians continued here, as they did at Notre Dame, until the Revolution. (The seventeen who died during their service were buried in the crypt.) It was here at Saint Louis that the Estates General met at the conclusion of the inaugural procession, 4 May 1789. In June and July, several of their sessions took place here. The last superior, Jean André Jacob (1740-1800), younger brother of the Vincentian superior at Notre Dame, had to surrender his pastorate to his confrere Jean Bassal (1752-1812), who eagerly took the various revolutionary oaths. In 1793, the church was closed to Catholic worship and became a Temple of Abundance, honoring farm workers. It later reverted to the

Street sign, Versailles

Church. Meanwhile, vindictive revolutionaries chiseled away the features of Saint Vincent from a medallion high on the outside walls of the transept. Their vandalism can still be discerned from the front of the priests' house.

Up to 1797, Versailles had been part of the archdiocese of Paris. In that year Saint Louis was chosen as the cathedral instead of Notre Dame, but its first legitimate bishop was installed only 27 May 1802. To visit the newly reopened church, Pius VII was received here 5 January 1805 during his lengthy sojourn in France. After benediction, he went to the palace and, fully vested with tiara, imparted his blessing from the balcony of the Hall of Mirrors. A barely legible plaque in the Mary chapel records the papal visit to the cathedral.

The exterior of the cathedral is a good example of an eighteenth-century building, classical and Baroque at the same time. The inside is elegant and harmonious, in the shape of a Latin cross. A large dome crowns the transepts. Noteworthy are the many paintings, mainly in the side chapels. One of them is another version of Saint Vincent preaching, painted by Noël Hallé in 1761. The canvas shows the saint in the pulpit of the church of Saint Étienne du Mont in Paris, recognizable from its elaborate *jubé*. The altar dedicated to him in one of the side chapels around the sanctuary has a fine bas-relief head of the saint in wood.

Another side chapel, the first on the left, contains a marble plaque: *To the memory of Blessed Jean Henri Gruyer, Lazarist, vicar of the parish of Saint Louis from 1784 to 1791. Massacred at the seminary of Saint Firmin in Paris, 3 September 1792. Erected in 1992 on his second centenary.*

The Vincentian *community house* is located to the right of the church. A plaque on the front mentions that Jean Henri Gruyer, vicar (or assistant) of the parish from 1784 to 1791, was massacred in Paris. He had spent most of his Vincentian life here in this house. *(4, place Saint Louis)* From 1711 the Daughters of Charity kept the parish school and served the poor two streets behind the church. *(Rue des Bourdonnais)* They returned in 1801 and continue their service elsewhere in Versailles today.

Three Vincentians were massacred in Versailles for refusing to take the prescribed civic oath: Jean Paul Galoy (or Galois), Mathieu Caron, and Jean Colin. These men had been imprisoned in the *queen's stables*, shortly after these had been turned into a prison. In the spirit of the massacres of 2-3 September in Paris, fanatics broke in and clubbed to death Galoy, sacristan of the royal chapel. The next day, they killed thirteen prisoners, including the other Vincentians. A plaque on the front of the buildings (now an appeals court) recalls its bloody history. Not all Vincentians, however, perceived the oath in such a bad light, and some took it. *(5, rue Carnot)*

To honor the century of Vincentian service, Versailles named a street after them, the *Rue des Missionnaires*. It runs along the Notre Dame parish cemetery. In addition, a small street, *Rue Saint Lazare*, runs directly behind and away from Notre Dame church. Nothing remains to identify the Vincentian mission at the chapel of *Glatigny*, another of the obligations of the Vincentians beginning in 1672. The present Capuchin friary and chapel is probably on the same property. *(Rond Point de la Chapelle)*

The modern city of Versailles, a wealthy bedroom community for Paris, has a population approaching 90,000.

The small village of **Viroflay** adjoining Versailles on the east had a *Maison des Missionnaires*. This was a country house for the Vincentians of Saint Louis in Versailles. Its large garden offered the priests and seminarians a respite from royal and parochial duties. Nothing remains of the house, and only a stretch of wall on Rue James Linard is believed to be left of the old enclosure. The parish church, *Saint Eustache*, likewise, contains no reminders of their

Rose chasuble worn by
Vincent de Paul, Villepreux

presence. The property was seized and sold in 1793. *(Clos Saint Eustache, rue James Linard)*

## VERT-LE-GRAND

Letter 311, from Vincent to Lambert aux Couteaux (1606-1653), is dated Vallegrand, 3 March 1638. This little town of 1500 people, then also called Val le Grand or Val grand, is located not far from Orsigny, south of Paris, on route D31 between Orsigny and Frenneville. The founder was probably here on business concerning these two properties, although his letter gives no

hint one way or the other. Perhaps he was giving a mission in this rural area. The reason for deducing this is that he was there long enough to have leisure to write, and he had access to a messenger to deliver his letter to Saint Lazare. The parish church of Saint Germain preserves no memory of his presence.

## VILLEPREUX*

Villepreux, among the oldest towns in the Ile de France, was part of the Gondi estates from 1568 to 1664 and included the lands at Versailles that the family eventually sold to Louis XIII as a hunting preserve. Vincent's name is connected with Villepreux in several ways. Although precise information is lacking, it is nearly certain that he stayed at the Gondi chateau occasionally while he was the family tutor (until 1617). In early 1618, after his return from Châtillon, he gave a series of missions nearby with two priests. One was Jean Coqueret (1592-1655), a friend of Francis de Sales, and later superior of the Discalced Carmelite nuns in France. The other was Monsieur Belin, the chaplain for the Gondis at Villepreux. Together, they established a Confraternity of Charity here, the second one after Châtillon. Madame de Gondi was present on 23 February for one of the mission events in the village church. The same Belin was probably one of the first companions of Vincent, along with Antoine Portail, but his work at Villepreux kept him from fully joining the Mission. (Letter 190)

Baptismal font, Saint Germain
church, Villepreux

It was probably here in 1629-1630 that Vincent met **Marguerite Naseau** (or more correctly Nezot), regarded as the first Daughter of Charity. She was living here with a few others and spent her time in educating children. These young women had come to attend the mission, and Marguerite later spoke to him about her vocation to serve the poor. Vincent also sent Louise here in 1630 to help support the Confraternity. The same Marguerite Naseau also returned for a time to Villepreux in the service of the Confraternity, although her various assignments are not that clear, since the Daughters of Charity had not yet been founded. Vincent visited again in December 1633, when he came to see the young Catherine de Gondi, the wife of his former student, Pierre de Gondi, eldest son of Vincent's patron, Philip

Emmanuel. The purpose of his visit is unknown.

After Philip Emmanuel's ordination to the priesthood as an Oratorian, and in his retirement, he lived for a period at the *chateau*. Cardinal Mazarin had expelled him from Paris because of the problems Cardinal de Retz, Gondi's third son, had caused him. Vincent visited Philip Emmanuel here from time to time. One visit of a week's duration is recorded in 1648. Vincent also visited in January of 1649 after his failed attempt to persuade the queen and Cardinal Mazarin to come to terms with the leaders of the Fronde. It was perhaps at this time that he recalled seeing the count in

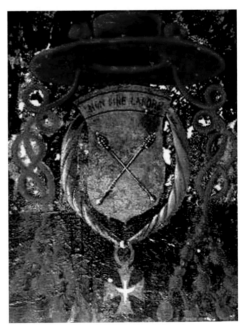

Gondi coat of arms,
Saint Germain church, Villepreux

Charité des Pauvres, Villepreux

a tattered cassock. He told the Daughters of Charity: *I have seen him when he was a courtier changing his clothes three times a day, when he was at Court, and since then I have seen him in a poor old torn cassock out at the elbows. I have seen that with my own eyes.* (Conference 82) Vincent also visited his friend and benefactor again here in the summer of 1655. Brother Robineau, the saint's secretary, recorded that while returning from this visit, Vincent stopped his carriage to give two women a lift into Paris. Moved by their age and weakness, he departed from his normal procedure. The old Gondi chateau, begun around 1600, was demolished in 1885. A new one was built and stands amid elegant gardens.

Close to the chateau is the village *church*, dedicated to Saint Germain. This church dates from the twelfth century and was the site of Vincent's early preaching. The apse chapel is dedicated to him, although there is nothing written

to indicate this. The church has an old rose silk chasuble which Vincent is said to have used. His work is presented in more detail in the **new church**, located in the quarter called la Haie Bergerie. Built in 1967, the parish church of Saint Vincent de Paul boasts an unusual façade. It shows the life of Saint Vincent de Paul (although without depicting him in any recognizable way), through prominent dates and places—among which is the 1618 mission in Villepreux.

Another of Vincent's undertakings is the **Charité des Pauvres.** *(1, rue Pierre Curie, formerly Grande Rue)* This building began in 1658, and the Gondis and others endowed it so well that funds remained until the nineteenth century. The Confraternity Vincent founded supported the charitable works carried on in this hostel, remarkable for its old corbelled façade. Daughters of Charity also worked in Villepreux from 1898 until

Saint Vincent de Paul House,
Charité des Pauvres, Villepreux

recent years. Their house, still standing, is entered from the side street. *(Rue Amédée Brocard, Rue du Docteur Alexandre)* A tiny statue of Saint Vincent placed in a niche adorns the front of the building, now used for the elderly. Today, Villepreux is a town of some 9000 people.

During his 1618 mission, Vincent did not limit himself to Villepreux alone. After the saint's death his friend Michel Alix recorded that he also traveled to Maisons-sur-Seine, today **Maisons-Laffitte**. This small city of some 23,000 today is the site of a sumptuous chateau, completed in 1651. Alix recorded that Vincent lodged in the old manor house, now demolished. He undoubtedly celebrated mass and preached in the old church, next to the chateau. This old church has been converted into the Musée Ianchlevici. *(Place de la Vieille Église)* Besides having the chateau, open to the public, the town also is a center for horse racing, continuing a tradition dating from before the Revolution. Daughters of Charity also worked in Maisons from at least 1663 until the Revolution.

Two locations west of Villepreux, **Maule** and **Crespières**, were also sites of the ministries of the Daughters of Charity in their earliest days. Two sisters were missioned to each place, where they worked for several years with the sick poor of the region. Although Louise came to visit, little is known of the work in either town. East of Maule is the small town of **Les Alluets-le-Roi**, site of a temporary mission to which Louise sent one or two sisters in 1654. In none of these three places is there any monument to their work.

# 3

# North

Seminary chapel, Cambrai

# Nord—Pas-de-Calais

*Although this northern region received the ministry of Daughters of Charity in the time of the founders, it is better known for being the site of brutality and suffering associated with the Revolution. Four Daughters of Charity were martyred here. One Vincentian, the future martyr Louis Joseph François, was born in this region.*

Grande Place and
Hôtel de Ville, Cambrai

## ARRAS, CAMBRAI*

The presence of the Double Family of Saint Vincent de Paul, the *Daughters of Charity* and the Congregation of the Mission, goes back in Arras for centuries. The Sisters arrived here early in 1656, under Vincent's direction to serve the poor and to keep a small school. In his instructions to them at their departure, Vincent said: *it may happen that you will be despised and that people will have a poor opinion of you. Even if some were to say that you keep the money that belongs to the poor and that you do not expend all the money that you receive for them, humble yourselves. . . .* (Conference 77) When they arrived, they received very poor lodgings, and were soon forced to go from door to door to beg food. Marguerite Chétif (1621-1694) was superior of the house when Vincent appointed her superioress general to succeed Louise.

The *Congregation of the Mission* had a house in Arras from 1677 to 1791, taught in the major seminary here and received many vocations from the diocese. Before all that, Guillaume Delville

(1608-1658), something of a free spirit, accepted in his own name the pastorate of Saint Jean de Renville in Arras—without informing Vincent. The founder was understandably distressed and left the elderly Delville mildly chastised, but in any case he did not live very long afterwards. Another free spirit was Philippe Ignace Boucher (b. 1631). He took his role as a military chaplain too seriously and started firing at the enemy. In so doing, he would have incurred a canonical penalty had he killed or wounded someone. Vincent worked on the issue.

What is of more historical importance is the ministry of the Daughters at the Revolution. The house where they lived from 1779 to 1794 is still standing. They returned after the Revolution, 1801, and remained until 1904. The house was probably rebuilt after the first World War, which damaged the town terribly. *(26, rue des Teinturiers)* The sisters have returned and continue their works in Arras.

At the time of the Revolution, seven Daughters were working in Arras. When the anti-religious laws came into force, one sister returned to her family, and two others went into hiding, escaping to Poland. The other four Daughters of Charity, *Sisters Marie Madeleine Fontaine, Marie Françoise Lanel, Marie Thérèse Fantou* and *Jeanne Gérard*, were arrested for refusing to take the oath in support of the constitution. They were also accused of anti-Revolutionary activities. They were imprisoned in the Hôtel de Beaufort in Arras from 14 April to 25 June 1794. Probably to avoid public outcry, the authorities transferred them by night to Cambrai.

When the sisters arrived in **Cambrai**, they were brought that same day to the major seminary. They would soon face the revolutionary tribunal, meeting in the former study room of the Jesuits. Their prosecutor was the notorious Joseph Lebon, mayor of Arras and deputy to the national assembly. This former Oratorian sent some 40 priests and 15 sisters to death by the guillotine.

After their summary trial and subsequent refusal to take the oath, the sisters were hustled to the guillotine for execution, according to the laws of the time. The Cambrai guillotine was erected on the main square, the Grande Place, but nothing now recalls its evil presence. The four Daughters of Charity were the last to die here. They had been in Cambrai, however, only one day, since they were executed on the day of their arrival, 26 June 1794. The sisters were buried in the town cemetery. In Section I, an engraved stone lists the names of the sisters and recounts the events of their death. Lebon himself suffered the same penalty in 1795. Many felt he richly deserved it. At least two of the Sisters have statues erected to honor them in their native towns: Blessed Lanel in Eu, and Blessed Fantou in Miniac-Morvan.

The seminary buildings were finished in 1614. A plaque on the exterior notes that the Revolutionary Tribunal sat here in 1794. By an odd coincidence, this seminary had been in Vincentian hands until 1791. Jesuits ran it until their suppression in 1764, and Vincentians arrived in 1772. It is regarded as one of the most elegant churches of northern France and was completed in 1694. (*Rue Grand Séminaire*) Besides Vincentians, there had also been Daughters of Charity in Cambrai from 1702 until the Revolution, and again afterward. The five sisters of the house were imprisoned in Cambrai, and later in Compiègne, but did not suffer martyrdom.

The *cathedral of Notre Dame* faces the old major seminary where the sisters were condemned, across the Place Saint Sepulchre. It was built in 1702 as a parish church. After the destruction of the old Gothic cathedral during the Revolution, it was chosen as the cathedral in 1804. Much of the building was restored and decorated in the nineteenth century. After the sisters were beatified in 1920, a modern stained glass window

Seminary chapel, Cambrai

Commemorative window,
Cathedral, Cambrai

was installed to honor them, depicted with the revolutionary soldiers. However, no inscription or anything else explains the meaning of the window.

The cathedral also contains the tomb of François de Salignac de la Mothe Fénelon (1651-1715), archbishop of Cambrai from 1695 until his death. This eloquent preacher also became involved in the struggles around Quietism and in the resurgent Jansenism of his period. Nevertheless, he was one of many bishops who wrote the pope to support the beatification of Vincent de Paul, who had known his uncle, Antoine de Salignac, marquis of La Mothe Fénelon (1577-1639). Vincent and he had worked together in a campaign to prevent dueling.

Vincentians returned to direct the Cambrai seminary in 1857, where they remained until their forced expulsion in 1903. The two Daughters who had fled Arras disguised as peasant women returned in 1801 and with four others began their service again in Rue des Teinturiers. A small statue of the Virgin Mary, said to be a gift from Vincent himself to the Arras house, is now in the Daughters of Charity motherhouse, Paris.

Today, Arras is a city of some 39,000 inhabitants; Cambrai is a little smaller.

## BUSIGNY

The small town of Busigny has no known connection with Vincent de Paul. Instead, it was the birthplace of *Louis Joseph François* (1751-1792). He spent most of the years from 1772 to 1790 teaching in Vincentian seminaries. He also was briefly the secretary general of the Congregation in 1786 and was a well-known preacher. In 1788, he was appointed superior of Saint Firmin, the seminary at the old Bons Enfants, in Paris. François's most important contributions were his ten pamphlets defending the interests of the Church in the revolutionary period. Most of his writings went through several editions and made him well known. In the summer of 1792, the seminary of Saint Firmin had been changed into a prison for clerics who had refused the constitutional oath. Early in the morning of 3 September 1792, death came for most of the clergy inside as they were killed in their rooms and hurled out of the windows to the crowd below. François, similarly treated, was finished off by a group of women who beat him to death with heavy wooden clubs. He was beatified in 1926. In all, 77 died in this massacre.

Two of his brothers, *Jean Baptiste* (1753-1839) and *Jean Jacques* (b. 1760) also entered the Congregation. By a strange coincidence and in contrast to their older brother, both took the constitutional oath. Jean Baptiste did so at Chartres and became the superior of the constitutional seminary there. Jean Jacques was assigned to Metz in 1791. He is thought to have become a parish priest and then married.

Besides Louis Joseph François and his brothers, two other Busigny natives should be noted. *Jean Antoine Joseph de Villette* (c. 1731-1792) spent his life soldiering. Probably because he was a relative of Jean Humbert Cousin (1731-1788), Louis Joseph's predecessor at Saint Firmin, he retired there and spent his days in prayerful service. This layman suffered martyrdom with his friend and was beatified with him. *Jean Jacques Dubois* (1750-1817) also joined the Congregation. During the revolutionary period he retained his ties as a Vincentian and worked to reestablish the community in France. He became the pastor of Sainte Marguerite parish in Paris. These two also received their secondary education with the Jesuits at Le Cateau.

The only thing to see in Busigny is the parish church of their baptism. Louis Joseph's statue is found here, but it is not well identified. In addition, a stained glass window commemorates Saint Vincent de Paul. Busigny is a town of perhaps 2500 people.

In *Le Cateau-Cambrésis*, the Jesuit school that the martyr attended is still standing. It is now used as a Lycée. Its chapel has been taken down, but other parts of the building remain.

## MONTREUIL, CALAIS

The count of Lannoy called the Daughters of Charity to take charge of the hospital and orphans in Montreuil, commonly called **Montreuil-sur-Mer**. Two sisters set out in 1647 but quickly encountered problems with the sisters of another community who had preceded them. Vincent's letter to Anne Hardemont, superior, is a model of directness and efficiency. He wrote on 9 May 1650: *Since there is still a lack of understanding with the former Community at the hospital, giving us good reason to fear that you will not find sufficient peace there, we think it advisable for you to leave and for us to withdraw you. Besides, we need you and your Sister here. Therefore, I ask you to take leave of the Governor, his lieutenant, and the town leaders. Thank them for the honor they have done you, ask them to excuse you for not giving them all the satisfaction they expect and say that you are sorry for being unable to continue to serve at the hospital because Providence has determined otherwise.*

Another short-lived work was at **Calais**. Anne of Austria called, in 1658, for Daughters of Charity to care for wounded and sick soldiers. Two of the sisters died in the work, and two others fell ill in their service. Vincent selected four others, and his words to them are still preserved. (Conference 100, 4 August 1658) The sister who copied down his words also noted that he often broke down in tears while speaking to them on this occasion. The work at Calais was later suspended but taken up again in 1760, lasting, in all probability, until the Revolution. Most of old Calais was destroyed in the second World War, but it has recovered and has a population of about 80,000. The Daughters of Charity have returned to Calais where they work in various pastoral ministries.

# Normandie (Basse)

*The modern region of lower Normandy was the site of only one of Vincent's early works. He planned to open a house here at a famous pilgrimage shrine, an apostolate that came to fruition only after his death.*

## DOUVRES-LA-DÉLIVRANDE

In 1657, Vincent agreed to accept the direction of a small seminary attached to the ancient shrine of **Notre-Dame-de-la-Délivrande**, one of the oldest in Normandy. Negotiations dragged on beyond his death, and at length, in 1692 the Congregation of the Mission began its work, which included the seminary and may have included the pilgrimages. The object of the pilgrimage is a wooden statue of the Virgin Mary and the child Jesus, itself a replacement of an early one. The Vincentians remained until the Revolution. At that time, one of the priests, **Jean Baptiste Hénin**, was arrested and imprisoned at Caen, where he died. The seminary buildings appear to have been demolished at that period. The present basilica dates from the nineteenth century, and serves as the parish church in this town of about 4500. The Délivrande seminary, whose site is not known, was a sort of annex to the seminary of **Bayeux**, whose site is well known, since it houses the famous tapestry depicting the conquest of England by the Normans. *(Rue de Nesmond)* Daughters of Charity were also present at the general hospital of Bayeux from 1704.

# Normandie (Haute)

*The modern region of upper Normandy is rich in Vincentian involvement: Vincent's early companion Calon came from Aumale; Vincent visited Forges for his health; he gave missions here; he worked as a vicar general in the Rouen area. Louise de Marillac also made several important Norman foundations of the Daughters of Charity.*

Collegiate church, Aumale

## AUMALE

Vincent is said to have given missions in the deanery of **Aumale**, at the time in the archdiocese of Rouen. It is clear from his letters that others gave missions here, however. The reason is that on 23 August 1629 Vincent and Louis Calon (or Callon) (d. 1647), doctor at the Sorbonne and resident at Aumale, had signed a contract. It bound Vincent to supply two priests each year to preach, catechize, hear general confessions of the poor people of the diocese of Rouen, and especially of the deanery of Aumale, Calon's birthplace. Later, the same priest established a Confraternity of Charity in this country town, and it appears that Vincent had something to do with it.

Whether he was here in person is unknown. Daughters of Charity served in the local hospital (part of which remains) from 1690 to the Revolution. Although the sisters spent three days in jail during the Terror, they were permitted to remain at the works. They resumed the habit in 1803 and remained until 1906. The large collegiate church, Saints Peter and Paul, has nothing to recall the work of Calon, of Vincent or of the Daughters of Charity. Aumale has a modern population of perhaps 2800.

*Louis Calon's* connection with Vincent de Paul went back to 1 July 1626, when he entered the College des Bons Enfants in Paris intending to become one of Vincent's first missionaries. Illness, however, kept him from this, and consequently he was not one of those who signed the act of association between Vincent de Paul and Antoine Portail, François Du Coudray and Jean De la Salle. Although not strictly a member of the Congregation, Calon continued his interest in it and gave missions as well. Daughters of Charity came to the hospital of Aumale in 1690, remaining until the Revolution. They resumed their work shortly after, and remained until 1965.

Aumale is not far from **Neufchâtel-en-Bray** nor from **Forges-les-Eaux** where Vincent certainly came to visit. Consequently, it might be presumed that he took the occasion to visit his erstwhile confrere Louis Calon when opportunity arose.

An old tradition has it that Vincent also came to **Thibouville**. The writer Veuclin, a priest from Rouen, cited the testimony of another priest, who claimed to have seen a letter written by Vincent and dated "Thibouville." This town is southwest of Rouen. Daughters of Charity were sent here perhaps as early as 1638 to help in a time of plague, but a formal foundation began only in 1680, lasting until the Revolution. They returned in 1824 and continue to work in this old mission in favor of children. A copy of a nineteenth-century painting by Frédéric Legrip shows Vincent bringing a foundling to the first Sisters at Thibouville, thus continuing the tradition of his presence here. The original of this painting is now in the hospital of **Bellême**, where the Daughters left it on their departure. They had been here from 1695 to 1990.

**Bernay** tells the same story: the Daughters of Charity came here in 1654 to help with the parish Charity and to instruct poor girls; perhaps Vincent came as well. A Confraternity of Charity had been founded here in 1650-1651, and it was the Ladies of Charity (with the count of Bernay) who requested the Daughters. A remarkable twentieth-century window in the parish church pictures Vincent with Daughters depicted as caring for children, the sick, and particularly orphaned girls, all dressed alike in blue. In this way Vincent's memory is kept alive in this district, along with **Beaumesnil**, because of the ministry of the sisters. Veuclin listed all these towns in his search for traces of Saint Vincent de Paul in the archdiocese of Rouen. Most of the towns Veuclin mentioned are small. The Daughters returned to Bernay in 1804, remaining until 1896 when the government suppressed their school. They continued to work in the orphanage until 1945. The hospital was under their administration from 1830 until 1980.

## ECOUIS*

During Vincent's early life, he was an absentee canon and treasurer of the collegiate church of *Notre Dame of Ecouis*. Like many other priests in his day, Vincent received income from his canonry. He was nominated to it by Philippe Emmanuel de Gondi, who, since he was baron of Plessis, near Ecouis, had the right to name a canon and treasurer. Vincent took official possession of this office in May 1615 and visited here 16-17 September. Records show that Vincent appeared in person at Ecouis, took the usual oath and invited his new confreres to a dinner, probably served in the canons' residence. With this office, together with his other benefices, Vincent was continuing his plan of making himself financially independent, much as he had written to his mother that he would do. (Letter 3, 1610) His office as treasurer, however, was not entirely problem-free. The canons registered a complaint with Monsieur de Gondi about Vincent's lack of residence and so summoned him to appear in person and explain. Vincent did not appear, and no records exist to explain what happened next.

Vincent later resigned his position or positions (as canon and/or treasurer), but the date for this remains unknown. Local historians have suggested that he may have held it for as long as 30 years. Even Pierre Coste was uncertain and spoke of Vincent's early resignation as only "probable."

The church building began in 1310 and a papal legate consecrated it on 9 September 1313. This splendid old church still stands, and it has continued to keep the elaborate choir stalls for the

Collegiate church
interior, Ecouis

Collegiate church,
choir stalls, Ecouis

canons. Although it has stalls for 36 persons, only about eight were listed in the documents concerning Vincent de Paul. The woodwork dates from the Renaissance and was doubtlessly new in 1615. The church also preserves fine old statues, many of which contain traces of their original polychrome painting. In the sanctuary is a large round plaque with the head of Saint Vincent de Paul, with the notation, "Canon of Ecouis, 1615." The plaque is undated, but the model was that used for the tercentenary of his death, 1960, celebrated solemnly here at Ecouis.

The little town, like the church, has managed to preserve many old houses that would have been here when the saint made his one and only visit here. Ecouis today numbers some 700 inhabitants.

A small community of Daughters of Charity should also be listed here, since it is in Normandy, although quite far from Ecouis. This house of **Sainte-Marie-du-Mont** opened in 1655, or perhaps as early as 1650. As elsewhere, the sisters worked in a small hospital and saw to the education of the children. They remained here until at least the Revolution.

## FORGES-LES-EAUX

Forges-les-Eaux is an ancient town, dating back at least to Roman times. The name Forges recalls the important iron forges here, also from the Roman period. Iron working continued through the Middle Ages and kept the town busy. Unfortunately, a fire destroyed most of the town in 1607 and reached as far as the parish church of Saint Eloi, a patron of metalworkers.

The name of the town changed in the seventeenth century through the addition of "les Eaux," (the Waters), showing the importance of the three medicinal iron springs of the area in that period. Monks at Bois de l'Epinay, west of the town, began in the medieval period to construct artificial ponds whose water was of thermal origin. The monks kept carp and other fish in them for their use and most likely to raise for sale.

In the seventeenth century, Forges became a fashionable place to visit for *medicinal cures* through the taking of certain waters. An old stone gate has been reerected near the site of today's main entrance to the park. A modern thermal establishment and clinic continues the centuries-old tradition. Vincent took the waters here, as did some of his other confreres (Marc Cogley, for example, in 1657, who returned no better) and Daughters of Charity, particularly as he recommended them. He wrote to Louise in Letter 29: *[My confreres] are strongly urging me to [go to Forges], because they have been told that the mineral waters did me some good in past years when I had similar illnesses. I have finally decided to offer no resistance . . . . In any case, Vincent was in good company since Louis XIII, Queen Anne of Austria and Cardinal Richelieu came here in 1632. Vincent admitted, however, that waters have never done me any good during my fever [malaria?] in Forges.* (Letter 394)

The neo-Gothic **parish church** was completed in 1878. It has nothing special to mark the presence of the saint in the area, who probably celebrated mass in the church. Forges today numbers about 3500 inhabitants.

The Daughters of Charity worked in **Serqueux**, just north of Forges on route D1314, beginning in 1645. Their works of charity extended as well to Forges, within walking distance. The sisters faced an unusual problem, since their confessor, the pastor of Serqueux, was deaf. Vincent told them to go to Forges instead. This same pastor, however, sent little boys who had misbehaved in school to the sisters for whippings. Vincent was not amused. (Letter 1546)

Commemorative plaque, Ecouis

189

Nevertheless, the work of the Daughters for the sick and in the school was significant enough to attract four girls from the same family to the Daughters of Charity: Françoise, Madeleine, Marguerite and Catherine Ménage. Françoise was assigned for many years to the hospital of Nantes. The Daughters left about 1705. The town suffered in various wars because of its strategic railway yards. Consequently, little remains of the pre-Revolutionary town. Even the parish church was rebuilt after the second World War. Serqueux has a population today approaching 900.

### GAMACHES-EN-VEXIN

The parish church of Gamaches, in the diocese of Evreux, conceals a secret unknown even to Pierre Coste. It is that on 28 February 1614, Vincent was named pastor here. Because of the death of its previous occupant, the post was vacant. Philippe Emmanuel de Gondi, baron of Plessis, had the right of presentation and did so on Vincent's behalf. A note accompanying the original document may suggest that Vincent never took up this new benefice. Further, no proof exists that he ever came here in person, exercised any responsibility for the parish, or received any revenue from it.

Gamaches today has about 300 inhabitants.

### NEUFCHÂTEL-EN-BRAY

The parish church, *Our Lady of the Assumption*, had a Confraternity of Charity, founded 12 November 1634 by Vincent himself. This Confraternity was called locally "La Miséricorde." Since this name was also used in Rouen, it might be concluded that the Confraternity was based upon theirs. It differed from the others that Vincent founded in that it was a work of the Company of the Blessed Sacrament. *Adrien Le Bon*, the prior of Saint Lazare who with his monks gave the property to Vincent, was a native of Neufchâtel. It has been suggested that he traveled here with Vincent to open the Confraternity. After living the rest of his years at Saint Lazare and gaining the high esteem of Vincent and his confreres despite his difficult character, he died in Paris, 9 April 1651. According to his wish, he was buried in Saint Lazare. A lengthy epitaph decorated his gravestone.

The parish church is Gothic in style, plain but quite large for a town of its size, today about 5500 persons. Louis IX, Saint Louis, came here in 1257, and windows in the church portray that visit. That church burned down in 1472. During the period of the early reformation, its successor was a Huguenot church (1562-1591). Like many other contemporary churches, this one has a fine Entombment of Christ (*Mise au tombeau*), with five figures instead of the usual seven. It dates from the sixteenth century. The church suffered grave damage during the second World War but has been largely repaired. There is nothing to recall the presence of Vincent or of Adrien Le Bon here. Daughters of Charity, however, had a house here in the nineteenth century.

Not far from Neufchâtel-en-Bray is *Eu*, birthplace of Blessed Marie

Françoise Lanel, Daughter of Charity, one of the martyrs of Arras. This important town, the seat of counts, commemorates this Sister with a statue in the collegiate church, where she was baptized. William the Conqueror was married here in 1050, Laurence O'Toole, exiled archbishop of Dublin, died in Eu in 1180. The city today numbers some 8000 inhabitants.

Saint Ouen interior, Rouen

## ROUEN

Vincent was vicar general of the commendatory abbot of *Saint Ouen* in Rouen from 1642 or 1643 to, in all likelihood, the last years of his life. Its two abbots, for whom the saint worked, were either too young or were prevented by the government from exercising their responsibilities. The first was Amador Jean Baptiste de Vignerod, a child of about ten at his appointment in 1642. His brother Emmanuel de Vignerod was not yet fourteen when his turn came in 1652. He took over from his brother, who decided he had no vocation to this state.

Vincent's connection with these two stems from Cardinal Richelieu's sister, Françoise Du Plessis, who married René de Vignerod, lord of Pontcourlay. Their daughter, Marie Magdalene de Vignerod (who also wrote her name with the letter W), married Antoine de Roure, lord of Combalet. On his death, she sought to enter the Carmelites, but her uncle the cardinal circumvented it, pushed her fortunes and persuaded the king to erect her lands at Aiguillon into a duchy. The marquise of Combalet, now the duchess of Aiguillon, became one of Vincent's most steadfast supporters. In addition, she also took care of the five children of her wayward brother, François de Vignerod. Two of these were the Vignerod boys who acceded to the abbey of Saint Ouen.

There is no clear explanation for why the saint became involved here, apart from his obligations to the duchess. He had work enough to do as superior general of two communities,

Houses, Rouen

the Vincentians and the Daughters of Charity. As vicar, he was responsible for selecting and presenting clergy for 80 pastorates and chapels depending on the old abbey. That he did so is clear from the many documents remaining in local archives. There is no monument to Vincent in the church, and it is unclear whether he ever came here, either in connection with his office of vicar general or otherwise. His care also extended to Marmoutiers, near Tours, and to the abbey of Saint Martin des Champs in Paris, both of which also had the Vignerod boys as commendatory abbots.

This might explain a problem in Vincent's information about the Rouen seminary. He believed that this institution, under Jesuit direction from 1617 to their suppression in 1762, produced few priests. It was, in fact, more successful. (Letter 2019)

The present church of *Saint Ouen* in Rouen dates from the fourteenth and fifteenth centuries and is noteworthy for its elegant style. Its lofty interior is filled with light, helped by the absence of many stained glass windows. The remaining old glass has been reset into modern settings after the devastation caused during the second World War. In the former cemetery behind the church, a monument recalls the public abjuration of errors that Joan of Arc made here. She was executed elsewhere in Rouen in 1431.

The great *cathedral* of Rouen, as well, was badly damaged and nearly destroyed by aerial bombardment. Its Vincentian connection is that it was the site of the consecration of the third Vincentian bishop at the time of the Revolution. *Jean Baptiste Gratien* (1747-1799) had been the superior of the seminary in Chartres. He supported the Revolution and was elected the constitutional bishop of Seine Inférieure, the new designation for the archdiocese of Rouen. He was ordained bishop 18 March 1792.

Daughters of Charity began their works of charity and education here in 1844, and they continue their pastoral works here. Modern Rouen is a city of more than 100,000 people.

Vincent de Paul and confreres, Folleville

# Picardie

*Picardy, north of the Paris region, was the site of many of the earliest efforts of Vincent de Paul and Louise de Marillac. Vincent saw the beginning of the Mission at Folleville and gave his first ordination retreats at Beauvais. Louise crisscrossed the area visiting and encouraging the Charities, and sending her Daughters here to serve the poor. Vincentians and Daughters of Charity continue these early works.*

Jesuit college, Amiens

## AMIENS**

Amiens, now a city of some 150,000 people and the capital of the ancient province of Picardy, stands at an important communications crossroads on the banks of the Somme. For this reason, it suffered ferocious destruction in the first and second World Wars. The many new buildings, particularly around the railway station, recall the terrible bombardments of the past.

The city has existed from ancient times, but the most important site is, naturally, the *Cathedral of Our Lady*, Notre Dame. It is the largest gothic building in France, built between 1220 and 1280. Since most of its windows were destroyed, it has none of the somberness of Our Lady of Paris (Notre Dame de Paris) or Our Lady of Chartres. Its premier relic is the head (actually, part of the head) of John the Baptist. Of Vincentian interest is the large statue of Saint Vincent de Paul, the work of the Aimé and Louis Duthoit, on the left side of the choir stalls. Much of Vincent's early work took place in this diocese, since the Folleville parish falls within its boundaries. It should be recalled, as well,

that Vincent requested help from the Jesuits, newly founded at Amiens, to hear confessions at Folleville. The Jesuit college (College Saint Nicolas) that he contacted has been taken over by various groups, including a school, but some of the old buildings remain behind the Gendarmerie Nationale. (*Rue des Jacobins, Rue Émile Zola*) As a resident of Amiens early in her life, Françoise Marguerite de Silly, Madame de Gondi took as a spiritual director one of the priests of the order of Minims. She sent Vincent to see him to get a copy of the formula of absolution at the end of 1616. A few traces of their convent are still evident, and their name is preserved in one of the university campuses. (*Ilôt des Minimes*)

Except for Antoine Portail, all of Vincent's first companions in the Congregation came from Picardy. Just why this happened is not clear. It appears, however, that the saint's mission work, taken up by the earliest members, attracted many others from the region to join their fellow Picards. Vincent himself understood the Picard dialect and tried to use it (Letter 560), perhaps even for his important sermon at Folleville. During Vincent's life, a Confraternity of Charity was established in Amiens, and he oversaw, at least from a distance, the life of the Visitation convent in Amiens.

In 1662, two years after the saint's death, Vincentians began to work in the *major seminary* of Amiens. Before Vincentian times, first the Oratorians and then the Sulpicians used the buildings, formerly belonging to the abbey of Saint Martin aux Jumeaux, as a semi-

Statue, Amiens cathedral

recalls that, according to ancient tradition, the monastery was built where Martin of Tours (d. 397), at the time a soldier, removed the lining of his cloak to clothe a poor man. A subsequent vision of Jesus moved him to be baptized and to embrace religious life. It is likely that the widespread use of the name Martin in one form or another (Martino, Martini, etc.) comes from popular devotion to this saint. Further, the term "chapel" comes from "cappa," a temporary shrine where the kings of France placed Saint Martin's cloak during their campaigns. Every "chapel" recalls his act of charity done here. *(Place d'Aguesseau)*

Beginning in the eighteenth century, the Congregation began to acquire land to build a seminary in what became

nary. Besides teaching in the seminary, the Vincentians also gave missions from this house in Amiens. The seminary training was, typically for the time, very short. It simply prepared candidates, already armed with degrees in philosophy and theology, with the basics of the pastoral life: liturgy, music, preaching, hearing confession, besides some practices of piety for their own spiritual life. In 1693, the Vincentians began to offer special retreats for the clergy of the area. The buildings are no longer standing, their place having been taken by the Palais de Justice. *(Rue Robert de Luzarches)* A plaque on a side street

Commemorative plaque,
Martin of Tours, Amiens

Saint Vincent, Father Étienne
and martyrs, seminary, Amiens

the normative style. It followed as much as possible the layout of Saint Lazare. This work began in 1736 and the community was able to move in during 1741. At the time of the Revolution, the community had to leave because its members refused to take the constitutionally prescribed oath supporting the state. Three of the priests of the seminary died in prison in 1793, Fathers Julienne, Bailly and Brochois. The buildings became in turn a military hospital and a home for beggars. The Vincentians were able to secure the buildings again in 1816 when the State agreed to restore some former Church property. The superior, *Amable Ferdinand Joseph Bailly* (1786-1864), a relative of the other Bailly who had died in prison, was the first to take vows in France after the Revolution. Since he did so during a period without approved leadersip in the Congregation, his vows were deemed to be invalid. Jean Baptiste Nozo, superior general, instructed Bailly to petition to renew his vows or to leave. He refused. Their mutual enmity embroiled them in lengthy and public

law suits and was one of the reasons for Nozo's resignation as superior general and for Bailly's estrangement from the Congregation. His brother and a former Vincentian seminarian, Emmanuel Joseph Bailly, worked with Frédéric Ozanam to found the Society of Saint Vincent de Paul in Paris.

During the first days of the Revolution, the superior general, Jean Félix Cayla de la Garde hid in the buildings. He was discovered and arrested but was able to escape, whereupon he fled the country. In the revolutionary period after 1830, his successor as superior general, Dominique Salhorgne, fled from Paris to Picardy and spent the year of

Seminary façade, Amiens

Perboyre family at prayer,
Saint Anne, Amiens

Perboyre family at prayer,
Saint Anne, Amiens

Perboyre family hearing catechism,
Saint Anne, Amiens

John Gabriel Perboyre teaching
catechism, Saint Anne, Amiens

John Gabriel Perboyre levitating,
Saint Anne, Amiens

Martyrdom of John Gabriel Perboyre,
Saint Anne, Amiens

1831 at this same institution. The Vincentians returned after the Revolution, in 1806, to resume their care for the seminary. They remained at their post until expelled in 1903. When the diocese closed the seminary, the army took over the buildings. The main chapel became a reading room, while an auxiliary chapel for the people (la chapelle basse) was for several years a military recruiting office. Hidden behind the modern ceiling, however, are some paintings honoring Saints Vincent and Louise, as well as other members of the two congregations. Figuring prominently among them is Jean Baptiste Étienne. The buildings themselves resemble in many details the former Saint Lazare and in turn provided a model for the present Vincentian motherhouse. (*Rue Jules Barni*)

When the Vincentians returned after the Revolution, they served the small chapel of an orphanage. From these beginnings developed the parish of **Saint Anne.** The present Gothic revival church dates from 1886, and it contains several works of art specifically

Charles Marie Aubert,
Saint Anne, Amiens

John Gabriel Perboyre and garments
of Clet, Saint Anne, Amiens

Vincentian in interest.

The side chapel dedicated to the memory of **John Gabriel Perboyre** has interesting and unique windows depicting him. These take their origin in the devotion of the Vincentian priest Pierre Charles Marie Aubert (1812-1887), a former student of Perboyre's in Paris, later the pastor and builder of the present church. The altar in Perboyre's honor was placed there in 1890 to mark the triduum celebrated for his beatification. The central statue depicts him after his execution.

The stained glass windows, were made in 1891 but installed only in 1931. Moving left to right, the first window deals with prayer. The main section depicts an event narrated by Aubert: the levitation of John Gabriel during the celebration of mass. The shadows of his feet appear on the carpet below, and the server is Aubert himself. The lower section shows the Perboyre family at prayer. John Gabriel is depicted with a halo. The text reads: "Martyrdom is all I wish for." The family table shown here still exists. The upper section shows a room furnished in Chinese style, with Perboyre at prayer.

The central window deals with his

Vincent as a child,
Saint Anne, Amiens

Three saints, Saint Anne, Amiens

death. The center portion portrays the moment after his passing. Artistic license has him clothed in his red prisoner's tunic and raised quite high off the ground. In fact, he was clothed merely in some ragged shorts and was tied only a few inches above the ground. A crowd is depicted, and perhaps includes the one Chinese Christian known to be present for his execution. A large luminous cross is shown in the sky above. The lower portion shows his trial, at the moment when the mandarin demands that he trample the crucifix placed on the ground in front of him. The text gives his answer: "But I will not renounce the faith of Jesus Christ." The guard at the far left carries a stout bamboo pole to beat him after his refusal. For this he was

stretched on the floor face down and beaten in the lower back and kidney area. The top section recalls the vision received by the Chinese scholar, Liu Jiu Ling, who had compassion on John Gabriel as he was being brought to another town for interrogation. In his vision, he saw the martyr holding two ladders, one white and the other red, leading up to heaven. Liu eventually became a Christian.

The third window depicts John Gabriel teaching. The center portion has him teaching his novices in Paris and showing them the blue Chinese robe of the martyr Francis Regis Clet and the cord used to strangle him. He is in a wood-paneled room, recalling the Salle Saint Augustin of the Vincentian motherhouse. The lower portion shows the young John Gabriel teaching catechism in front of his home, Le Puech, near Montgesty, whose church appears in the background. The text reads: "To go to heaven, you must make sacrifices." In the upper portion he is shown teaching catechism to the Chinese people seated before him. Across all three windows runs the text: "Blessed John Gabriel Perboyre, martyred in China, 11 September 1840, born at Le Puech, France, 6 January 1802."

By the side of the altar is a lengthy inscription recalling the life and works of Father Aubert, buried under the floor. He died in 1887 and, as the founder of the church, was given the honor of burial in a side chapel. He himself chose one that had not yet been dedicated in the hopes that one day it would be dedicated to Perboyre. His intuition was correct.

In the right transept is a series of five large paintings of Saint Vincent, the work of Charles-Alexandre Crauk (1819-1905), about 1882. They portray Francis de Sales and Jane Frances de Chantal; foundlings; Vincent glorified; Vincent singing to the Moslem woman in the fields during his supposed captivity; and Vincent as a child, accompanied by his dog, giving alms to a poor man. This latter canvas shows the old tower of the church in Pouy, now destroyed. Below these paintings are several fine wood carvings: Vincent giving the rules to the Daughters; his first mass; taking the chains of a galley convict; giving the rules to his confreres. The main altar has a traditional statue of Vincent with two children. Below is a carving of Vincent as

he was dying.

The Daughters of Charity arrived in Amiens in 1647 to work in the hospital of Saint Charles. Their services developed and they have had several houses in Amiens before and after the Revolution. They remained at the hospital until 1905. When they had to leave because of the anti-religious laws of the time, the people of Amiens presented them with an elaborate bust reliquary of Saint Vincent. This can be seen in the museum at the Vincentian motherhouse. The sisters have returned and continue their pastoral work.

## BEAUVAIS*

One of the great sights of France is Beauvais' cathedral of Saint Peter. Had it been completed, it would have been the tallest of all the Gothic cathedrals, and its tower would have surpassed that of Strasbourg. Various problems kept it from being completed, however, such as fire and wars, but the worst was that the engineers and architects lacked proper skills. The nave suffered a partial collapse in 1284, and only part of the transept remains. It is still astonishing for its daring size. Vincent saw it approximately in its present incomplete state.

Besides conducting various missions and other works in the diocese, Vincent himself began the practice of *ordination retreats* here. Bishop Augustin Potier of Beauvais (d. 1650) suggested a retreat for his ordinands "to instruct them in what they should know and the virtues they should practice in their calling," as Abelly summarizes it. Vincent and two secular priests held these retreats in late August and September of 1628 at the bishop's palace. Today this is the departmental museum, located next to the cathedral. More exactly, these retreats were held in the chapel of the residence, but this has now been demolished. All the subsequent seminary work of the Vincentians can be traced from this first undertaking. Bishop Potier continued to support and encourage Vincent and served with him as a member of the Council of Conscience during the regency of Anne of Austria. Vincent also came here on other occasions. He paid at least three official visits to the Ursuline nuns of Beauvais, for example. One of his letters (number 631) was written in *Bresles*, a small town a few kilometers east. In this, he mentions yet another visit to Beauvais, but it is unclear whether he was preaching missions, although it seems likely.

Vincentians gave missions in the diocese, and they served in its major *seminary* from 1679 to the Revolution. Its superior, the elderly Jean François Henri Grillet (1725-1802), administered the diocese as best he could during the absence of the bishop at the time of the Revolution.

Louise also came here and lodged with Madame de Villegoubelin, a Lady of Charity. It had been decided to have only one *Confraternity of Charity* for the city of Beauvais, but this led to several problems of organization, since several hundred women belonged. Vincent recalled this later in a conference to the Daughters of Charity: *I saw this myself at Beauvais where at first the people wished to adopt the former method and established one Confraternity for the whole city. It lasted for some time but was not a success, so a branch was established in every parish and this turned out to be much more successful.* (Conference 77) One of these Confraternities served the area around the cathedral. The credit for the success of these Confraternities was due in large measure to Louise's attention and care for them.

In his lifetime, the *Daughters of Charity* were also established in Beauvais, where they continue in service. The city today numbers some 55,000 people.

## FOLLEVILLE,*** GANNES*

Although the village of Folleville dates from the fifth century A.D., some traces of a large Roman camp, dating from the first Christian century, are visible to the south. The name Folleville probably comes from a Latin word for a leaf *(folium)*, referring to its rural setting. The town had been strategically placed on a hill to observe those passing by on the Roman road leading from Lyons to Senlis, Amiens, Boulogne and Britain beyond. This road was located in the valley of the Noye below. Barbarian tribes devastated the area from the third to the fifth centuries. In the seventh century, the king designated the area as a fief of the great abbey of Corbie, located not far away. In the ninth or tenth century, the lords of Folleville began to fortify the area against the Normans.

The most famous lord was *Raoul de Lannoy*, born of a Flemish family. He was chamberlain and counselor of three

Postcard, parish church
exterior, Folleville

kings: Louis XI, who decorated him with a golden chain for his warlike valor, then of Charles VIII and Louis XII. Louis XI spent the night in the castle amid great splendor in 1477, Charles VIII visited here in 1492, as did Francis I in 1546. Henri II arrived for the baptism of Henri, son of Louis de Lannoy, his godson. The eldest daughter of this same Louis de Lannoy, Marie, wed Antoine de Silly in 1572, and he thus became the lord of Folleville. His daughter Françoise Marguerite de Silly married Philippe Emmanuel de Gondi, general of the galleys, in 1610. She spent part of her childhood here, and eventually the property came into her possession. She exercised responsibility for the peasants on her lands, with the customary right of proposing priests to the bishop as pastors.

In 1615 and 1617 Vincent resided at Folleville as the tutor of the children of the Gondi family. Antoine Portail, his earliest follower, perhaps joined him, although he was ordained a priest only in 1622. One of the children, Jean François Paul, became the notorious and worldly Cardinal de Retz, known for his

part in a rebellion against Cardinal Mazarin. During a period totaling about eighteen months (divided into three periods: 1615, 1617, 1620), Vincent preached and gave missions in the surrounding parishes. The names of two of these are known, Sérévillers and Paillart, where he established Confraternities of Charity in 1620. Vincent also began to experience sickness here, the ailments of his legs which he suffered throughout his adult life. After 1655 the Community celebrated the events of the "first sermon of the Mission" on 25 January, and the saint's recollections (although he is not recorded as mentioning the name

Postcard, parish church
interior, Folleville

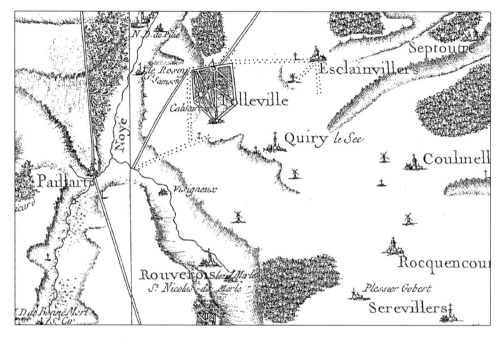

Eighteenth century map of Folleville, Paillart and Sérévillers

Folleville) are preserved in a repetition of prayer on 25 January of that year, as well as in a conference of 17 May 1658.

This sermon, delivered on a Wednesday probably in the course of a longer mission, remained in his mind as a founding moment of his life's work. He had previously been giving missions, and already had the practice of urging general confessions, as is known from his petition to the archbishop of Sens on the subject, dated 1616. He probably took up the recommendation of Francis de Sales, who in the *Introduction to the Devout Life* (1609) urged the practice. In addition, the experience of Madame de Gondi was crucial. She went to confession to the local pastor, a resident of

Folleville for at least the previous fifteen years. He, however, did not know the formula for absolution, and the thought that so many people might die without having made a good confession horrified her. She had Vincent obtain a copy of the formula from her spiritual director in Amiens and had the priest read it when she made her confession. Having outsiders like Vincent and others hear general confessions would right these wrongs.

At various times in Folleville's history, Vincentians came to visit. One group gave a mission in 1770 and, on concluding this mission, presented a reliquary and dedicated a side altar to Saint Vincent. During the nineteenth century,

Parish church interior, Folleville

Parish church interior, 1861, Folleville

many Vincentians and Daughters of Charity came on pilgrimage. Many of these people also contributed to the restoration of the church.

Bishop Jacques Boudinet of Amiens asked Father Étienne to send some Vincentians to take over the parish, which they did in late 1869. The bishop had other plans as well. A large piece of property was bought in 1874. Like the Berceau, to which it was compared, the bishop believed that Folleville too should have some Vincentian presence. His first plan was to receive orphaned boys. Daughters of Charity came for this purpose in 1875. Further, he negotiated the building of a train station at La Faloise, and it in turn began to attract pilgrims to Folleville. Meanwhile, because of the deaths of superior generals and bishops and, because of both anti-clerical laws in France and the first World War, the orphanage closed and the Daughters left in 1904. Another work then developed: a training school for Vincentian brothers, beginning in earnest in 1926. The Vincentians purchased the castle and worked to main-

Marble sarcophagus, Folleville

Jesus and Mary Magdalene, Funerary niche, Folleville

tain it. Other buildings were gradually restored and new ones added. This work was later closed and sold. A large statue of Saint Vincent is still to be seen over the main entrance of the school, located across the road from the castle. Today, the town consists of a few houses and numbers perhaps 70 people.

The present stone *church*, in Gothic style, replaces a church dating from about 1360. It is divided into two parts: the nave, built in the fifteenth century, for the use of the people, and the sanctuary, begun in 1510 and consecrated in 1524, for the family. The nave, built first, was dedicated to the apostle Saint James the Greater. His statue is in the niche behind and to the left of the pulpit. This church was one of the many on the

medieval pilgrimage route, the "Route of Paris," to Compostela, Spain. A modern sign by the door of the church as well as an old statue of Santiago above and to the left of the door recall this. Several elements make it clear that the family spent more funds on decorating their part of the church than the people did. The vaulting of the nave is of oak and has eight beautifully carved figures at the base of the ceiling. The vaulting of the sanctuary, however, is carved stone. The windows in the nave are plain, those in the sanctuary more elegant. The floor of the sanctuary is marble, while that of the nave is stone and brick. In both parts of the building there are traces of paint on the columns, and painted crosses recall the bishop's consecration of the church.

Virgin and child, floral rosary, Folleville

The sanctuary area, the "choir," was added to the church to serve as the mortuary chapel of the lords of Folleville. It is dedicated to Saint John the Baptist. In earlier years, it was separated from the nave by a wooden altar screen, a *jubé*, taken down at the Revolution. The items that follow describe the parts of the sanctuary, beginning on the left.

(1) The *family niche*, easily heated, used by the seigniorial family to attend mass. Old gate closings on its front are still visible. From it, they could look through the small opening directly onto the tomb of their ancestors.

(2) An elegant white marble *sar-*

*cophagus* of Raoul de Lannoy (d. 1513) and Jeanne de Poix (d. 1524). This is an excellent example of Renaissance work, carved in Genoa in 1507 by Antonio della Porta at the time when Raoul was governor of that city, and where he died. Among the elements to be noticed are the letters R and J intertwined, a Pietà, Saints Anthony, Sebastian and Adrian, and the representation of the beheading of John the Baptist (patron of Jeanne). Above is the coronation of the Virgin; she is depicted as surrounded with a floral rosary. This rosary, in medieval fashion, is made of wild roses, with five petals each, the only kind of rose in France before hybridizing. Below are four children weeping, holding the epitaph and the coats-of-arms of the families. Representations of skulls are numerous. The tombs were emptied during the seventeenth-century wars of religion. Raoul and Jeanne were the great-great-grandparents

Lannoy family sarcophagus, Folleville

Stained glass window, Folleville

of Marguerite de Silly, Madame de Gondi.

(3) The *tomb* of François de Lannoy (d. 1548), son of Raoul, and Marie de Hangest, pictured kneeling, carved from local stone. Above the figures on the wall behind are carved heads. Below on the lowest register are the four cardinal virtues. This tomb is sur-rounded with a fine marble frame in Renaissance style. Both tombs have the figures facing the niche that used to hold the sepulcher of Jesus. This couple were the great-grandparents of Madame de Gondi.

(4) Above the *funerary niche* and under the central window are angels bearing the instruments of

the Passion. In the center is the risen Christ appearing as a gardener to Saint Mary Magdalene. He holds a shovel, symbolic of his nourishment of the tree of life. This shovel is typical of the time and the region: although stone, it depicts a handle and blade of oak, with a small crescent of wrought iron on its lower edge. The carved sepulcher of Jesus that used to repose here was removed in 1634 to the parish church of Joigny, the main seat of the Gondi family, when Pierre, Marguerite's son, sold the Folleville castle. It follows the same style as the marble sarcophagus mentioned above.

(5) The *main window*, the crucifixion, dates from the sixteenth century. On the right hand is a mounted soldier—a portrait of François de Lannoy, shown wearing his golden chain of office. In its upper registers angels appear with the instruments of the Passion. The *ceiling vaults* are richly decorated, recalling the sculptures of the tomb of Lannoy and Poix. The artist responsible for the window also did those in the neighboring village of Paillart.

(6) The *niche* used for the wine and water for mass is a sixteenth-century work, adorned with the initials of Raoul de Lannoy and his wife.

(7) Next to the niche and high in the wall is a small *iron door*, the remainder of a sixteenth-century

Vincent de Paul and confreres, Folleville

tabernacle for holy oils. The interior was finished in wood and still has traces of cloth glued to it.

(8) The present *sacristy* has some of the oldest paving stones in the church.

(9) A side chapel, containing a *shrine of Saint Vincent de Paul*, in imitation Gothic, bears the date 1899, with another representation of angels with the instruments of the Passion on the upper wall of the sanctuary. Inside the chapel are figures of saints representing the four cardinal virtues. To one side is an old door leading to a tower; it also gave access to the jubé. This area was formerly the sacristy, and the remains of an outer door, now blocked up, can be seen in the left-hand wall. It gave the family access to their part of the church.

(10) Above is a *modern window*,

dated 1869, the design of Charles Bazin. Its upper section features several words written on scrolls: Meekness, Simplicity, Humility, Zeal, Mortification, Religion; and then two titles of Saint Vincent in Latin: *Cleri Parens, Pater Pauperum* (Parent of the Clergy, Father of the Poor). There are four figured sections: (a) Vincent hearing the confession of the dying peasant at Gannes; with the text in French: "25 January, day of the Conversion of Saint Paul;" (b) the conversion of Saint Paul, the feast day with the first sermon of the Mission; the text reads: "The conversion of a notable inhabitant of Gannes;" (c) Vincent preaching at Folleville; with the text: "Saint Vincent de Paul preaches the sermon of his first mission at Folleville," which also pictures the *jubé*; and (d) Vincent teaching the three Gondi children, with the text: "Tutor of the three sons of Monsieur Philip Emmanuel de Gondi, lord of the area." It should be noted, however, that this responsibility lasted only until Vincent's return from Châtillon and, that, furthermore, only Pierre, the oldest son, born in 1606, was of an age to profit from the saint's teaching. The others, Henri (b. 1612) and Jean François Paul (b. 1613), were probably too young for him and would have been in the care of others.

Below these pictures are the emblem and motto of the Congregation

Wooden statue, 18th century, Folleville

of the Mission (text: "On 25 January 1617, Saint Vincent de Paul projects the establishment of the priests of the Mission"); Cardinal de Retz archbishop of Paris (text: "The Cardinal archbishop of Paris approves the Congregation of the Mission"); the Daughters of Charity (text: "In 1633 the institution of the Daughters of Charity took place"); and Urban VIII (text: "On 15 March 1655, Pope Urban VIII approves the institution of the Priests of the Mission"). (The windows are not in the right order to correspond with the texts below them, since they were taken down and repaired and put back incorrectly—[a] and [b] being inverted.)

(11) Across the sanctuary, on the wall, is a ***tablet*** commemorating

Gondi pulpit and pews, Folleville

Postcard, Gondi pulpit, Folleville

donors from the Congregation of the Mission and others to this Vincentian shrine, together with a statue of John Gabriel Perboyre, who visited here while he was teaching at Montdidier before his ordination.

(12) The *high altar* dates only from 1874. On it, however, is displayed a small wooden statue of Vincent, dating from the eighteenth century. The style and gestures of this piece are unusual, and its provenance is unknown.

In the nave are the following elements, from left to right beginning at the door of the church.

(13) The *confessional*, apparently dating from the early seventeenth century, in earlier days faced the pulpit. Vincent may have gestured toward it during his mission sermon of 1617. It more probably dates, however, from his second mission in 1620.

(14) The marble *baptismal font*, carved in 1547 for the baptism of Louis de Lannoy. It is mounted on a pedestal of local stone. On the exterior of the basin are four coats-of-arms and the Lannoy chain of office.

(15) The *paintings* on the walls are copies of those prepared for Vincent's canonization. They hung

213

previously in the Vincentian house at Montdidier until their transfer here in 1913.

(16) An old *crucifix* was removed from the *jubé* and placed on the wall facing the pulpit. It was painted (again?) in the seventeenth century. Two statutes accompanying it were stolen in 1970.

(17) The stone *statue* of Saint James the Greater replaced, in the sixteenth century, the original one brought from Spain by one of the lords, Jean de Folleville, who had made a pilgrimage there. The present statue has often been repainted but keeps its original colors. It sits in a niche, the remains of an old staircase that led to the *jubé*. With the decline of the use of this altar screen, it began to fall into disrepair, and all that remains of it are some pieces of vaulting visible on the walls. It was replaced by the next item.

(18) The oak *pulpit* was carved in Montdidier. Recent research has shown that this in all likelihood is not the pulpit where Vincent preached what he later recalled as the first sermon of the Mission, since it appears to date from 1620. Philippe Emmanuel de Gondi and his wife gave this pulpit to the church after their chaplain returned from his brief pastorate in Châtillon, perhaps as a way of locally implementing the decrees of the Council of Trent. This old pulpit, with a seat inside, was restored in 1868. It stands on a small carved leg in the Louis XIII style. Six panels, sculpted with various designs, constitute the body of the pulpit. The back board was replaced in the eighteenth century, and a carved inscription dates from 1868: "On January 25, Feast of the Conversion of Saint Paul, 1617, Saint Vincent de Paul preached his first sermon of the Mission in this pulpit. It was repaired with the help of the Congregation of the Mission in 1868." An iron grille was added at that time to protect the pulpit from the pious pilgrims who had, over the centuries, removed parts of it for their own devotion. At the foot of the pulpit are two carved stone portraits. The head facing right is that of Raoul de Lannoy.

(19) The *pews* probably date from 1620, ordered at the same time as the pulpit. Before Vincent's time, men and women were separated in the body of the church, each group with its own altar. The men remained on the right, and their altar was dedicated to James. This altar also served as the main altar for the parishioners. The women were on the left, and their altar had Mary as patron. A niche (*piscine*) in the wall by the pulpit, used for holding wine and water, gives an idea where one altar was placed. These two altars blocked the view of the high altar, but it should be remembered that the church building was divided into two sections:

Aerial view, Castle, Folleville

the more elaborate (closed off with a gate in the *jubé*) belonged to the lords, who had their own chaplain, and the older and more common part belonged to the people, who had their own pastor—doubtless a cause of confusion.

(20) The *graffito* scratched into the wall to the right of the pulpit. This is barely legible but recalls the gift of an ex-voto, placed here by a parishioner after a pilgrimage to Compostela.

(21) The stone *statue* of Saint Sebastian over the back door, now unused, is very old.

(22) The *carved figures* at the lower end of the ceiling vault, mentioned above, are difficult to identify. One is clearly Santiago, known from the scallop shell on his cap. Others are grimacing, bearded, nude, etc., but their meaning is not known.

Outside the church, the differing rooflines demonstrate the various ages of the buildings. Also the statue of Mary,

fourteenth century, probably comes from the previous church building. She holds the child Jesus on her right arm, but his figure has been partially removed. The small round section held the staircase leading to the altar screen. Below the statue of Santiago by the main entrance is an old sundial, useful in times when clocks were rare.

The De Lannoy family may take its name from the river, La Noye, which runs in the region. In any case, one branch of the family is named Delano, associated with Franklin Delano Roosevelt (d. 1945), president of the United States. His widow Eleanor came to visit this ancestral area in 1952.

By the front door of the church

Folleville Castle

Votive chapel, Folleville

stand the remains of an old gate, leading into the castle. Directly on the left is a modern building replacing an ancient pilgrim hospice. Originally a wooden structure situated on a mound, a stone *castle* gradually took shape. The major work dates from the eleventh or twelfth century. Jean de Folleville, at one time ambassador to Spain, restored the castle in the late fourteenth century. At its greatest extent, twice the present size, the castle was surrounded by a dry moat, with access guaranteed by a drawbridge. It was well decorated inside, plastered and hung with tapestries, a luxurious setting, although this is difficult to perceive today. The inner section of the castle, the *donjon* (the "keep"), is most of what is visible today and dates from the thirteenth and fourteenth centuries. At

various times it held prisoners, and some of the graffiti they left became visible during archaeological excavations carried out in the 1930s. Large fireplaces are still in evidence, proof of the need to warm the main rooms in the winter. The family had rooms on the upper floors around a central hall. The large circular tower room on the right was that traditionally used by the priest, and therefore by Vincent. The large tower on the left enclosed the kitchen, and below it are storage rooms, restored in 1996. The castle did not fall into ruins but was intentionally demolished by the count of Mailly, one of its owners, to acquire materials for the Château of Mailly-Raineval, a process that began in 1777. The Vincentians, who purchased the castle in the early twentieth century, sold it in 1965. Since 1988, a local association has worked to preserve and improve it.

To one side in the garden is the *Pavillon*, a former residence for the caretakers of the castle, dating from before the time of the Gondis. Recent archaeological work has shown that some ceiling beams from the castle were reused in this house. Some are decorated and bear the

Parish church exterior, Gannes

painted initials AM, probably for Antoine de Silly and his wife Marie de Lannoy, the parents of Madame de Gondi. The building now houses a small museum.

To the southwest of the town can be seen, when weather permits, the outlines of the *Roman camp*. This large camp had much to do with the eventual development of the hillside town now called Folleville. Along an old Roman road *(the chemin de la Chapelle)* lying below the town is a tiny *votive chapel*, originally dedicated to Saint Vincent de Paul. It is dated, in its present condition, to 1880.

One of the villages belonging to Madame de Gondi was *Gannes*, a few kilometers south of Folleville and which today, with 300 inhabitants, is larger than Folleville. Abelly tells us that it was there that she learned of an elderly man wishing to go to confession. Vincent heard his confession. The dying man was so grateful that he announced widely that he would have been condemned to eternal punishment had it not been for this general confession. Vincent took the occasion on the following feast of the Conversion of Saint Paul, 25 January 1617, probably during a mission, to preach to the parishioners of Folleville on the subject. This led, at least in the founder's mind, to the founding of the Congregation of the Mission. Vincent had, however, promoted and heard general confessions during the missions that he gave before this time. His most important achievement, therefore, was ultimately to move the Gondis to endow a congregation to continue this work,

Engraving, parish church, Gannes

something they did in 1625.

Local tradition makes the dying man the miller, and the ruins of the old mill can still be seen. There was also a chateau here, but few traces remain of it.

The church in Gannes, set on a small hill, is a Gothic building, with well-carved hanging keystones in the arches of the sanctuary. The building has been much restored and added to. On the outside is a sundial dated 1660. Inside the church are the following:

(1) *Statue of Saint Vincent de Paul* and a plaque installed in the 1940s by the pastor of Folleville to com-

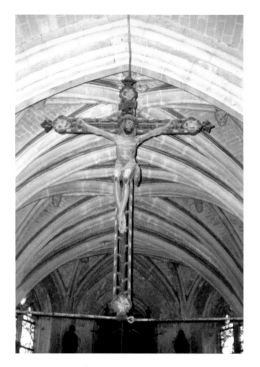

Jubé crucifix, parish church, Gannes

memorate Vincent's ministry in Gannes. The date of December 1616 appears, but it could as easily have been January 1617. Another statue of him is in the sanctuary.

(2) The *heart of François de Lannoy*, lord of Gannes. He was the great-grandfather of Madame de Gondi, and his heart was entrusted to this church, while his body was buried at the Folleville church. A long inscription on a marble plaque near the statue of Saint Vincent commemorates the event. It names, among other things, his lands, including Folleville, Paillart and Sérévillers.

(3) The *jubé* was a grille surmounted with a crucifix. The grille has been removed, but traces of it can be seen on the choir stalls in the sanctuary. The old crucifix remains, probably dating from the seventeenth century.

(4) The *pews*, from the seventeenth century, accommodate about 200.

(5) The *baptismal font*, in carved local stone, which might well be seventeenth century.

A short distance east from the church is the little chapel of *Our Lady of Bon Secours* (traditionally translated as Prompt Succor). This wayside shrine dates from the Middle Ages. In 1689, the chapel was repaired to commemorate an event in the village. Two men bringing their goods from Beauvais had threatened a young village girl with abuse. She was able to escape through the help of the Blessed Virgin, who caused villagers to come to her aid. The criminals left their horses and cart behind; these were sold and provided the funds for the shrine. A pilgrimage grew up which continues to this day. Inside the chapel are old statutes of Mary, and Saints Joachim and Anne, along with various offerings to the shrine. On the front of the chapel are the Latin inscriptions: *Regina Angelorum* and *Salus Infirmorum*, "Queen of Angels" and "Health of the Sick." This old chapel has no real connection with Vincent, although he probably passed by it and prayed here on his travels.

## HEILLY

During the years of Vincent's stay with the Gondis at Folleville, a cousin of Monsieur de Gondi, Marie, lived at the *chateau* of Heilly with her husband, Louis de Pisseleu. Heilly is a few kilometers northeast of Amiens. An old tradition has it that Vincent came here with the Gondi boys in his charge to visit their cousin Marie. During these visits, he probably strolled their property and prayed at the chapel of an old priory located here, Saint Laurent des Bois.

One day he heard the sound of clashing swords coming from a clearing and discovered two noble guests of the chateau fighting a duel. Managing to calm the duelers Vincent effected a reconciliation. Marie de Gondi had a cross erected there in 1617 to recall the event.

Some time later, again according to documents whose present whereabouts are unknown, Vincent blessed the chapel of the cemetery at the chateau. This took place in 1625 and might have happened in connection with a mission that he preached in the area. This little chapel has disappeared, as has most of the chateau. Some remains of the chapel were to be seen up until the end of the nineteenth century. In 1897, following a mission that Vincentians preached in the town, the local inhabitants undertook the erection of a new monument, the *Calvaire de Saint Vincent*, near where the previous one had stood. Vincent's presence here was celebrated in the course of the tercentenary of his death in 1960.

The monument consists of a large crucifix rising out of a grotto. Inside the

Postcard, Vincent Calvary, Heilly

grotto is a Pietà. Flanking the grotto are two statues: Saint Anne with the Virgin Mary, and Saint Vincent de Paul. This is located beside the parish church. *(Rue de Grande Carrière)* No signs in the town mention it, however, nor is there anything to explain the meaning of this unusual grouping of rocks and stairs, grotto and crucifix, and two somewhat dilapidated statues. The town itself has fewer than 500 people.

A purely local tradition connects Vincent with **Albert**, a larger town a few kilometers east. Daughters of Charity came here to staff a hospital and school beginning in 1697 and lasting until the Revolution. Like most of the town, it was destroyed or replaced after two world wars. *(Rue Tien-Tsin)* The site of the shrine of Sainte Marie de Brebières, its parish church, dedicated in 1896, preserves the memory of yet another miraculous statue discovered by a shepherd. A side altar in Vincent's honor recalls his presence here. The bust of him over the altar follows a possible, but disputed, portrait of him said to be the work of Philippe de Champaigne.

Vincent Calvary, Heilly

A few kilometers south of Albert is **Bray-sur-Somme**. The Daughters of Charity came here to staff a hospital in 1700, located probably on the site of the Maison de Retraite near the parish church. One of the women who entered the Company from Bray was *Marie Antoinette Deleau*, the last superioress general before the Revolution. When she had to leave Paris after dispersing the Sisters, she returned here. When the hospital was reopened on the last day of 1795, she was able to encourage the Sisters to resume their work in the hospital, but in lay clothes. *Jeanne Antide Thouret* had also served in the hospital for several months from 1791 to 1793, when she too left for her home. A large portrait of her adorns the parish church.

## LIANCOURT

Although Vincent came here at least once, Louise came here often. Her purpose was to visit and help the Confraternity of Charity, established here in 1635, and the Daughters of Charity. The duchess of Liancourt, Jeanne de Schomberg (1600-1674),

endowed the Charity, a seminary, and other good works. Their family chateau has been demolished. Today, the town has a population of about 6500.

One intriguing document mentions Vincent's presence on 10 or 11 June 1635, when Vincent was asked to help resolve a legal matter, probably as an external mediator. Two men, perhaps brothers, shared parts of the same building. One wanted to block up a window that allowed the other man look into his brother's private family courtyard. The case was resolved, and a formal document was signed and duly witnessed before the local notary. Many such documents must have existed at one time. Vincent, as the prior of Saint Lazare, had responsibility for the execution of justice

Vincent bust, parish
church, Albert

on his property, and perhaps he was invited to take part in this case for that reason.

Daughters of Charity arrived in 1636. Their years here were difficult, in particular because of some calumny spread about the sisters. Coste reports that their confessor accepted the evil said about them and told them to find another: "You come here and accuse yourself of little faults and conceal enormous sins; look for some other confessor, for I have no absolution to give you or your two companions." (*Life*, I, 416-17) Their mission here terminated after 1652.

The rules for the Liancourt *Charity* are in existence but have apparently not been published. The parish church, dedicated to Saint Martin, does not, however, have the traditional painting of the "Lord of Charity," sent to some, if not all the Charities in Vincent's lifetime.

Eventually, the duchess and her husband took the side of the Jansenist party, probably out of their religious devotion. This turned them away from Vincent. He undoubtedly had them in mind when he spoke to his confreres of two persons, who had once lived holy and self-sacrificing lives, but who had allowed themselves to be carried away by Jansenist opinions. It reminded him simply of hell: that is, they had rejected the supernatural order of things (submission to the pope) to cling to the human order (trusting their own thinking). (Conference of 27 April 1657)

Also, Vincent mentioned that Louise should "take the waters" here at Liancourt. (Letter 616) However, since Liancourt is not known for its thermal springs, this strange expression probably refers to her traveling upstream by a water taxi on the waters of the Oise, a common mode of transport.

## MONTDIDIER

The town of Montdidier, some 100 kilometers north of Paris, with a current population of about 6000, lies in the department of the Somme. The Congregation of the Mission presided over the direction of the Ecole Saint Vincent, a *collège* or boarding high school, from the year 1818 until 1903. In that year, the French government dismissed all religious communities from their teaching positions. During those 85 years, the Congregation worked with devotion at the task of educating young men.

The town takes its name from Didier, king of the Lombards, imprisoned here by the Normans. For centuries, the Benedictine priory of Saint Pierre, founded from Cluny, assured education for boys. This ceased at the Revolution. The new foundation dates from 1804, when the buildings again received students. In 1806, the Fathers of the Faith (*Pères de la Foi*) took the school over, but they remained only until 1814. In 1818, at the initiative of Pierre De Wailly, at the time Vincentian superior of the major seminary at Amiens, the Congregation reopened the school. (De Wailly was the first superior general after the Revolution but remained in office only 22 months, from January 1827 until his death in October 1828.) Over the years, the Vincentians undertook large construction projects to accommodate

Tax office, Montdidier

the needs of a school: classrooms, dormitories, dining room and kitchen, chapel, etc.

Of greater interest is the presence of *John Gabriel Perboyre* in this school. He was sent here in the autumn of 1824 as a subdeacon and after having completed his theological studies in Paris. He lived in a little room over the chapel. While here, he had charge of the younger students. To nourish their piety, he directed a little sodality, the Congregation of the Holy Angels. Working through it, he was able to care for his students' spiritual development. In his second year, he was assigned to teach a course in philosophy for the oldest class, a task he performed well. He found himself quite busy, from 4:00 in the morning to 9:00 or 10:00 at night. At the conclusion of this second year, John Gabriel returned to Paris to prepare for his ordination. Bishop Louis William Dubourg, who had earlier invited the first Vincentians to the United States, ordained him a priest. In his last years, this Sulpician bishop had returned to France. Dubourg ordained John Gabriel in the chapel of the motherhouse of the

Daughters of Charity, on 23 September 1826. Besides Saint John Gabriel Perboyre, the college also numbered among its alumni many other important personages, including bishops and generals.

The town suffered greatly during the first World War and was left nearly in ruins in 1918. Consequently, nothing remains today of the old school buildings, except the pre-existing ramparts and gardens used by the Benedictines. The tax office, dating from the twelfth century, faces the school, now renamed the Ecole du Prieuré.

The *parish church* of Saint Peter, named after the monastery, was rebuilt after the first World War but faithfully copies the fourteenth-century church. Inside is a side altar in honor of Saint Vincent. The modern statue of him, carved in 1952, matches others in the church. In the same side chapel is a plaque recalling the history of the college. At the bottom are two brass plaques inset into marble, with the heads of Saint Vincent and John Gabriel Perboyre. Each also has a small embedded relic.

Other noteworthy items are the tomb of Raoul of Crepy (d. 1074), the polychrome stone Entombment of Christ (about 1550), a fine Romanesque figure of Christ in the sanctuary, and the ancient baptismal font (eleventh century).

The Daughters of Charity also had works in Montdidier. A school for the poor opened in 1777, and resumed in 1818, the year the Vincentians arrived. The Sisters also ran the town hospital, beginning in 1824, probably lasting until about 1905.

Because of the success of the school here, the authorities in nearby **Roye** invited the Vincentians to take charge of a boys school. They began in 1826 on the promise of funds from the town to help with the expenses. When these did not arrive, the priests left, 1 September 1834. A notable event was that the body of Saint Vincent was moved in great secrecy to Roye from Paris during the 1830 revolution. The Vincentian community purchased a small house next to the school, built an oven, inserted the relics and then walled up the supposed oven. Here the relics remained until about April 1834, when conditions allowed their return to the Paris motherhouse chapel.

Local tradition associates Vincent himself with the pastor of Roye, Pierre Guérin. He had begun a small community of sisters, the Daughters of the Cross, to teach in his parish school. Vincent took a hand in the examination of their founder, accused of spreading false doctrine. He acquitted Guérin, remained his friend and confidant and aided the sisters.

## MOUY

According to his biographer Pierre Collet, Vincent came here in 1647, in his mid-sixties, to give a *mission* and found a Confraternity of Charity. The church of Saint Léger, in this town of the diocese of Beauvais, dates to the thirteenth century. It suffered much during the wars of religion as well as during the Revolution. The lord of Mouy, Louis de Vaudrey, became one of the Calvinist

Parish church, Mouy

leaders but was assassinated in 1569. The sanctuary of the church was given to Protestants during that period, while the body of the church served as a stable. Catholics had to build a small chapel elsewhere. In Collet's time, about a century after its foundation, the Confraternity was still flourishing. During the Revolution, the parish church was used for political meetings and also for some small manufacturing. Perhaps because of these difficult events, there is no memorial of Vincent's passage here. The town today numbers some 5000 inhabitants.

## NOYON*

Noyon, an Ancient Roman city of strategic importance, has alternated between glory and suffering over the centuries. On 9 October 768 Charlemagne was crowned in the Noyon cathedral as king of Neustria, the western part of the Frankish dominions. Hugh Capet, the first king of France, was also crowned here. John Calvin, the reformer, was born here in 1509 and, although not a priest, held a canonry here until 1534.

Cathedral library, Noyon

During the Revolution, the great cathedral saw its sanctuary turned into a dance hall and the nave into grain stores. The porch suffered as well. Vandals systematically removed every trace of the ancient carvings over the doors and the small statues that surrounded them. The exterior of the cathedral clearly shows the impact of the bombing during the first World War that virtually destroyed the building.

Vincentians first came here to help the clergy. The priests of the diocese had founded a clergy conference in 1637 on the model of the Tuesday Conferences in Paris. In 1643, some priests came from Saint Lazare to preach retreats. Vincentians returned in 1650, however, because of tragedy. Vincent sent his confreres throughout the regions of Picardy and Champagne to provide relief to the war-ravaged area. Beginning in 1655, the bishop of Noyon began to ask Vincent to send his confreres to staff the diocesan seminary. The founder deferred his response, and in the meantime the bishop died. His successor, after Vincent's death, received a positive response from René Alméras, the second superior general. The work of the seminary began in 1662, therefore, and continued until 1791.

The *seminary* was located on a piece of ground behind the cathedral, bounded by Rues Saint Pierre, Saint Jean and Charles de Gaulle. The parish church of Saint Pierre was on the same lot. At the time of the Revolution, the

Vincentians took in refractory priests, allowing them to live at the seminary and celebrate mass in the chapel. After the expulsion of the Vincentians, the buildings became a prison. The buildings were later sold and demolished. Nothing remains of what was regarded as a beautiful brick building, except for a few pieces of the wall and some foundations in brick and stone of a large building incorporated into another construction. The last superior was Simon Bruno Fontaine. When he had to leave, he fled the country for Italy and fled again when Napoleon arrived. Fontaine then moved to Ljubljana in modern Slovenia, where in 1805 he died of disease after his hospital ministry, a martyr of charity. Only one Vincentian at Noyon took the oath of Liberty and Equality. The other priests and brothers were deported or otherwise dispersed.

A pioneer Vincentian from the diocese of Noyon was *Adrien Gambart* (1600-1668). He was received at Saint Lazare in 1634, probably before his ordination. He left at some point but continued to enjoy good relations with Vincent, whom he admired greatly. Coste, mistakenly, identified Gambart as one of the first companions of Vincent and Antoine Portail, whom they paid a salary to for going with them on the missions. Gambart wrote a series of mission sermons regarded as typical of the simple style that Vincent espoused. These were published beginning in 1668. Vincent entrusted him with various responsibilities, such as being confessor of the Visitation nuns in Paris.

The Daughters of Charity also served in Noyon at the *Hôtel Dieu*, the local hospital. This institution, founded in 1178, remained in use until 1918. Its 740 years of service must be a record of some sort. The hospital has been taken down, but part of the cloister walk was restored in 1984-1987. (*Rue de l'Hôtel Dieu*) The sisters remained until the Revolution. Their house was located near the seminary. (*6, rue Saint Pierre*) Next door was the residence of Jean Louis Guyard de Saint Clair. This priest, a canon of the cathedral, was in Paris during the Revolution. He was among the number of those massacred on 2 September 1792 at the abbey of Saint Germain des Prés. Along with the Vincentian martyrs of Saint Firmin, and many others, he was beatified in 1926. A plaque outside his residence recalls his memory. Modern Noyon is a city of some 15,000 inhabitants.

South of Noyon is **Attichy**, today a town of about 1700 people. Its importance is twofold. First, it was the family seat of Louise's wealthy in-laws. The names of several of them figure in her correspondence, as they do in letters to and from Vincent. Louise's husband, with her approval, took charge of the minor children of two of their Attichy relatives, a charity which cost them considerable time and money, and which was not reciprocated. Second, the Daughters of Charity had a small community here beginning in 1656, where they served the sick poor and cared for the children, and probably remained until the Revolution. Louise may have visited Attichy and prayed in the local parish church, but there is no record of this, nor anything in the church to commemorate the presence of the Sisters.

East of Noyon is **La Fère**, with 3000 inhabitants. Here the Daughters of Charity served in the hospital beginning in 1656. One of its outstanding superiors was *Mathurine Guérin* (1631-1704). Four times superioress general, she had served in several houses of the Company, was Louise's secretary, the directress of the seminary (or novice directress), and treasurer. Her term at La Fère, however, lasted only a few months in 1659 and 1660. This town, with its major military facilities, was nearly obliterated during the first World War. It has been largely rebuilt.

## PAILLART,* SÉRÉVILLERS

These two towns in Picardy, located on the estates of Madame de Gondi, are mentioned together, since Vincent founded early Confraternities of Charity here. The Confraternity was founded simultaneously for Folleville, Paillart and Sérévilliers at the Paillart church. The first one was for women (11 October 1620) and, some two weeks later (23 October) another one for men. These foundations, it should be noted, took place before the foundation of the Congregation of the Mission (1625).

In **Paillart**, the Gothic parish church still stands. Its pews are old, probably contemporary with Vincent. The remains of its altar screen, the *jubé*, are visible, and now a wrought-iron screen marks its place. In 1867, Bazin, the same restorer who worked in Folleville, restored the late-medieval windows, dating from 1544. The windows in the two churches are consequently similar in artistic treatment. Despite Vincent's presence here, there is nothing in the church to commemorate him. Paillart has about 600 inhabitants. In **Sérévillers**, nothing commemorates Vincent's ministry. The village numbers less than 100 people.

Old documents concerning Madame de Gondi mention the town of Saint Martin as her estate. Vincent probably would have visited there on his mission rounds. This parish, no longer existing, is today a part of Conty, a town of some 1500 persons.

## SENLIS

Senlis, a city of some 15,000 people, received the Christian faith, it is said, as far back as the third century. Walls from that period are still visible. Its Gothic cathedral and quiet old streets give it a special character.

Vincent came to Senlis in 1636 to see Louis XIII, present with his troops. The king received him and asked for *chaplains*, whom Vincent had offered. The place of their meeting cannot be easily determined, since the king was

Parish church, Paillart

encamped. The occasion was an invasion of Spanish troops at the beginning of the French period of the Thirty Years War. Vincent sent some fifteen priests and brothers and wrote a short rule of conduct for them. He looked on the work of the chaplains as a sort of mission and had them conduct several others both at Saint Lazare and in the surrounding areas.

In 1641, an attempt was made at a foundation of the Congregation of the Mission in Senlis, but it did not take place. Daughters of Charity worked in a parish from 1682 and served in the hospital from 1696 to the Revolution. One of them was able to remain to care for the sick during that period, but only in lay clothes.

They had another foundation, beginning in 1641, at **Nanteuil-le-Haudoin**. The sisters here served in the hospital and kept a small school. They came at the invitation of Marie de Hautfort, duchess of Schomberg (1616-1691), sister-in-law of Madame de Liancourt, both Ladies of Charity. These great ladies, however, could provide them lodging only in the hospice alongside the beggars. The Rue de l'Hôtel-Dieu still exists, but its buildings are long gone.

## SOISSONS

The city of Soissons, today with some 30,000 inhabitants, took its name from the Suessiones, a tribe of the Gauls. It later became a capital of the Frankish kingdom. Its splendid Gothic cathedral testifies to its continuing importance.

According to his biographer Collet, in 1621 Vincent made an important retreat here, perhaps in one of the abbeys in the city. Although nothing is known of either the exact date or the place, the retreat at Soissons helped him to master his temper. *I addressed myself to God to beg him earnestly to change this curt and forbidding disposition of mine for a meek and benign one. By the grace of our Lord and with some effort on my part to repress the outbursts of passion, I was able to get rid of my black disposition.* (Abelly 3, 163) In a letter written some years later, Vincent mentioned another benefit of this retreat. He had found himself too eager and too pleased with the idea of starting the Mission. During the retreat, he became more balanced in his approach. Consequently, his resolve to found a congregation, conceived at Montmirail, became more focused. His time in Soissons marked a starting point for his later works. (Letter 580)

Vincent sent his missionaries to help in the region of Soissons when it had been devastated by war. The Congregation of the Mission then had a house here from 1772 to 1791. This was the major and minor *seminary of Saint Léger*, founded in the old abbey of the same name. The work was begun again after the Revolution, and the Vincentians cared for it from 1859 to 1886, when it finally closed. The municipal museum occupies the buildings today.

Daughters of Charity had many houses in the diocese, both before and after the Revolution and continue their service here.

## VERNEUIL-EN-HALATTE

Vincent preached a mission here, as is known from Letter 16, dated Verneuil, 8 October 1627. This town forms part of a series of small places in the Oise valley, visited by Vincent, such as Loisy-en-Brie (Marne), as we learn from Letter 12, dated 30 October 1626. After the foundation of various Charities during the course of his early missions, he sent Louise in 1633 to Verneuil to visit the Confraternity. Nothing in this town of 3500 persons points to their presence here. However, a cooking pot sent here by Louise for the service of the poor is now kept in the Hospice de Condé in nearby Chantilly, where the Daughters had a house.

Vincent also wanted Louise to go to "Pont," now **Pont-Sainte-Maxence**, likewise to visit the Charities. Her interesting notes on these visits refer to the conditions she encountered at Verneuil, Pont, Gournay (now **Gournay-sur-Aronde**), Neufville (now **Laneuvilleroy**), and **Bulles** in February 1633. She may have paid a later visit to these Charities in May 1636.

## VILLERS-SOUS-SAINT-LEU

Vincent de Paul came to Villers-sous-Saint-Leu some time before 1640. He came here in the company of Jean André Lumague, the father of Marie de Lumague, Mademoiselle Pollalion (1599-1657). Lumague, the lord of Villers, was a friend of Vincent's. His daughter Marie, born in Paris, became a widow early in her life. She took Vincent as her spiritual director and worked closely with Louise to visit the Charities and other works. With Vincent's encouragement she also founded a community of sisters, the Daughters of Providence. These sisters cared for wayward girls and provided a refuge for women whose virtue was threatened. After her death, Vincent took care of the affairs of her congregation.

Vincent came here to give a mission around the same time. The thirteenth-century church where he preached still stands, but there is no souvenir of his ministry here. The Lumague chateau is in ruins. Louise stayed here with Mademoiselle Pollalion on occasion. She had invited Louise to come to stay with her for a rest.

Parish church, Villers-sous-Saint-Leu

Brother Claude Gesseaume (b. 1615) was a native of this place. His sister, Henriette, became a Daughter of Charity, as well as two of her nieces. A nephew, Nicolas Chefdeville, followed Claude as a brother in the Congregation of the Mission. Villers today has about 500 inhabitants.

Not far from here is **Chantilly**, today a modern city of more than 11,000, known for its castle and modern racetrack. The Daughters of Charity came to Chantilly in 1647 to begin an establishment for the sick, and to care for the needy children of the area. In so doing, they were responding to the initiative of Charlotte de Montmorency, princess of Condé. Unfortunately for the two Sisters, funds for their support were often late in coming. In 1653, they had even sold their furniture to pay debts and, in the next year, it was decided to withdraw them altogether. Nevertheless, conditions improved, and the Sisters remained until the Revolution.

# 4

# West, Center

Miniature of Vincent de Paul, probably painted during his lifetime. Paris, Motherhouse.

# Auvergne

*Vincentian connections with the Auvergne region begin in Vincent's time and involve "taking the waters" at Bourbon. Later, the seminary of Saint-Flour saw the early ministry of John Gabriel Perboyre and inspired many vocations to the Vincentian congregation.*

Bourbon Castle, Bourbon-L'Archambault

## MOULINS, BOURBON-L'ARCHAMBAULT

Moulins, the traditional capital of Bourbonnais, takes its name from its mills *(moulins)*, property of the dukes of Bourbon. Later, the dukes made the town their residence. Moulins owes its growth to the castle (1340), now partly demolished, and to the collegiate church (1368). This church, still existing in part, has been incorporated into the nineteenth-century cathedral. In 1616, Jane Frances de Chantal came here to found a Visitation convent. She also died here during another visit, on 13 December 1641. This convent has become a girls school and retains its old chapel. Moulins today is a town of some 24,000 people.

Besides service by the Daughters of Charity here since 1684, the Vincentian connection with Moulins comes from René Alméras, Vincent's successor as superior general. Alméras came to Moulins after spending some time taking the waters at **Bourbon-l'Archambault**, a few kilometers west. (Letters 2255, et al.) After a relapse, he was in danger of death at Bourbon, and Vincent wanted him to go to Moulins, since he believed that the *weather is better*. Alméras enjoyed the hospitality of the Oratorian house in Bourbon. There are no "waters" at Moulins, however, although Vincent says so in Letter 1065, where he is probably referring to Bourbon.

Other Vincentians also came to Bourbon for a cure. Brother Claude Le

Gentil (b. 1620), later a priest, was to come here in September 1648, and Brother Jacques Rivet (b. 1620) in May 1654. Vincent took great interest in the health of his confreres. Local tradition has it that Vincent came here, but no documents support this.

The lords of Bourbon gradually advanced in power and gave their name to the ruling house of France, with branches elsewhere, such as today's royal house of Spain. Not to be forgotten is Bourbon County, Kentucky, where the famous Bourbon whisky is made. It is doubtful that the French Bourbons ever developed a taste for it.

The Romanesque church of Saint Georges preserves a relic of the True Cross, a gift of Saint Louis, king of France, to his sixth son, Robert de Clermont, who became lord of Bourbon. It has been in the church since the end of the thirteenth century. Daughters of Charity worked at Bourbon-l'Archambault from 1665, where they helped in the hospital and in a residence for the elderly. In recognition of their service, the town permitted the sisters to bury their deceased members in the parish church. They continued their work for patients and the local poor from 1866 until about 1903. They have returned to continue various pastoral works here. Bourbon-l'Archambault has about 2700 people.

Pierre Coste, probably incorrectly, connects Alméras with **Bourbon-Lancy** (Saône-et-Loire). This city of some 6000 people is a few kilometers east of Moulins and still popular for its thermal springs. The name "Bourbon" refers to an old Celtic deity, Borvo, associated with thermal springs. Both Bourbons, therefore, have waters, but the other Bourbon (l'Archambault) is more likely where Alméras had visited, as one of Vincent's letters (2411) makes clear.

The parish church of Bourbon-Lancy dates from the nineteenth century. This town too had a Visitation convent, now the site of the major thermal hotel that has made use of some of the old buildings, notably the cloister colonnade. If Alméras and the other Vincentians came to this Bourbon, perhaps they were able to lodge with the chaplain of the Visitation.

## SAINT-FLOUR

The small city of Saint-Flour, population 7500, has been the seat of a bish-

Visitation convent chapel, Moulins

op since 1317. The present Gothic cathedral dates from the fifteenth century. Its place at the edge of the plateau on which the city is perched gives it a dramatic view over the Auvergne countryside.

The history of the Congregation of the Mission in Saint-Flour is complex. A seminary for the diocese began in 1653. Its founder, Bishop Jacques de Montrouge (1612-1664), had come under the influence of the great religious personalities of his day, including Vincent. However, the bishop turned to Jean Jacques Olier, a native of the diocese of Saint-Flour, for Sulpicians to run his seminary. They arrived in 1650 but in 1653 handed over the institution to the diocesan clergy. In 1673, the next bishop invited the Vincentians to staff the seminary, and they began their work the following February. They continued to govern it until the Revolution. A new building, still standing, was begun in 1753 to replace the first, which was too small. The Vincentians left it in 1791. Daughters of Charity also came to work in the Saint-Flour parish, beginning in 1681, and returned after the Revolution.

When the seminary property was restored to the Church in 1803, Vincentians were invited to return as well. Lacking anyone to send, the Vincentian vicar general could not resume the work. The Sulpicians came instead, but Napoleon forced them to retire in 1811. After various other starts and stops, the Congregation of the Mission returned in 1820, remaining until 1903. Their expulsion from all the seminaries of France was not followed, in this case, by a return to Saint-Flour, as

they did in a few other dioceses, once conditions changed.

*Jean Gabriel Perboyre*, a priest for only a few weeks, came to the Saint-Flour seminary in 1826 to teach. After a year, the bishop asked John Gabriel to direct his incipient minor seminary, which he did until 1832. The chapel contains a stained glass window commemorating Perboyre's life and ministry, particularly at the seminary. In his second floor room, a plaque records his stay here and his eventual martyrdom in China. The design of the seminary had in some way come from the old Saint Lazare, a claim also made for the former major seminary at Amiens.

An alumnus also shared in the grace of martyrdom. **Jacques Berthieu** (1838-1896) joined the Jesuits and was missioned to Madagascar. He died there and was beatified in 1965.

Among many other Vincentians who either came from this diocese or taught here were: Jean Marie Aladel (1800-1865), later director general of the Daughters of Charity; Antoine Fiat (1832-1915), superior general from 1878 to 1914; Guillaume Pouget (1847-1933), a professor of science and theology; and Charles Léon Souvay (1870-1939). At the expulsion of the Congregation, Souvay came to the United States where he taught in Saint Louis until being recalled to Paris. He was superior general from 1933 until his death. The Saint-Flour seminary, where Souvay taught sacred scripture, closed in 1959. Since then, it has served as a retirement home. *(7, rue des Planchettes)*

# Bretagne

The deeply Catholic region of Bretagne (Brittany) has preserved many of its Celtic roots, notably its Breton language. Vincent de Paul sent his confreres here for missions and seminaries, and he visited these foundations in 1649. Vannes was the home of Pierre René Rogue, a Vincentian martyr at the Revolution. Daughters of Charity also worked in several different houses in this region during the time of Louise de Marillac.

## SAINT-MÉEN-LE-GRAND*

At the end of the sixth century, a Welsh monk, Mewen, founded a monastery here, which in later years took his name. Normans destroyed it in 919, but it took on a new life in the following century. After flourishing for several centuries, it entered a period of decline. By the seventeenth century, only two monks lived here to exercise the works of the Benedictine order.

The bishop of Saint-Malo, Achille de Harlay de Sancy (1581-1646), who was also commendatory abbot of Saint-Méen, decided to establish a *seminary* in his abbey, the first major seminary of Brittany. The bishop, an Oratorian, invited his confreres, but they soon left, and Vincentians replaced them. The two remaining Benedictines agreed to this new situation, but their confreres elsewhere in Brittany did not. The matter reached the courts, and the Vincentians, although at first allowed to stay, were then forcibly expelled. The bishop responded by sending in troops, and the Vincentians were restored after a nearly comic siege. This is probably the most difficult foundation Vincent undertook. So difficult that it became one of the leading objections put forth by the so-called "devil's advocate" during the process for Vincent's beatification.

Some old seminary buildings are still standing, and one of the most visible elements is the central wooden staircase. The present main building, however, dates from the eighteenth century replacing the old monastic residence. The seminary building has been turned into apartments. (*Rue Saint Jean*)

The *abbey church* still serves the parish. It is Romanesque with Gothic portions and has some important frescoes from the fourteenth century. The stained glass windows, among the oldest in Brittany, date from the fourteenth and fifteenth centuries. When the Vincentians came to Saint-Méen, they inherited the Benedictines' obligation to chant the Divine Office in choir. Some Vincentians objected to this, and later their obligation was scaled back somewhat. The Congregation opened an internal seminary (novitiate) here in 1673, without great success. Besides teaching in the seminary and caring for the church, the Vincentians also worked out of Saint-Méen giving missions from 1645 until their departure at the Revolution. They rebuilt part of the church in the eighteenth century, and the altars they installed are still in place.

Daughters of Charity worked here in the *hospital*, beginning in 1640. During the Revolution, four sisters remained, supporting themselves and the poor by opening a small grocery. When the Daughters finally left in 1962, the town erected a monument in the cemetery located behind the abbey church. Their old hospital forms part of the present retirement home at the other end of the Rue Saint Jean from the seminary.

## TRÉGUIER

Another Vincentian project in Brittany was the Tréguier major seminary. At the invitation of Bishop Balthasar Grangier de Liverdis (1606-1679), Vincent agreed to this foundation in 1648. On his one and only trip to the region, in 1649, he visited his confreres in Tréguier. Their service in the seminary was not altogether peaceful and they suffered from misunderstandings with the bishop and the chapter over finances and ecclesiastical privileges. Nevertheless, the Vincentians remained until the Revolution. After the revolutionary period, in 1819, the buildings housed a minor seminary and, with the expulsion of congregations at the beginning of the twentieth century, the commune took over the property. Such parts as remain are now used as a technical college, the Lycée Mixte. The seminary chapel, built only in 1894, is now a theater.

The small cathedral, named after Tugdual, the British monk who founded a monastery here in the sixth century, is Romanesque with Gothic elements. Its oldest parts date from the eleventh century, and the Gothic section (the nave and choir) dates from the fourteenth century. The cathedral recalls the memory of Saint Yves, buried here in 1303. Saint Yves, a native of the region, is one of the patron saints of lawyers, who often come on pilgrimage.

Further to the east, and close to Saint-Brieuc, the Daughters of Charity had a small work of charity for the sick poor in *Saint-René*, now a part of **Hillion** on a peninsula overlooking the bay of Saint-Brieuc. This mission probably began in 1646, but little is known of it. The Vincentians staffed a seminary in Saint-Brieuc from about 1664 to 1791, and the Daughters worked here from 1715 in service of the poor. They returned in 1803.

## VANNES*

In 1643, Sébastien Rosmadec (1585-1646), the bishop of Vannes, invited Vincent to send priests to run the diocesan seminary, but the project had to be abandoned since the financing was unstable. A more successful seminary began in 1701. Its most famous professor was the beatified martyr, *Pierre René Rogue*. He was born in Vannes, 11 June 1758. One family home, Rue de la Monnaie, no longer stands; but two others are known. *(31, place de Lices; 11, rue des Tribunaux)* Rogue made his studies in the Collège Saint Yves in Vannes, now Collège Jules Simon. He was ordained as a diocesan priest on 21 September 1782 in the seminary church, now taken

Vannes Porte Prison

down. Four years after his ordination, he entered the Congregation of the Mission at Saint Lazare, 25 October 1786. Because his health was weak, he soon returned to Vannes from Paris to complete his novitiate and to serve as professor of theology in the major seminary. The seminary itself, now the Foyer de Mené, was located next to the parish church, Notre Dame de Mené. *(9, rue Emile Burgault)* The church that Rogue knew, however, has been demolished.

The revolutionary government approved the Civil Constitution of Clergy on 12 July 1790 and mandated an oath to support it. Since the text of the oath seemed to weaken the authority of the Church, Rogue, along with other Vincentians at the seminary, refused to take it. Rather than leave for exile, he remained in Vannes to serve in secret. Two of his hiding places are known. *(14, place Cabello*, at the corner of Rue du Four and Rue de la Tannerie, and *9, rue de Trussac*, now *Rue de la Salle d'Asil)* He escaped police capture for some time but was spotted as he was leaving his hiding place while about to bring Communion to a sick person on Christmas Eve, 1795. A plaque outside the old seminary commemorates his arrest.

Rogue was held at the Porte Prison, the imposing towers at one of the gates of the city. During his time here, he acted as a kind of chaplain to the other prisoners, bringing them whatever consolation he could. He was tried at the chapel of the Retraite des Femmes on 2 March 1796. Condemned for refusing to take the constitutional oath, Rogue was to be guillotined within 24 hours. His mother, who had visited him in prison, almost certainly witnessed his martyrdom. *(Place de l'Hôtel de Ville)*

His body was buried first at the Boismoreau cemetery in an unmarked grave, but his mother remembered the location. Pius XI beatified him on 13 June 1934, as part of the celebration of the Holy Year of 1933-1934. On that occasion, his body was moved to the Cathedral of Saint Peter, but it is now not exposed for the veneration of the faithful. Instead, a wax model has been placed in the chapel of the Rosary, and a plaque explains Rogue's ministry and martyrdom. The image shows him lying in death, vested as a priest, holding a ciborium to his chest. The cathedral also contains the tomb of Saint Vincent Ferrer (c. 1350-1419), who died in Vannes. A splendid tapestry, dating from 1615, commemorates him. Vincent honored him as one of his patron saints.

Among the many signs of veneration for their local martyr, the town designated the street that leads into the Rue des Lices where he was born as Rue Bienheureux René Rogue. Vincentians returned to the seminary in 1804 but remained only until 1833.

Daughters of Charity were present in Vannes beginning in 1682, and six of them were arrested and imprisoned here in the period 1793-1795. None was executed, however. They returned after the Revolution to continue their hospital ministry (beginning in 1802).

The Daughters also served in the hospital at **Hennebont**, some distance west of Vannes. Louis Eudo de Kerlivio (1621-1675) had studied at the Bons

Enfants in Paris, where he came to know Vincent and the Daughters of Charity. As the vicar general of the diocese, he invited the sisters, and two arrived there by 1650 to serve the sick poor, many of whom spoke only Breton. Several letters from Vincent to this community still exist. During the Revolution, the sisters were hounded from their two hospitals. One group, after evading discovery, went to Paris and were sent to open a house in Turin. Traveling with three Vincentians, they brought with them a quantity of items, including clothes belonging to the saint and, most importantly, his heart. This relic had been secreted in a large book whose pages had been hollowed out to receive it. After this turbulent period, the Daughters returned. Hennebont, greatly damaged during the second World War, is today a city of around 14,000 people.

Another small establishment of the Daughters was the fortress hospital of **Belle-Ile**, often called Belle-Ile-en-Mer. This work was another foundation of Nicolas Fouquet, who had purchased the island from Henri de Gondi, Cardinal de Retz, marquis of Belle-Ile. Because of Fouquet's family connections with them, he favored the Daughters of Charity. He asked that they come to care for the prisoners and for the instruction of the poor young girls of this island located off the Brittany coast, not far from Vannes. In 1660, Vincent sent as the first superioress Mathurine Guérin, who had already held important posts in the Company. She would be superioress general on four different occasions. The apostolate here lasted only until 1666.

Saint Vincent's lodging,
Vincentian house, Richelieu

# Centre

*The region now called Centre was the site of several Vincentian works, some during the lifetime of Vincent de Paul. One of the most important was at Richelieu, a place Vincent visited several times. For Daughters of Charity, Chartres has a special meaning because of Louise de Marillac's dedication of the Company to the Virgin Mary there.*

Seminary corridor, Chartres

## CHARTRES**

Among the great sights of France is the cathedral of Chartres. It dominates the medieval town and the surrounding countryside. A Romanesque cathedral was built in the eleventh and twelfth centuries, but it was damaged by fire in 1194. Its crypt, the towers, and base of the western façade remain. The present cathedral was consecrated in 1260 and offered to the piety of the faithful the great relic of the tunic of the Blessed Virgin. For centuries this drew many pilgrims. Today, the magnificent carvings and the stained glass windows (twelfth and thirteenth centuries) are the object of visits and studies.

*Louise* came here on pilgrimage, 14-17 October 1644. *I offered the said company entirely to [God], asking Him to destroy it rather than let it be established contrary to His holy will. I asked for it, through the prayers of the Holy Virgin, Mother and Guardian of the said Company, the purity of which it stands in need . . . . I asked Him for the grace of fidelity for the Company through the merits of the Blood of the Son of God and of Mary.* (Spiritual Writings, L. 111) Vincent, however, was not here with her. He came at least once to pray about an important transfer of a bishop who the saint believed should receive a more important diocese. Other visits are likely, but no records exist.

The foundress prayed in the old crypt, where a modern statue of Notre Dame de Sous-Terre (that is, of the crypt) is enshrined. Vincent probably prayed here as well. The ancient statue came from an early Christian sanctuary here, said, in turn, to have been venerated by the pre-Roman inhabitants of the region. At the Revolution, the statue was burned. To reach Chartres, the two

Street sign, Chartres

founders probably followed the traditional pilgrim route: Paris, Palaiseau, Orsay, Gometz, Limours, Saint-Arnoult, Gué de Longroi, Chartres. Although references to these towns and, more generally, to the diocese of Chartres, occur in Vincent's correspondence (because of various business affairs and missions), Chartres did not play a large part in his works. Daughters of Charity continue the practice of a pilgrimage here to pray for the Company.

Vincentians staffed the Chartres *major seminary* from 1680 until the Revolution. It was located at Beaulieu, just south of the city. Today, the area is an industrial zone, bisected by rail lines. The Congregation also ran the *minor seminary* of Saint Charles from 1719. This seminary was located to the left of the Evêché, the bishop's residence. Today it houses the departmental archives. (*Rue du Palais de Justice*) In the chapel of this seminary an unpleasant event took place at the time of the Revolution. Two confreres publicly took the constitutional oath, 6 February 1791. The event was intended to influence non-juring clergy to follow them. The superior of the seminary, *Jean Baptiste Gratien* (1747-1799), later became the constitutional bishop of Rouen. His companion, Jean Baptiste François, was a brother of Blessed Louis Joseph François, later martyred for his opposition to the same oath. Daughters of Charity began their service in the city hospital in 1664 and after the Revolution returned in 1854.

Near here is **Gallardon**, where a Confraternity of Charity began in 1634. Whether Vincent was present to inaugurate it is not known. Louise probably came to visit its members.

## CHÂTEAUDUN, VARIZE

In 1654, Daughters of Charity opened their work in Châteaudun in the *Hôtel Dieu*, the city hospital. The discussion about which sisters to assign here was recorded in the minutes of the Council. Vincent insisted on sending virtuous sisters, and the council chose Jeanne Lepeintre, present at the meeting. Reflecting on the building of Solomon's temple, built with precious stones, the founder asked Sister Jeanne: *Will you be a precious stone? Will you be a ruby or an emerald?* She replied, characteristically, *Father, I don't know what I'll be; I'm really afraid that I'll be nothing but mud.* She had her work cut out for her, since the hospital was badly arranged. Her place was taken by the redoubtable *Barbe Angiboust* (1605-1658), who quickly brought order. Barbe had headed whatever houses she had been assigned to and exercised an influence second only to Louise herself. She died here, 27 December 1658. The hospital began in the eleventh century, but the building presently standing dates only from 1762, and it no longer receives patients. The Daughters of Charity remained here until July 1976. Local tradition has it that Vincent came here himself to inaugurate the work of the sisters. (*Place de la Madeleine*)

Dominating the region is the castle that gave its name to the town. It was long the home of the Longueville family, with whom Vincent had various dealings, especially concerning their support

Parish church, Varize

of the Jansenists. Châteaudun has a population of about 15,000.

Before coming to Châteaudun, the sisters had begun a small house in **Varize**, a short distance east. Two had arrived here in 1652 to work for the sick and to teach the children. Daughters of Charity remained in the service of this small town until 1780. They left because the local lord was no longer interested or able to support their work. The old castle and the parish church remain, but the Prussians burnt the rest of the town in 1870 in retaliation for being attacked by its defenders. Consequently, the Daughters' house and school are probably no longer standing.

Some 40 kilometers south of Châteaudun is the city of **Vendôme**. It was here that a relic of Jesus was venerated: a tear shed by him at the tomb of Lazarus (actually a piece of quartz with a visible drop of water inside). This supposed relic disappeared after the Revolution and, in any case, was spurious. Nevertheless, several miracles had been reported concerning it in the early part of the seventeenth century. When asked whether one or more of the sisters at Châteaudun could go there on pilgrimage, Louise did not forbid it. (Letter 587) The former Benedictine monastery church of the Trinity, which housed the relic, is today a parish church.

West and south of Vendôme is the tiny village of **Lublé**, today numbering about 130 people. Again, in the lifetime of the founders, about 1654, the Daughters of Charity had a small work for the poor: a hospital and school. Little is known of this work, however.

## FONTGOMBAULT

The abbey of Notre Dame de Fontgombault has over the centuries sheltered a remarkable number of different religious families. Benedictines lived here from the late eleventh century. Trappists were here from 1849 to 1903, but Benedictines are again in possession of this foundation. Vincentians were here for a few years (1742-1779) as part of their work in the seminary for the archdiocese of Bourges. Nothing in the great church or in the public part of the abbey recalls their work—something the modest founder would have probably approved. The small town of Fontgombault is home to about 1000 people and certainly owes its origin to the abbey.

Another abbey, some 20 kilometers east on route D6, is better known for someone who spent practically no time here, Jean Duvergier de Hauranne, known usually as the abbé of *Saint Cyran*. The old abbey of Saint Cyran, from which he took his name, is in **Saint-Michel-en-Brenne**, a town of some 500 inhabitants. Most of the abbey has been taken down, but some old buildings remain. In light of later developments, it might have been better for the Church had Duvergier come here to stay and not propagate the teachings known

as Jansenism. Vincent, however, agreed with the abbé's request for his confreres to give missions in the parishes depending on this abbey.

## LIMOURON

Limouron (or Limoron) was a hamlet (just a farm today) by Villamblain, near Châteaudun. Vincent came here in June 1638. The reason for his visit was that this property was at the time the Benedictine priory of Saint Mary Magdelaine, ceded some time previously to Adrien Le Bon, prior of Saint Lazare. Le Bon did not live here and was only its titular prior. This title passed to Vincent when he took over Saint Lazare from Le Bon. Vincent described it as *a simple little priory we have, two leagues from Orléans . . . . It consists of a farm, where there are two farmers, each having two plows for tilling about four hundred (arpents) [about 600 acres] of land, in one piece all around.* (Letter 992, 2 October 1647) Vincent's presence here demonstrates his interest in matters agricultural, something he pursued all through his life. He also admired the faith of its inhabitants: *That place belongs entirely to God . . . how admirable is the effect of His goodness on those people!* (Letter 330, June 1638)

## ORLÉANS

The important city of Orléans often figured in the letters of Vincent and Louise. We have one letter that he wrote from here (Letter 1091), dated 25 February 1649, and it is clear that Louise was also here. The main reason seems to be the location of the city on the transportation routes. Otherwise, there was no house of the Congregation of the Mission or the Daughters of Charity in this city before the Revolution. The Vincentians opened a mission house in 1869 and remained until about 1903. Today, Orléans is a city of more than 150,000.

A few kilometers southwest of Orléans is **Cléry-Saint-André**. This town of some 2500 people is notable for its enormous basilica, Notre Dame de Cléry. The origin of this pilgrimage site is lost in legend (a statue of the Virgin Mary found in a bush by peasants), but it can be traced to the thirteenth century at least. The present church, dating from the fifteenth century, contains the tomb of Louis XI (d. 1483) and his wife. It can be supposed that Louise stopped here at various times, although this cannot be proven from existing records. Vincent mentions the town in one letter to Louise (Letter 410), apparently relying on personal experience. The two founders must have visited many such shrines.

Aerial view, Richelieu

## RICHELIEU**

In 1621, Armand Jean Du Plessis (1585-1642) purchased Richelieu from family members, a small village with the manor house that had been family property since 1350. When Du Plessis, former bishop of Luçon, became a cardinal, he assumed the name of this fief. To honor his principal minister, Louis XIII made the town the center of a duchy-peerage in 1631, attaching to it several outlying fiefs. The cardinal saw to the building for himself of a sumptuous chateau and park here to replace the traditional family home. His magnificent and prideful chateau was demolished after 1814, but the park with its entrance gates and

Notre Dame church, Richelieu

City gate, Richelieu, postcard

walls, some seventeenth-century out-buildings, and the foundations of the chateau remain. A large statue of the cardinal stands at the main entry.

The small town of around 2500 people, built on a rectangular plan in Renaissance style, is still surrounded by interesting ramparts and moats. Two city gates remain, as do remarkable private and public buildings. On the Market Square, in front of the church, the Halles are noteworthy for their seventeenth-century woodwork.

Richelieu's parish was officially erected in 1638, and the church was built during that year. *Notre Dame de l'Assomption* is built in a classical style, as befits the classically designed town. The main altar, however, dates from the

Vincent in glory, parish church, Richelieu

eighteenth century, and the Blessed Sacrament chapel is dedicated to Saint Vincent—the main items being the painting in the dome, and the large painting over the altar, depicting Vincent preaching. The sacristy houses some elegant woodwork, paintings from the chateau, as well as a chalice and paten, which the duchess of Aiguillon, the cardinal's niece, presented to the saint. A copy of this chalice is in the Vincentian museum of the Paris motherhouse. The

Saint Vincent's chalice and paten, parish church, Richelieu

Vincentian house, Richelieu

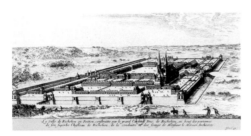

View of city of Richelieu,
17th century engraving

organ was begun in the seventeenth century. The baptismal font is original, dating from 1637. The cardinal's coat of arms figures prominently on the vaults over the altar. His cardinal's hat is depicted with six rows of tassels, one more row than most ordinary cardinals possessed, probably because Richelieu was also a duke and peer of the realm, and the king's principal minister. (The

hat itself, drooping and dusty, hangs above Richelieu's tomb in the chapel of the Sorbonne.) Several Vincentians were buried under the floor in the middle of the church, between the four main pillars, but their graves are not marked.

The cardinal, seeking an active religious congregation for his duchy, offered a residence to Vincent, the contract for which was signed in 1638. By it, Vincent agreed to send ten priests. Four were to serve the parish, prepare the ordinands of the diocese and give priests' retreats. The other six were to give missions so that the whole duchy would be evangelized every five years. Although Vincent reluctantly acceded to the cardinal's demands, he insisted that Notre Dame become a model parish. The cardinal agreed to provide a steady source of

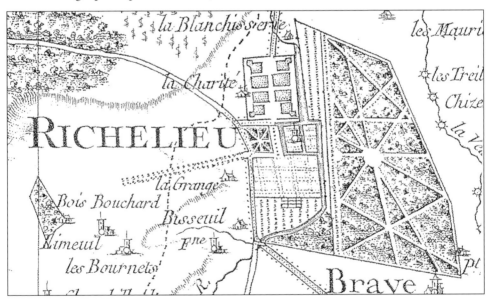

Eighteenth century map of Richelieu and Braye

Vincentian house, Richelieu

Daughter of Charity house, Richelieu

funds for their support, including income from properties such as rental houses and farms. Vincent wrote several letters on the subject of this foundation and in later years even began a novitiate in the house. After the cardinal's death, his favorite niece and heir, the duchess of Aiguillon, continued to provide support.

Vincent visited here several times (1638, 1639, 1640, 1642, and 1649). He mentioned the good order and piety of the people and observed that the taverns were not much frequented, especially on Sundays and feast days. The Vincentian pastors erected a Confraternity of Charity. During the Fronde, he sent the novices from Paris to Richelieu for their safety.

Because the cardinal was the king's principal minister, chief and general superintendent of navigation and commerce, the court came to call. When they did, the pastor of Richelieu would be called on to officiate at solemn functions. Vincent wrote Bernard Codoing (1610-c.1678) on how to behave himself in the presence of twelve-year old Louis

XIV and his court. *[The King] does not like long speeches, so do not make any. Tell him, however, that you have come to offer His Majesty the services of the Company and to assure him of its prayers that God may be pleased to bless him and his armies, to preserve him for many years to come, to grant him the grace of subjugating the rebels and of extending his empire to the ends of the earth; in a word, that God may reign over his States.* (Letter 1234, dated 1650, after the cardinal's death) Unfortunately for the king, the letter arrived too late. In 1660, the king returned with his new wife, his mother, and an enormous following. René Alméras celebrated a baptism at which His Majesty was the godfather.

Two Daughters of Charity also came to Richelieu in 1638 to work for the sick and teach poor girls. Louise came here to visit her sisters. Vincent addressed several letters to that community of Daughters, one of the earliest outside Paris and the first outside the Ile de France. The location of the Sisters' hospital occupied a large section, fronting on the Place des Religieuses, extending to the walls at the northwest corner, ending at the Porte de Chinon. They remained here until the eighteenth century, possibly until the Revolution. The Revolutionaries also seized the church building and there installed the Goddess of Reason. Later still, public meetings were held as well, while the few remaining Catholics were permitted one side nave for their worship.

A large *community house*, built by the cardinal and located behind the church, is only partly used. Poorly furnished at the beginning, it was for a while one of the novitiates of the Congregation. Vincent recalled that his confreres recited their office in common, not in the parish church, but in an oratory in this house. (Conference 213) The Richelieu house is one of the oldest community houses still standing, but Vincentians no longer occupy it. The commune seized it at the Revolution and has since sold part of it. In that section is to be found the room which the saint is said to have used. Vincentians returned briefly as pastors from 1876 to 1885. Today, the entire pastoral area of Richelieu and several surrounding villages is called the parish of Saint Vincent de Paul.

On the dark side of things, the Richelieu Vincentians house became involved in the notorious cases of demonic possession of nuns at Loudun, Chinon and Louviers. The formerly Protestant town of **Loudun** had seen Catholic worship and communities reestablished after much neglect. The appointment in 1617 of a pastor, Urbain

Saint Vincent's lodging,
Vincentian house, Richelieu

Grandier, whose appreciation for and practice of celibacy was negligible, led to much disorder. The prioress of the Ursulines thought she was possessed, and Grandier agreed to become the convent's spiritual director, with predictable results. Public exorcisms did not put an end to the problems, but a shabby trial led to Grandier's being burned alive, 18 August 1634, in the presence of thousands. All this, of course, took place before the arrival of the Vincentians in Richelieu. The alleged possessions continued, however, until 1641. Vincent even cited some sentences for the Daughters of Charity concerning the need of conversion, said to have come from demons speaking through the nuns. (Conference 87, 18 November 1657) The Daughters had a hospital in Loudun from 1684 to the Revolution.

In a related case, some women in **Chinon**, a few kilometers north, pretended to be possessed and made damaging accusations against two local priests. They were led in this by another priest who had been one of the exorcists at Loudun. In 1640, an unnamed Vincentian at Richelieu supported their cause from the pulpit. Vincent reacted quickly and had the man reprimanded. (Letter 459)

A third case broke out in 1643 at **Louviers** and lasted until 1647. In this town in Normandy, some distance north of Richelieu, a monastery of nuns was affected with problems of three priests involved in sacrileges, magic and sorcery. The principal subject was burned alive as a sorcerer, and his two accomplices, already dead, also had their corpses burned. Although the Richelieu Vincentians were not involved, Vincent was, as a member of the Council of Conscience. These strange episodes give some context to the ministry of the early Vincentians in Richelieu.

## SAINT-DYÉ-SUR-LOIRE

Vincent wrote a letter from here to Antoine Portail (13 October 1644). Neither in this letter nor elsewhere does he mention his reason for coming here. Because of its location on the river Loire, it is possible that it was merely a stopping place. Geneviève Fayet, Madame Goussault, a close collaborator of Vincent and Louise, reported to him that she had come here also but only to dine. *I found the church very well looked after, and the poor and the children better instructed than anywhere else.* (Letter 135, 16 April 1633) Other than that, there is no indication of any Vincentian activities here, nor even a Confraternity of Charity, such as might have been founded if Vincent had come here to give a mission. Saint-Dyé is still a small town, with fewer than 1000 inhabitants.

Saint Vincent's chalice and paten,
parish church, Richelieu

# Limousin

*The region of Limousin, taking its name from the porcelain center of Limoges, has little of Vincentian interest. Two towns, however, Le Dorat and Ussel, have a connection with Saint Vincent himself.*

## DORAT (LE)

Determined Vincentian pilgrims will appreciate visiting the motherhouse of the Sisters of Marie Joseph et de la Miséricorde at Le Dorat, since these sisters succeeded the Congregation of the Mission at Saint Lazare in Paris. In 1850, the French government committed to them the care of the women prisoners kept in the old priory.

The sisters left as the buildings were gradually demolished in the 1900s. They took with them some of the keys used in the old institution. These, along with a bell, the gift of Anne of Austria to Vincent, are kept in a small building on their motherhouse grounds. This bell,

Plaque for Saint Lazare bell,
Sisters of Marie Joseph, Le Dorat

erroneously called a silver bell (it is bronze, probably with some silver added to give it a good tone), was originally used to summon the ordinands to their spiritual exercises. When the sisters arrived, they placed it in a new location as their main bell. After their departure, they received the bell as a souvenir.

Le Dorat today numbers about 2500 people, living in the shadow of an impressive Romanesque collegiate church.

## USSEL

This city located in the central hill country of France was the capital of the duchy of Ventadour. The duchess of Ventadour, Marie de La Guiche de Saint Gérand (d. 1701), devoted herself to charitable works after her husband's

Saint Lazare bell, Sisters of
Marie Joseph, Le Dorat

death. She was one of Louise's main supporters and was present at her deathbed. At the request of the duchess, two Daughters of Charity had come here in 1658.

The sisters had hesitated to come, given Ussel's distance from any Vincentian house. Vincent gave them this advice: *This is the main point for you—to make God known by your spiritual service to the poor, while serving them corporally, as it is our principal purpose to instruct and then serve the sick poor.* (Conference 94, 1658) When the sisters arrived, they found that their work was to aid the sick and keep a school. They lived in an isolated house and had great difficulty with the dialect and the local food. Since the work got on their nerves they sang for their amusement. (Louise didn't want them to be heard outside.) A local tradition holds that the sisters left Ussel and went to meet Vincent at Moulins, but he urged them to go back: *Return, my daughters, return to Ussel. Providence will take care of you.* Indeed, the Daughters did not leave this apostolate, the civil hospital, even at the time of the Revolution. They were compelled to leave, however, when the hospital was put under lay control early in the twentieth century. Nevertheless they continue in other works here.

Ussel, today with a population of about 12,000, has preserved the small ducal home of the Ventadours. Several ancient buildings exist in the old town, among which is the old hospital, today housing the Hôtel de Police and several other civic organizations. Nothing in the parish church recalls the presence of the Daughters.

Church window, Lézigné

# Pays de la Loire

*Many sites in the region of the river Loire were blessed by the ministry of Vincent de Paul and Louise de Marillac. The hospital at Angers, in particular, is well known. Also, the tragic events of the Revolution profoundly touched these Vincentian works.*

1640 – 1940

TRICENTENAIRE DE LA FONDATION
DES SŒURS DE S<sup>T</sup> VINCENT DE PAUL

C'EST A ANGERS, ALORS RAVA-
GÉE PAR LA PESTE, QUE FUT FONDÉ PAR
S<sup>T</sup> VINCENT DE PAUL LE PREMIER ÉTABLIS-
SEMENT DES FILLES DE LA CHARITÉ ET
INSTALLÉ DANS CETTE SALLE DE L'HÔPITAL
S<sup>T</sup> JEAN PAR M<sup>LLE</sup> LE GRAS NÉE LOUISE DE
MARILLAC AVEC 9 SŒURS.

1<sup>ER</sup> FÉVRIER 1640.

VISITE DE M<sup>E</sup> VINCENT 1649.

DON DE EUGÈNE PROUST. *Maire honoraire d'Angers*.

M<sup>GR</sup> JEAN COSTES. *Évêque*.

VICTOR BERNIER. *Maire*.

E. ROBERT *vic. gén. des Lazaristes*.

Commemorative plaque,
Hôtel Dieu, Angers

## ANGERS**

The city of Angers, the capital of the old province of Anjou, extends along the banks of the river Maine. With a favorable climate and location, its vines have flourished for centuries. Angers began in Celtic times, fell to the Romans, and in the ninth century was assaulted by Normans. During the Middle Ages, it was under the control of the counts and dukes of Anjou. One of them, Henry II Plantagenet, became king of England. Because of these connections, it was only in the fifteenth century that Angers became definitively united to the French crown. The dukes of Anjou had their seat in Angers and were buried in the cathedral of *Saint Maurice*. The city suffered greatly under the revolutionary government, and many believers were martyred for the faith. The cathedral commemorates these martyrs visually in a beautiful bas-relief on the altar of the south transept. Noteworthy in the cathedral are its exceptional windows and extensive tapestries. Today the city has some 160,000 inhabitants.

Vincent came to Angers in 1649, following Louise, who had visited twice before (1640, 1646). She saw to the installation of the Daughters of Charity in the ancient hospital. They arrived because of the persistence of Guy Lasnier (1602-1681), the abbé of Saint

Hôtel Dieu, Angers

Étienne de Vaux. He had met Vincent at Saint Lazare during a retreat and determined to ask Daughters of Charity to staff the hospital. Abbé de Vaux became a great benefactor and counselor of theirs. He also had the foresight to preserve many letters from the founders. Ladies of Charity, organized on the same model as those at the Hôtel Dieu in Paris, also helped serve the sick at the hospital.

The *hospital of Saint John* where the Daughters and the Ladies served was founded in 1175 by Etienne de Marçay, an official of Henry II, in reparation for the murder of Thomas Becket (1118?-1170). Daughters of Charity were in this important hospital, the oldest surviving one in France, from 1639 until the Revolution, and afterwards from 1806 to 1854. At that date, the hospital became a museum. Its main exhibition hall had been used for the sick and contained more than 200 beds. This meant that

Chapel of Avrillé, outside Angers

there would sometimes be more than 200 patients, since many would share beds in times of epidemics. The main hall remains as it was when the Daughters of Charity were here but without the beds. The pharmacy contains ancient vessels and utensils used to prepare medicines. It was here that Sister Odile Baumgarten worked from 1777 to 1794, when she was executed for the faith. At the door of this large hall, a plaque recalls the service of the sisters and the visits by Louise and Vincent. In 1854, the Daughters of Charity left the old hospital to be with the sick transferred elsewhere. The sisters remained there until 1869 but have since returned to other works.

In the old hospital chapel, modified in the eighteenth century, are two small altars built in 1740; one of them was dedicated to Saint Vincent but now holds a statue of the Sacred Heart. The enclosed cloister walk is an architectural jewel, a masterpiece of twelfth-century carpentry. Louise and Vincent certainly strolled along the pavement in this cloister. At the end of the garden is a large building used, among other things, as a storeroom. Sister Marie Anne Vaillot worked here up to the time of her arrest.

*Marie Anne Vaillot* (b. 1734) and *Odile Baumgarten* (b. 1750) were among 35 Daughters who worked at the hospital. Bans on religious congregations and on religious and ecclesiastical dress were enacted in 1792. Certain religious houses were allowed to continue, however, such as the hospital at Angers. Consequently, the Daughters of Charity remained until the summer of 1793, at which time the

Chapel entry, Hôtel Dieu, Angers,
19th century engraving

Lorient, the port for the embarkation, saved them from their fate.

At **Avrillé**, a town adjacent to Angers on the northwest, route N162, is the Field of the Martyrs. At the time of the trials, it was a simple field. The condemned were led here and lined up before trenches dug to receive their bodies. Amid prayers and singing led by the Daughters, they were shot and dumped into the waiting graves. These ten common graves contain about 2000 individuals, although only about 800 can be identified from records. In an effort to limit the number of beatifications, 100 candidates were chosen based on the records that they left behind stating that they died for the faith. The others, presumably, were killed for political or social reasons. Since the executions, the Field of the Martyrs has become a place of pilgrimage, prayer and reflection. The small chapel, begun in 1848, is dedicated

local revolutionary council demanded that the sisters should take the revolutionary oath and put aside the habit. A few did, but the majority refused. The oath became obligatory in the following January, three Daughters were arrested for not supporting it. One was freed, but Sisters Marie Anne and Odile were tried, found guilty, and then sentenced to death by firing squad. On 1 February 1794, they and some 200 others, tied together in pairs to a central rope, were paraded from the prison through the city to the killing field. On the way, Sister Odile dropped her rosary, hidden beneath her clothes, but the guards kept her from retrieving it. Another woman did, and it has been preserved until today. The other Sisters were arrested and condemned to deportation to French Guyana. Grateful citizens in

Hôtel Dieu interior, Angers,
19th century engraving

to Saint Louis. Its windows depict the various scenes of the executions. In the chapel's sanctuary are plaques listing the names of the beatified martyrs. One was a priest, Noël Pinot, beatified 31 October 1926; Pope John Paul II beatified the other 99 on 19 February 1984. Of those, twelve priests and one Benedictine nun were guillotined. The other 84, mainly poor women and Daughters of Charity, were shot during the period from 12 January to 16 April 1794. Two major pilgrimages are held each year: 1 February, the liturgical feast of the martyrs; and 25 August, to honor Saint Louis.

Although Vincentians had earlier given missions in the diocese of Angers, it was only in 1674 that a permanent *mission house* began here. In 1692, a novitiate opened in the same house, although it was never as important as the Paris novitiate. Jean Henri Gruyer made his novitiate here, however, a fact that adds some luster to the institution. It was located in the former Hôtel des Granges, Rue Valdemaine, although no trace of it seems to exist today. This mission house continued here until the Revolution. The church attached to the house became one of the Angers prisons during the revolutionary period, beginning in 1794. The Vincentians began a new mission house in 1860, and it continued until 1903. It has since been demolished. *(18, rue de la Meignanne)*

Vincent's departure from Angers was, like his arrival, marked by an accident and misadventures. As related below, he nearly drowned near Durtal before arriving and, on leaving for **Rennes**, his horse was spooked while crossing a wooden bridge. The noise of a nearby mill frightened it, and the horse and its saintly rider nearly fell into the millpond. In the evening, he arrived at a shabby inn that he had to share with the innkeeper's drunken friends. Later, when Vincent arrived in Rennes, an anti-royalist sympathizer recognized him and threatened to kill him. Another priest saved his life, and Vincent was able to continue unharmed the following day.

Daughters of Charity came to Rennes in 1675, and took up work in the parish as well as in the local prison, unusual work for them at the time. One of the sisters, *Jeanne Montagnier* (d. 1802), devoted her life to this work. At the Revolution, since she too refused the oath, she was condemned to the same prison for a year. During her imprisonment she continued to minister as best she could to her fellow inmates. The Daughters returned in 1808 and continue various works in the city.

## FONTENAY-LE-COMTE

Local tradition has it that Vincent visited here, though on what occasion and for how long is unknown. His friend, *René Moreau* (1605-1671), received him here. This priest was later the vicar general of the diocese of Maillezais. Beyond this, nothing is sure, since this Moreau does not appear in any of Vincent's extant writings. Since Fontenay was not far from other places that Vincent visited in 1649, he might have taken that occasion to see his friend. Also, Fontenay is not far from Richelieu, which the saint visited several times.

A Vincentian *mission house* existed in Fontenay from 1676 until the Revolution. Daughters of Charity worked in the hospital here from 1726 to the Revolution, and afterward until 1903. The Vincentian house was located in the chateau of Terre-Neuve. *(Corner of rues Rapin and Jarnigande)* Fontenay today is a city of more than 14,000 inhabitants.

## LE MANS*

Vincentians came to Le Mans in 1645 under Bishop Emeric Marc de La Ferté (1608-1648). He established them in the former hospital of *Notre Dame de Coëffort*, which became an important house for the Congregation. The Vincentians were hospital chaplains at the Hôtel-Dieu, received seminarians, gave retreats to ordinands and preached missions all around the area. At the time of the difficulties of the Fronde, Vincent considered sending some of his confreres to Le Mans to get them out of Paris. This did not happen. Instead, Vincent had to absent himself from Paris and took the occasion to visit Le Mans (in March of 1649). As a member of the Council of Conscience, he had not recommended its bishop for ordination, something the bishop knew. The situation was potentially embarrassing. Nevertheless, Vincent asked the bishop's permission to stay at the seminary, and the bishop responded graciously. Vincent is also believed to have preached in the cathedral here on that occasion. He later found it necessary to encourage one of his confreres, Guillaume Cornaire (b. 1614), who had written complaining of the boredom of his apostolate. (Letter 1228) Shortly after, Cornaire's life became more exciting: his confreres had to hide items from soldiers in the area to prevent pillaging. (Letter 1460)

In its later history, the Le Mans seminary endured many trials, especially financial problems involving its many lands, woods, houses and dependent chapels. Its most distinguished alumnus was probably *Pierre Collet* (1693-1770). He entered the Congregation of the Mission in 1717 and became a much-published theologian and biographer. His life of Vincent de Paul was the great biography of the eighteenth century. The seminary continued until 1791. In the revolutionary era, one Vincentian professor who suffered was *Jean Guibaud* (1761-1794), who went into hiding. A woman desiring the promised reward betrayed his location. He was then arrested and executed in Le Mans. Another faculty member, *François Martelet* (1760-1798), was also condemned for not taking the constitutional oath. He was arrested and shot at Besançon.

Daughters of Charity were sent here to the Le Mans hospital in 1646

Notre Dame de Coëffort, Le Mans

Notre Dame de Coëffort, entry, Le Mans

Notre Dame de Coëffort, interior, Le Mans

because of their good work at Angers and since the hospital chaplain and the superior of the seminary were both Vincentians. Their foundation did not succeed, however. They returned in 1802 to a more successful apostolate in the hospital, lasting through the century. They continue their pastoral works here.

The church building had been the main hall of the former hospital, and it has recently been restored to its early layout, similar to that of Angers. Closed to the public for many years as the army was using it, Notre Dame de Coëffort was restored to the Church for worship 28 October 1951. One window on the façade retains the image of the seal of the Congregation of the Mission. The old hospital property has now become

Notre Dame de Coëffort, interior, Le Mans

the Lycée Gabriel Touchard. The square in front of the hospital/church was at one period called Place de la Mission, but its name has been changed to Square Washington. One street leading into the square, however, is still called Rue de la Mission. Modern Le Mans is a city of around 150,000 people.

Abelly recounts that, while going from Le Mans to Angers, about two kilometers southwest of **Durtal**, Vincent's horse stumbled down the steep bank of a small creek, swollen by rain, and probably pinned his rider under him. Vincent's traveling companion, a priest, saw him and saved him from drowning. Completely drenched, Vincent remounted his horse, went quickly to a nearby farm to dry out and not surprisingly grew feverish. This unnamed priest left

Church window, Lézigné

Pouillet creek bridge, near Durtal

the Congregation but asked several times to be readmitted. When he reminded Vincent that he had once saved his life, Vincent wrote that he should return to Saint Lazare, where he would be received with open arms. The creek has various names, but it is called Pouillet, near the Durtal road (N23). A small farm, La Goilerie, could be where the saint and his companion stopped. A modern window in the village church of **Lézigné**, south of Durtal, recalls this event, dated to March or April 1649. (Letters 1097, 2004) The window, dated 1937, depicts Saint Vincent catechizing the children of the family while their mother dries his cloak by the fire.

## LUÇON

In 1638, when Cardinal Richelieu, the retired bishop of Luçon, invited Vincent to send missionaries to Richelieu, he also asked for missionaries for his former diocese, which members of his family had served as bishops for many decades. The two parties signed a contract to this effect, and missionaries came to the diocese of Luçon. Vincentians were to remain here from that year until the Revolution.

The saint himself traveled to the city of Luçon, perhaps in 1633, and later to visit his confreres. He did so probably in early May of 1649 during his long absence from Paris, partly as a way of distancing himself from the troubles of the Fronde. While here, he lodged at the seminary *(Rue de l'Hôtel de Ville)*. Luçon today has a population of around 9000.

The cardinal provided a large house suitable for the missionaries as well as for ordinands. The country house of Pont de Vie, located at **Le Poiré-sur-Vie**, was their ordinary residence from 1641 to 1680. It does not appear to be extant. The Vincentians also had a house in Luçon itself, designed to care for the "New Converts" from Protestantism. Little is known about this work. The diocesan seminary, which the Vincentians directed from 1771 to 1791, is more tangible evidence of a Vincentian presence. Their

seminary became a military barracks but was demolished in the 1930s.

During Vincent's western journey, a tradition holds that he visited **La Roche-sur-Yon**, the most important town in the region. Here his friend Jacques de La Boucherie lived in the parish of Saint André d'Ornay, a short distance west of the town. Another tradition associates Vincent with a visit to **Fontenay-le-Comte** at the same time (see above). The fact is, however, that it is exceedingly difficult to track the saint's movements. Nevertheless, we know some of the places he visited, and he had to pass through others. Hence, it is likely that these old traditions have some basis in fact.

The missionaries had a country house at Beaulieu-sous-Mareuil, a farm area on the outskirts of **Mareuil-sur-Lay-Dissais**, a few kilometers southeast of La Roche. Eventually they also received responsibility for the local parish, Saint Pierre (from 1678). The building itself was used both as an ordinary residence and as a country house. When the confreres received care of the seminary in Luçon itself, they also lodged seminarians at Beaulieu. Vincent, of course, did not come here.

## NANTES

At the lower end of the Loire valley stands Nantes, today a city of some 250,000 inhabitants. For centuries it disputed the title of Capital of Brittany with Rennes—Rennes won. On one of its many islands, which have recently been reclaimed from the river and incorporated into the city, stands the *Hôtel Dieu*, the city hospital. In August 1646, Louise herself came here with six sisters to open the house. It is located on one of the former islands and maintains its traditional appearance. *(Quai Moncousu)*

Vincent visited the sisters here on his lengthy journey through Brittany, arriving about 19 April 1649. He remained here for around ten days. René Alméras, as the director of the sisters, also visited, as did other Vincentians in their turn. One of the reasons for these repeated visits was difficulties between the sisters and the hospital administrators. The hospital prospered, however, and the sisters remained until the Revolution. They returned to Nantes in 1819.

Unconnected with the apostolate of the sisters was the occasional presence of Vincentian missionaries embarking for or returning from Madagascar. Nantes was and is an important port.

Its name lives on in the **Edict of Nantes.** Henri IV promulgated this document in 1598 in Nantes to give a measure of religious toleration to French Protestants. The growing power of the Huguenots, as they were called, and their quasi-independent status within France, led Louis XIV to revoke his grandfather's edict in 1685. A great exodus of French Protestants ensued, and the galleys gradually began to fill with pastors and others who had refused to obey the law.

## SAUMUR

The most notable Vincentian feature of the city of Saumur is the shrine of Our Lady, Notre Dame des Ardilliers. The story is that, in 1454, a farmer dis-covered in his field a statue buried in the ground, perhaps hidden there to keep it away from the depredations of soldiers. It was a Pieta, the Virgin Mother with the dead Jesus on her knees. This farmer eventually placed the statue by a spring that arose near where he discovered the statue. People came to see and pray, and then believed in the miraculous effects of the spring. So was born the pilgrimage that continues to the present. The people of Saumur built a chapel (consecrated 1553), and the Oratorians developed the pilgrimage, particularly to challenge the many Protestants in Saumur (after 1585). Louis XIII contributed to the reconstruction of the shrine and gave it thereby the status of a Royal Chapel.

Cardinal Richelieu, despite his reputation for being more interested in politics than religion, took responsibility for building a chapel to the left of the nave in 1634. It is here that the pilgrimage statue is venerated today. In 1940, the ensemble suffered major damage from a battle, but it was restored and blessed anew by the future Pope John XXIII, then nuncio to France.

It appears that Vincent came here at least once, and he recommended that Louise do the same on her travels. This is known from several letters dated 1638 and 1639. In addition, she and the first sisters sent to Nantes stopped here in 1646 on their way to open the hospital there. Otherwise, there is nothing to recall their presence here. Modern Saumur has a population of about 30,000.

# Poitou-Charentes

*Since the region of Poitou-Charentes is far from Paris, it did not have much connection with visits or ministry of the two founders, Vincent de Paul and Louise de Marillac. Before Vincent's call to found the Congregation of the Mission, he was the titular abbot of Saint Leonard de Chaume in Dompierre. The other sites in this region are principally associated with the work of the Vincentians and are especially noteworthy for the effects of the Revolution on the Congregation. (Poitiers, the capital of Poitou, is treated under Richelieu.)*

## ANGOULÊME

As often happened, the diocese of Angoulême received Vincentians in the founder's day to preach missions, beginning in 1634. The local clergy had previously had a good experience with a type of Tuesday Conference for priests and some retreats for ordinands. Consequently, the bishop invited Vincent to send priests for a seminary, but it was only with the expansion of the Congregation of the Mission into more seminaries after the founder's death that a permanent house in the city of Angoulême was founded. In 1704, Vincentians began a *seminary* and ran the parish of Saint Martial attached to it. This work continued until 1791. The seminary used a former Carmelite convent, although the building no longer stands. *(Boulevard Berthellot)* A new church dating from 1853 has replaced the former Saint Martial. Vincentians returned to serve in the major seminary from 1856 to 1903, when they were expelled from nearly all their houses in France. They returned again to serve from 1919 to 1959. Apart from a small relic of Saint Vincent, nothing in the church recalls the Congregation's service here. *(Rue de l'Eglise Saint Martial)* An important pilgrimage chapel, dating from the thirteenth century, was attached to the same parish. Notre Dame d'Obézine (also written Aubézine, even Bézines) drew so many pilgrims that the Vincentians undertook the building of a larger chapel, which served from 1732 to 1897. The present chapel was completed in 1929. *(Rue des Bézines and rue de Montmoreau)* Angoulême today num-bers about 43,000 inhabitants.

The fate of the community attached to the seminary and parish demonstrates what happened elsewhere at the Revolution. The superior was banished and went to Turin. One priest, Louis Janet, died of ill treatment aboard the "Washington," in the harbor of Rochefort, 10 September 1794. The other three priests were deported and probably died in exile. The brother, Jean Eloi Paris, was put on the "Washington" as well but was later released, only to be put back into prison, at age 68. His subsequent history is not known.

Commemorative cross,
Saint Leonard de Chaume

# DOMPIERRE-SUR-MER

Among the many murky areas in Vincent's early life is his being the abbot of *Saint Leonard de Chaume*, near La Rochelle. Indeed, the very name of the abbey has fallen out of local consciousness, and all that remains is a small settlement south of town on route D108, with perhaps a dozen houses, called collectively "the Abbey" (*L'Abbaye*). A sturdy stone cross stands on the site, bearing only the word PAX and the date 1610. The parish church of Saint Pierre, however, has a plaque commemorating the saint's presence in the parish.

In his desire to provide himself with an income, Vincent did what many other priests of his day were also doing. He became an *abbé*, that is, an absentee abbot of a non-existing community, with rights to the income but also with certain obligations. According to extant documents, the abbey was in ruins, apart from a couple of houses and walls. To fulfill his obligations, Vincent came here in 1610, performed all the required symbolic acts (visiting the ruins of the chapel, opening and closing some doors) and then dealt with the people living in his buildings. He also appointed a

Historical plaque, parish church, Dompierre-sur-Mer

procurator to handle the affairs of the abbey lands. Besides this property, Vincent also succeeded some feudal rights to the administration of justice. It is clear, however, that his tenure was not peaceful. Unable to satisfy his legal obligations, he became embroiled in lawsuits. Wisely, he got out of this affair by 1616. Perhaps reflecting on his experience, he said to his confreres in 1659: *Experience has taught many the difficulty of obtaining [benefices]. They have been cheated of their hopes, and are now objects of derision to the world. They are regarded as persons who have allowed themselves to be deceived, like children chasing butterflies, or, indeed, like those who wish, as they run, to capture their shadows. . . . Everything seems to be made of gold and silver, but, in reality, there is nothing but lead.* (Conference 219)

The modern town of Dompierre has fewer than 2000 inhabitants.

## LA ROCHELLE

In the late sixteenth century, the city of La Rochelle became a semi-independent Protestant stronghold. As a

Farm buildings, Saint Leonard de Chaume

result, its Catholic inhabitants gradually diminished in number. In a sermon on the catechism, delivered between 1613 and 1617, Vincent reflected on the impact of teaching the catechism in La Rochelle. *At La Rochelle there are about 1500 Catholics, and all the others are Protestants. These Catholics did not know what they believed in fifteen or sixteen years ago, until God sent them a good doctor who began to catechize the children. Little by little he did so well that, by the grace of God and by this little catechism, he made those people so good that I am ashamed of myself when I am with them and I see that they surpass me greatly in charity.* (Coste, 13, 29) Just what Vincent had been doing in La Rochelle remains to be determined, although it was probably because he was titular abbot of the Chaume abbey. The doctor may have been a friend of his. Louis XIII and Cardinal Richelieu both determined to reclaim La Rochelle politically and religiously, in part because of the city's strategic location on the Atlantic. The cardinal himself led the siege of La Rochelle (1627-1628), and the novelist Alexandre Dumas used this event as one of the settings for his novel *The Three Musketeers.*

After the crown recovered the city from the Huguenots, the government was able to bring about the erection of La Rochelle as a *diocese.* Vincent had a hand in this. As a member of the Council of Conscience, he proposed the bishop of Saintes, Jacques Raoul de La Guibourgère, for the new diocese. Vincent counted La Guibourgère as a friend and esteemed his abilities. The new diocese was constructed from the former diocese of Maillezais and from parts of the diocese of Saintes.

The bishop needed a cathedral, and the former Protestant church sufficed until it was accidentally destroyed by fire. The cathedral of **Saint Louis** began in 1742 but was completed after the Revolution and consecrated only in 1862. Its façade remains unfinished, and its interior furnishings date only from the nineteenth century. This church has a major window in the choir dedicated to Saint Vincent de Paul, shown with poor young children, as is typical of the nineteenth century. Whether this window takes its origin in Vincent's general care for the poor or in the presence of his confreres in La Rochelle is unknown.

The Jesuits had a royal college (a secondary school) and a seminary here beginning in 1629. When they were expelled in 1762, Vincentians were invited to replace them for the seminary, and they did so in the following year. They remained in charge of the *major seminary* from 1763 until 1790, when the Revolution suppressed all religious congregations. The seminary has been changed into a high school, the Lycée Dautet. The institution had extensive properties and gardens, located against the old ramparts, but some of the property has been sold off. *(Rue Dalayant)* Some buildings of the old Jesuit college remain, but only the chapel dates from before the Revolution. The familiar Jesuit coat-of-arms is still visible on the façade of this chapel. The institution is still in use as a collège. *(Rue du Collège)*

In the nineteenth century Vincentians returned to the seminary. It was refounded in a new location in 1851, and they remained there until 1903. This seminary originally incorporated elements from the church of Saint John, but this latter has completely disappeared. In addition, no sign of its former use remains on the façade of the present building. *(26, rue Saint Jean, now 6, rue de la Monnaie)* The Daughters of Charity opened a school here in 1831 and continued with other works of charity.

Another Vincentian connection is that in Vincent's time several of his confreres embarked here for the Madagascar mission. One of them, *Charles Nacquart* (d. 1651), left a description of how he and his fellow-missionary, *Nicolas Gondrée* (d. 1649), spent a month here in 1648. With the bishop's permission, they spent the morning in the hospitals and, during Easter week, served prisoners as best they could. (Letter 1179) Today, La Rochelle is a thriving city of around 75,000 persons.

## POITIERS

Although the ancient city of **Poitiers**, now with a population of about 80,000, did not have a Vincentian house in the time of the founder, his confreres from Richelieu were active in the diocese giving missions and ordination retreats. At length, in 1681, the bishop invited the Congregation of the Mission to assume the direction of the major seminary, which it continued until the Revolution. The buildings, many times rebuilt, still stand and today house the administrative offices of the Banque de France. *(Rue des Carmelites)* In 1710, the Vincentians began the minor seminary, Saint Charles. This building, too, remains, having been transformed first into a military barracks (1795-1945), and then into apartments. *(3, rue du 125e. de l'Infanterie)* One of its students, who later attended the major seminary, has been canonized (1933). André Hubert Fournet (1752-1834), a priest of the diocese of Poitiers, founded the Daughters of the Cross, known as the Sisters of Saint André. His collaborator in this work was Jeanne Élisabeth Bichier Des Ages (1773-1838), also canonized. A small street near the cathedral, Rue Saint Vincent de Paul, commemorates Vincent's presence here in his sons and daughters. Poitiers is a thriving city of some 80,000 residents.

## ROCHEFORT*

The river Charente runs to the sea through Rochefort. Although the city had a church from the eleventh century, Rochefort owes its religious and economic growth to the military port built here in the seventeenth century. The government also built a naval hospital here, probably because of its river, its seaside location and its hot springs. The buildings of the former naval hospital of Rochefort have been transformed into residential apartments. The city has a population of about 25,000.

In 1683, Vincentians were invited to open a special *seminary* here to prepare navy chaplains. The background for this choice appears to have been the seminary in Marseilles where Vincentians had been preparing chaplains for the royal galleys. The Rochefort

Monument to victims, Ile Madame

seminary for naval chaplains was one of three founded by the crown between 1683 and 1686. The other two, at Brest and Toulon, were confided by the king to the Jesuits after the Vincentians refused to take them. According to the contract of foundation, eight priests and four brothers would constitute the personnel of this new institution.

In 1687, the Vincentians next received the "royal parish" of *Saint Louis*. Located at the time outside the walls of the small town, the parish was erected for the Vincentians to better serve the arsenal, the ships and those living nearby. Ladies of Charity also served the poor in this parish in the pre-Revolutionary era. At the time of the Revolution, the Vincentians steadfastly

Mass grave, Ile Madame

refused to take the oath of *Liberty and Equality*. Only one was executed, Alexis Lucas, at Nantes (17 November 1793). He had fled to Vannes but was arrested. Their firm purpose contrasts with that of the Capuchins and other clergy in Rochefort, all of whom took the oath.

The Vincentian church buildings were then sold to profit the state. With the restoration of Catholic worship, the former Capuchin chapel of Saint Francis was rebuilt and took the name of the former Vincentian parish, Saint Louis. Of the previous church, the only remnant is the bell tower, now a signal tower, and a large room used at one time for fencing practice. Nothing in its present reconstruction and decoration, dating from 1835, speaks of the Vincentians or of Saint Vincent de Paul. *(Rue Toufaire)* One reason might be the conflict between the people and their Vincentian pastors, accused of concentrating too much on the sailors and too little on their other parishioners.

The Daughters of Charity served in Rochefort too. Beginning in 1673, they ministered in the town hospital serving the sailors and others. They also worked in a small hospital established in 1731 for the townsfolk, otherwise not admitted to the naval hospital. The grateful town named the civil hospital **Saint Charles** after the Vincentian Charles Jouvenon (1677-1741), "father of the poor," who began it. Its name lives on in the Rue de l'Hôpital Saint Charles on one side of the large general hospital that has replaced it. This small street runs into Rue Thiers, formerly the Rue Saint Jacques. The deaths of six young sisters who contracted a plague while serving the sailors in 1745 are still remembered.

The sisters also labored in the parish school, located on the Rue Saint Pierre. The more recent Maison de la Charité has been transformed into a part of another Catholic school. *(9, rue Victor Hugo)* During their service, they also kept an orphanage for the children of sailors and naval officers. *(19, rue Martrou)*

One unanticipated part of the Daughters' work was their ministry to the prisoners, whom the revolutionary tribunals were sending to Rochefort. The sisters put aside the habit and continued working as previously. The prisoners were mainly clergy and religious. Since there was no room in the prison in town, most of the prisoners were confined on floating hulks in the harbor. Many died during their imprisonment, since they were generally left to perish of diseases such as typhoid. The greater number were destined for execution elsewhere. Among those who died in the harbor were two Vincentians priests, *Jean Louis Janet* and *Nicolas Parisot*, imprisoned on the "Washington," a gruesome honor to the first president of the American nation. These two priests were in their thirties.

The sickest prisoners were put ashore on **Ile Madame** to be cared for in a crude hospital. Despite the somewhat more humane treatment they received, many died here. The dead, including Fathers Janet and Parisot, were buried in a mass grave. The gravesite is marked with local stones laid out in the shape of a cross. A plaque at the entry reads: "To

Saint Vivien parish, Saintes

the memory of the 829 priests and religious deported on the hulks of the Year II (1794)." A yearly pilgrimage originating in La Rochelle keeps alive the memory of these deportations of the clergy. A submersible causeway, accessible at low tide, connects the mainland with this island, now a vacation colony. People come here today to gather seafood, particularly oysters and mussels.

An important monument to the martyrs is at **Port-des-Barques**, where the land joins the causeway to Ile Madame. This monument, a tall obelisk flanked by statues of Saints Peter and Paul is part of a larger open-air shrine where mass is regularly celebrated. No names appear on these monuments, which state only that priests and religious perished here. Pope John Paul II beatified 64 of the priests (but not the two Vincentians) on 1 October 1995.

Also of historic interest at Port-des-Barques is a commemorative plaque and bust of Gilbert Du Motier, the *marquis of Lafayette* (1757-1834). He embarked from here on 10 March 1780 to go to America, where he served as an officer of the American revolutionary

forces. He then returned to France where he served the revolution as well.

After the revolutionary period, the Daughters of Charity were able to resume their habit and renew their vows. The Vincentians who had remained in hiding had left by 1793. Despite the tragic end of the Vincentian work at Rochefort-sur-Mer, their apostolate here was fruitful. It led to other establishments in the region: the mission house at Fontenay-le-Comte and the seminary at La Rochelle.

## SAINTES

Vincent opened a house in Saintes in 1644. Its purpose was the preaching of missions, as elsewhere. A seminary began at the same time, and several extant documents demonstrate how it was supported financially—principally through the income from various parishes. One of these was the church of *Saint Vivien* in the city of Saintes. This church today has no reminders of the work of Saint Vincent, although the old seminary was located beside it. Today, the seminary is used as a military barracks. Just behind this church is the Petit Rue du Séminaire, leading up to the old property.

In 1656, Louis Rivet, the anxious superior of Saintes, heard strange noises in his house every night. He thought that there might be ghosts and so informed Vincent. The latter analyzed the issue carefully and offered two avenues of investigation. First, he recalled that *certain individuals [at Saint Lazare] made strange, lugubrious sounds with their voices in order to frighten others.* Maybe they were up to no good, perhaps counterfeiting money in the basement. Second, however, if *you cannot give any other explanation, have recourse to the blessings of the Church, repeated if necessary*. Rivet might even try to have the bishop perform them. Vincent wisely suggested that the superior not become upset. (Letter 2140) The confreres continued their works at Saintes until 1791. What happened to the nightly visitors is a mystery.

In 1857, long after the Revolution, Vincentians resumed their work in the seminary. In that same year, they took charge of the ancient parish church of *Sainte Eutrope*. This eleventh-century church is still one of the glories of Saintes, although Huguenots damaged it considerably. The seminary eventually moved to another location but still exists. Street names mentioning the seminary lead to it. The Daughters of Charity also came to Saintes, beginning

in 1700. They returned in 1872 to undertake the care of orphans and other works of charity.

The last bishop of Saintes was Pierre Louis de La Rochefoudauld Bayers (1744-1792). Killed at the Carmelites in Paris during the September massacres, he was beatified 17 October 1926. Hundreds of others, including his brother, François Joseph (1736-1792), the bishop of Beauvais, and two Vincentians, Louis Joseph François and Henri Gruyer, perished at the same time. A special chapel is dedicated to Pierre Louis in the *cathedral*. Saintes lost its official status as a diocese in 1648 when it was partly absorbed by the new diocese of La Rochelle. The name of the diocese, however, carried on until the Revolution. The modern city of Saintes has a population of about 25,000.

# 5

# South

Saint Vincent de Paul parish, Pouy

# Aquitaine

Vincent de Paul, a native of the region of Aquitaine and the most famous son of the Landes, was ordained to the priesthood here for the diocese of Dax. Although he did not do much work in this region after the foundation of the Congregation of the Mission, he sent his confreres here. He continued to have friends here and to be interested in his native region throughout his life.

## AGEN

So far as is known, Vincent never came to Agen. He accepted a house here in 1650, however, to serve as a seminary, with the proviso that the Vincentians should to be able to understand the local Occitan language. Previous attempts at a seminary had been unsuccessful, and problems continued after the Vincentians arrived, mainly involving insufficient funds and a negligent bishop. Vincent had wanted to close the seminary, but his confreres remained until the Revolution. The *seminary* in Vincent's time had been at what is now called Place des Droits de l'Homme. These old buildings became the School of Commerce and Industry, lasting until at least the 1930s.

The diocesan seminary was then rebuilt elsewhere, and it continued in this new location until the Revolution. Afterwards it too continued in use as a school, now the Lycée J.B. de Baudre. The buildings have been converted to their new purpose. The chapel has been taken down, for example. (*Place Verdun, formerly Place du Grand Séminaire, on rue Maréchal de Lattre de Tassigny*)

Agen is also important in Vincentian life since it was the the see of the first Vincentian bishop, *François Hébert* (1651-1728). He had been the superior of the house in Versailles when, on 6 April 1704, at age 53, he was ordained by the archbishop of Paris. Vincent had considered others of his confreres as possible bishops in mission areas, such as Lambert Aux Couteaux, but Hébert's selection so worried the then superior general, Edme Jolly, that he asked that it

not be repeated. He reasoned that it seemed not in keeping with Vincentian ideals. It was not until the Revolution that another French Vincentian was consecrated a bishop. Undoubtedly because Hébert was the spiritual director of Madame de Maintenon, a Lady of Charity and later wife of Louis XIV, the king hoped he would be elected superior general. When that did not happen, he proposed him to the pope for this diocese. Hébert's memoirs, published only in 1927, shed an interesting light on Versailles, particularly its religious life. He died in Agen.

Among the Vincentians at the Agen seminary at the time of the Revolution were two who took the constitutional oaths. *Antoine Labarthe* (1740-1820) was elected constitutional bishop of Lot-et-Garonne (the new designation for Agen). He quickly refused the office and later retracted his oath. He survived the Revolution and continued as a parish priest. The other, *Antoine Cautenet* (1761-1796) took all the oaths and then abandoned the priesthood during the Terror. He soon fled to Spain, however, and died in Barcelona. After the Revolution, until about 1810, at least two Vincentians served the seminary until the Congregation could get reestablished.

Daughters of Charity came to Agen in 1686 where they worked in the hospital and ran a school. Following the Revolution, they returned to the school in 1836 and took up the hospital again in 1885, and they continue their work here today. In 1733 one of the Daughters reportedly was cured from various ail-

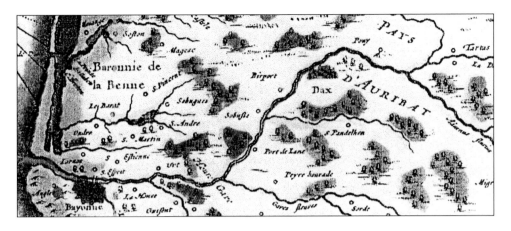

Seventeenth century map of the region around Dax

ments by the Water of Saint Vincent. This sacramental involved drinking or otherwise using water blessed with a relic of the saint. The same results were reported from waters blessed in honor of other saints. Today's Agen is a city of about 30,000 inhabitants.

## BERCEAU-DE-SAINT-VINCENT-DE-PAUL✸✸✸

*Vincent de Paul was born in the Landes of Gascony, in the diocese of Dax. The term "Gascony" refers to that region of southwestern France that extends from the Garonne river south to the Pyrenees, and "Landes" refers to a part of Gascony that is relatively flat and generally not fertile. It is interesting to note that, because of the closeness of Gascony with the French Basque region, the names "Gascony" and "Basque" have the same origin (gascon in early French – vasco in Latin - basco in the local dialect).*

*Because of the abundant material concerning the birthplace and other loca-tions associated with Vincent, this text is divided into the following sections: I. The De Paul family, II. The Berceau (his birthplace), III. Pouy (the local town), IV. The countryside where he lived and worked, V. Buglose and Gourbera, VI. Dax (where he attended school), and VII. Sites in the Dax region.*

### I. The De Paul Family

What did the name **De Paul** mean? In many parts of France the particle "de" is a sign of some noble origin. In Gascony, however, the particle "de" meant nothing other than joining the given name of an individual to the name of his or her house. A person was named after a saint at baptism and, since several persons often bore the same name, it was customary to follow it with the name of the house where they lived or the property that they farmed, using the particles "de" "du" or "de la" between the two. With the passage of time the names thus

283

joined became family names. In the religious records at Pouy, all the inhabitants in the seventeenth century, even the humblest, had "de" or "du" before their name. Vincent always signed his name as Depaul, in one word, a practice followed sometimes even by nobility for their own names. Beginning as early as 1628, Louise and others began to call him Monsieur Vincent, never Monsieur Depaul. In addition he always spelled his first name in the Gascon fashion, with a final s: Vincens, not Vincent, with a final t.

We can presume that the name "De Paul" had this kind of origin. However, the earliest registers, from the cathedral chapter of Dax, record the name Paul (in the forms de Paul, or even Pol) from as early as the 1400s. This offers a solution to the meaning of "Paul." This name has nothing to do with Saint Paul the apostle nor with Latin paulus *("little, small")* but rather with *palo* (Latin *palus*, a marsh) It seems to be a southern version of a common French family name, *de Marais* ("from the marsh"). It is common enough, also, in northern Spain, in the form Paúl. Which marsh is meant? This is harder to define, but half way between the Berceau and Buglose runs a stream called "Pont de Paul," and near the shrine of Buglose is a house called "Paul". Distant ancestors of his may have lived in that house or on the banks of the marshy stream. Hence that name might have passed to their descendants. Some members of the De Paul family still live in Pouy, and others with the same name, spelled Depaul, live in the surrounding area. Nevertheless, there were De Pauls in Pouy from at least 1509, one of them being named Vincence.

The family of *Vincent's father*, Jean de Paul, numbered several important rural officials: Jean de Paul (1545), a royal sergeant; another Jean de Paul (1564), a canon of Dax; and Etienne de Paul (1577), prior of Pouymartet at Gourbera, seven or eight kilometers north of Pouy. The family of *Vincent's mother*, Bertrande de Moras, was also of some importance. She had several lawyers and clergy in her family, people with important posts in Dax, Bordeaux and elsewhere. Besides, her family was related to the more important ones in the area: particularly to the Saint Martin and Comet families—names occurring in Vincent's biographies. A cousin, Dominique Dusin, was the pastor of Pouy with whom Vincent lodged when he returned in 1624 to visit his family.

The date of *Vincent's birth* has aroused lively discussion. Abelly, his first biographer, gave it as Easter Tuesday of

Descendants of the DePaul family,
20th century photograph

1576. Easter Tuesday of that year was 24 April. Vincent's own testimony, however, is different. Depending on what weight one gives to various citations, he was born either in 1580 or 1581. As to the day and month, his birthday could have been 24 April, however, which Abelly converted to Easter Tuesday. If not, Easter Tuesday of 1580 was 5 April, the feast of Saint Vincent Ferrer, Vincent's second patron; and the same day in 1581 was 28 March. Vincent himself said his birthday fell in April, but no one seems to have celebrated it in his lifetime and not until the nineteenth or twentieth century. Baptismal and civil records, in addition, have disappeared and so cannot resolve the case. Consequently, the exact day, month and year are still open to question. Scholars point to his ordination date in 1600 at age 19 or 20 as the reason why Abelly's collaborators presumed that Vincent must have been the proper canonical age of at least 24. Whether they changed his birth year to conceal this problem, or did so without knowing all the facts, is also unknown.

*Vincent's brothers* were: Jean de Paul, who lived at Lachine (Leschine), a nearby property, larger than his father's place; Bernard; Dominique (also familiarly called Menjon and Gayon); *his sisters* were: Marie, called Mengine; and another Marie, called Claudine, married to a man named Gregoire.

## II. The Berceau***

The Berceau-de-Saint-Vincent-de-Paul is officially part of the commune of Saint-Vincent-de-Paul. In the Berceau *(cradle)* is the farmhouse called *Ranquines*, perhaps from the Gascon term *ranqueja*, to limp. The name may recall the fact that Vincent's father limped, but it seems unlikely, the confusion coming from the fact that the property on which it stands is also called Ranquines. Vincent was born here, not in this same building but in an earlier one on the same site. He often described his father as a *pauvre laboureur*, meaning not a simple "laborer" or farm worker in English, but an owner of property who was able to work it. In this the De Paul family differed from many others who did not own land. The term *pauvre* here referred not to his poverty, which would be *laboureur pauvre*, but to his condition in having to work for a living. He once wrote: *it must be said that I am the son of a peasant [laboureur], and that I pastured swine and cows.* (Letter 1372) Although the family owned the property of Ranquines, they owed some feudal taxes, as Vincent recalled in later life, to the duke of Ventadour, who was also the marquis of Pouy. Vincent himself inherited land from his father, as he testified in an early will written in 1626.

Only 22 years after the death of Vincent did the question arise of the house where he was born. Guillaume Lostalot (b. 1660), a native of Dax, wrote to his confrere Melchior Molenchon (b. 1653), speaking of Bernard de Paul, Vincent's grandnephew. "He wrote me that the house of Monsieur Vincent fell to the ground, but that the room where he was born has been preserved intact." Another witness wrote that in 1682, when the house fell over, a cross was placed over the ruins.

On 14 February 1706, the ecclesiastical judge of Dax received in the presence of Father de Cès, who knew the area, four testimonies given under oath in preparation for the beatification and canonization of their countryman. Each one has its own interest, even now, and several are worth mention.

The first testimony came from Louis de Paul, grandnephew of the saint and owner of the Ranquines property. He was 66 years old, a farmer, and declared that: "Monsieur Vincent, [his relative], had never given anything to his relatives to bring them out of their poverty. I heard it said that when Monsieur Vincent was young, he gave away his clothes and a part of his bread to the poor. Monsieur Loustalot, pastor of the parish, had a cross placed over the site of the house where the late Monsieur Vincent was born to preserve the memory of his person, for whom he had a special devotion. I have seen several people cutting and carrying away bits of the wood from this cross because of their esteem for Monsieur Vincent... The room where Monsieur Vincent was born remained standing a long time after the rest of the house fell down and, since the room had been nearly ruined, Monsieur Loustalot had a small chapel built there where he placed an image of the Blessed Virgin. He had a picture of Monsieur Vincent painted kneeling before it. Many individuals, even the processions which go to Our Lady of Buglose, stop there to pray to God, to show the veneration which they have for the memory of Monsieur Vincent." It should be remarked, however, that this grand-nephew was not well informed about Vincent's help. His official will, dating from 1630, bequeathed land and money to his family and to their children.

The fourth testimony came from Pierre de Pasquau Darose, inhabitant of Pouy, 70 years old, a master carpenter. He said: "By order of Monsieur de Loustalot, pastor of Pouy, I myself made the cross and built the chapel which are at present on the place of the house where Monsieur Vincent was born. People come to cut off bits of wood from the cross and to pray to God, in this way showing their veneration for the memory of Monsieur Vincent."

Two traditions about the location of the family house exist. The older one, probably the more accurate, places it under the nave of the present large chapel. The more recent tradition separated the chapel from the house, and thus dictated the house's placement. In any case, the entire site is holy.

In its first *position* the present house was by the side of the road, turned toward it, facing east. The land on which the house stood was purchased only in 1841 to become part of the present Berceau property. In 1864 the house was shifted a little closer to the chapel, with the result that only a small part of the two placements remains the same. Also, it was then turned to face north for reasons of symmetry.

The current *six-room house* and loft, 12 by 8.5 meters in size, is a typical house of a Gascon landowner, with its exposed wooden joists and compressed earth floor. The marks of the original

Postcard, Ranquines,
about 1920, Berceau

reeds left their imprint on the bricks that dried on them and, on the inside, only posts and joists were in evidence. In fact, even though this house was not the one that Vincent knew, it is certainly quite similar to it. It evokes him near the very place of his birth. Some of the old beams may have come from the De Paul house. The first crossbeam at the entry, however, has the date 1744 carved in it, coming from one of its reconstructions. Since the *outer* walls were unstable and frequently repaired, they have been filled with brick and plastered over. The house had a kitchen (the main room) with a fireplace, rooms for the eldest son, the parents, Vincent and his brothers, the daughters, and a lean-to, now the oratory. Above is an empty loft. In an earlier time the front section of the loft was used to store hay, brought in through an opening in the front; and the rear held grains. In addition, the original house was another 1.5 meters wide on the west side—a space for animals and tools.

Below an old altar in the boys' room are preserved some relics and other reminders of the saint: a pair of his shoes, a standing crucifix (marked LA CROIX DE NOSTRE R. P. VINCENT DE PAUL), a white linen cloth used to bandage his legs, a fragment of a horse-hair belt used as an instrument of penance, a red or violet stole said to have been used by him at Folleville, and two small physical relics. All these items came from the original Saint Lazare and were given to the Berceau by Father Jean Baptiste Étienne, superior general of the Congregation. A copy of a letter written to Vincent's mother, 17 February 1610, recalls that she most probably received it here. The furnishings of the house are not original.

The place where Vincent's birth is commemorated is now found under the sloping roof in the back of the house, where people come to pray and often to celebrate the eucharist. Because the positioning of the house has been changed, this spot is where the second room on the left, the parents' bedroom, was originally located.

The kind of *countryside* that Vincent lived in during his childhood was not the extensive pine forest of the Landes that one sees today, since it did not exist in the sixteenth and seventeenth centuries. The forest was planted in the nineteenth century to inhibit the spread of wind-blown sands from the Atlantic shore. Formerly, the Landes were very sandy and easily became marshy. The area of Pouy is located in a bend of the river Adour, still an area somewhat sandy, which often has flooded pastures. This area, more than any other, resembles the land as it was in Vincent's day.

The family certainly owned what

every small landowner had in the region: a farmyard for cows, pigs and sheep. The Ranquines property was very small, only 30 by 34 meters, but enough for a house, garden and one or more outbuildings. North of the property where the large chapel now stands was a commons, used by the family and their neighbors. Following the usage of the small pastures of olden times, Vincent used to walk along the dusty paths, perhaps using the stilts typical of the Landes, his eyes fixed on the animals confided to his care, and carrying his provisions in a sack. It is not certain that he returned home every evening. There were few large stretches of pasture, and so he would have had to go looking for the more fertile land.

The De Paul **diet** differed markedly from that followed today. There were no potatoes, tomatoes, corn, even beans, since these originated in the New World and were only then being gradually brought into Spain. Instead, his family ate the local produce: carrots, turnips, broad beans, lentils, and even millet, at the time an important grain. In general, eating meat was not common. They would also have had access to birds (ducks, geese, pigeons, etc.) and their eggs, fish, and small animals, such as rabbits. Wine and cider were in current use as drinks. Milk was normally served only to babies, and water was often unsafe. Vincent recounted years later to the Daughters of Charity how the people of the Landes would eat: They are very plain in their eating. The majority are often content with bread and soup... In the region where I come from, we eat a small grain called millet, which we cook in a pot. At mealtime, it is poured into a bowl, and the family gathers around to eat, and afterward, they go out to work. (Conference 13) I am the son of a tiller of the soil. I was fed as country people are fed and now that I am Superior of the Mission, shall I grow conceited and wish to be treated like a gentleman? (Conference 85) He also recalled that the use of cider (instead of wine) was common in the region and good for the health.

All his life Vincent showed the qualities typical of peasants: good sense, patience, confidence in Providence, hard work, and modesty. Like Jesus himself, Vincent was born among humble workers, and always demonstrated love for the poor, the little ones.

The first accounts of *veneration* for Vincent in his native area date from 1706 and come from his relatives. Louis Depaul, a farmer at Pouy and owner of Ranquines (mentioned above) and Jean Depaul, another grandnephew, aged 74, lived at Saint-Paul-lès-Dax. He testified, perhaps with some sourness: "I have heard it said by my father that he went to meet Monsieur Vincent while he lived in Paris, to ask his advice about a promise of marriage he had made to a girl whom he had abused. Monsieur Vincent told him that he was obliged to go and marry her. And he gave my father on his return only 10 écus and a letter for Monsieur de Saint Martin. Monsieur Vincent never gave us anything to help lift us out of the low condition in which we were living." Perhaps referring to the same period, Vincent himself admitted to his confreres that some of his relatives were forced to live on alms (Conference 148, 1656) *and still do.* (Conference 204, 1659) This condition might easily have been caused by the problems of the Fronde. During this time, some of Vincent's friends helped them, as he did himself. In any case, Jean Depaul, mentioned previously, was badly informed about his grand-uncle, Vincent.

Vincent also made a *family visit*, most likely in 1624. He recalled it in a conference to the missionaries on 2 May 1659: *I fear, thought I, becoming in like manner attached to my relatives. And that is what happened. I spent eight or ten days with them to instruct them in the ways of their salvation and detach them from the desire of possessing riches, so far as to tell them that they had nothing to expect from me, and that even if I had chests of gold and silver, I would give them nothing, because an ecclesiastic who possesses anything owes it to God and the poor. On the day of my departure I felt so much grief at leaving my poor relatives that I did nothing but weep, and weep almost unceasingly all along the road. To these tears succeeded the thought of giving them assistance, and putting them in a better condition, of giving this to one and that to another. In my mind, deeply moved as I was, I portioned out to them in this manner what I possessed, and what I did not possess. I say this to my shame. And I say it because it may be that God has permitted this to make me more sensibly perceive the importance of the Evangelical maxim of which we speak. For three months I was worried by this troublesome passion of advancing the fortunes of my brothers and sisters. It was the constant burden of my poor mind. However, when I found myself somewhat free, I prayed to God to be pleased to deliver me from this temptation, and I prayed to Him so earnestly that, in the end, He had pity on me and delivered me from those tender affections for my relatives.* (Conference 204)

He perhaps referred to the same

Postcard, oak tree and
seminary, Berceau

Ranquines and 19th century
oak tree, Berceau

event in Letter 1481: *When parting time comes, there is nothing but sorrow and tears, and what is worse, the servants of God are often left with nothing but distractions. Their minds are full of images and sentiments very little in harmony with their state, and they sometimes lose the attachment they had for their spiritual exercises.* It should be noted, however, that Vincent made a will three years after his visit, and disposed of his property in and around Dax by giving it all to his family. (Coste 13, Document 27)

Besides this visit, he also sent his confreres to give *missions* in the area. At least one is known from the year 1652.

The great *oak tree*, called *Lou Bielh Cassou* (the old oak) in Gascon, is centuries old. The fall of one of its huge branches in 1939 allowed a piece of its wood to be sent for analysis to Bordeaux. The conclusions of specialists showed a planting date of between 1200 and 1230. Young Vincent certainly rested in its shade, although it was not part of the family property, since the road passed it on either side. The oak is one of several ancient trees preserved in the Landes.

At the Revolution, agitators tried to burn it. The tree's worst enemies, however, have been indiscreet pilgrims who took away bits of the bark as a souvenir of the saint. We have such important witnesses as the duchess of Berry and the duchess of Angoulême. Even a spiritual son of Saint Vincent, Blessed Frédéric Ozanam, wrote about events of 2-3 December 1852: *I send you, my dear friend, a leaf from a blessed tree. It will dry out in the book where you leave it, but charity will never wither in your heart... I saw in it a symbol of the foundations of Saint Vincent de Paul. They never seem held to the earth by anything human, and nevertheless have been triumphing for centuries and growing amid revolutions.* The pastor of the place had an entire branch cut down for the founder of the Society of Saint Vincent de Paul, destined for the General Council of that society. The Vincentians at Buglose gave a cross and rosary to Pius IX in 1856, using wood from the tree. Such treatment clearly compromised the future of the oak. In earlier days a retired soldier was stationed to guard it. Protective enclosures were built in 1824 and 1857. In recent years a barrier has been built around it and the tree reinforced with iron rings and cement plugs. It measures about 12 1/2 meters (38 feet) in circumference.

In 1868 the oak was believed to be dying, especially since someone had set a fire in it in 1865 to rid it of hornets. Fortunately, the son (*Lou Hilh* in Gascon) is vigorous. This sprout, planted in 1857, is taller than its parent and shades Ranquines. Some acorns have also been taken away and in many countries other descendants of the oak are flourishing.

In 1951 it was decided to make a selection of the best acorns. Experts performed what was called the "marriage of the oak," since they placed a huge white veil over the tree to assure that the tree would have acorns of a pure type. Ceremonies with music and dancing accompanied the event, but, mysteriously, that year, for the first and last time, not a single acorn appeared on the entire tree.

It is certain that, as they are today, oak trees were part of the countryside familiar to Vincent the young boy. Calvet wrote in his biography of the saint: *Around each house a clump of oaks developed. They were protection against the west wind, a shelter for pigs that fed on the acorns, shade in the summer, and a noble decoration in any season.* The account of Vincent placing a small statue of Mary in a fold of the trunk and then praying there, is legendary, dating only from the nineteenth century.

In 1706, a small chapel had been built next to the house. Then, to respond to the increasing devotion of the faithful after Vincent's beatification in 1727, another *chapel* opened in 1730, probably built on the site of his birthplace. Blessed at the end of 1751, it lasted for exactly a century. At that time it gave way to the present chapel, built on the same site. On 6 August 1851, the first stone was laid in the presence of the prefect of the Landes, and the bishop celebrated mass under the old oak. The chapel itself was loosely modeled on the Val de Grâce in Paris. Progress in building was slow because of a lack of funds. Contributions from the Vincentians and the Daughters of Charity, together with a national lottery, allowed work to continue. A barely legible inscription over the main door recalls its inauguration thirteen years after it began: ANNO DOMINI MDCCCLXIV DIE XXIV MENSIS APRILIS HOC SACELLUM D.O.M. FUIT SOLEMNITER DEDICATUM IN MEMORIAM ORTUS S. VINCENTII A PAULO ("On 24 April in the year of Our Lord 1864 this chapel was solemnly dedicated to God in memory of the birthplace of Saint Vincent de Paul"). The architect was initially Jacques Ignace Hittorff, who had had designed the great parish church of Saint Vincent in Paris. His elaborate plans were simplified by a disciple, Gallois, the architect of the Vincentian motherhouse chapel in Paris.

Over the main door of the chapel is a carving of young Vincent aiding a poor man. The inscription reads QUIS PUTAS PUER ISTE ERIT ("Who do you think this boy will be?"), a citation from

Postcard, chapel, Berceau

Chapel, Berceau

Luke 1:66. Above the door is a large statue of the saint similar to that in the Vincentian motherhouse. It shows him in a gesture of openhanded charity. Below are figures of faith, hope and charity, dated 1864. The text, PERTRANSIIT BENEFACIENDO ("He went about doing good"), is a citation from Acts 10:38. The sculptures are the work of M. Forget, a Parisian artist.

On 14-15 July 1947, a great *fire* broke out, destroying several buildings. Among them, the chapel burned and its dome collapsed. Because of the energy of two Vincentian priests, Fathers Pierre and Descamps, and the work of Nazi prisoners of war, it reopened 1 December 1948. A modern painting of Saint Vincent in heaven, with angels, now fills the dome. Various outdoor plaques honor former students of the Berceau who served in the second World War and Indochina as well as the many more who died in the first World War.

Thanks also to the generosity of many donors, especially followers of Vincent, the chapel has taken on new life. The most recent altar, built of Bordeaux limestone, was consecrated 27 November 1980 by the bishop of Aire and Dax.

In 1980 Victor Feltrin of Paris carved a strong wooden statue of Saint Vincent. The same artist did a matching statue of Mary the following year. The inside decoration is relatively sober. The letters SV, either intertwined or separated, are nearly the only specifically Vincentian element in stone. The stained glass windows, dating from 1864, closely copy those in the Vincentian motherhouse, depicting incidents in his life and after his death. The central window behind the main altar depicts Vincent escorted by angels into glory. The transept windows, in the shape of a fan, recall his presumed birth date, 24 April 1576, and the dedication of the chapel, 23 April 1864.

A plaque in the right transept reads: "To the memory of the priests and brothers of the Congregation of the Mission and of the Daughters of Charity of the Berceau of Saint Vincent de Paul, who dedicated themselves to children and youth from 1864 to our days. Their Grateful Students." The first Vincentians and Daughters at the Berceau repose in a crypt under the chapel.

The small organ—one manual, seven stops—was the work of the famous builder Cavaillé-Coll. Jean Baptiste Étienne paid for it personally from his family inheritance, and it was installed in 1873. In 1998, it was renewed and enlarged.

The *mission of the Berceau* was developed early in the nineteenth century under the inspiration of the prefect of the Landes and the bishop of Aire and

Postcard, seminary, Berceau

Dax. It perpetuates the memory of the saint in his birthplace. At the beginning, it was decided to have all his major works represented here. The first to open was a house for elderly bereft of resources, and for poor orphans. The elderly would receive proper care, and the orphans would receive education and training. The Vincentians and Daughters of Charity were to assume charge of the work under the responsibility of a board. Frédéric Ozanam spoke enthusiastically of the project, and Napoleon III authorized a national lottery to help accomplish it. The work began in 1864 and received civil recognition the next year. The emperor had assigned a military architect to design the buildings, which explains their style, reminiscent of nineteenth-century military barracks from the Paris region. A modern Catholic school adjacent to the old buildings continues the primary and secondary schools begun in the nineteenth century. Its first student was one André Depaul, a distant relative of Vincent.

The hospice became a retirement center and has gradually been modernized. One of the wings admits aged sisters. The active sisters work in the retirement center and bring care to the homes of the needy.

After the other constructions, the Vincentians had a minor seminary built in 1868. It also received émigré Spanish Vincentians in 1869 during a revolution and French Vincentian students during the wars of 1870 and 1939. This seminary graduated some 350 members of the Congregation of the Mission, including seven missionary bishops. The

Saint Vincent de Paul parish, Pouy

chapel, built in 1934, has several striking stained glass windows, particularly one of Saint John Gabriel Perboyre. After 1971, the building became a diocesan "collège" (a residential secondary school). The priests no longer have responsibility for it but continue as its chaplains. They do typical Vincentian works and, with the sisters, receive pilgrims through the work of the Vincentian Center, located in two buildings across the road from Ranquines. These are arranged for groups and present exhibits.

### III. Pouy/Saint Vincent De Paul**

The old name of the village, Pouy, is related to Latin *podium* or platform, marking an elevated area. The elevation of the village can easily be seen below

Sign, Saint-Vincent-de-Paul

Parish church, 19th century
photograph, Pouy

from the banks of the Adour. There are several other places in France called Pouy, or, more usually, Puy. (Vincent spelled it Poy in Letter 992.) In those cases, the name refers to local volcanic hills. Vincent's Pouy was the center of a rural community, but it was also the seat of an important barony, with rights to dispense justice. One of the judges of Pouy was Monsieur de Comet, who had a home at Préchacq, about five kilometers east of Pouy. The judge received Vincent, his young relative, into his home in Dax as tutor for his children.

King Charles X approved the *change of name* from Pouy to Saint-Vincent-de-Paul on 3 December 1828. To honor its most famous son, the inhabitants of the village had requested the name change, and they changed the title of the patron of the parish to Saint Vincent de Paul at the same time. The name Pouy still persists in some ways, however. (Another village called *Saint-Vincent-de-Paul*, a few kilometers north of Bordeaux, has no apparent connection with the saint. The history of its naming is obscure.)

The old *village church*, dedicated to

Saint Vincent de Xaintes,
parish church, Pouy

294

Vincent de Paul at the plow,
church window, Pouy

Saint Peter in Chains where Vincent and his family worshipped, was demolished in 1913 after severe damage from lightning the previous year. The baptismal font, a copper bowl set into a carved stone base, comes from that church and is still in use. A marble plaque records Vincent's baptism there. He received the name Vincent ("the victorious") perhaps because one of his godparents had that name, or more probably out of devotion to Saint Vincent of Xaintes, a martyr, the first bishop of Dax and principal patron saint of the diocese. During his 1624 visit to his home after moving to Paris, he renewed his baptismal vows in that church. Also, Vincent's biographer Abelly noted that he recalled his baptismal anniversary regularly and publicly asked pardon of the community on that day for his faults. The date commonly given is 24 April 1581. Vincent most probably made his first communion in this same church. On 15 August 1628, he also acted as godfather in this church to a nephew, also called Vincent de Paul. The modern church seen today was completed in 1924. Vincentians from Buglose were pastors here as well, from 1706 to 1792, and again from 1955 to about 1997.

The modern stained-glass windows narrate events in the life of Vincent: (1) praying; (2) giving money to a beggar; (3) plowing with oxen; (4) celebrating his first mass; (5) blessing poor men; (6) teaching; (7) ransoming captives [a symbolic depiction]; (8) sending out missionaries; (9) with a child [based on the statue by Alexandre Falguière]; (10) taking on the chains of a galley convict;

Typical house of Landes with
oak trees, near Pouy

(11) with a bishop and priests; (12) with Ladies and Daughters of Charity; (13) presenting plans for a church; (14) with the pope [a symbolic depiction of the approval of the Congregation]; (15) at the deathbed of Louis XIII; (16) his deathbed; (17) taken up in glory. Antoine Fiat, Vincentian superior general, with the mother general of the time, Marie Maurice, donated the elaborate Stations of the Cross. (A marble plaque recalls this donation.)

The church has preserved the old wooden panels taken from the high altar of the previous building, the altar Vincent knew. They are: (1) Jesus giving the keys to Peter (recalling the previous dedication to Peter in Chains); (2) the tabernacle and four side panels with scenes from the life of Saint Peter; (3) Saint Paul, with the sword of the spirit (Eph 6:7); (4) a saint-bishop, probably Vincent of Xaintes; (5) God the Father with a globe; and (6) a statue base with the head of an angel. These are placed in the right side altar chapel and above the main door. The large main crucifix also comes from the old church, but it appears to be later than the seventeenth century.

Vincent's parents were undoubtedly buried in the old *cemetery* east of the church, but no trace remains of their graves, probably because of the frequent floods of the Adour. Several Vincentians and Daughters of Charity are buried in simple graves marked by crosses in the new cemetery begun in 1846.

The *De Moras house*, located to the west of the former presbytery, was probably the "town" house belonging to Vincent's mother's family. The name de Moras is widespread in the Landes, with such forms as Morar, Moras, Mauras,

Landscape in forest of
Landes, near Pouy

Demoras, Dumoras, with and without an *s*. His mother's family belonged to the local nobility, and many of his relatives on both sides of the family had held, and would later hold, important positions in the Church and in the state.

The modern post office is on the site of the home of the saint's sister, where she moved after her marriage to Monsieur Gregoire. The house was named "Paillole," and the site kept that name until the building of the post office in 1930.

The property called *Leschine*, part of Vincent's inheritance, is located north of Pouy facing Route N 124. Its name, however, lives on only in official docu-ments, not on the modern buildings themselves. A small portion of the same road has been renamed Route de Monsieur Vincent.

## IV. The Countryside

The *Holy Wood* is a two-hectare area of imposing old oaks located on the banks of the Adour river, on the road from Yzosse. Local tradition claims that the young Vincent forded the river here (there was no bridge until 1897) to pasture his animals. This is impossible to prove, but this oak grove is typical of the area. In the saint's time, the village carefully maintained an extensive oak forest. Many other oak groves still exist near the

Grain mill, Pouy

Common lands, Barthes, Pouy

Grain mill, 19th century
engraving, Pouy

banks of the Adour.

The name *Barthes* designates the marshy bottomland on the banks of the river Adour. The river Adour rises in the Pyrenees and enters the Atlantic just north of Biarritz. The Barthes is common land, flooded twice a year, and various animals graze on it. During the winter, when the river rises, one can easily form an impression of how the entire area looked in the time of the saint's boyhood.

A tradition recounted at the canonical inquiry leading to Vincent's beatification has it that he brought to a local *mill* the grain that his parents had gathered. It would be ground and served as nourishment for the family and their animals. The pious young Vincent, according to what he said about himself, once gave some of his family's grain to a poor man whom he met on the way. On one occasion, he is even said to have given all his meager savings to a poor beggar. These two charitable events became part of the standard series of pictures detailing his life.

Today one can see a remaining mill, on private property on the N 124 east of Pouy. It is no longer in working condition, being unnecessary in modern times. The millstream runs out of the pond, mentioned below. It is not clear if the young man came here or to one of several other mills in the region.

### V. Buglose,** Gourbeba

On the busy route D27 leading to the shrine of Buglose is a small oratory, *Our Lady of the Brier*. From the year 1622 the faithful had begun making pilgrimages to Buglose. Beginning in 1803 the pastor of Saint-Paul-lès-Dax, Father Lesbazeilles, erected a series of Stations of the Cross along the road. These stations disappeared over time, but the remaining one led to the construction of a small oratory. In 1876 Eugène Boré, superior general, had it restored to mark the presumed tercentenary of the saint's birth. The statue of Mary placed here copies that of the Miraculous Medal. In 1947 the oratory and its grounds were repaired. In 1974 the little shrine was again completely renovated. Since brier *(bruyère)* grew there in the sandy soil, the title Notre Dame de Bruyère (Our Lady

Our Lady of the Brier,
near Buglose

of the Brier, or Heather) was given to the oratory in that year.

The creek running to the Pouy mill takes its various names from the properties through which it flows. At the place where the road to Buglose crosses it, it is called the *De Paul Creek*. The bridge is an old stone construction, visible at least from its west side. The creek runs into a pond *(Étang de la Glacière)*. It seems possible that the young De Paul children came here to swim or fish. The pond has been developed into a public park. Its outlet, called the Mill Stream, runs into the old rural mill mentioned above.

Street sign, De Paul quarter, Buglose

De Paul house, Buglose

Our Lady of Buglose,
church window, Tilh

In the village of Buglose are an old home and a series of apartments called the *Quartier de Paul*. The building on the east side, located at present behind the Hôtel des Pèlerins, is called Paul. It has been proposed that the creek and the house gave its name to the family. Since the name Paul is so old in the Dax area,

Vincent's mass at Buglose,
church window, Buglose

shrine, as his biographer Collet relates, Vincent came here on pilgrimage. He walked barefoot from the Pouy church, celebrated mass at Buglose, and shared a meal with his family on the day before his departure. Vincent, however, did not mention this visit in his own recollections of this visit home, dated probably to the spring of 1624.

The present church (finished in 1864) has the rank of minor basilica. It houses the old pilgrimage statue of the Virgin Mary and the child Jesus. She is seated, crowned, holding the child in her lap. The child, in turn, is smiling, his hand held up in the traditional gesture of a pontifical blessing. It is said that a poor peasant found the statue as he was plowing. His attention was drawn to it because one of his oxen was licking it clean of the mud that covered it. The heavy stone statue, probably a gift from

Vincentians, seminarians
and poor men, Buglose

however, this supposition seems unlikely. Nevertheless, it shows that the name is widespread in the region.

*Our Lady of Buglose* is a pilgrimage site of the Landes dating from the beginning of the seventeenth century. It was not here during Vincent's childhood. A chapel was built here in 1622, which the bishop dedicated on 16 May of that year. After giving a mission for the galley convicts in Bordeaux, Vincent returned to see his family (his mother probably had died before this time). During that visit, and shortly after the dedication of the

the bishop to Pontonx, a neighboring parish, around 1500, had reportedly been hidden at the time of the wars of religion, about 1570. The legend states that the people named the site "ox tongue," Buglose (although Vincent himself spelled it Burglosse in Letter 992). Instead, the name seems of Basque origin, and refers to a plant known in French as "ox tongue." Pierre Coste recounts great doubt cast on certain aspects of the story. In any case, Vincent came here. A plaque and a window in the church, showing him saying mass, recall his visit. The text below the window reads: "How Saint Vincent de Paul prayed before the statue of Our Lady of Buglose." Windows elsewhere preserve the story of Vincent coming here as a boy to pray at the ruins of the church allegedly destroyed by Huguenots. In fact, there is no evidence for this presumed destruction. It is almost certain that there was no church here before 1620—only a small shrine, perhaps, similar to Our Lady of the Brier.

The church building has recently been restored, and is known for its large carillon of 60 bells, blessed in 1895.

Statues of four angels crown the square bell tower. Inside are tombs of the local bishops, as well as commemorative plaques from priests ordained here. Noteworthy, too, are two early woodcarvings placed in the left-side chapel. These show the Vincentians (with diocesan seminarians or priests—known from their typical French collar—and two poor men), and Daughters and Ladies of Charity (with poor children). They are important, that of the missionaries is one of the oldest known depictions of Vincentians. They adorned the altar dedicated to Saint Vincent in the previous church. The elaborate Renaissance pulpit likewise comes from that building. In the right-side chapel are two other polychrome carvings, depicting Mary Magdalene in the grotto of La-Sainte-Baume, near Marseilles, where she is said to have received communion from an angel.

Behind the church is the *Chapel of Miracles*. This old chapel marks the original pilgrimage site. A plaque behind the chapel, now incorporated into a large outdoor shrine, completed in 1960, reads: "In 1623 [=1624] in this chapel

Postcard, outdoor Buglose shrine

Postcard, Vincentian house
and Buglose church

Saint Vincent de Paul came to pray with his family." Near the chapel is a small spring with the two following notices: "Here from 1570 to 1620 was hidden the statue of O[ur] L[ady], which is found in the basilica." "Miraculous spring of Our Lady of Buglose." A large statue of Saint Vincent is found nearby, as is the Synod Cross, a large wooden cross placed there in 1993 to recall the synod held for the diocese of Aire and Dax.

In 1647 the bishop of Dax asked Vincent to send missionaries here. He was unable to do so, but his successor sent some in 1706. To the left of the main entrance of the basilica is the large old *community house* where the Vincentians lived during many years of service at Buglose. They gave missions in surrounding dioceses, and retreats to clergy and laity in this house, known locally as "the monastery," until the Revolution. Since they were the pastors of Pouy and cared for the chapel at the Berceau, the devotion of the Buglose Vincentians for their founder encour-

Mill, Pouymartet

aged veneration for Vincent de Paul at Pouy. For their support, they purchased the barony of Pouy in 1715. Their community house, which the bishop recovered after its confiscation during the Revolution, is still in use as a pilgrim center and a residence for the diocesan priests who now staff the shrine. Buglose, like the Berceau, is part of the commune of Saint-Vincent-de-Paul.

West of Buglose lies the small village of **Gourbera**, with some 200 inhabitants. Near here are the remains of the mill of **Pouymartet**. Close by are scattered remains of a brick building. This is believed to have been the priory of Pouymartet that formerly undertook the care of poor and sick pilgrims on their way to the Spanish shrine of Santiago de Compostela. Etienne de Paul, a likely relative of Vincent's, was its prior, and may have been instrumental in teaching Vincent the basics of his education before he went to Dax. It has been suggested that this relative resided there,

Typical home, Gourbera

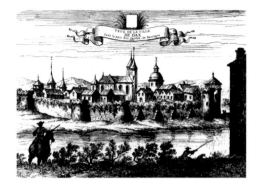

Engraving, 17th century, Dax

and that the young Vincent walked from Ranquines through the fields for lessons with him. Since the mission of this priory was to care for the poor and the sick, Vincent may have received a taste for this kind of service here. The Pouymartet hospital continued in use until the late eighteenth century. There is no proof, however, of Vincent's presence here.

## VI. Dax**

Dax, where Vincent attended school after learning the rudiments, was a *walled town*. Some of its ramparts remain today, built on foundations from the ancient Romans who first built them in the fourth century. That these walls still stand testifies to the vigilance of its inhabitants, who kept Dax virtually free of the various phases of the religious wars during the sixteenth century. Vincent and his schoolmates certainly walked over them. One of the town gates is named Porte Saint Vincens, not after Vincent de Paul but after Vincent of Xaintes, the town's first bishop. An ancient thermal spring, the Fontaine Chaude, called Nèhe after the Celtic goddess of water sources, gave the city its name (*ad aquas* - d'Acqs - Dax).

Dax today, with nearly 20,000 inhabitants, is still famous for its many *thermal springs* treating rheumatism and other disorders. It is the second most popular thermal town in France, after Vichy. These springs attracted the Roman emperor Augustus Caesar, his daughter Julia Augusta, as well as countless others. The Musée de Borda, named after a local scientist and benefactor of the Congregation of the Mission, has a collection of local prehistoric and his-

Seventeenth century map of Dax, Pouy

Comet home, Dax

toric relics and displays Roman ruins visible under nearby buildings. The city bullring demonstrates the area's close ties with Spain, since Dax was an important junction for merchants and travelers using the passes of the Pyrenees, as well as an important river port. The ancient bridge from Vincent's time exists no longer, carried off in 1770 by a huge flood. A second bridge was added in 1970 to relieve the increasing traffic.

In Dax, on the site where the post office and police station are now located, was a Franciscan friary. These religious had a *collège* to receive boarding students, who paid about 60 livres a year. The students included boys from the country whose parents wanted to assure

a secondary education. Vincent came there at age twelve and probably spent four years living first with the Franciscans and then with M. de Comet, while attending classes at the municipal school adjacent to the friary. We know one incident from those years that he related to his confreres in a conference on obedience, 19 December 1659: *I remember that when I was a young boy my father brought me with him into town. Because he was badly clothed and limped a little, I was ashamed of walking with him and of admitting that he was my father.* He recounted a similar story to Madame de Lamoignon: *I remember that once, at the school where I was a student, someone came to tell me that my father, a poor peasant, was asking to see me. I refused to go to speak with him. In this I committed a great sin.* (Coste, Life, 1, 14)

At 17, rue des Fusillés is the family *home of Monsieur de Comet*. This has been recently restored and on the outside bears a plaque, dedicated in 1960, recalling the presence of the young Vincent here. Monsieur de Comet was an attorney at Dax and judge of Pouy, and related by marriage to Vincent. He lodged him in his home and confided to him the education of his children, while also giving him time for his studies. Monsieur de Comet served at the courts, still located a few doors north of the home, although now in newer buildings. Young Monsieur Depaul also knew the old bishop's residence, now the city hall. At 27, rue Cazade lived his cousins Saint Martin. In 1658 one of these cousins discovered Vincent's intriguing letter relating his Tunisian captivity. He had written the letter to this man's father-in-law more than fifty years previously.

The old Gothic cathedral of *Sainte Marie*, dating from the fourteenth century, fell into ruins and was taken down in 1638-1643. In Vincent's time, the bishop worked to rebuild it, and Vincent was able to get Louis XIV to donate a large sum to help with construction. Rebuilding started in 1644, but the church was consecrated only in 1755. In 1894, when the façade and towers were completed, the Portal of the Apostles, the main (west) door from the previous cathedral, was installed inside in a transept. The present cathedral has some nineteenth-century souvenirs (statue, windows, painting) of Saint Vincent de Paul, as well as some other remnants of the cathedral that Vincent knew, such as a few choir stalls in the right transept. Remarkably, one of the canons of the cathedral proposed a special chapel to be set aside in Vincent's honor supposing that he would one day be beatified; this happened during the founder's lifetime.

The *Hospital of Saint Eutrope*, where the Daughters came in 1712, also

Vincent and peasant of Gannes, seminary chapel, Dax

has Vincentian connections in that Sister Marguerite Rutan (b. 1736), its superior, was accused of anti-Revolutionary activities. (*Now Hôpital Thermal, rue Labadie*) This Daughter of Charity was imprisoned in the **Carmelite convent** with other religious (*11, rue des Carmes*) and then received a show trial in the former bishop's residence. That same day, 9 April 1794, she was paraded in a cart through the city to the place of execution. A condemned priest was tied back to back to her during this spectacle. They were guillotined in the square by the castle, now replaced by the Hôtel Splendid. Her burial place has never been identified. The cause for her beatification was introduced in 1931, but it has not progressed.

An ancient *monastery* enclosed the tomb of Saint Vincent of Xaintes. A new church, built in 1893, replaces it. It also displays remains from the Gallo-Roman period. Vincent regarded Vincent of Xaintes as his patron and honored him on 1 September, his feast. (Another namesake, Saint Vincent Ferrer, he regarded as secondary patron, keeping his feast as well.) The location of Xaintes

Postcard, Notre Dame du Pouy seminary, Dax

is unknown; it may have been the city of Saintes or even the part of present-day Dax where the bishop was martyred.

After the Revolution, in 1799, several individual Vincentians returned to the diocese and put themselves at the disposition of the bishop. But only much later did they receive a home with a chapel, dedicated to the Immaculate Conception, and inaugurated as *Our Lady of the Pouy* in Dax on 21 November 1845. In 1880 a newer building was finished. For many years it was the major seminary and/or novitiate for the Congregation in France. The building still stands, and the chapel can be visited. Of the original small chapel, only the area around the present altar remains. The present chapel holds many memories for Vincentians from other parts of the world as well as France, since so many studied and were ordained here. During the last years of the seminary's presence, paintings in Byzantine style were completed in one of the transepts and in the back of the chapel, where they symbolically represent the episode of the peasant at Gannes, among others. The superior of the time had wished that the artist, Nicolas Greschny, would cover the church with these paintings, but events overtook his plans. The chapel includes tombs of the Borda family, the former owners of the property.

Saint Jean Gabriel Perboyre was honored here, and the stained glass windows recall him as well as Saints Francis Regis Clet and Louise de Marillac.

The building, apart from the chapel and library, now serves as a hotel for

De Paul family grave, Pontonx-sur-l'Adour

guests taking the thermal cure. Adjoining the property, further up the hill—the *pouy* from which the seminary took its name—is the present retirement home for Vincentians of the Toulouse province. Fronting the home is Rue des Lazaristes, while on the side is the Rue du Père Perboyre.

A small community of Christianized Jews of Portuguese and Spanish origin (Marranos) existed in Dax in Vincent's period. Interestingly, almost nothing is recorded in Vincent's correspondence or biographies concerning his observations on contemporary Jews.

### VII. Sites in the Region of Dax

The places in this section are divided into those roughly north and/or east of Dax, still in the Landes; and those south of Dax, called the Chalosse, leading into the foothills of the Pyrenees mountains.

**Pontonx-sur-l'Adour** is a town north and east of Buglose, with about 2000 inhabitants. Its church, dating only from the nineteenth century, contains a statue, painting and window in honor of the saint. Of general interest is the old communal laundry. This still has in place the sloping antique stones before which the women of the village would crouch to wash their clothing. In the town cemetery are grave markers for the Depaul family (descended from the saint's brother), and the Mora (Moras) family, related to his mother. It has been suggested that the saint's mother took her name from a hamlet, **Moras**, in the small village of **Sainte-Eulalie-en-Born**,

some 70 kilometers north and west of Pouy. Without documentation, this is difficult to prove.

About 20 kilometers northeast of Dax is the town of **Tartas**, the birthplace of Pierre Coste (1873-1935). He entered the Berceau at age eight, as an orphan. He later edited the correspondence of his countryman Vincent and wrote the most comprehensive modern biography of the saint. Tartas numbers some 3000 people.

A few kilometers farther east is the little village of **Cauna**, population 400. The duchess of Ventadour, mentioned above, was marquise of Pouy, Téthieu, Buglose and Cauna, among other places

Priest's residence, Tilh

Street sign, Saint-Paul-lès-Dax

in the Landes. In her will, dated 1634, she left Vincent a sum of money to found a mission house in Cauna. He never made the foundation, however, since he could not acquire the promised funds.

Closer to Dax is *Téthieu*, a village of perhaps 500 people. Its church of Saint Laurence, located near the old Pouy mill, has a modern window showing Saint Vincent as, among other things, a shepherd. A side altar and its traditional painting show local veneration of the saint. This parish is now joined with that of Pouy.

The town of **Saint-Paul-lès-Dax** is built where the Roman aqueduct of the Aquae Tarbellicae, an early name for Dax, began. The apse of the present parish church dates from the eleventh or twelfth century, having outlived the ancient church buildings in Dax. Its exterior has rich carvings on columns, depicting such figures as mythological beasts, acrobats, lions and birds. These probably come from Spanish sculptors. There are several carved panels on the outside of the apse. Vincent knew this town, as he and his family had property

in the area, but there is no monument to him in the church. The church building is also interesting in that the old tower keeps the traditional shape in use in Pouy in the saint's time. Its population today numbers about 10,000 people. A large boulevard, named after Saint Vincent, keeps his memory alive.

About 25 kilometers southeast of Dax is the town of **Tilh.**\* A Basque influence is evident in the town: the bullring, the *fronton* (handball court), and some local family names. This parish, Saint Pierre, in the hilly area south of the see city was where, probably in 1598, his protector, M. de Comet had put forth the name of the future Father de Paul. He would need this pastorate, or canonical title, to assure his advancement to ordination. Plaques inside and outside the church recall his appointment, although he was never able to exercise his ministry here. Above the exterior

Commemorative plaque,
parish church, Tilh

plaque, installed in 1960, is a bronze profile of Vincent, with a line in Gascon. It preserves the traditional pronunciation of Vincent's name and the final *s* that he used in his signature: LOU BOUN MOUSSU BINCENS [The Good Monsieur Vincent]. A Father S. Soubé (Sansoubé, Soubès, perhaps even Saint-Loubès) appealed Vincent's appointment in Rome, and the new priest had to abandon his claim. It was perhaps at that time that Vincent traveled to Rome, probably for the Holy Year of 1600. As such, his non-appointment was a providential turning point in his life. Tilh today numbers about 800 people.

To the east of the Berceau in the hilly Chalosse area is the town of **Amou**, population 1500. A native of Amou, Bertrand Ducournau (1614-1677), was destined to become Vincent's personal secretary. As a child Ducournau traveled on pilgrimage to Buglose. After his education, he worked in Saint-Jean-de-Luz, on the Atlantic coast, and then in Bayonne. There he met Louis Abelly, at the time vicar general of the bishop. He also met Jean Duvergier de Hauranne, later known as the abbé of Saint Cyran,

Château of Montgaillard, Orthevielle

the great promoter of Jansenism. A native of Bayonne, Duvergier urged Bertrand to enter religious life, which he did after a retreat at Saint Lazare in Paris. He died at Saint Lazare. The town of Amou has commemorated its prominent son by naming a street in his honor, designating his family home, and identifying the font in the parish church where he was baptized.

In the village of **Orthevielle**, north of the Gave, is the chateau of Montgaillard. Vincent is believed to have pastured his animals in this area, probably coming from his mother's family farm **Peyroux**, located just north on D6. A local tradition says that the future saint learned to read and write here. Vincent told the bishop of Saint-Pons, Persin de Montgaillard, whose family came from the area: *I knew it well. I kept flocks when I was young, and I used to lead them out there.* (Collet, II, 195) The sixteenth-century church, a fortified building with small windows, has an unusual old statue of Saint Vincent, more Spanish than French, and a window depicting Our Lady of Buglose.

De Moras family home, Peyroux

Abbey buildings, Arthous

museum of prehistory and early artifacts discovered through archaeological research.

One of the abbots of Arthous was Salvat Diharse (1576-1648), himself of Basque ancestry, and whose family castle was located at nearby Labastide-Clairence. He was a commendatory abbot, only in minor orders, but he drew revenues from the lands. He could not live here because the monastery was in ruins. His uncle and namesake was the bishop of Tarbes and would ordain Vincent to subdiaconate and diaconate there. The younger Diharse would, in turn, succeed his uncle as bishop of Tarbes.

Farther south, and approaching the Basque country, is the small town of **Bidache**\*, with a population of around 1000 people, which, together with Arthous, was in the diocese of Dax in Vincent's day. In the parish church of Saint James the Greater, the young Vincent received tonsure as well as the four minor orders from Bishop Diharse, the elder (d. 1603), on the same day, 20 December 1596, the Friday of Ember Week. The bishop, perhaps a relative of Vincent's mother, or at least a family friend, had been a member of the chapter at Bidache. He possibly chose this collegiate church since it was near Peyroux and near his own diocese. Vincent received minor orders in Bidache and not in Dax since his home diocese had no bishop at the time. The present church, however, built in 1880, stands on the site of the earlier one.

A side altar, with a window depicting his tonsure at the hands of the bish-

Otherwise, nothing else recalls the saint's presence here. One Vincentian connection dates from 1799, when Antoine Célières (b. 1730), became pastor. The last Vincentian superior at Buglose, he had fled to Spain at the Revolution but returned when the bishop offered him the post. Just below the church is an old communal washing shed *(lavoir)*, recently restored. Orthevielle has about 750 inhabitants.

South of the Gave is the old Norbertine abbey of **Arthous**. Founded about 1160, it suffered over the centuries from wars and invasions. It was located here to take advantage of good farmland and it was, moreover, on a pilgrimage route to Compostela. Nevertheless, Arthous suffered because of its location on the frontier between Spanish and French domains and was ruined in 1571 because of the wars of religion. Louis XIII helped to restore it, but it was suppressed at the Revolution. The present buildings, now state property, have been extensively restored, and their rich architectural details are especially interesting, such as the sculpted capitals showing the capital sins. The buildings also house a

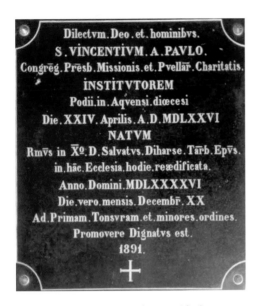

Commemorative plaque, Bidache

dows do not mention, however, that the saint was about fifteen years old at the time and took tonsure and minor orders to be qualified to begin his theological studies. Vincent chose Toulouse since it was the nearest university with a theological faculty. In about 1880 the present church, however, replaced the one on the same site where Vincent was ordained. It has been suggested that, because of the Spanish Basque character of the area, he first went from here to Zaragoza in Spain for his theological studies. From Spain he then went to Toulouse, according to this theory.

Facing the church a short distance north is the ruined *chateau* of the dukes

op, has two commemorative plaques (in French and Latin). The first reads: "Bishop Salvat Diharse, bishop of Tarbes, deigned to promote to first tonsure and minor orders in this church, today reconstructed, on 20 December 1596, Saint Vincent de Paul, beloved of God and man, founder of the Congregation of the Priests of the Mission and of the Daughters of Charity, born in Pouy, in the diocese of Dax, 24 April 1576." The second reads: "This altar and this window have been given to the parish of Bidache by Father Antoine Fiat, superior general of the priests of the Mission, and Madame [*sic*] Havard, superioress of the Daughters of Charity, as a witness of their filial devotion to Saint Vincent de Paul, their illustrious and glorious founder, on the feast of Saint Vincent, 19 July 1891." The win-

Château, Bidache

Château, Bidache

of Gramont. Duke Antoine II had proposed the younger Diharse as bishop but retained some rights to receiving income from his diocese, a situation that left the young bishop poor and insecure, and having to rely on the duke. This nobleman was able to do so since his small duchy was somewhat independent of the French crown, and Bidache was his principal fortress. His relative independence—he was styled "sovereign of Bidache," in addition to several other noble titles—also had the effect of allowing Jews expelled from Spain and Portugal to settle here. Their synagogue was in use until the Revolution. The old cemetery has maintained some headstones with bilingual inscriptions in Hebrew and Portuguese. The dukes of Gramont from the period after the Revolution are interred in the crypt of the parish church.

Although not directly connected with Vincent de Paul, the Basque town of **Espelette** (Ezpeleta) is of interest as the birthplace of *Jean Pierre Armand David* (1826-1900). In 1862, shortly after his ordination, this young confrere of a scientific bent was sent to China, and made

observations (insects, plants, birds, fish, etc.) for various interested parties in France. The Museum of Natural History in Paris supported several of his expeditions to Mongolia, Szechwan and Tibet, and Central China. David's name has been given to several of his discoveries, in particular "Père David's deer." His is noted, in particular, as the first European to have seen and described the Giant Panda, in 1869. The World Wildlife Fund erected a commemorative plaque on his birthplace *(355, karrika Naguisia)*, now a private residence. His parish church preserves many features of Basque style. The David family tomb is visible in the parish cemetery. In nearby **Hasparren** a

Jewish tombstone, Bidache

Bilingual road sign, Espelette

Catholic school bears his name (*Lycée Agricole Armand David*).

South of Dax, guarding a bridge on the Gave de Pau River, is **Orthez**. This was an ancient capital of Béarn, an old province of the kingdom of Navarre. Orthez began to develop in the thirteenth century. As happened with Pau, its larger neighbor, its citizens took to Protestantism in the sixteenth century and treated Catholics harshly. The old bridge, situated high above a rocky bank, was the scene of several battles between the two groups, and many lost their lives as they plunged off this bridge into the swift waters below. Protestants still live and worship in the area. Jeanne d'Albret, queen of Navarre, founded a Protestant university here in the sixteenth century, and the renowned Theodore Beza (1519-1605) taught here. Vincent's idyllic existence at the Berceau must have been affected by the memory of so much violence in this area. The Daughters of Charity had a public hospital and a school here from 1767 until the Revolution. Today, Orthez, with its pop-ulation of about 10,000, is also known for its wine production.

**Pau**, like Orthez, guards a river crossing over the Gave, its great castle recalling the kingdom of Navarre and its rulers. Pau was the hometown of Henri IV, whose mother, Jeanne d'Albret, was the daughter of Marguerite d'Angoulême, the sister of François I, king of France. Henri inherited his mother's Protestantism and his granduncle's lineage. He was thus a claimant for the throne of France when the male Valois line was extinguished with the death of Henri III. Jeanne d'Albret imposed a rigid observance of the reformed faith and led a fierce persecution against Catholicism in her realm. Churches were "reformed," that is, purified of religious pictures and statutes, and many priests

Armand David home, Espelette

313

Cathedral, Tarbes

the Pyrenees, Pau today has some 82,000 inhabitants.

In the small cathedral of **Tarbes**,* Notre Dame de la Sède, the same Bishop Salvat Diharse (or d'Yharse), the elder, ordained Vincent to subdiaconate and diaconate during the required Ember Days in September and the following December. The Society of Saint Vincent de Paul donated a plaque to the cathedral: "Saint Vincent de Paul was ordained subdeacon, 19 September 1598, and deacon, 19 December 1598, in the cathedral of Tarbes by Bishop Diharse, bishop of the diocese. Erected 21 April 1912." This bishop ordained Vincent since his own diocese was vacant at the time, the new bishop not having received

Commemorative plaque, cathedral, Tarbes

were imprisoned or executed. As at Orthez, the continuing Protestant-Catholic struggles here surely influenced Vincent's early years and outlook.

From 1686 to 1790, the Congregation of the Mission served in the *diocesan seminary* of Pau. Perhaps because the institution burned down accidentally in 1731, little information exists about its history. The founder was the duchess of Gramont, the same family mentioned above concerning Bidache. Daughters of Charity also had several works here, the most noteworthy being the hospital that they served from 1688. They were expelled at the Revolution but were so missed that the authorities invited them back in 1793. The Sisters developed many other works here in the course of the next century. Esteemed for its fine climate and spectacular views of episcopal ordination. The Tarbes cathedral today does not have the same decoration as it did in the saint's time, since it had to be repaired several times after Huguenot attacks. The altar and its furnishings date from the eighteenth century. Troops were guarding the building from attack at the time of his ordination and remained until 1613. Daughters of Charity came to Tarbes sometime before 1792 and then returned in 1803 to work in the hospital, located a few steps away from the cathedral. They continue their work, but in another location. A statue of Saint Vincent adorns the façade. (*Hôpital de l'Ayguerote, Placeta de l'Espitau*) Tarbes today has about 48,000 inhabitants.

## BÉTHARRAM

For some centuries a pilgrimage *shrine* at Bétharram had honored the Virgin Mary. According to one account dating from the sixteenth century, a young girl of the neighborhood was about to fall into the rushing waters of the river Gave, in the Pyrenees. She recounted that Mary extended a beautiful branch (*bet arram*) to pull her out. To recognize this event, the bishop repaired an old chapel in 1614. In 1616, a large cross was erected on the hilltop above the little shrine chapel. Damaged in a storm, it was seen to reerect itself, and the shrine became known as Our Lady of Calvary. Bétharram rapidly became a center of pilgrimage, attracting crowds of the blind and the lame. A congregation of priests, called Our Lady of Calvary, was founded to minister here beginning in 1621.

In 1659 the founder of the Calvarians with the bishop of Lescar, the local diocese, invited Vincent to send missionaries here, perhaps on the model of what he had done at the shrine of La Rose some years previously. Vincent described Bétharram as *a place of great devotion, and if it is not the second, it is at least the third most frequented shrine in the kingdom.* (Letter 2877) Vincent wrote of the miracles that occurred. Although he appointed a superior, Vincent saw several problems with the proposal. Nothing came of it in the end because the bishop's response went astray, and perhaps also because Vincent's health was declining and death was impending. There is nothing especially Vincentian about the shrine today, which has incorporated some of the elements of the seventeenth or eighteenth century church in its construction. It is now a part of Lestelle Bétharram, a town of fewer than 1000 people. Bétharram is also known for its large caves and grottoes.

A saint associated with Bétharram is *Michael Garicoïts* (1797-1863), founder of the priests of the Sacred Heart of Jesus of Bétharram. He taught at the major seminary then at Bétharram and, when it was moved to Bayonne, he stayed here and attracted others to live with him to undertake works of evangelization and education. His tomb is in the Bétharram shrine. He was greatly influenced by Vincentian spirituality. Garicoïts was canonized in 1947 together with Jeanne Élisabeth Bichier Des Ages (1773-1838), a foundress who had helped him in his works and profited from his counsel.

Widow at prayer, 17th century wall painting, Notre Dame de Garaison

Procession, 17th century wall painting, Notre Dame de Garaison

Another saint, a pilgrim to Bétharram in her early years, was Bernadette Soubirous (1844-1879) from neighboring **Lourdes**, on the banks of the same Gave. She came here often with her mother or members of her family, particularly a few days before her own experiences at Lourdes began.

As to the great shrine of Lourdes today, catering to the million or more who come on pilgrimage, there is not much of a Vincentian character. In recognition of his being one of the great saints of France, Saint Vincent is represented by a large statue at the left along the great ramps leading to the upper basilica. At the time of her first visions at the grotto (1858), Bernadette, a member of the Children of Mary, was wearing a Miraculous Medal, which by then had been widely distributed in France and elsewhere. The city also remembers Vincent in a Rue Saint Vincent de Paul.

Lourdes has more than 16,000 full-time residents today. It might be noted that this area of the Pyrenees is known for other earlier shrines to the Blessed Virgin Mary in honor of visions at vari-ous periods: Notre Dame de Médoux at Asté, Notre Dame de Mouillan at Moutoussé, and Notre Dame de Garaison at Monlong.

The shrine of **Notre Dame de Garaison** was staffed by Pierre Geoffroy, who founded a community here about 1608. Its purpose was the reform of the clergy and the preaching of missions in the country areas. In addition, members of his community came to Bétharram to staff it beginning in 1615. The church at Garaison preserves extraordinary wall paintings from the end of the seventeenth century. They depict mainly healing miracles, and show people in their daily occupations. After the Revolution, this shrine was restored, and another congregation of priests continued the ministry of the previous congregation. These Missionaries of the Immaculate Conception were the first to develop the shrine at Lourdes. Today, despite some efforts to demolish Garaison, it continues to function together with Bétharram, and reflects very well the life and activities of Vincent's period.

Many of these shrines are associated, as well, with miraculous springs and continue to draw numerous pilgrims.

## BORDEAUX

The city of Bordeaux is the capital of the ancient province of Aquitaine, where Christianity was introduced as early as the fourth century. Part of the murky history of the young Vincent is the story of a visit he made here in 1605 for some purpose today unknown. Abelly wondered whether it might not have concerned the offer of a bishopric by the duke of Epernon, uncle of two of Vincent's pupils at Buzet-sur-Tarn. In any case, Vincent never mentioned it afterwards.

Vincent also came to Bordeaux to give a mission for the personnel of the *galleys*, meaning the convicts, sailors and officers. Galleys had been brought here in 1622 to prepare for a siege of La Rochelle, which took place the following year. Since this was still in the period before the foundation of the Congregation, Vincent, as the chaplain general of the galleys, turned to other clergy and religious, such as the Jesuits, to help with this work. After his visit to Bordeaux, dated 1624, he took the advice of two of his friends and visited his family at Pouy. This was his well-known visit home.

He also sent missionaries to the diocese in 1634, an occasion blessed with success. At some unknown period, a conference of clergy was established in the diocese, on the model of the Tuesday Conferences in Paris. Daughters of Charity came here in 1690 and worked in parish schools and hospitals. At the Revolution the sisters were maltreated and assaulted by crowds in the city. Some were forced to work at paving the city streets. Even though they put aside the habit to appear in public in approved dress, they were recognized and often ridiculed and insulted. They returned following the Revolution and stayed until the expulsions of 1905. They have resumed several works here.

Despite Vincent's contacts here, it is not known how he came to know *Jean de Fonteneil* (1605-1679), a priest of the diocese. This priest, a Bordeaux native, became a friend and imitator of his. Fonteneil's excellent qualities contributed to his rise in the Church. Among other things he became dean of the Bordeaux cathedral and vicar general of the archdiocese. An extensive correspondence between him and Vincent has been preserved. Fonteneil also showed himself helpful to the Congregation as well as to the Daughters of Charity in their various works, and he assisted Vincent's relatives. He founded a community of priests, the Congregation of the Clergy, to give missions and retreats, and to form the clergy, but this group survived him by only three years.

On Fonteneil's death and, with the dissolution of his community, the Congregation of the Mission inherited all the properties, rights and duties of the Congregation of the Clergy. Among the obligations was the *diocesan seminary*. It came to the Congregation of the Mission in 1682. At the beginning the seminarians lived and studied in two houses next to the parish church of Saint Siméon, where Fonteneil had been pas-

Saint Siméon church, Bordeaux

tor, and which the seminarians used for their religious exercises. This church, no longer in use, remains standing, and its name lives on in the street, Rue Saint Siméon. This seminary was later enlarged and moved to another location. The new institution opened in 1739 and continued until the Revolution. It is no longer standing. *(Corner Rue Judaïque and Rue du Palais Gallien)*

Among the Fonteneil properties was the renowned **Haut-Brion**. Fonteneil had received this land in 1650, and the Vincentians, in turn, held it from 1682 until the Revolution. The missionaries used it first as a country house for the Bordeaux seminarians but gradually improved the vines until the vineyard developed an excellent reputation, particularly as mass and table wine for bishops. The Vincentians also built a small chapel here for their own use; it still stands, although no longer used for worship. At the Revolution the property was sold to benefit the state. The vineyard, however, retains the name of the congregation: Château la Mission Haut-Brion. Its wine is highly prized. *(Cours de*

*Maréchal Galliéni, Talence)*

The seminary staff also had charge of the pilgrimage chapel of **Notre Dame de Montuzet**. This is located on route D135 between Bec d'Ambès and Blaye, and is a hamlet now called **Montuzet-lès-Arnauds**, part of **Plassac**. It, too, was inherited from Fonteneil's community, some of whose members retired here. Becoming a separate house in 1708, it served as a retirement home for elderly Vincentians from 1737. Nothing remains of the chapel and house today, apart from an ancient stone cross standing in front of the old site. Overlooking the river Gironde and set at the edge of a vineyard, however, is an elevated statue of Our Lady. The statue and site are not otherwise identified.

Stone from Saint Lazare, La Mission Haut-Brion, Talence

Entry, Château la Mission, Talence

Also of Vincentian interest is that the founders of the Vincentian mission in the **United States**, Fathers Felix De Andreis, Joseph Rosati, Joseph Acquaroni, Brother Martin Blanka along with several other non-Vincentians stayed in Bordeaux preparing to embark

Bishop's castle, Château-l'Évêque

for America. Their visit lasted from 1 February to 13 June 1816. A total of thirteen made that voyage.

Bordeaux is now a city of more than 210,000 inhabitants.

## CHÂTEAU-L'ÉVÊQUE***

As would make sense, the town of Château-l'Évêque is named after the fortress and residence of the bishops of Périgueux, ten kilometers to the south. It has borne this name officially, however, only since 1831. The bishops used this fort-residence from the fourteenth century to the Revolution. Its importance

Postcard, Château-l'Évêque

came from its location at a significant point in the Beauronne valley water system. The chateau underwent major repairs in the fifteenth and sixteenth centuries. In the sixteenth century, Protestant (Huguenot) forces often attacked it. In fact they succeeded in assassinating the bishop of Périgueux in 1575. The castle is now in private hands.

Next to the chateau is the parish church of Saint Julian. Since the name Julian, a patron of sick travelers, was often was attached to hospices for travelers, it can be presumed that this chapel

**319**

was originally used for pilgrims and travelers. It has since been incorporated as a side chapel in the small parish church. It keeps its original orientation, facing away from the present main altar.

Thanks to the efforts of Father Jean Baptiste Étienne, the parish church was restored beginning in 1874. The windows (dated 1887) in the nave present original themes from Vincent's life. The first two depict "Saint Vincent de Paul in the Landes," and "The family of Saint Vincent de Paul." The second set shows the "Entry of Saint Vincent de Paul in Chateau l'Eveque," and "Saint Vincent de Paul at Buzet," where he had a small school. These windows, however, depict the Berceau as it was in the nineteenth century, full of young pine trees. Instead, in Vincent's time, it was less wooded. Another large window in the side chapel compares the life of Vincent with that of Joseph: the death of Joseph and the death of Vincent; Jesus at work with Joseph, and Vincent helping a poor man, and holding an infant; the marriage of Mary and Joseph, and the ordination of Vincent. A small altar has some reliefs portraying his ordination, teaching and first mass. A plaque recalls his ordination there, as do copies in Latin and French of his ordination document.

The remains of the early chapel consist principally in the two pilasters at the edge of the sanctuary (the three double Gothic columns are nineteenth century), and the stones in the floor of the sanctuary. Above the sanctuary was an attic, in an area now demolished. It was there among old papers that a copy of the saint's ordination record was found in the nineteenth century.

Several questions have arisen concerning Vincent's *priestly ordination*. Why did he obtain written permission (dimissorial letters) from the diocese of Dax but not use the permission for more than a year? Also, why was he ordained by François de Bourdeille, the bishop of Périgueux, and not by his own bishop of Dax, to whose diocese he belonged until the foundation of the Congregation of the Mission? No one knows the answer to these questions. Vincent's delay may reflect his hesitation to submit to ordination in a diocese whose relatively new bishop, Jacques Du Sault (1570-1623), was something of a reformer. However,

Vincent, flocks and parents,
church window, Château-l'Évêque

Original chapel, Château-l'Évêque

Vincent in Château-l'Évêque, Vincent
teaching, church window, Château-l'Évêque

ordained someone, he would probably
have had some difficulty in ordaining a
man of nineteen or twenty (even though
Vincent's dimissorial letter repeated the
standard formula that he was of "legitimate age"), and who would not finish
his theological studies for another four
years. However, since his bishop had
been chaplain for Queen Marguerite de
Valois in Paris, he may have had a hand
in nominating his young priest, Father
Depaul, to the same position. This may
demonstrate that the bishop had no
problem with him. In any case, François
de Bourdeille was not a bad bishop. He
had been active in reorganizing his dio-

Historical reconstruction,
Château-l'Évêque

the young newly-arrived bishop was in
conflict with the canons of the cathedral
(1600-1604), and could not ordain anyone there. Besides, even if he could have

321

Ordination, plaque in parish church,
Château-l'Évêque

cese, holding synods, etc. He died 24 October 1600.

Another possibility is that Bishop de Bourdeille had helped Vincent financially in his studies, and he, in return, helped to educate Bourdeille's nephews at his school in Buzet. This, at least, was the tradition among the bishop's relatives, recounted as late as the mid-nineteenth century.

Why was Vincent ordained here and not in Saint Étienne cathedral in Périgueux? First, the Huguenots still held power in Périgueux and it would have been difficult for the elderly bishop to travel. Second, in any case, the bishop no longer lived in Périgueux (since his residence had been destroyed), and he had no usable cathedral (since the Protestants had partially demolished it).

Where exactly was he ordained? The bishop called the chapel his "church" in the official ordination document, as does the diocesan register of ordinations. This leads to the conclusion

that he did not ordain Vincent secretly or privately in his domestic chapel, as some have suggested, but in the chapel on the public road by his castle.

When he was ordained is clearly reported in the ordination document, 23 September 1600. The same document also records that the date was Saturday of the Ember Week, one of the days stipulated for ordinations. This may explain the expression in the document "general ordinations," but it does not prove whether Vincent was ordained alone or together with others.

Château-l'Évêque today is a small village of 1800 persons. The Daughters

Original entry, parish church,
Château-l'Évêque

Commemorative plaque,
Château-l'Évêque

of Charity run a retirement home here (begun in 1869) and receive guests as lodgers for retreats, etc. Some Vincentians lived here from 1877 to 1883 and returned later as chaplains to the sisters. During the second World War, the body of Saint Vincent was moved here, where it was hidden in their chapel and basement, then returned for veneration (from 20 May 1940 to 3 June 1945). Nazis lived in the sisters' buildings but never bothered them or the Vincentians.

At the south edge of town is a road leading to Périgueux said to have been laid out in the time of the ancient Romans. *(Voie Romaine)* To the left, before this road begins, are signs for the Calvaire, a modern series of Stations of the Cross leading up the hillside.

Many years later Vincent reflected on his priesthood. *As for myself, if I had known what it was when I had the temerity to enter it—as I have come to know since then—I would have preferred to till the soil than to commit myself to such a* formidable state of life. I have said this more than a hundred times to poor country people when, to encourage them to live contentedly as upright persons, I told them I considered them fortunate in their situation. Indeed, the older I get, the more convinced I am of this because day by day I discover how far removed I am from the state of perfection in which I should be living.* (Letter 2027)

A few kilometers west of Château-l'Évêque is **Bourdeilles**, the seat of the noble Bourdeille family. Their large castle witnesses strongly to the power of this family, which provided several bishops for Périgueux, including François, who ordained Vincent.

## PÉRIGUEUX*

The region known as Périgueux has been inhabited since prehistoric times. The tribe of the Petrocori gave their name to both the region (Périgord) and the city (Périgueux). Julius Caesar mentioned it in his account of the Gallic wars. In Roman times the city grew and prospered, owing some of its wealth to its natural springs and to the river Isle that runs through it.

Aerial view, Château-l'Évêque

Its old Roman amphitheater survives as a city park. Envious of this area, successive tribes raided and destroyed it: Alemans, Visigoths, Franks and Normans. Its condition deteriorated so badly that even its Roman name, Vesuna, was forgotten, and it became called simply the Cité, the city.

Périgueux's first bishop was *Saint Front*. A small sanctuary over his tomb, begun in the sixth or seventh century, led to the development of an adjacent town, Puy Saint-Front, rivaling the old Roman settlement. In the eleventh century, the Romanesque church was consecrated, only part of which remains. It was enlarged after a fire in 1120, changing it into a Byzantine-style church in the form of a Greek cross (i.e., with equal arms), finished in 1173. This church is called Saint Front. Since it was not on the site of the old town, called simply the Cité, it was not the cathedral.

Saint Front, however, gradually took over the prerogatives of the earlier cathedral, called *Saint Étienne de la Cité*. This latter is also very ancient, with remains of a third-century wall, and a baptistery dating from 1150. Like Saint Front, it has two Byzantine style domes remaining from an earlier total of four. It was the cathedral until 1669. After the Revolution Saint Étienne became a storehouse until it was restored to worship in 1816. An enormous carved wooden altarpiece is a work of the seventeenth century, formerly part of the major seminary. Had the church not been ruined, Vincent might have been ordained here instead of at the bishop's chapel in Château-l'Évêque.

In the sixteenth century a

Saint Front cathedral, Périgueux

Protestant community was organized in Périgueux. The Protestants eventually devastated Saint Front, destroying the tomb of the saint and pillaging the treasury. By the next century, however, the cathedral had been rebuilt and restored to Catholic use. The old rivalry between the two churches (Saint Étienne and Saint Front) ended when Saint Front was repaired and designated the cathedral in 1669. The Revolution wreaked havoc, but Périgueux survived. In the nineteenth century it underwent a cultural and religious renaissance.

Important personages from Périgueux include the writer Montaigne (1533-1592), Alain de Solminihac, Fénelon (1651-1715, tutor of Louis XV, author, archbishop of Cambrai), Guillaume Joseph Chaminade (1761-

Postcard, Saint Front
cathedral, Périgueux

1815, founder of the Daughters of Mary and the Marianists), and the convert author Léon Bloy (1846-1917). Périgueux today has a population of about 30,000.

Although Vincent was ordained in the diocese of Périgueux, he had no other youthful connection, so far as is known, with this diocese. In later life, however, his friend Alain de Solminihac requested he see to the appointment of *Philibert de Brandon* (1597-1652) as bishop. A former lawyer and widower, Brandon was one of the founders of the Seminary of Saint Sulpice in Paris. He came as bishop to Périgueux in 1648, where he remained until his death four years later.

Bishop Brandon invited Vincent to send two men to open a seminary. His responses to this invitation show clearly the complexity of the negotiations involving both finances and apostolic activity (i.e., the requirement of a firm financial base, and a seminary being attached to a mission house). Vincent wanted to send at least four men, two for the seminary and two for the missions. In the end he bowed to pressure

and sent only two for the *seminary*. Shortly after, the bishop's brother, the priest Balthasar de Brandon de Bassancourt, who was also his vicar general, managed to get the Missionaries expelled, and Vincent had to recall them in 1651. The major and minor seminaries of the pre-revolutionary period were somewhere on the site of the present Cité Administrative, practically adjacent to the old cathedral. The Lycée Jay de Beaufort probably occupies the site of the major seminary. The Congregation returned to direct the major seminary from 1672 to 1792, and again from 1916 to 1969. Perhaps in their memory a large square between the cathedral and the river was called Place de la Mission, now surviving as Rue du Séminaire.

Near Périgueux is the *abbey of Notre Dame of Chancelade*. This ancient foundation, begun about 1100, was in the hands of Clercs Regular of Saint Augustine in Vincent's day. His friend, Blessed Alain de Solminihac, had agreed in 1614 to succeed his uncle as abbot and entered the community. He made a brief novitiate, took vows and was ordained a priest in 1618. His monastery, however, had only three other members. Studies in Paris brought him into contact with leading religious circles, likely including Vincent de Paul. Back in Chancelade, he was installed as abbot in 1623 and set to reforming the abbey. To help in this, he was to enlist Vincent, but the interminable problems of reform lasted well beyond both their lifetimes. There is, however, no indication that Vincent came here at the time of his ordination,

Portrait, Alain de Solminihac,
Chancelade

Commemorative stone,
Chancelade

although some have conjectured that he might have made a pre-ordination retreat in the decrepit abbey. Inside the twelfth-century church are relics and objects belonging to Solminihac, who continued as abbot while being bishop of Cahors (1636-1659). Pope John Paul II beatified him on 4 October 1981. Remains of the *jubé* are visible in the walls of the nave, as well as several fourteenth-century murals. Their survival in this humid location is a marvel.

Near the front of the abbey is a Romanesque chapel dedicated to Saint John, probably built for the people of the region as their own. Consecrated in 1147, it is still used for Sunday liturgies and is interesting for its antiquity. Across the road, on the abbey side, is the old communal washing shed *(lavoir publique)*, no longer in use. Most medieval towns had one or more of these.

## SAINT-LIVRADE-SUR-LOT

Marie de Wignerod de Pontcourlay (1604-1675), marquise of Combalet, and duchess of Aiguillon, wanted to endow a house for the Vincentians in the diocese of Agen. One reason for her foundation was that Agen lay within the territory of her duchy of Aiguillon, which she purchased in 1637. **Aiguillon** itself, however, preserves an old ducal palace, but the adjacent parish church has no monument either to the first duchess or to Saint Vincent.

Reliquary, Alain de Solminihac,
Chancelade

The duchess was able to secure for the Vincentians the shrine of *Notre Dame de la Rose*, an old pilgrimage chapel outside the town of Sainte-Livrade-sur-Lot, on a Roman road from Aiguillon. This was the fourth house of the Congregation (after the Bons Enfants and Saint Lazare in Paris, and the house in Toul).

Before Vincentians arrived, the chapel had fallen into ruins, but it was rebuilt by 1624 through the help of a royal judge who lived nearby. The local clergy then started to look for some help with the increasingly important chapel. For its part, the town council offered land to anyone willing to staff the shrine. Vincent completed the agreement in 1639. Previously, beginning about 1637, at least two priests had been in Aiguillon in a house endowed by the duchess. In 1640, these men then moved to the shrine near Sainte-Livrade. Vincent expressed a wish to visit here, but was never able to do so. Some confreres had problems with the local dialect, a problem the founder could appreciate, since it was a form of his own native language, Occitan.

The confreres handled both the pilgrimages and parish missions—these were their two principal works. In 1646, one unfortunate Vincentian, Bernard Jegat (b. 1610), was in La Rose probably to recover his health. At his doctor's orders, he was to go swimming in the nearby river Lot, but he drowned in its placid waters. Jegat was only 36 and, since few others knew him, Vincent asked his confreres at La Rose to draw up an account of his life.

The Vincentians remained here until 1791. The pilgrimage chapel has disappeared, as has the confreres' home. The name "La Rose," however, remains attached to parcels of land south of the town. The pilgrimage statue of Mary and the child Jesus, of gilded wood, now rests in a chapel adjoining the parish church of Sainte-Livrade. Today, Sainte-Livrade has a population of about 6000.

## SARLAT-LA-CANÉDA

Sarlat, to give it its usual name, is a town of some 10,000 inhabitants and one of the Europe's most noteworthy medieval sites. A monastery began here after 820, and a town gradually grew up around it. It became a diocese in 1317. Ruined during the Hundred Years War,

Saint John Chapel, Chancelade

Road sign, Notre Dame de la Rose

the town was rebuilt and its cathedral finished by 1500. The town boasts many beautifully restored private homes.

Vincent greatly esteemed *Nicolas Sevin* (1613-1678), bishop of Sarlat. He was named to this post in 1647, on the recommendation of Alain de Solminihac to Vincent and the other members of the Council of Conscience. He appreciated Sevin's holy life and example, his virtue, learning, health and experience. Again on Solminihac's recommendation, Sevin became coadjutor of Cahors and finally its bishop after Solminihac's death. Sevin lodged for a time with Vincent after resigning Sarlat and before moving to Cahors, and he preached an ordination retreat at Saint Lazare. Other than this connection, the Congregation had no permanent work in the diocese of Sarlat in Vincent's lifetime. Afterwards, however, Vincentians staffed the major semi-nary beginning in 1683 and preached missions in the area. They left at the Revolution and lost at least one confrere to revolutionary justice, *Jean Élie Bories* (1720-1794), a Sarlat native and the superior of the seminary. He was executed in Périgueux for refusing to take the constitutional oath. Vincentians later returned to the same work in the seminary, transferred from Périgueux, but this time they remained only from 1817 to 1821. The Daughters of Charity followed them here in 1818 to begin a parish school and to work for the poor.

A few kilometers southeast of Sarlat is **Carsac-Aillac**. An old, perhaps reliable, tradition says that Vincent made his ordination retreat here. The reason for suggesting this is that the lord of Carsac is thought to have been the parent or close relative of one of the students whom Vincent taught at Buzet.

# Languedoc-Roussillon

   As in the east of France, so in part of the south, the works of Vincent de Paul and Louise de Marillac were not extensive. Nevertheless, several foundations here date from their time: Agde, Alet, Montpellier and Narbonne. These were not great successes in human terms, however.

## AGDE

François Fouquet (1611-1673), bishop of Agde, called Vincent to open a *seminary* in his diocese of Agde. The city took its name from the Greek word referring to good fortune, *agatha*. One of the oldest cities in France, Phoenicians lived here before the Romans arrived. In the seventeenth century, it was still recovering from the ravages of the wars of religion. Fouquet had been a good friend of Vincent's from his days as a member of the Tuesday Conferences, and Fouquet's mother was prominent among the Ladies of Charity. Vincent did not agree with details of the bishop's proposed contract (concerning the Congregation's independence and its finances), but at length he told his confreres to leave for the Agde seminary and its attached parish (1654). Further, he foresaw troubles since the climate was difficult and epidemics common. In fact, Pierre Du Chesne, whom Vincent regarded highly, died here (3 November 1654) only a few months after opening the seminary. Vincent never seems to have visited Agde, since it is so far from Paris. Vincentian work here took its normal course, however, with the arrival of new candidates for the Congregation, preaching occasional missions.

The bishop's youngest brother, Louis (1633-1702), succeeded him as bishop of Agde and had a new contract drawn up with the Congregation. The result was not promising and the Vincentians left in 1671. They moved from here to Narbonne to continue their seminary work, but the real reason for their departure was the bishop's overt hostility. Apparently nothing remains of the old seminary buildings in Agde itself.

The same bishop François Fouquet in 1656 called the Daughters of Charity to serve in Agde. Their important works in the hospital began, however, only in 1761. Although one sister was imprisoned, some were able to stay during the Revolution, and others returned afterward to the same hospital. They had various houses here until 1903. Today, Agde is a small town of about 5000 people.

## ALET-LES-BAINS

The town of Alet-les-Bains, to give it its current name, lies in the foothills of the Pyrenees. Its good elevation and hot springs assured its importance, even in ancient times. It became a diocese in 1318. Bishop Nicolas Pavillon of Alet (1597-1677) was a friend and admirer of Vincent. In preparation for his episcopal ordination, for example, Pavillon spent several days in retreat at Saint Lazare. The diocese he inherited had suffered greatly from religious wars in the preceding decades. Vincent sent his confreres to Alet to give missions and to staff a *seminary* in this poor diocese, which they did only from 1639 to 1642. A Tuesday Conference was founded here as well, in imitation of the first one in Paris. Differences with the bishop led Vincent to withdraw them. Nevertheless, the two brothers Chandenier, both diocesan clergy and close friends of Vincent, came to Alet in 1652 to preach a mission, thus keeping alive a relationship with the Congregation. In his later years the bishop became involved with Jansenism and caused his friend Vincent some anxieties. The bishop was buried in the abbey, but his grave is unmarked. Alet today has about 500 inhabitants.

The Vincentians were lodged in the ninth-century abbey adjoining the present cathedral. The abbey, destroyed by Huguenots, is still in ruins. Its altar and furnishings were removed to the village church of **Espéraza** a few kilometers away. Although an early church in Espéraza can be dated to the eleventh century, it was renovated in the seventeenth century following the wars of religion. The altar and its furnishings date, as well, from the eighteenth century, and thus were not contemporary with the presence of the Vincentians.

## MONTPELLIER

The mission of Montpellier was not one of Vincent's successes. He was called to open a seminary here in 1659. He agreed but quickly discovered that he had acted too hastily, perhaps because of his advanced age. In any case, Vincent learned from another bishop that the bishop of Montpellier, dissatisfied with his seminary professors, was planning to close the institution. Vincent withdrew his confreres the next year, citing a lack of solid financial support.

As happened elsewhere, the Vincentians returned after the Revolution. They resumed their seminary apostolate in 1844, housing both major and minor seminarians in the same institution, the former monastery of the Recollects. They remained until forced to leave about 1903. One of the professors had been *Antoine Fiat* (1832-1915), superior general from 1878 to

Guillaume Pouget

1914. The Vincentians took charge of the seminaries once again: the minor seminary, 1918-1953, and the major seminary, 1918-1973.

*Daughters of Charity* came to Montpellier in 1664. After the Revolution, they too returned to continue their work in the general hospital, with orphans and other works of charity. The well-known portrait of a Lady of Charity, often identified, incorrectly, as Marguerite Naseau, hung in this hospital. The sisters have continued various works of charity here.

Montpellier today is a city of some 210,000 inhabitants. It is relatively young by the standards of the sunny south, dating only from the ninth century. It suf-

Guillaume Pouget

Cardinal Désiré Joseph Mercier (1851-1926), several meetings of Anglican and Roman Catholic theologians, including Portal and Halifax, were held at Malines, Belgium, between 1921 and 1925. These "Malines Conversations" gave impetus to the ecumenical movement.

## NARBONNE

A year before his death, Vincent agreed to send three confreres to take charge of the *seminary* here in this ancient city. Archbishop François Fouquet (previously bishop of Bayonne and then of Agde) had invited them, as he had done when he was bishop of Agde. The negotiations dragged on until interrupted by Vincent's death. The peevish bishop wrote him just a month before his death: *let this be the last letter I am obliged to write to you on this matter, and free me of the greatest trouble and chagrin I have in my diocese at present and which is such a headache for me. If not, resign yourself to receive every week letters longer than this one...* (Letter 3229) Vincent's successor in office, René Alméras, signed the contract on 10 September 1661. The Vincentians moved to the newly-built seminary and remained until 1791. There seems, however, to be no trace of either the old seminary, regarded as large and magnificent, or its attached parish, *Notre Dame de Maiour.*

The Gothic *cathedral*, begun in the thirteenth century, has never been completed. However, it has a side altar with a statue, a painting and a stained glass window of Saint Vincent de Paul. Today, Narbonne, with a population of 45,000,

fered during the wars of religion, and its ancient churches were systematically destroyed. The cathedral is one of its oldest buildings.

A native of Montpellier, of interest to Vincentians, is *Fernand Étienne Portal* (1855-1926). After his ordination, Portal taught in various seminaries. Weak lungs brought him to the Vincentian seminary on Madeira. There he met Charles Lindley Wood, Lord Halifax, whose daughter was recuperating. Their friendship blossomed into an interest in Anglican-Roman Catholic dialogue, urged on by Leo XIII. Leo's successor, Pius X, was not so anxious to continue this. Portal was effectively censured and forbidden to teach in Paris, but tolerant superiors allowed him to continue his work privately. Under the presidency of is a part of the diocese of Carcassonne. It keeps traces of a rich history, including Romans, Jews and Moslem Arabs. It was here that, by order of the Emperor Diocletian, the Roman soldier Sebastian was first shot with arrows (he survived) and later clubbed to death. His cult became widespread in the Middle Ages.

The archbishop also invited the **Daughters of Charity** to come here. In an instruction given to the sisters at the time of their departure, the founder had some sharp observations to make: *Do not expect to have only roses, there will be thorns as well. The people there are clever and hard to please. You must expect to be laughed at. They are good, but all their inclinations tend to what is evil. The vice of impurity is, above all others, prevalent there.* (Conference 112, September 1659) As some reflection of this warning, the Daughters were given lodgings in a jail for prostitutes. The situation improved, but the sisters did experience difficulties living apart from their other sisters. They continued here, working in the hospital and keeping school, until the Revolution.

Vincent's school, Buzet-sur-Tarn

# Midi-Pyrénées

*Vincent de Paul spent important years in the region of the Midi-Pyrénées: philosophical and theological studies in Toulouse, teaching at Buzet, and one of his first masses at Notre-Dame-de-Grâce. In later years his friendship with Blessed Alain de Solminihac led him to send his confreres and Daughters of Charity to the bishop's diocese of Cahors. The future saint, John Gabriel Perboyre, was born in this region and obtained some of his schooling with the Vincentians at Montauban.*

## BUZET-SUR-TARN,** NOTRE-DAME-DE-GRÂCE**

The village of Buzet-sur-Tarn numbers today some 500 inhabitants and is located on the left bank (south) of the river Tarn, about 40 kilometers north of Toulouse. It is a *bastide*, one of a series of forts built throughout southern France in the thirteenth century, generally on the same plan. All the bastides look similar, with a rectangular layout, often surrounding an existing building; and with walls and towers, regular streets running at right angles, and similar houses. The castle of Buzet used to adjoin the church; only its tower remains. Its castle guarded the river Tarn between Albi and Montauban, since the only bridge in the area crossed here; only its access ramp and some pillars (and a modern suspension bridge) remain after a devastating flood in 1930.

Buzet is important in Vincent's biography since it is believed that in this village he began a small *school* for some local boys during the time of his studies in Toulouse. The story is confused and uncertain in many respects, but it seems well founded that the young cleric had some connections here. Since it would not have been possible for him to come and go quickly to Toulouse, his work here presumes a continuous presence of some months, at least in the summers and at other holiday periods, unless he hired someone to help him in his absence. It is commonly believed that Vincent undertook this work to help pay for his schooling. He seems later to have moved the school to Toulouse, thus obviating the travel problems.

The parish **church** of Saint Pierre is Gothic, dating in its present form from the fifteenth century. It was much restored in the late nineteenth century, and has kept an imitation of the typical painted walls and ceilings characteristic of the *bastide* churches. The brick octagonal tower, 33 meters in height, is visible from some distance. Its lower section served as the watchtower of the castle, now long gone. At some later period the top section of the tower was added. In side chapels are paintings of Saint

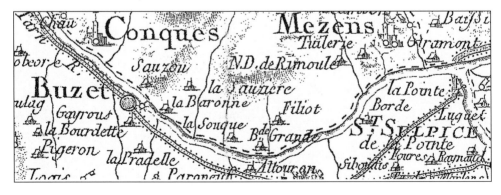

Eighteenth century map of Buzet, N.D. de Rimoule

Church tower, Buzet-sur-Tarn

Vincent, particularly teaching in his school at Buzet. The students in the school are portrayed as elegantly dressed, carrying on the tradition of their noble status. Another large painting represents the saint with children; angels display a ribbon with the words *charité, humilité, simplicité*, traditional virtues of the Daughters of Charity. Stained glass windows also recall his ministry in Buzet. He certainly would have prayed in this church and probably celebrated mass here. It is extremely difficult to be certain about the saint's whereabouts or about his chronology during this period.

Two statutes are of interest in this church. The first likely depicts the

Parish church, Buzet-sur-Tarn

Vincent's school, Buzet-sur-Tarn

Commemorative plaque, Buzet-sur-Tarn

Egyptian princess rescuing the infant Moses from the Nile. It may be an offering after someone was saved from perishing in the Tarn. The second is a statue commonly seen in local churches: Saint Germaine of Pibrac, patroness of young farmers. She is depicted here carrying a load of roses in her apron. She died in 1601.

The *house* where Vincent lived is confidently shown. Its location, however, is based only on local tradition. The back of the house is at the end of a small impasse off the Grande Rue des Fleurs, between numbers 82 and 96, and fronts on the recently-named Impasse St. Vincent de Paul. A plaque on the build-

ing says: "In this house Saint Vincent de Paul taught school from 1596 to 1597." The house had two large rooms that could have served as a small school. They are not in good condition at present.

A plaque outside the little brick chapel of **Notre-Dame-de-Grâce** reads: "Chapel of Our Lady of Grace, fourteenth century. Saint Vincent de Paul celebrated one of his first masses here in 1600." This is based on the local tradition reported by Collet. This chapel, a foundation of the Benedictines at Conques and earlier in the diocese of Montauban, has been a place of pilgrimage at least since the end of the 1500s, and it is not difficult to reach from Buzet. Today, one crosses the river, goes through the village of Mézens and climbs the hill by route D35 to the "little chapel in the woods," to cite Collet. Vincent, however, probably took the small path through the woods leading

Postcard, Notre-Dame-de-Grâce

Notre-Dame-de-Grâce

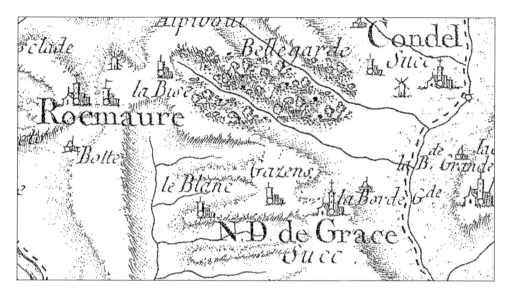

Eighteenth century map of Notre-Dame-de-Grâce

up the slope to the plateau where the chapel is, a half-hour walk. This chapel is not exactly in the woods anymore, since it is mainly surrounded by farmlands, but it lies on the top of the ridge. When Vincent came here, the chapel was about twelve meters long by five meters wide and did not have its side chapels. After these were added in 1842, the chapel could accommodate about fifty people. Its tall flat façade is typical of others in the Toulouse region. Also, like other country chapels, this one has been restored many times, such as in 1825, 1850, and 1973 after a period of neglect.

The object of devotion is a small statue of Mary and the child Jesus. It is not original but a copy. The tabernacle, on a side wall, is in the shape of an urn with a representation of a bible on top, an original design dating from the eighteenth century. It used to be in the side

chapel dedicated to Saint Vincent de Paul.

In this side chapel, restored in 1980, is to be seen a bust-reliquary of Saint Vincent, donated by the Daughters of Charity in 1851. It was said to be a copy of an original now in the South Kensington museum in London; but the face is that of a local winegrower, with red cheeks and broad nose. The painting

Commemorative plaque,
Notre-Dame-de-Grâce

339

in this chapel depicts Saint Vincent teaching. The altar has a bas-relief head of the saint carved on the front of the altar and apparently dates from the nineteenth century.

The facing side chapel has a large painting of the traditional glorification of Saint Vincent, shown with Saint Louise. In the foreground are the two books of the Common Rules of the Congregation of the Mission and the Daughters of Charity. Another large painting depicts the first mass, celebrated with an archpriest. Abelly says that Vincent was there alone, with only a server and an assisting priest. Might one not also think of students who could

Our Lady of Rimoule
site, near Mézens

easily have accompanied their teacher on the day of his first mass?

At the back of the chapel is a large painting of the crucifixion, with two depictions of the Red Scapular, a devotion with roots in the Daughters of Charity. Behind the church is an old cemetery and meeting rooms for catechesis.

The chapel used to contain the altar taken from *Our Lady of Rimoule*. That chapel, now destroyed, was located across the Tarn just west of Mézens. A small cross identifies its place. Some have claimed it as the chapel where Vincent celebrated his first mass, or perhaps one of his first masses. Since it does not fit Collet's description as on a hilltop, amid woods, its place is less secure than the one he described. Nevertheless, nothing would have prevented the young priest from celebrating mass there as well. In any case, a modern marble altar was installed in Notre-Dame-de-Grâce during the restoration of 1989, and the old Rimoule altar was removed.

This chapel is still the site of a pilgrimage in honor of Our Lady of Grace on Pentecost Monday; another recalls Saint Vincent and is held on 27 September. A Vincentian mission here is recorded as early as 1677. During the Revolution a pious neighbor bought the chapel, thus saving it for the future. In the nineteenth century, various pilgrimages of Vincentians and Daughters of Charity came here. Jean Baptiste Nozo, the superior general, sent relics here from Paris in 1837. His successor, Jean Baptiste Étienne, together with the superioress general, visited in 1851. Charles Souvay, another superior general, visited in 1936, as others have since.

Not far from Buzet is **Albi**. The Congregation of the Mission ran the seminary for this important diocese from 1774 until the Revolution and, with some gaps, from 1806 to 1903, and again from 1918 to the 1970s. They saw to continuing the tradition of a Vincentian presence at Notre-Dame-de-Grâce. Daughters of Charity, similarly, served in Albi after the Revolution until the forced secularization of their works in 1907.

## CAHORS*

Cahors is an ancient Gallic town located in the bend of the river Lot. In Roman times, it had a 1000-seat theater, thermal springs and an aqueduct. In the period of the barbarian migrations, Visigoths (472) and Saracens (732) sacked it, followed by Normans and even Hungarians. The cathedral of Saint Étienne is Romanesque with some Gothic additions, as usual. In keeping with medieval tradition, it preserved a dominical relic, that is, a relic of the Lord *(Dominus)*. In this case, it is the Holy Coif, or the linen said to have

Saint Barthélémy church entry, Cahors

wrapped his head in the tomb. This relic is exposed today in a nineteenth-century reliquary. A statue of Saint Jean Gabriel Perboyre is prominently placed in a side chapel. Perboyre was a native of the diocese; his birthplace is only twenty kilometers away.

In the twelfth century, Cahors was a financial center and, under English administration, had Thomas Becket as its governor. Another notable inhabitant became Pope John XXII, one of the Avignon popes (1316-1334). In 1332, he created a university here that continued until its suppression in 1751. The area also produces a fine wine.

***Blessed Alain de Solminihac*** (1593-

Valentré bridge over the Lot, Cahors

Saint Barthélémy tower, Cahors

1659), a friend of Vincent de Paul, was bishop of Cahors from 1636 to 1659. In his ecclesiastical career, he quickly became known as a forceful religious reformer. Vincent remarked to the Daughters going to Cahors that *the great austerity with which he treats himself may render him a little severe. His Excellency is a man who would make it a matter of conscience before ever paying a compliment.* (Conference 104) This severe and unbending man was called the French Borromeo (a painting in the nave commemorates this). Four years before his priestly ordination in 1618, he became the titular abbot of Chancelade, near Périgueux, and succeeded in reforming

it. In 1636, he became bishop of Cahors (by which he also became its count and baron, with civil responsibilities). He was so zealous in holding pastoral visitations and synods that he stirred up much opposition from disaffected priests. He saw to the preaching of missions in his diocese and the foundation of a seminary in 1643, which he confided to the Congregation of the Mission. Pope John Paul II beatified Bishop Solminihac in 1981. He was originally buried in the chapel of the canons of Chancelade in Cahors. His body was brought to his cathedral in 1791 and placed in the chapel of the Blessed Virgin. An inscription on the tomb reads: "The body of the Venerable Alain de Solminihac, bishop of Cahors, which reposed in the church of the Canons Regular [of Chancelade] for 132 years, has been transferred and put here on 7 August 1791." Besides this burial chapel, another one dedicated to him is also in the cathedral.

As part of their pastoral ministry the Vincentians also served the parish church of **Saint Barthélémy** for a time,

Seminary chapel, Cahors

since it was attached to the seminary. A large painting of Saint Vincent de Paul in glory is the only sign of the Vincentian presence in this parish. The original seminary building was turned into a military installation, part of which is still standing, as the east wing of the Caserne Bessières. Vincentian novices were also accepted here beginning about 1690. *(Rue P. Mendès France)*

At the Revolution, the pastor, Jean Baptiste Bégoulé (1751-1808), took the prescribed constitutional oath. As the other Vincentians ostracized him, he later retracted his oath. He then had to flee the country, but he returned, as his confreres did. The revolutionaries pillaged the church. After the Revolution, the Vincentians opened the seminary in another building, formerly the house of the canons of Chancelade and now divided between the Maison de Retraite and the Maison des Oeuvres. A bust of Vincent de Paul and a statue of John Gabriel Perboyre identify the property. The Vincentians maintained this seminary until 1903; the institution itself closed in 1906. *(Rue Joachim Murat)* Besides various members of the Perboyre family, many other notable Vincentians came from this diocese, including three missionary bishops. One Vincentian also suffered death in Cahors during the Revolution, François Bergeon, executed here on 17 May 1794.

The Daughters of Charity came to Cahors in 1658 and opened an *orphanage* for boys—the first one in their long history. An orphanage for girls followed in 1683. They also served in the city hospital from 1697 until the Revolution and

again afterward. One of the sisters, Jacquette Paujad, was imprisoned in Cahors during the Revolution for her faith. Little is known about her. Another sister, the superior of the hospital, lost her mind over having to resume work after the disasters of the Revolution. Sisters and orphans alike suffered from deprivation, disorder and even famine.

Near the city on a prominent hillside is **Mercuès**, a small town (800 persons) dominated by the chateau of the bishops of Cahors. It is located on the site of a Roman fort and a temple to Mercury. The present chateau was built in the fifteenth century and, after Protestants had burned it, the building was rebuilt in the seventeenth. Alain de Solminihac lived there and wrote several letters to Vincent from there. The bishops used Mercuès as their residence until

Château, Vilary near Catus

the beginning of the twentieth century. The chateau is now in use as a luxury hotel.

The same bishop was also responsible for the shrine of the Virgin Mary at **Rocamadour**. The bishop called it "the most celebrated in the kingdom," and he worked to restore devotion and pilgrimages there. It is unknown what Vincent thought of this shrine, or whether he actually went there. (Letter 1220) The year-round population of Rocamadour is about 700.

## CATUS, LE PUECH,** MONTGESTY**

The importance of these three places for Vincentians is that they are connected with *Saint Jean Gabriel Perboyre.* He was born at the hamlet of Le Puech (a form of the word *puy*, meaning an elevated place) near the town of Montgesty, 6 January 1802, and was ordained a priest 23 September 1826. He was novice director at the Vincentian motherhouse in Paris but nourished a desire to go to the foreign missions. On 29 August 1835, he landed in China near Macao. He exercised his ministry among the Catholic people of China until one of his students betrayed him. He was thereupon arrested, tortured and executed, 11 September 1840. He was beatified 10 November 1889 and canonized 2 June 1996. In this, he became China's first saint.

His uncle, Jacques Perboyre (1763-1848), a seminary professor in Montauban, greatly influenced his vocation. This priest, ordained before the Revolution, had been forced to hide out

Saint Martin de Graudène ruins, near Catus

in the region for several years during the revolutionary period. After which the young Jean Gabriel was sent to school with his uncle, again in Montauban. The old man is reported to have regularly slept in a coffin for the last years of his life as an act of penance. He died there peacefully and was buried simply.

The small town of **Catus**, population 800, is built around the former Benedictine priory of Saint Jean, now dedicated to Saint Astier. Its Romanesque church was begun in 1115 and was modified in the fourteenth and sixteenth centuries with some Gothic additions, such as the side chapels. There are superb Romanesque carved capitals on the pillars. Little remains of the monastic buildings, apart from sections of the cloister walk and the chapter hall. Several medieval houses can be seen in

Menhir de Courtis,
near Montgesty

from the sixteenth century. The only entrance was through a ladder, but now access has been made easier by adding doors on the ground level. Nearby on the west side of route D23 are the ruins of the Romanesque chapel of Saint Martin de Graudène. The young Perboyres knew this place, now hidden amid trees and bushes.

**Montgesty** is a village of legends, such as one about Roland, the nephew of Charlemagne. He is said to have fought the Saracens here before going on to Rocamadour, where his sword was planted in a rock. In the region of Montgesty are ruins from the Neolithic period (a standing stone, dating from

the town. After the Revolution, the church was repaired several times, particularly after the great floods of 1960. Members of the Vincentian province of Toulouse briefly served this parish, and twelve associated parishes in the region, beginning in 1995. Since Catus was the parish for Vilary, Jean Gabriel Perboyre would have attended this church during his family visits to Vilary.

South of Catus on route D13 is the hamlet of *Vilary*. One of the houses, now in other hands, remained, until the middle of the twentieth century, the property of a branch of the Perboyre family. Pierre Perboyre, the father of the martyr, was born here, as was Pierre's brother Jacques. To call it a chateau overstates the case, but the main body of the building was a tower of refuge for nobles in time of war and insecurity; it dates

Early main altar, Montgesty

Eighteenth century map of Montgesty and Catus

around 2500 B.C., the *menhir de Courtis*), the Gallo-Roman period, and burial sites from barbarian times. In the Gothic church dating from the 14th century can be seen a large image of Christ in the Spanish Baroque style. The church also has several reminders of Jean Gabriel Perboyre: an altar, a window depicting a rather pudgy young priest, and a plaque commemorating his baptism. In front of the church is a large statue of him, dedicated in 1897. Montgesty today has fewer than 300 people, as the entire region has been depopulated due to changes in rural life.

One of the hamlets associated with Montgesty is **Le Puech**, the birthplace of Jean Gabriel Perboyre. It is some six or eight kilometers south of Montgesty and preserves the old buildings of the Perboyre farmhouse. Part of their family home dates from the fourteenth or fifteenth century. A large statue of the martyr in Chinese dress stands at the entrance to the property. Here were born four sons and four daughters. Two became Daughters of Charity, one of whom died in China. Another sister resembled her martyred brother so much, that her likeness was used to depict him—except for her eyes, which explains why John Gabriel is shown with eyes downcast. Three of the sons became Vincentians. Jean Gabriel, the martyr, was the eldest. Jean Louis (1807-1831), left shortly after his ordination for

China, but died at sea. Jacques Jean (1810-1896) entered the Vincentians as a lay brother, but later resumed his studies and was ordained a priest in 1845. He attended his brother's beatification in Rome and afterwards celebrated mass at his altar in the motherhouse. Another Perboyre was Jean Gabriel (1808-1880), their cousin. He became a renowned historian of the Congregation. The Le Puech farm is still the property of descendants of the family. The entire area, however, is depopulated because of changes in agriculture and modern life.

MAISON OU EST NÉ LE BIENHEUREUX JEAN-GABRIEL PERBOYRE
PRÊTRE DE LA CONGRÉGATION DE LA MISSION (6 JANVIER 1802)

Le Puech, near Montgesty,
19th century engraving

Tower and entry, Montgesty

Commemorative plaque,
parish church, Montech

Vincentian house,
Notre-Dame-de-Lorm, Castelferrus

## MONTAUBAN, NOTRE-DAME-DE-LORM, MONTECH

Saint Theodard founded a monastery in Montauban in 820. The city, one of the *bastide* type of fortresses, was founded in 1144. Like all bastides, it was built on a rectangular plan around a central town square, with fortifying walls. A great bridge was built over the Tarn in 1297, and it has withstood floods for seven centuries.

The city became a diocese in 1317, turned Protestant in 1536, but Richelieu reconquered it for the Church in 1629. The cardinal minister celebrated mass in the cathedral at that time, although the Protestants had removed its roof and nearly ruined the building. After the Revolution, the diocese was reestablished in 1817.

The city now numbers about 55,000 inhabitants. It is in a region that spoke the southern dialect, called Languedoc, or Occitan. Some Vincentians there found it difficult to understand. This language is undergoing a revival, and is, for example, an option on local school examinations.

Bishop Anne de Murviel (1568-1652), bishop of Montauban for 52 years, had two Vincentians evangelizing in his diocese from 1631 and 1640. He noted in a letter to Vincent the presence of sorcerers and witches in his diocese who, mercifully, disappeared after these Vincentians preached their mission. (Letter 684) Pope Alexander VII also recalled their successes in his bull uniting Saint Lazare to the Congregation, 1655. A community house in the diocese began in 1652 in **Castelferrus** at the shrine of *Notre-Dame-de-Lorm*. The old pilgrimage church has been destroyed, and the original statue (found in the trunk of an elm, *orme*), the object of the pilgrimage, has been moved to the present parish church. The large building next to the

Martyrdom of John Gabriel Perboyre,
Saint-Étienne de Sapiac

shrine church may have been the Vincentian residence, although this is not clear. Vincent described this place as suitable for Firmin Get (1621-c.1681) to recover his health: *Notre Dame de Lorm, in the diocese of Montauban, where the weather is good, the countryside is lovely and the Garonne, a beautiful river, flows through it.* (Letter 2664) Castelferrus today is a village of about 400 people. Despite their good work in Lorm, someone attempted to burn the place down in 1659. (Letter 2809) The Vincentians also had charge of the neighboring parish of **Saint-Aignan**, which the community accepted in 1657 as a way of helping the bishop.

The priests began the seminary in **Montech**. It then transferred to Lorm and next to Montauban in 1660 when it was again safe for Catholics to be there. Vincent oversaw this change during the last two weeks of his life. (Coste 13:182) A plaque in the church of Notre Dame de la Visitation in Montech recalls the presence of the congregation there. "To the everlasting memory of the religious hospitality given to the bishop of Montauban, to his chapter, and to the Lazarists for twenty years by the town of Montech at the time of the wars of religion. This marble plaque was engraved and placed by the pious zeal of Mr. Leon Roussoulieres, pastor of Montech, and Dr. J. Larramet, the mayor of Montech, 1876." The seminary appears to have been located on the grounds of the present retirement home near the cathedral. Nothing seems to remain of the old seminary buildings. A small statue of Saint Vincent has been placed in this southern Gothic church, which dates from the fifteenth century. Montech today has about 3000 inhabitants.

Vincent was also somewhat involved in the **Labadie** affair. Jean Labadie (1610-1674) was a Jesuit for fifteen years but left the Society. He was a popular preacher but given to sensual mysticism and became first a Jansenist and then a Calvinist at Montauban in 1650. Vincent wrote about him. (Letters 1345, 1549, dated 1651 and 1652) Quickly dissatisfied with Calvinists in Montauban, Labadie moved to Geneva, then to Holland, and ended up founding his own church. His followers survived him only until 1744.

In 1808 two Vincentians founded a sort of *minor seminary* in **Montauban** in a former Carmelite monastery. The Perboyre brothers, Louis and Jean Gabriel, nephews of Jacques Perboyre, one of the founders, made their studies here. The future saint attended here from 1817 through 1820. This seminary is now a public school, and its chapel has been set aside for Protestant worship. It was in this chapel that Jean Gabriel made up his mind to become a priest. *(2,6 Grand' Rue Sapiac)* The studio of the renowned painter Ingres, located in Montauban, was responsible for the first painting in honor of the new martyr, dated 1844. It is found today in the church of *Saint Étienne de Sapiac*, a building dating from 1680. This painting is more historically accurate than today's standard versions, but some details are not (Jean Gabriel in a black cassock, for example, whereas he was clad only in shorts). (Another copy is in the Daughter of Charity house.) A stained glass window depicts Perboyre more in keeping with the usual depictions and serves as a point of comparison. This painting is probably here since Jacques Perboyre was vicar of Sapiac from 1815 and made his first attempts at a minor seminary here (the site is unknown) before moving it to the Carmelite building.

Vincentians also directed the major seminary of Montauban from 1929 to 1958, when it was joined with that of Toulouse. The Daughters of Charity were in Montauban from 1685 to 1792 to serve the sick poor in the hospital. They returned in 1869 to run a parish school.

Near Montauban is the old fortified town of **Villemur-sur-Tarn**. The principal attraction for Vincentians is the Grenier du Roy. The Daughters of Charity used this former royal salt warehouse as a hospital from 1860. It dates from the seventeenth century and is now a well-preserved municipal building. Vincent would have known this town during his travels down-river from Buzet. Today it has about 5000 inhabitants.

A few kilometers west of

Family home, Evariste Huc, Caylus

Montauban, on D926, is **Caylus**. It, too, has a connection with John Gabriel Perboyre, since it was the birthplace of **Régis Evariste Huc** (1813-1860). This young Vincentian arrived in China in 1841, the year after Perboyre's death. With another Vincentian, Joseph Gabet, he set to work among the Mongols. Huc's gift for languages, his daring and bravery, as well as his precise observations, helped him in many adventures in Mongolia, China and Tibet. Gabet and Huc reached Tibet in 1846 in hopes of converting the lamas there, but were quickly escorted away. Huc's many books inspired popular interest in China. On the centenary of his death his hometown dedicated in his honor a section of the main road running in front of his family home, which has a large plaque describing his exploits.

## RODEZ

*Louis Abelly* (1604-1691), Vincent's friend and first biographer, named bishop of Rodez in 1662, was ordained for this diocese in 1664. Because of a stroke in 1665, Abelly retired to Saint Lazare, remaining until his death in 1691. Probably because of his short tenure, there are no monuments or references to him in the cathedral, Notre Dame.

The Vincentians had a *seminary* here, however, from 1767 to 1791. When the Jesuits were suppressed in 1761, the bishop initially placed members of the diocesan clergy in his seminary but finally invited the Congregation. The first superior of the new institution was Jean Félix Cayla de la Garde (1734-1800), a Rodez native and the last superior general elected before the Revolution (1788-1800). Because of the relatively short life of this Vincentian undertaking, not much information is available. The Romanesque church of Saint Amans served the seminary as well as the people of the parish. After the Concordat between the Holy See and France the seminary buildings continued in use as a seminary for philosophy until 1905. The church building, demolished in 1752, was quickly restored and still stands.

Daughters of Charity also worked in Rodez beginning in 1859. The city today has a population of about 25,000.

## TOULOUSE**

Toulouse is more than 2000 years old. Originally founded by Celts, Toulouse was occupied by the Romans in 118 BC. The Gallo-Roman city was a center for the making and distribution of wine. The ancient city contained 25,000 inhabitants and had a theater for 6500 people. Today Toulouse has around 400,000 inhabitants.

The first bishop, Saint Sernin (Saturninus), died about 250, during the Decian persecution. A university existed in the city from its early centuries. The Visigoths conquered the city in 413 and made it their capital. The Franks conquered them in turn. Clovis, their first king, entered the city in 508. Charlemagne (Charles the Great) organized a dukedom at Toulouse, making it the base for his conquest of the north of Spain. He also founded the basilica of Saint Sernin, which Pope Urban II consecrated in 1096. The church and its treas-

ury are well worth a visit. Because of its importance, it is certain that the young theology student, Vincent de Paul, visited here to pray, and perhaps to celebrate mass during the four years he lived here after his ordination.

Toulouse was also a center of planning for the First Crusade, to free Christian holy places in Palestine, as well as a center of Catharism, a heretical movement. Saint Dominic founded his order, the Order of Preachers, at the beginning of the thirteenth century and made Toulouse his headquarters. Toulouse had been relatively independent up to the end of the thirteenth century, but through marriage alliances it became French. In this period the Dominicans built their dramatic church to receive the relics of *Saint Thomas Aquinas* (c. 1225-1274). Although he did not teach at Toulouse, Thomas's Dominican confreres sought to have his remains transferred to their main church. The Franciscans, too, built a church and convent, but only a few traces remain.

Unlike the majority of aspiring priests in his time, who studied privately, Vincent undertook his theological studies at the University of Toulouse, probably between 1597 and 1605. It is difficult to be certain about the exact dates. He lived at *Collège de Foix* for the majority of his time. The name of the college (i.e., a residence) comes from Cardinal Pierre de Foix, who had it built and endowed between 1453 and 1457. This building still exists and is one of the finest and rarest examples of the local architecture of the fifteenth century. Fortunately, its

Bilingual signs,
College de Foix, Toulouse

Entry gate, College de Foix, Toulouse

appearance has not changed much since Vincent's day. It consists of a central court surrounded by a cloister, and a rectangular building, the *donjon*. This section contained a renowned library, of which the vaulted ceiling alone remains in the present chapel. There were student rooms above. The original chapel at the side of the college was taken down in 1850. In his time, it received some 25 students of civil and canon law and theology, together with professors. The name of his college lives on the Rue du Collège de Foix. Today the Collège de Foix is the motherhouse of the congregation of the Sisters of Our Lady of Compassion, founded by Maurice Garrigou (1766-1852). This priest, known as the "Vincent de Paul of

Toulouse," secured this property for his new congregation in 1817.

Pierre Coste recounts how unsettled the University of Toulouse was in Vincent's time. Thousands of students from many countries attended lectures there, and it is no wonder that troubles broke out. Not fortunate enough to secure a scholarship, Vincent had at least enough money to enable him to begin his studies. His father's will, dated 7 February 1598, asks the family to help Vincent continue them. He may also have spent some time at the University of Zaragoza in Spain, since it was not uncommon for students to travel and hear famous lecturers when and where they could. It is likely that Vincent began his studies in Zaragoza and continued

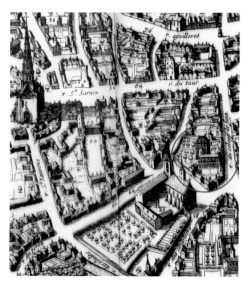

Eighteenth century engraving,
College de Foix, Toulouse

Aerial view, College de Foix, Toulouse

them in Toulouse.

Vincent was ordained in 1600, in the midst of his studies, and expected to become a pastor shortly after. Since 1600 was a Holy Year, he also traveled to Rome, perhaps to ensure his appointment to the parish of Tilh. During that visit, he saw Pope Clement VIII, an event he recalled for the Daughters of Charity later in his life. *I have seen a pope, it was Clement VIII, a very holy man, so holy indeed that even heretics used to say: Pope Clement is a saint. He was so touched by God and had the gift of tears in such abundance that when he went up what is called the Holy Stairs, he bathed it in his tears.* (Conference 30) Toward the end of his time in Toulouse, Vincent took in students at Buzet, and later in Toulouse itself, ten boys, "whom he taught and raised to the service of God," as Brother Robineau reported. After about seven years of philosophical and theological studies, he earned his degree of bachelor in theology, receiving the title of *maître*. It is possible that he taught theology briefly at Toulouse, something his degree allowed. Other adventures then occurred in the life of this young priest.

Members of the Congregation of the Mission gave missions in the diocese of Toulouse beginning in 1632. However, the community was established in the city only from 1707, likewise to give missions. Funds for a house in Toulouse had been received at Saint Lazare in Paris in 1632, and Vincent looked for the opportunity to open a house from that time

Commemorative plaque,
Jesuit college, Zaragoza, Spain

Hôtel Dieu Saint Jacques, Toulouse

until his death. In 1752 the diocesan seminary was given to the care of the Vincentians. With the expulsion of the Jesuits in 1762, the *seminary of the Mission* was transferred to their former novitiate and house of continuing formation for their members. It lasted until the revolutionary period and closed in 1792. At that point it became a military installation, the Caserne de la Mission. Today it is a school, the Lycée/Collège Pierre de Fermat, facing the Jacobins. Among the many Jesuits who made their novitiate here was Saint Jean François Regis (1595-1640), a missionary in Canada, and namesake of the Vincentian martyr Francis Regis Clet.

The first Daughters of Charity came to Toulouse in 1689 to work in the Hôtel Dieu Saint Jacques. The sisters returned to this splendid complex, still standing next to the Pont Neuf, in 1800.

During the Terror, however, the superior spent ten months in prison, and 30 others were imprisoned at least briefly. The sisters also had several other houses in Toulouse and continue their works to this day. Vincentians returned in 1892, and the city is now the headquarters for the Vincentian province of Toulouse.

The first *American Vincentians* were the guests of the seminary toward the end of January 1816. They then moved on to Bordeaux, from where they embarked for the United States. This seminary has become the university library. *(Rue de Taur)*

# Provence—Alpes—Côte-D'Azur

*Vincent's work in this Mediterranean region is not well known, since he is so regularly associated with Paris. In his younger years, however, he knew Marseilles well since he was chaplain general of the galleys of France. His confreres continued his work on behalf of galley convicts and of Christian slaves in North Africa.*

Major seminary entry, Avignon

Baptistry, former Vincentian
chapel, Marseilles

## AVIGNON

Avignon, the seat of the papacy from 1305 to 1377, is significant to Vincent's life as the place where he wrote his first extant letter, 24 July 1607. In it he recounts for his patron, Monsieur de Comet in Dax, his captivity in Tunis. He wrote a somewhat different account in Letter 2, dated Rome, 28 February 1608. Whatever the historical truth of these letters, they are authentic. Doubts have arisen about his supposed captivity, and experts are divided on the issue. In any case, Vincent seems to have known Avignon. One of the great sights is the papal palace, the Palais des Papes, where

Pietro Montorio (1558-1643) was vice-legate. Vincent mentioned him, but not by name, in the two captivity letters. The church of Saint Pierre, cited in the same report, still stands. *(Place Saint Pierre)*

Vincentians served the Church in Avignon from 1705 to 1791, leaving at the Revolution. Since the area of Avignon was papal territory, Vincentians came to staff the *major seminary* here from Italy, rather than from France. At the time of the Revolution, this territorial inconsistency was remedied by the seizure of the territory, and the Italians were expelled. The seminary site is at the north corner of Avenue de la République and Rue Joseph Vernet. A side street, Rue du Collège d'Annecy, preserves the seminary's earlier name, and its dilapidated chapel façade is still visible there. After the Revolution, Vincentians did not take up the work again in Avignon. Daughters of Charity, however, came here in 1854 for service in the hospital, and they continue their mission here. The city today has about 90,000 inhabitants.

Associated with Vincent's account of his captivity is **Aigues-Mortes**, a town on the coast where he and his companion supposedly landed before making their way to Avignon. Louis IX, Saint Louis, founded the city to serve as a Mediterranean port, from where he embarked on two different Crusades. It was, similar to the bastide fortresses, rectilinear in layout and encircled with stout walls, towers, and a moat. This small city of some 5000 inhabitants has kept its original layout. Nowadays, however, it is several kilometers from the sea.

## MARSEILLES, LA-SAINTE-BAUME

Marseilles, with 800,000 residents, is, depending on which statistics are used, either France's second or third largest city, a size demonstrating an importance dating from classical Roman

Former Vincentian chapel, Marseilles

times. Vincent is connected with this important port in several ways. He traveled here in 1619 as the chaplain general of the galleys, a post created for him, and perhaps at two other times (1618, 1622). He came also to console Monsieur de Gondi on the death of his wife (1625), since the latter was then on duty here as general of the galleys. Vincent later sent his confreres here. Known for various reasons as the Priests of the Mission of France, the Vincentians arrived in 1643. Their purpose was to carry on work for the galley rowers, whether volunteers, convicts or slaves, as well as for the crew and the officers. The priests served as a sort of Red Cross, providing parcels or funds sent to the men, as well as advocacy in cases of illness or other needs. Their house also was the center for the ransom of captives in Tunis, Algiers and elsewhere in North Africa. Nearly everything to do with their ransom passed through the hands of the Vincentians. One ceremony was especially spectacular. On their return and release, they would assemble in the Vincentian church for Benediction of the Blessed Sacrament. At a signal, still holding their chains, the former captives let them crash to the floor simultaneously in an outburst of joy.

In keeping with their traditional Vincentian charism, the members of the Marseilles house also cared for the poor country people by preaching the traditional missions, and they ran a seminary for the training of the galley chaplains from 1648. It was also a seminary for Marseilles from 1673 to 1791. Among those who worked in the house was the martyr *Jean Le Vacher* (1619-1683), killed in Algiers.

Vincent himself probably worked at one of the great forts to the side of the Old Port. It was here that the galleys were assembled and maintained, and the rowers lived and worked. The Arsenal, the principal building for the service of the galleys, has been demolished, but some seventeenth-century buildings used also for naval purposes still stand behind the site of the Arsenal.

The story of Vincent assuming the chains of a galley convict is centered in Marseilles. It is unlikely, inasmuch as substitution was punishable by mutilation and death, and, besides, as chaplain general, Vincent had the rank of a naval officer. The story has captured popular imagination, but it is generally discounted today. However, the depiction in the film *Monsieur Vincent* of the charitable priest impetuously replacing a brutalized prisoner has much to commend it. Something like this may have been the kernel of the story, repeated even in the saint's lifetime.

The chapel dating from the time of the founder is located on Rue Tapis Vert. The *community house* adjoining it was the first to have displayed the coat of arms or emblem of the Congregation on its building. This has now disappeared. At the time of the Revolution, the members of the house left or were expelled to Nice, at that period part of Savoy. Ten years later, in 1801, they returned but had no funds to buy back the property. At the north side of this building is a small street, the Rue de la Mission de France using the local name for the Congregation of the Mission.

Father Charles Verbert, however, founded a parish after the Revolution not far from the old chapel. The church of *Saint Vincent de Paul* is known generally as Les Réformés since it began in the chapel of the monastery of reformed Augustinians previously located here. Toward the middle of the century, the plan developed to build a new church. It is a large neo-Gothic edifice. The façade, dating from 1867, is unfinished. There is also a Rue Saint Vincent de Paul to further keep his name alive. However, it is only one block long and not near any Vincentian site.

The government gave the old house and its chapel, Rue Tapis Vert, to others after the Revolution since the Vincentians could not afford to buy it back. First, it went to the Poor Clares (1806-1839), then to the Jesuits, who rebuilt the chapel and added the present façade (1860). They remained until their expulsion in 1880. After various non-religious uses (concert hall, storage, etc.) and damage during the second World War, it was reopened in 1983 for the followers of Archbishop Marcel Lefevre, the Fraternity of Saint Pius X. The furnishings of the old chapel are long gone and the present ones are mostly modern. A plaque inside the chapel recalls its current dedication to Pius X, by the archbishop himself. The site of the church is close to the painter David's house where the French national anthem, known popularly as La Marseillaise, was first sung. (*25, rue Thubaneau*)

Many missionaries departed from the port of Marseilles. One especially important group was the first band of Daughters of Charity to leave for China. They did so in October 1847. Daughters had been at work in a hospital in Marseilles since 1763 and involved in several other works beginning in 1845.

East of Marseilles is the shrine of **La-Sainte-Baume** (literally, the holy grotto). According to legend Mary Magdalene came here and lived in the cave that is the focus of the shrine. It is located high in the hills and requires a stiff climb of about one half-hour to reach it from the car park on D95. In August of 1625 Vincent made a much lengthier pilgrimage visit, as he reported in a conference to the Daughters of Charity, 17 April 1653. *[Mary Magda-*

*lene] went up to a high mountain, so steep and toilsome that several days are needed to climb and descend it, so cold that I myself, who was there in the month of August, had to wrap myself up, the cold was so intense; and yet when we reached the foot of the mountain we found it excessively hot.* This twelfth-century shrine was badly damaged in 1793, but it has regained its former interest.

Besides the port of Marseilles, **Toulon** was also the home for the galleys at various times. The Congregation did not have an established house here, but some Vincentians did accompany the galley convicts here. As in times past, Toulon continues to be a major French naval base. It is a city of some 170,000 inhabitants.

# 6

# East

Fireplace, Labouré home,
Fain-lès-Moutiers

# Bourgogne

The region of Burgundy (Bourgogne), famous for its rich foods and wine, was well known to Vincent de Paul and Louise de Marillac. Both of them traveled and worked in this area. Vincent's pioneering work, the Confraternities of Charity, and his emphasis on general confessions during missions, were refined in Burgundy. Catherine Labouré, the visionary of the Miraculous Medal, was born here and felt the influence of the work of the two founders.

## ALISE-SAINTE-REINE

The name Alise is a later form of Alesia, the site of a battle between the Romans and Vercingetorix, a Gaul known from Julius Caesar's *Gallic Wars*. According to Christian tradition, a young virgin, Reine, suffered martyrdom in the town in the third century, whereupon a miraculous fountain sprang up. Even in the seventeenth century, the cult of this local saint drew many pilgrims, who used the waters for curative purposes. The water from this fountain was so appreciated that it was bottled and sent as far as Paris. Vincent, probably in 1658, agreed to found a pilgrims *hospice* here. He did so with the help of Queen Anne, various Ladies of Charity, and the Company of the Blessed Sacrament. One letter to Vincent from Jean Desnoyers, the head of the hospice and one of its two founders, remains. (Letter 3157) Opened in 1659, this was Vincent's last foundation, but he did not live to see its completion.

Hospice entry, Alise-Sainte-Reine

The town itself, numbering about 650 people, is on the side of the great strategic plateau where the Romans built a fortress and town. A good museum displays the items uncovered in archaeological excavations. The hospice (or hospital) follows the standard model of small medieval hospitals, such as the one in Moutiers-Saint-Jean. That is, a chapel stands in the center, with the men's ward on one side, and that for women on the other. Large doors could open to allow the patients to assist at mass. **Jeanne Antide Thouret** spent one year here, 1788-1789. It is said that the Daughters of Charity took the civic oath at the Revolution and so were able to remain in service. Statues and relics of Saints Vincent de Paul, Louise de Marillac, Catherine Labouré and John Gabriel Perboyre have been placed in the chapel, still used for worship. Although part of the hospital is set aside for small exhibitions, the rest remains in service. In addition, the first rules of the hospital still exist, as well as a great store of archival materials. The Daughters served here until 1968, a tenure of 302 years.

On a lighter note, the renowned Canon Félix Kir (1876-1968) was born here. He became mayor of Dijon and bequeathed to French people a special

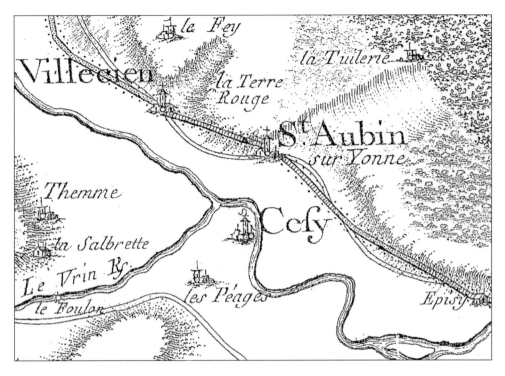

Eighteenth century map of Villecien and le Fey, near Joigny

aperitif modestly called the Kir. It is made of local white wine and *crème de cassis* from Dijon. This priest regularly served it to his guests.

## JOIGNY**

Philippe Emmanuel de Gondi (1581-1662) became count of Joigny on the death of his uncle Cardinal Pierre de Gondi (1533-1616). Vincent in his capacity as tutor and chaplain for the Gondis often stayed in this important family home. The church of **Saint John**, adjacent to the Gondi castle, was probably located on the site of a former monastery chapel dating from the tenth century. Stout walls later fortified the site, whose strategic value is clear from its location above the valley of the river Yonne. The church was dedicated on 28 May 1504 but was ruined by the great fire of 1530. It was then rebuilt, and its magnificent barrel vault ceiling dates from between 1557 and 1597. An arcade of bays supports this vault on each side and above the columns stand the apostles. During the Revolution, the church was given over to the worship of the goddess Reason. Some original stained glass windows remain, but aerial bombing destroyed the majority on 15 June 1940. The town has revived and today

Postcard, Gondi castle, Joigny

has about 5000 inhabitants.

In a chapel on the right side is a noteworthy sculpture of the entombment of Christ, the work of Mathieu Laignel, a sixteenth-century artist. This piece had been in the parish church at Folleville, where Vincent would have seen it. It was located there behind the main altar. Pierre de Gondi (1606-1676), son of Philippe Emmanuel, had it removed in 1634 and brought to Joigny when he sold his parents' Folleville property. He placed it in the family castle where it remained to 1723, when it was moved to the church. The marble carvings recall those in Folleville. For example, the front of the sarcophagus depicts the profiles of Raoul de Lannoy and his wife. These statuary groups became popular in northern Europe after the

Saint John church, Joigny

Street sign, Joigny

scourge of the Black Death in the late fourteenth century, which prompted new reflections on the sufferings and death of Jesus. Besides the main group, there are also three small statues of kneeling angels, holding armorial shields of the ancestral families of Madame de Gondi. Because of their size, they are not exhibited.

Near this sculpture is another of Adelais, countess of Joigny, dating from the thirteenth century. Her tomb, too, like the entombment sculpture, was transferred here centuries later, around 1892.

An altar honors Saint Vincent. The modern windows above it depict the chapel at the Berceau and his silver coffin at the motherhouse in Paris.

A *castle* has stood on this spot since 996; the monks who had previously lived here were removed at that time. Over the centuries the castle grew and the town with it. Together with the church, an earlier chateau burned down in 1530. The present chateau began in 1569 and became habitable after 1603, when Philippe Emmanuel's brother Henri, Cardinal de Retz (1572-1622) bought it. Intricate Renaissance details give the building a sense of great dignity. The building, however, has remained unfinished. Once restored, the Gondi chateau will be open for visitors. Philippe Emmanuel de Gondi died in this castle after 35 years of priesthood but was

Entombment of Christ sculpture, Saint John church, Joigny

Plaque, Saint Vincent's residence, Joigny

Bailiff's house, Joigny

17th century sculpture,
Saint Thibault church, Joigny

buried in Paris at the Oratorian church of Saint Magloire, now demolished.

A staircase behind the castle leads to the street below. A *house* identified as that where Vincent stayed is now a private home, not open to the public. *(10, rue Dominique Grenet)* A plaque identifies it: "Saint Vincent de Paul lived in this house." His visits here can be precisely dated up to 1618. He made others in 1628 and 1629 and gave a mission lasting four months in 1638-1639. His confreres also gave missions in Joigny and throughout the region, as they were required to do in virtue of the foundation that the Gondis established. This work continued at least until the early 18th century.

Outside the gate in front of the

Postcard, Saint André church, Joigny

and other works of art. A window recalls Vincent's presence: "In memory of the Confraternity of the Ladies of Charity of Joigny, 1613." This confraternity, the third that he founded, covered the whole town and included as members the pastors of Saint Thibault and the two other parishes. The window is dated 1927.

The church is also important as the baptismal church of *Madeleine Sophie Barat* (1779-1865). She was born in Joigny—her birthplace is preserved and may be visited—and was baptized the following day, 12 December 1779. She made her first communion in this same church in 1789. Stained glass and marble plaques record these events. Her brother Louis studied at the Saint Firmin seminary in Paris, the former Bons Enfants. Madeleine Sophie went on to found the Society of the Sacred Heart. One of the sisters of the Society, *Philippine Duchesne* (1769-1852), founded the first house of the community in the diocese of Saint Louis, Missouri, in the United States. Philippine Duchesne knew and

church is the bailiff's house, the most impressive timbered house in Joigny. It was built after the fire of 1530, with many Renaissance details. Unfortunately, the bomb that destroyed the stained glass in the church also destroyed the façade of this house. It has been rebuilt, but the side on Ruelle haute Saint Jean is original. Vincent would have passed it often and possibly entered since the bailiff in the founder's time signed the document establishing the confraternity of Joigny.

Joigny also features the important church of *Saint Thibault*. Begun about 1450, it was completed in 1529, the year before the great fire. The tower was finished in the seventeenth century. The building contains important statuary

Confraternity of Charity chapel, Joigny

Confraternity housing, Joigny

esteemed Felix De Andreis, the first Vincentian superior in America. She was canonized in 1988. Mother Barat, as she was called, was canonized in 1925. *(11, rue Davier)*

The third parish of Joigny was **Saint André**, now no longer used. *(Place de la Republique)* Its pastor was one of the three who, under the guidance of Vincent de Paul, founded the confraternity of women (1618) and then the mixed confraternity of men and women (1621).

The headquarters of the confraternity was the chapel of the **Saint Antoine Hospital**, a foundation dating from the twelfth century. This was part of a larger building, some of whose walls are still

standing. After the Revolution, hospital services were transferred to another old establishment, still in use across the Yonnne *(avenue Gambetta)*, and the Saint Antoine buildings became first a secondary school (1848-1968), and later a music school. The old chapel is now the city's school of dance. *(24, rue saint Jacques)*. Vincent also received two houses from members of the confraternity for various charitable uses. *(Maison de Charité, 2 bis and adjoining house, rue du Four Banal)* This charitable work lasted from 1620 to 1661.

The city also has a church of **Saint Vincent de Paul**. Begun in 1960 to serve a new housing development, it recalls Vincent's presence among and care for the people of Joigny.

Vincent also went at least once to the Carthusian monastery, Valprofonde, located near Joigny, on the south side of the Yonne. Some seven kilometers from the river is Béon and, two kilometers farther south on D943, a small access road leads to the farm, still called Les Chartreux (the Carthusians). The present buildings, while old, probably are not the original Carthusian foundation,

Hospice, Saint-Fargeau

which would normally have a distinct architecture allowing for a semi-eremitic life for the monks. Vincent recalled the advice given him during his retreat, which helped him overcome temptations he suffered while hearing confessions. (Letter 477)

The small town of **Villecien** is a short distance west of Joigny. A pastor, Jean Maurice, was the first moderator of the Confraternity of Charity of Joigny. The name of the town also appears once in Vincent's correspondence. (Letter 23, February 1628) He was here after giving a mission on one of the estates of Antoine Hennequin, Sieur of Vincy (d. 1645). His father had built the family castle, still standing, and it is likely that Vincent stayed in the castle. Monsieur de Vincy, as he was called, continued to befriend and support the saint. Indeed, on his deathbed he received permission to join the Congregation of the Mission, and was buried in the Saint Lazare chapel. His sister, Isabelle Du Fay (also Du Fey or Fays, d. 1635) lived here as well. Both were close confidants of Louise and Vincent, perhaps because they were related to her through Michel de Marillac, her uncle. The parish church generally preserves the appearance it had in Vincent's day. Its elaborate presidential chair and baptismal font were there in his time. Members of the Hennequin family were also the lords of Clichy when Vincent was pastor there.

Local tradition also associates Vincent with **Paroy-sur-Tholon**, a small town south of Joigny on D955, probably one of several depending on the Confraternity of Charity in Joigny.

Nothing exists in the town or in the parish church to recall his ministry.

South of Joigny is **Saint-Fargeau**. Daughters of Charity came here to work in the hospital and opened a small school. They arrived in 1657 at the initiative of the duchess of Montpensier, Anne Marie Louise d'Orléans (1627-1693). She had been a rebel leader in the Fronde and is known for opening the gates of Paris to the prince of Condé's army. This act was ultimately fruitless, as the Parisians rejected the rebels and welcomed the king, his mother and Cardinal Mazarin back in their midst. The life of the Daughters in Saint-Fargeau was attractive enough to draw several others to join their Company. Their house, already old when they arrived, is still standing and serves as a retirement home. The town today numbers fewer than 2000 persons. (*Maison de retraite, rue du Moulin de l'Arche, and rue de l'Hôpital*)

## MÂCON*

It was probably on a visit to Châtillon in 1619 or 1620 that Vincent passed by Mâcon. By that date he was already chaplain general of the galleys and thus a person of some importance. He came across many poor people on the streets, probably because they had heard that the Aumône, the local charitable confraternity, was dispensing help. Since the confraternity no longer could manage to do so, and perhaps with the support of the Oratorians, with whom he had been associated previously in Paris, Vincent spent a week reorganizing it. He returned and helped it further by

Vincent serving the poor,
Saint Pierre church, Mâcon

joining his Confraternity of Charity with the Aumône. Afterwards, the new group was called the Association of Saint Charles of Christian Charity. During this latter visit, which lasted three weeks or a month, he stayed with the Oratorians in the new seminary, near the Cathedral. These details come from Father Guillaume Desmoulins, the Oratorian superior. He likewise described how the poor were also to go to confession monthly and fulfill other religious obligations.

Vincent, too, described it to Louise. *When I set up the Charity in Mâcon, everyone made fun of me and would point at me in the streets, but when the deed was accomplished, everyone wept for joy. The town magistrates paid me so much honor on my departure that not being able to stand it, I was compelled to leave in secret to avoid the applause.* (Letter 198c) The Charity of Mâcon was one of the oldest in France and became a model cited by the French clergy at their 1670 assembly in Pontoise. It is unknown whether Vincent ever returned to Mâcon after this time.

To honor Vincent, a side chapel of the church of **Saint Pierre** recalls his activity with a large mural painting of him as well as two stained glass windows. The left window quotes from the rules: "The purpose of this assembly is to be able to help the poor." The right window reads "St. Vincent de Paul began this charity on 16 September 1621 in the church of St. Nizier." More historically important is the original painting by Jean François de Troy of Vincent preaching. This was one of the series painted for his canonization that hung in the original Saint Lazare. It is found in the left apse. This church, however, was built only in 1865, in neo-Romanesque style. *(Place Saint Pierre)*

The patron of the **cathedral**, Saint Vincent, is not Vincent de Paul but

Jean François de Troy, "Vincent preaching," Saint Pierre church, Mâcon

Turn, Hospital of the Charity, Mâcon

rather the patron of winegrowers, since Mâcon is in an important wine-growing area. This Saint Vincent Cathedral, opened in 1816, was built under Napoleon I, and was originally called Saint Napoleon, an ancient martyr (Neopolus of Alexandria) whose feast was joined to that of the Assumption, 15 August, beginning in 1806. It was later altered to Saint Louis when Louis XVIII came to power, and then to Saint Vincent, the title it keeps. The Old Saint Vincent has kept some of the parts of a medieval church but has largely been rebuilt.

The church of **Saint Nizier**, mentioned in the foundation records of the confraternity, no longer exists, having been demolished shortly after the Revolution. It was probably located where the Musée Lamartine now stands. It was an annex of the church of Saint Pierre le Vieux, and a chapel of the Penitents in the seventeenth century. The Ladies of Charity too assembled there for their spiritual nourishment.

The old **Hospital of the Charity** also recalls Vincent's work in Mâcon. Its famous "turn" is visible from inside and outside the building. Originally a feature of cloistered convents, it came to be used for those who were abandoning children. They placed them in it, pivoted the "turn" toward the inside and then notified the hospital personnel by ringing a bell. Abandoning children here offered a better future than leaving them outside a church in the cold, where someone might steal them or the children might die of exposure. *(249, rue Carnot)* At the Revolution the hospital became a prison for elderly priests who had refused to take the constitutional oath. The Revolutionary cult, Theophilanthropism, was moved to the hospital chapel here in 1796, but the chapel reverted quickly to the parish, which used it beginning in 1802. The Sisters of Charity of Nevers directed the hospital from 1804 to 1973. The building itself was built from 1752 to 1762. The structure replaced an earlier one set up in 1680 in memory of the original Charity Vincent founded in 1620. Although the intriguing "turn" does not date from Vincent's period, it is nevertheless one of the rare specimens still in existence and illustrates a dark chapter of history. Modern Mâcon has around 40,000 inhabitants.

Vincent's fame had preceded him to Mâcon, as we read in a document dated September 1621. The town officials knew that "a pious priest of the general of the galleys" had acted as he had previously done in "Trévoux and in other surrounding towns." (Doc. 134) A confraternity at **Trévoux**, a few kilometers southwest of Châtillon, may show that Vincent's work extended farther

Collegiate church, Tournus

than just his parish. In any case, nothing is known about his activities here or elsewhere in the district apart from this enigmatic reference.

The great abbey church of **Tournus**, mentioned above as the titular abbey of Louis de Chandenier (d. 1660), is still standing, a few kilometers north of Mâcon. Vincent likely came to visit as he passed through the region of Mâcon. The institution ceased to be a monastery in 1627, and thereafter a series of secular priests became its titular abbots. Louis III de Rochechouard, as he is listed in the abbey church, held the post only from 1645 to 1647. After this time, he apparently had some rights to a pension and so continued to be called the abbot of Tournus. This priest was so attached to

the Congregation of the Mission that he asked and received permission on his deathbed to join the community. Daughters of Charity served the poor in the hospital here from 1764 until the Revolution, and then again from 1853 until about 1900. The tenth-century abbey church and its grounds still dominate this town of about 7000 people.

## MOUTIERS-SAINT-JEAN*

The village of Moutiers-Saint-Jean is the site of a former monastery (or *moutiers*). A local saint, John of Rhéaume (or Réôme) began a monastic life nearby. After his death about the year 540, his followers moved his body to Moutiers, a more suitable location. One of the monks of this ancient abbey, Aurelian, wrote the first treatise applying the rules of Greek and Latin composers to the music of the Church. This happened about the year 850. Another date of great importance was about the year 1020, when the liturgical feast of the Blessed Trinity was inaugurated here. This monastery was partly destroyed at the time of the Revolution, and historic pieces of it, particularly from the chapel, were sold at public auction. Some of them reached museums in the United States. What remains has been turned over for housing. The Jardins du Coeur du Roy, the elegant abbey garden, a Renaissance design, can still be seen outside the walls of the monastic enclosure.

Claude Charles de Rochechouart de Chandenier (d. 1710), formerly abbot of l'Aumône, in the commune of La Colombe, in 1655 became the abbot of

Moutiers-Saint-Jean. His life from 1650 to 1660 is frequently and easily confused with that of his brother Louis, the (titular) abbot of Tournus. Their mutual love and affection was such they did not wish to be separated, although each one was offered a bishopric. Both of them named Vincent, for whom they had a great respect, as their vicar general. He thus had responsibilities toward the abbeys that the brothers governed, here at Moutiers and at Tournus, which would have let him name pastors for the parishes dependent on Moutiers. Unfortunately, no documents to this effect survive. Vincent held these offices from October 1650 to June 1652. Claude died 18 May 1710, and Collet, Vincent's second biographer, quotes the text of his long epitaph. (Vol. 1, pp. 584-88) In the

Simon François portrait,
hospice chapel, Moutiers-Saint-Jean

chapel of the former hospital hangs a rare early portrait of Saint Vincent. The work of Simon François, it portrays Vincent in choir dress and was probably made for Claude de Chandenier. It may likewise have been painted for him by one of the monks of the monastery. Claude de Chandenier is buried in this chapel.

It is believed that, on missionary journeys, Vincent might have visited the abbey. Even so, this would have been before Claude de Chandenier became its titular abbot. Perhaps because of his visit, a *Confraternity of Charity* existed here beginning 4 June 1656. Daughters of Charity apparently worked for the Charity beginning in 1660. On 4 March 1681, the bishop of Langres authorized the opening of a hospital (now a retirement home), with the help of the Mesdames Vernot. The Daughters of Charity took up this work around 1710.

Hospice chapel entry,
Moutiers-Saint-Jean

During the Revolution, they remained, sometimes attending mass celebrated secretly in an attic. When the sisters withdrew from this house in the 1980s, they also left behind the famous portrait. In the former hospital, the pharmacy,

Bourchardon statue, hospice sacristy,
Moutiers-Saint-Jean

Vincent's pitcher, hospice pharmacy,
Moutiers-Saint-Jean

with its antique containers for medicines, contains a porcelain pitcher and basin said to have belonged to Vincent, as well as a plate with an egg-cup and salt cellar attached, useful for serving the sick.

As a young girl, *Catherine Labouré* (1806-1876) used to attend mass in the hospital chapel. The young Catherine did not see the portrait of Vincent, since the sisters kept it in their common room. The circular relief of him on the façade of the chapel, however, was presented only in 1868. In addition, a small *statue* of the Blessed Virgin Mary is still to be seen. This statue, similar to the painting in Catherine's parish church, before which she probably prayed as a child, was kept in the hospital chapel. Both the painting of Mary and the statue are based on a design by the popular sculptor Edme Bouchardon, the model that the archbishop of Paris chose for the Miraculous Medal.

In the *parish church* a series of modern windows depicts events in the lives of local saints. These windows show Saints Benedict, Vincent de Paul and Louise de Marillac, and Catherine Labouré. She attended Sunday mass here and made her first communion in this

Parish church, Moutiers-Saint-Jean

376

Vincent de Paul, parish,
Moutiers-Saint-Jean

Alphonse Ratisbonne window,
parish, Moutiers-Saint-Jean

church, 25 January 1818. The town has fewer than 300 inhabitants.

A short distance away, up the D103 and astride an old crossroads, is **Fain-lès-Moutiers**. This was Catherine's home village. The Daughters of Charity have acquired her birthplace and some of the property and now welcome retreatants and other guests.

The *home* of the Labourés, one of the leading families of Fain, can be visited. The main room today was originally two rooms: the girls' room on one side and the other containing the kitchen and eating area, the center of the home. At one side is the original area where cheese was prepared; this has been left nearly as it was when the house was last purchased. After the death of Catherine's mother and the departure of her older sister to enter the Daughters of Charity, Catherine took over the management of the family estate and was also a surrogate mother to her siblings. She was only twelve years old. Her parents' bedroom preserves pictures and items of furniture either from the family itself (the original cradle, a wardrobe) or from the period. The boys lived upstairs. In the farmyard is the large dovecote, Catherine's responsibility. The family raised the doves to sell in the market for their eggs and meat.

Across the road from the house is the Romanesque *parish church*. At various times the Labouré family cared for it. The infant Catherine was baptized here. A well-known and evocative paint-

Farmyard, Labouré home,
Fain-lès-Moutiers

ing of the Blessed Virgin (as the Immaculate Conception) is to be seen in the body of the church, where it has hung since before Catherine was born. It closely resembles the design on the Miraculous Medal. A side chapel was the special responsibility of her family. Stained glass windows in this chapel depict her and Saint Vincent de Paul. During his brief term as vicar of the abbot of Moutiers, Vincent was responsible for naming the pastor here. Records are lacking to show whether he ever named anyone.

Catherine often walked along the road leading from Fain to Moutiers-Saint-Jean to attend daily mass since in her days no resident priest lived in the village. Fain today has about 150 inhabitants.

A short distance north of Fain is Saint-Remy, home of Catherine's aunt and uncle, the Jeanrots. After the latter's death, and after the death of her own mother, Catherine lived with Aunt Marguerite (d. 1853) from the autumn of 1815 to early 1818. Because other relatives resided near by, Catherine has also been associated with visits to other villages: Vassy, Cormarin, and perhaps

Fireplace, Labouré home,
Fain-lès-Moutiers

Senailly, her mother's birthplace.

When Catherine decided to enter the Daughters of Charity, she made her postulancy at the house in Châtillon-sur-Seine, at the source of the Seine some forty kilometers north of Fain. She had also stayed here from 1824 to 1826 with a cousin *(7, rue Saint Vorles)* before moving to Paris to help her brother as a waitress in his pub. She then returned to join the Sisters, but nothing remains of the house she entered on Rue de la Juiverie, except that its wrought-iron grilles are at the municipal library. After three months, in early 1830, she moved from here to Paris where she entered the novitiate at the Rue du Bac in mid-April.

## SENS

The city of Sens has a long history. Its archbishop held the important title of Primate of the Gauls and Germany. The diocese of Paris too was subject to him until 1622, at which time Paris became an archdiocese in its own right. Nevertheless, Sens did not figure much in Vincent's history. He did have some dealings with the archdiocese early in his career, since Joigny, the seat of the Gondis, was in its territory. In 1616

Labouré home,
Fain-lès-Moutiers

Vincent was giving missions on their lands and heard general confessions. When he met with cases reserved to the bishop, he wrote to ask general permission to grant absolution. All of this may appear overly legalistic, but it shows that he had already begun to preach missions and hear general confessions even before the foundation of the Congregation of the Mission (1625). Perhaps his experience at Gannes and Folleville (1617) urged him in this direction.

The date of Vincent's visit to Sens is 20 June 1616, when he wrote for permission to absolve reserved cases. Since the vicar general wrote his reply on the same day, it appears likely that Vincent had delivered the petition in person. Otherwise, we know of no other time when he was in Sens.

Vincent's congregation ran the *seminary* in Sens from 1675 to the Revolution and, in 1839, returned to the same seminary until the expulsion of 1903. Among its other responsibilities, in pre-Revolutionary times the seminary served as a clerical penitentiary. Another of its obligations was to serve the parish of *Notre Dame de Sens*. Daughters of Charity had an orphanage and various primary schools here beginning in 1854.

There is little if any reminder of Vincent in the great Gothic cathedral of Sens. For English speakers, the presence of the exiled archbishop of Canterbury Thomas Becket (1118-1170) at Sens is important. His memory remains alive here, and among the relics is Becket's chasuble, famous for being part of the oldest complete medieval vestments in existence.

Shrine church, Épine

# Champagne-Ardenne

*Although the Thirty Years War ended officially in 1648, it continued in various forms in northern France, particularly in Champagne and Picardy, for some years. Marauding armies from the Spanish Netherlands competed with those of the French in brutalizing the population. Church institutions were not spared, since the devastation took on the character of a religious war. Vincent de Paul, Louise de Marillac and many others energized the Ladies of Charity to undertake works of relief. Daughters of Charity served the sick poor, among whom were sick soldiers. Vincentians fanned out throughout the provinces to bring spiritual and financial aid, collected mostly in Paris. One of the most important methods of raising funds was the Relations, a publication of letters describing the horrors that the missionaries and others were encountering. The grateful magistrates of Rethel, one of the towns in Champagne, wrote in a similar vein, but added their thanks for the help received. The very words they used are still horrifying: cheating, starvation, barbarous and cruel acts, unbearable licentiousness, malice, generalized brigandage, desolation, horrible necessity. (Letter 1381, 17 July 1651)*

## CHÂLONS-EN-CHAMPAGNE, ÉPINE

Vincent sent his missionaries to preach in the diocese of Châlons (also called Châlons-sur-Marne). One reason for doing so was his friendship with Félix Vialart (1613-1680). This man was the son of Michel Vialart and Charlotte de Ligny, another of Vincent's many influential women supporters. Félix was, in addition, the cousin of Jean Jacques Olier. Vialart became bishop of Châlons in 1640. These complex personal relations illumine the basis of much of Vincent's work. Louise visited the Charities of the diocese, and the Daughters of Charity came here in 1653 to serve war victims in the city hospital. They served in various schools and the hospital from 1692 and then after the Revolution until 1907.

Vincentian service in the *seminary* began, however, only in 1681, lasting until the Revolution. Vincentians returned in 1833. The superior at the time was Jean Baptiste Nozo, who remained until his election as superior general in 1835. The seminary was suppressed from 1866 to 1883, when the Vincentians again returned and remained until 1903. The city today has about 50,000 people.

Possibly the seminary's most noteworthy professor *Buenaventura Codina* (1785-1857). A Spanish Vincentian, he had come to France when the Congregation was suppressed in his country. He would return home as provincial superior and director of the Daughters of Charity. His saintly reputation led him to be named bishop of the diocese of the Canary Islands, with residence at Las Palmas (1848). He was distanced but not expelled from the Congregation for accepting the episcopacy without the superior general's permission. The bishop's cause for canonization has been introduced in Rome.

The basilica of *Notre Dame de l'Épine* dominates the plateau above Châlons. This pilgrimage church began, as often happened, with the report of a miraculous statue of the Virgin Mary that appeared in a thorn bush *(épine)* in flames. The present church, of cathedral size, began in the fifteenth century. It is one of the few churches in the country to have kept its altar-screen, or *jubé*, under which is kept the pilgrimage statue.

Notre Dame de l'Épine

Vincentians became part of its long history because they served in the seminary at Châlons. The bishop united this shrine parish to the seminary in 1725, and two priests arrived to care for it. The reason for this was undoubtedly to secure a source of income to support the seminary. A separate Vincentian house existed here from 1732 until 1758, when it was turned over to diocesan clergy. Épine has a population of fewer than 700.

Early statue of Saint Vincent, Chaumont

## CHAUMONT

Daughters of Charity came to staff the **hospital** of this city, also called Chaumont-en-Bassigny, in 1672. The interest in Chaumont lies in that one of the oldest, if not the oldest, statues of Saint Vincent is in the chapel of their former work. The sculptor Jean Baptiste Bouchardon, a Chaumont native, carved it in 1730 and placed it with two others on the chapel altarpiece. This small gilded statue depicts Vincent in a pose that was scarcely copied after this time: holding a book in his left hand and a heart surmounted with flames in his right. This heart, a feature of charitable saints, and perhaps derived from the iconography associated with Saint Augustine, is among the earliest symbols associated with Vincent de Paul. He is joined here by a similar statue of Mary, in the center, and Mary Magdalene on the right, the patroness of the hospital. The Daughters returned to the hospital after the Revolution, and remained until about 1903. In keeping with their long service here, other statues of Vincent and Louise have been placed in the hospital chapel. Chaumont today has a population of about 28,000. (*Centre Hospitalier, 66, avenue Carnot*)

## LANGRES

The city of Langres, whose medieval walls still stand, numbers about 10,000 inhabitants today. There is no indication that Vincent ever came here, but he had some contact with its powerful bishop, Sébastien Zamet (1588-1655). Vincent appreciated his

Road sign, Saint-Nicolas-de-Grosse-Sauve

Priory building,
Saint-Nicolas-de-Grosse-Sauve

opposition to Jansenism. His name and coat of arms appear in several places in the cathedral, although there is nothing recalling Vincent here.

In February 1624, while Vincent was still pastor of Clichy, he took possession of the small priory of *Saint-Nicolas-de-Grosse-Sauve*, formerly in the hands of his Oratorian friends. As was typical in his day, a priory served as a source of income, like a modern real estate investment, rather than a religious house. There is nothing to show that Vincent ever came here, and records are lacking to show that he gave up the priory. He probably did so around the time of the founding of the Congregation of the Mission, in 1625 or 1626. That we know this much is due to a fragment of parchment used to bind an old missal. It was discovered and deciphered in 1897. How many more discoveries might be made is anyone's guess. Subsequent discoveries have confirmed the original document.

The former priory and hospital is now a farm, southeast of Langres, on D136, a Roman road. The only early

Former chapel,
Saint-Nicolas-de-Grosse-Sauve

building is part of the old chapel, now a garage and barn. As its name indicates (*sauve*, from Latin *silva*, or woods), it is in wooded country.

The Vincentian community had planned a house in Langres (1672), but it did not open. The Daughters of Charity, however, worked in two hospitals and two parishes from 1690 until the Revolution, and again afterwards. **Jeanne Antide Thouret**, the future saint, spent her postulancy at the city hospital and returned in 1789 to serve for a few months in the military hospital, Saint Laurent, also run by the Daughters.

## MONTMIRAIL**

Vincent lived in Montmirail with the Gondi family, since Philip Emmanuel, the general of the galleys, was baron of Montmirail-en-Brie and had a chateau here. Vincent, of course, was the family tutor, with responsibilities for the education of the children. The household where he worked numbered between 20 and 25 attending Madame alone, not counting others who worked for the general. One of the sons, Jean François Paul de Gondi, became the notorious Cardinal de Retz, later the first archbishop of Paris. He was born in the chateau of Montmirail in the fall of 1613, probably when Vincent first

Parish church, Montmirail

Blessed John de Montmirail as a knight, parish church, Montmirail

Vincent de Paul in Montmirail,
parish church, Montmirail

arrived here. Vincent's conference to his confreres on the duties of a chaplain in a noble family (Conference 14) undoubtedly reflects his own experiences here. Brother Robineau, his secretary, recounts how Vincent accompanied the pious Madame de Gondi in her rounds to feed the sick poor.

Montmirail (a name meaning "hill of surveillance") was important, even in Roman times. The church of *Saint Étienne* itself may have been built over a pre-Christian building. The present church began in 1122. It has been expanded and renovated several times, particularly because of the town's exposed location on main roads. The last great change in the church took place at the Revolution, when the ancient funeral monuments of the lords of Montmirail were destroyed. Montmirail, with about 4000 inhabitants today, was also on the escape route of Louis XVI and his family, attempting to flee in 1791 to the safety of France's Austrian enemies. He was recognized here and arrested at Varennes, farther along the highway. This sealed his fate and led him and the queen to the guillotine.

Of particular interest in the church is Vincent's pulpit. This wooden pulpit bears an indication that the saint used it in 1613. In his time, it also had individual statues of the twelve apostles, but they were removed at the time of the Revolution. Located in the body of the church, the pulpit faces a large crucifix, below which were the seats for the parish trustees. Perhaps Madame de Gondi and her family also sat here. In the fashion of the eighteenth century, the seats are enclosed and face the pulpit directly. Brother Louis Robineau, the saint's secretary, recalled that Vincent had begun a weekly service in the parish church on Saturday evenings to honor the Blessed Virgin. It continued for many decades. Vincent also founded his fourth Confraternity of Charity here (1618) even before the beginning of the Congregation of the Mission, and he visited it at least in May of 1629. (Letter 39) Louise also came to visit in 1630, and Daughters of Charity arrived, probably in 1650.

The stained glass is not old. In the 1880s, the pastor had planned to install a

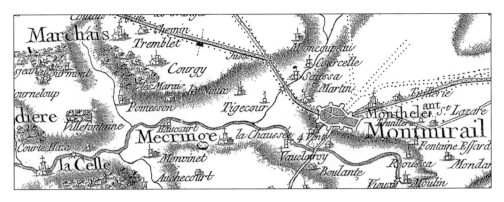

Eighteenth century map, Marchais and Montmirail

series of windows depicting the life of Saint Vincent. Only two of these are extant. The first, in the body of the church, depicts the Montmirail church. In this window, Saint Vincent is shown preaching, cross in hand, with a bell at his feet to summon the people. He stands on a raised platform. Below him are gathered the Gondi family members, clergy and the people of the area, both rich and poor. The second, in the left transept, depicts the saint encouraging the Ladies of Charity in Paris not to abandon their support for the

Postcard, Gondi castle, Montmirail

foundlings. Below is an extract from the text of his address to the Ladies: "If you abandon them, they will all die."

One modern statue depicts Saint Vincent bending down to recover an abandoned infant. Based on the Stouf model, it dates from 1897. Other much older and more important statues decorate the walls: an ancient Pietà and a relief of Saint Martin on horseback.

The various memorials of Blessed Jean de Montmirail (1165-1217) are noteworthy. He had been the local baron and a close friend of King Philip Augustus, with whom he was raised. At age 45 and after a life of soldiering, he became a monk. Vincent mentioned this local saint in a conference he gave to the Daughters of Charity. (Conference 28, 22 October 1646) He noted that Jean had had a problem that he confided to the prior of his monastery: he could not bear to clean his own shoes. The prior himself eventually did this for him. Jean later admitted his fault and took to cleaning them himself—an incident Vincent offered to the sisters of the power of

Vincent reliquary, parish
church, Montmirail

good example, the prior's, in bringing order to a community house. In 1208 this same Jean founded the hospital that the Vincentians and later the Daughters of Charity were to run.

The church also preserves an important relic of Saint Vincent: a bone from his foot. Also important was a miraculous cure, associated with this relic, of a Benedictine nun from Montmirail. The Holy See accepted it as an element of Vincent's canonization process.

An old side chapel, with traces of older painted decoration, has been transformed into a Blessed Sacrament chapel where daily mass is celebrated. The Blessed Sacrament is preserved in a modern tabernacle set into the niche formerly used to keep it in medieval times. Also in this chapel is the entry into the adjoining chateau, and above the chapel is a room whose windows look out onto the sanctuary. The family used it to attend mass in noble privacy. It was probably in this chapel, named after Saint Nicholas, that Vincent founded the Confraternity of Charity. He probably prayed in this chapel as well.

A large *Vincentian house*, used for many years, also exists in the town. This eighteenth-century building, at the end of Rue St. Vincent de Paul, has been transformed into a public building, the Centre Social La Rochefoucauld, and it may be visited. The large relic of Saint Vincent displayed in the parish church was formerly kept in this Community house. From here, the Vincentians went out to give missions and also helped to organize the relief of the province of Champagne, devastated by wars during the founder's lifetime. They also directed the Confraternity of Charity, which had important work among prisoners.

Adjoining the church is the *chateau*. Formerly the property of the

Road sign, Montmirail

Vieux Moulin farm, Montmirail

Gondi family, it passed into the hands of the Rochefoucauld family, which recently sold it. Tradition assigns Vincent a particular room, located directly over the entrance. In front of the chateau stretches a broad avenue of trees. In 1620, Madame de Gondi invited three Huguenots to this chateau for Vincent to instruct in the Catholic faith. Two of them renounced their Calvinist beliefs, but the third did not. His caustic remarks about the Catholic clergy so struck Vincent that they became, in some way, a turning point in his life.

The supervisor of the Gondi property, its *intendant*, was **Martin Husson** (1623-1695), a Montmirail native. Vincent admired his abilities and got this young man to accept the office of French consul in Tunis, where he went in 1653. As a layperson, he had fewer problems than the Vincentians did in that office. Nevertheless, the Tunisian authorities expelled him in 1657 and, on his return to France, he became the intendant of the duchess of Aiguillon.

It was perhaps in the chateau that a natural wonder was kept, one which excited Vincent's interest. *Those who have been to Montmirail have seen a tree trunk changed into stone. But how did this happen? I do not know by what power wood came to be changed into stone. The one changed into the other such that what was wood appears to be stone. The wood that is there is wood. Your eyes tell you that it is wood. The moss that envelops it, its visible features and seams tell you that it is wood. But touch it, and you know it is stone. This is an illusion, my brothers.* (Conference 214) He used this example in a conference to his confreres on truth and illusions. The whereabouts of this fossilized tree are unknown today.

Leading east out of town is a section of road called the Little Saint Lazare, a name given to a small hospice for lepers and contagious cases. Before the Congregation lived in town, it had a country home at **Fontaine-Essart**, a hamlet just east of Montmirail. The per-

Parish church, Marchais-en-Brie

Parish church, Courboin

that of *Vieux-Moulin* (Old Mill), located on D43, below the Montmirail hill, where a mill still operates. Both of these farms, Fontaine-Essart and Vieux-Moulin, were in the parish of Courbetaux. Louis Toublanc, secretary of the duke of Retz, willed these two properties to the Congregation in a document dated 14 July 1644.

In keeping with the methods of the time, the missionaries in Montmirail and the Daughters of Charity received income from the old pilgrim shelter at *La Chaussée*, in the floodplain below Montmirail. As it happened, all three of these properties, Fontaine-Essart, Vieux-Moulin and La Chaussée, were in the diocese of Troyes, whereas Montmirail itself was in Soissons. This caused complications in securing title and finances. The Daughters lived at La Chaussée from 1648 or 1650, until the hospital and the sisters transferred into town. They took up the hospital in Montmirail again after the Revolution, remaining until about 1900.

sonnel stationed in Montmirail lived here from 1644 before moving into town in 1678. Vincent addressed several letters to his confreres here (e.g., Letter 2678, in 1658). Nothing remains today to distinguish one set of old farm buildings from another, or to point out the Vincentian site. In any case, the old house burned down early on. The missionaries at Fontaine-Essart had much to suffer in the Fronde because of marauding armies. After moving into town, the Vincentians kept this country property until the Revolution, a pattern repeated elsewhere.

Another local Vincentian farm was

As part of their mission work, three Vincentians at Fontaine-Essart founded a Confraternity of Charity in nearby **Sézanne** in 1657. The members of the confraternity received the chapel of the martyrs in the parish church of Saint Denis to use for their prayers. Daughters of Charity were present here from 1681, in the Hôtel Dieu, until the Revolution and returned in 1802. There is nothing in the parish church, however, to evoke the work of the Vincentians or the Daughters.

At a short distance west of Montmirail is **Marchais-en-Brie**, where an old village church still stands. In 1621, Vincent and some other priests and religious were preaching a mission here. Vincent encountered again the recalcitrant Huguenot whom he had met in Montmirail and gradually won him over. To prove what Catholics believed about the honor given to statues, Vincent called on a child from the congregation. The child's wise answer was the man's deciding moment, and he remained faithful to Catholicism throughout life. The statue of Mary in the church, the subject of the discussion, thereupon became famous. During the Revolution, some "madmen," as Coste calls them, removed the statue and mutilated it. One of the townspeople saved the head, and it is now in the Vincentian museum of the motherhouse in Paris. The church itself is in a poor state and has nothing reflecting the presence of Vincent or of his confreres who came here later to give missions.

Although the next few sites fall within the bounderies of modern Picardy, they are included here because of their connection with Montmirail. North of the city, toward Château-Thierry, is **Montlevon**. Vincent gave a mission here with other clergy while in residence at Montmirail. The pastor recalled the young priest's humility. Further to the north is **Courboin**, one of the fiefs belonging to Madame de Gondi. According to a contemporary document, she and Vincent were present here on 19 June 1622 for the establishment of a Confraternity of Charity. A side chapel, renamed the Chapel of Jesus or of the Charity, was set aside at the time for the

members. The village church of Courboin has kept many of its old features (pews and benches, the old flooring), but the chapel in question did not continue. The same document names Chamblon and other villages belonging to Madame, probably including Montlevon. Chamblon is today's La Ville-Chamblon, southwest of Courboin. This Chamblon had a farm depending on the Vincentian house of Montmirail, as well as a Confraternity of Charity, but there is nothing to distinguish it today. (Vincent mentioned it, for example, in Letter 733, written in 1644.) One further fief of Madame de Gondi was Trosnay,

Parish church, Liesse-Notre-Dame

Vincentian house, Sedan

today's **Thoult-Trosnay (Le)** a few kilometers east of Montmirail. Since Vincent identified her in Letter 26 as baroness of Trosnay, the implication is that he must have given missions also in this parish, since he was obliged to preach on her lands.

The pilgrimage site of **Liesse-Notre-Dame**, some distance north of Château-Thierry and east of Laon, has a long history. The earliest records date the building to the twelfth century. The structure has been rebuilt and improved several times since then. Our Lady of Joy attracted the royal family of France as well as Vincentians and Daughters of Charity, although it is unknown if

Vincent or Louise ever visited here. The pilgrimage statue (replaced after the Revolution) is one of many black virgins in Europe. The church has kept its *jubé* (altar screen), one of the few left in France. In the town, now with about 1200 people, is a well reputed to be miraculous.

## SEDAN

At the beginning of his final illness, Louis XIII personally asked Vincent to send his missionaries to Sedan, with the

Saint Charles church, Sedan

Street sign, Sedan

express purpose of working for the conversion of the Calvinists. Sedan had been an independent principality until 1642, when Frédéric Maurice, the last prince, ceded it unwillingly to Louis as reparation for his part in a conspiracy. The prince had been raised a Protestant, and his family furthered the development of Reform by sponsoring a Protestant theology faculty in Sedan. He became a Catholic, however, in 1637.

The Vincentians left for Sedan on 14 May 1643, a week before the king's death. They assumed the pastorate of the town's only parish, **Saint Laurent.** From here, they went out on mission. This church suffered from age and was mostly demolished in 1692, except for the choir, which was finally taken down in 1792-1799. The site of the church is now an open area between houses facing on the Place de la Halle, Rue de Mulhouse and Rue des Voyards. There are some vaults underneath which had been used for burials, even until recent times. The whole section is now called Place Saint Laurent and is used mainly as a car park.

The house across the street, opposite the entrance to the yard, formerly called the Hôtel des Trois Écus, was the *Vincentian house* after 1666. It is not known where they lived previously. In the same house, the missionaries received priesthood students for their philosophical training. In keeping with the Vincentian mission, they also held regular conferences for the clergy and gave parish missions. *(43, rue du Menil)*

With the revocation of the Edict of Nantes (1685), which dispossessed Protestants of their principal rights in France, their "temple" in Sedan became available for Catholic worship. The Vincentians saw to its expansion and decoration. Both **Saint Charles** *(Place d'Armes)* and Saint Laurent remained in use until the latter's closure. One of its most active Vincentian pastors was

Hospital entry, Sedan

*Nicolas Philbert* (1724-1797). At the time of the Revolution, Philbert decided to take the constitutional oath to help reform the clergy, and he was soon elected bishop of the Ardennes, the new designation for the diocese centered at Sedan. Saint Charles, where he had been pastor from 1762 to 1791, became his cathedral. This situation lasted only three years, when he was arrested (but escaped), and the church was sacked. Saint Charles then changed successively into a temple dedicated to the goddess of reason and to the Supreme Being. When it returned to Catholic worship in 1802, the revolutionary diocese ceased to exist. Philbert's pulpit, pipe organ and extensive woodwork remain. In the rear of the church is a traditional statue, marked "Saint Vincent de Paul, Pastor of Sedan 1643." This is stretching history somewhat, particularly since Vincent never came here.

A huge fortress, suitable for a frontier, dominates the city. Sedan, on the river Meuse, is just a few kilometers from the Belgian border today. To care for troops and civilians, a *hospital* was begun in Sedan as early as 1521. Daughters of Charity came here for the hospital in 1639 (or perhaps 1641) and later added a school; this was their first house outside the Paris area. They remained during the Revolution, staying at least until the 1920s. The present old hospital buildings, however, date from the period 1757-1760 and have been expanded in recent years. Philbert, mentioned above, is remembered as one of the many benefactors of this hospital. Its chapel, still in use, commemorates Saint Vincent with a statue at the pinnacle of the façade. Over the door is the inscription HIC PAUPERES EVANGELIZANTUR ("Here the poor are evangelized"). Further, the area by the current main entrance of the hospital has been named Place Saint Vincent de Paul. One event that clearly garnered the support of the local population was the extensive aid arranged by Vincent during the Fronde in 1650. To help the poor of Sedan, a Vincentian founded a small diocesan women's community here in 1695. The Sisters of the Holy Family of Sedan did not continue after the Revolution.

A further reference to the presence of Vincentians is the name of the street and shaded promenade in front of the fortress, the *Promenoir des Prêtres*, the "Priests' Walk," meaning the Priests of the Mission. Their house was just a few steps away from the fortress and their garden was private. Vincentians remained here until the Revolution.

Sedan suffered greatly at various periods. The French endured a humiliating defeat near here in 1870, losing the emperor Napoleon III and some 80,000 soldiers to capture by the Prussians. This defeat marked the end of the empire, and a new republic was proclaimed in Paris. In both World Wars Sedan was badly damaged, as the many pockmarked buildings, ruins and abandoned properties still testify. Sedan, partly reconstructed, has a current population of some 21,000.

Vincent had several things to say to the Daughters (Conference 61, 23 July 1654) and to the missionaries about their work here. Above all, he encouraged them not to dispute with heretics, *neither from the pulpit nor in private. [The king, Louis XIII] knows that this does little good and often produces more noise than fruit.* (Abelly, Book 2, p. 26)

## TROYES

In 1637, Vincent opened a house in Troyes to give missions and to train seminarians. He was able to do so with the help of his friend and patron, Noël Brûlart, Commander de Sillery. Of the buildings from Vincent's time, only the transept of the church remains, since another major seminary was built on the same site. A large bell that Vincent donated to this house has been moved to the bishop's residence. This bell dates from 1644 and bears copies of the seal of the Congregation. Vincent came here with the Commander in July of 1639, and on that occasion wrote to Jane Frances de Chantal, outlining for the first time *what constitutes our humble way of life.* (Letter 383)

Because of the presence of Irish regiments here in Vincent's time, he sent an Irish confrere, John McEnery (regu-

larly called Ennery) to minister to them. Louis Joseph François had been superior here until summoned to be secretary general in Paris in 1784. He was later martyred as the superior of the Bons Enfants (then called the Saint Firmin seminary) in Paris. After the Revolution, Vincentians returned to the seminary from 1876 until their expulsion in 1903, and again from 1921 to 1970. Troyes today has a population of about 60,000.

The Vincentians lived for two years near by in the village of **Sancey**, now called **Saint-Julien-les-Villas**. Sébastien Gouault, a citizen of Troyes, had lent them the house. The saint addressed several letters here in the years 1639-1641.

In the Daughters of Charity school in Troyes, where the Sisters had been since 1718, *Sister Apolline Andriveau*

Street sign, Troyes

Saint Vincent's bell, Troyes

(1810-1895) began to have her experiences concerning the Scapular of the Passion. She was noted for her intense prayer life and her regularity. Beginning in 1846, she experienced visions concerning the Passion of Jesus and saw him handing her a red scapular. Eventually this scapular was approved for devotional use, and it spread through the work of the Daughters of Charity and the Vincentians. Father Jean Baptiste Étienne, superior general, had a chapel dedicated to the Passion built in the Vincentian motherhouse in Paris. He also called for Vincentian chapels and

Lord of Charity, parish church, L'Huitre

churches to have similar altars. Because of the similarity of this devotion to that of the Holy Agony in the garden of Gethsemane, propagated by Father Antoine Nicolle, the chapel today serves also as the headquarters for the Holy Agony devotion. This house of the Daughters began in 1682 and reopened in 1802.

Various Confraternities of Charity, some with paintings of the Lord of Charity, existed in the area around Troyes. These paintings take their origin in a plan by Louise and Vincent to link the confraternities. They sent large paintings, or models for them, to the Charities, depicting the resurrected, charitable Jesus, arms outstretched downwards, presiding over the work of the confraternities. Generally, works of spiritual and corporal charity were also

Lord of Charity, parish church, Boulages

depicted. They are or were found in the following locations, listed in alphabetical order. At **Arcis-sur-Aube**, the Confraternity began 27 September 1662. Nicolas Des Guerrois, canon of the cathedral of Troyes, donated funds for missions to be given in Arcis, his home parish, every five years. **Boulages** has one of the paintings, mistakenly titled "Sacred Heart." The missionaries came here in 1653 and again in 1658. **Bouilly** also had a painting, but no Confraternity of Charity is known to have existed there. Perhaps records are lacking. In **Brienne-le-Château**, the confraternity began 24 September 1655. The confraternity was probably located at the hospital of Brienne, where the Daughters of Charity served. Local tradition has it that in 1653 Vincent himself came here to inaugurate the work of the sisters for war victims. Sister Barbe Angiboust, at least, was here the previous year for that same work. A famous student at the military school of Brienne, who made his first communion in the school chapel, perhaps under the gaze of the Daughters, was Napoleon Bonaparte. **Chavanges** has a painting dated 1642. It is remarkable in that one of the vignettes depicts Vincent as a younger man with light brown hair, giving communion to a sick person. If it is Vincent, it is the earliest known depiction of him. **Chennegy** had a Confraternity founded 10 March 1647. **Lhuître** has a painting, dated 1650, with a good likeness of an elderly Vincent giving communion to a sick person. Farther afield is **Loisy-en-Brie**, in the champagne-raising area. Vincent came here in 1626, and Louise followed

in 1631. The present church building is in poor condition. **Mailly-le-Camp** was reported to have had a Lord of Charity painting, but it is no longer in either of the churches in this little town. Although both **Nogent-sur-Seine** and **Rilly-Sainte-Syre** had missions in 1657, Vincent probably did not give them. He is said to have founded the confraternity at **Soulaines-Dhuys** in 1658. However, because of his health and age, it is not likely that he came here.

Besides these towns, some others are known through references to visits that Louise made. Vincent himself suggested that she go to several small towns located near each other: **Bergères(-lès-Vertus)**, **Le Mesnil(-sur-Oger)**, **Soudron**, **Soulières**, and **Villeseneux**. Her purpose was to encourage the work of the Confraternities of Charity in these places on Gondi lands. (Letter 77, 1631)

Lastly, Marguerite de Silly, Madame de Gondi, was also baroness of **Dampierre**. One of her ancestors, Pierre de Lannoy (d. 1523), probably a great-uncle, was buried in the parish church. Only his sarcophagus remains. There is nothing in the church to recall her presence here or that of Vincentians perhaps obligated by the foundation contract of the Congregation to give missions on her lands here. Adjoining the church property is the chateau, a later construction. Its imposing tower and gates, however, date from the fifteenth century.

Vincent de Paul in Montmirail,
parish church, Montmirail

# Franche-Comté

    The works of Vincent de Paul and Louise de Marillac did not extend during their lifetimes to the east of France. Nevertheless, Blessed Jean Henri Gruyer, a martyr of the Revolution, was born here. Saint Jeanne Antide Thouret was also born here and founded her community in Besançon.

"Basilica," Sancey-le-Long

## BESANÇON*

Besancon, a major city of about 125,000 persons, is an ancient fortified site dominated even today by its fortress. It had a bishop as early as the third century, and one of them was Saint Antide, whose name was given to a daughter of a poor country family. **Jeanne Antide Thouret** (1765-1826) sought an active vocation in favor of the poor and so entered the Daughters of Charity in Paris. She remained a Daughter of Charity for eight years until the sisters were dispersed because of the Revolution. After a time of flight and discernment, she began a school, pharmacy and kitchen for the poor of Besançon in 1799. The young women she attracted eventually formed the Sisters of Charity. Their motherhouse, purchased after her time, offers an exhibit about her life and her foundations, as well as a couple of items belonging to Vincent de Paul. *(131, Grande Rue)* Many other places in the city where she opened works for the poor still exist. She died in Naples and is buried there. She was canonized in 1924.

## DOLE

Dole, with about 4000 inhabitants, has no known connection with Vincent. However, **Jean Henri Gruyer** (1734-1792), the future martyr, was born here. Little is known about him. After his ordination as a diocesan priest, he joined the Congregation of the Mission in 1770. He served the two Vincentian parishes in Versailles (Notre Dame and Saint Louis), and when the Constitutional clergy took over the parish, he returned to his home region. In August 1792 he made a trip to Paris and had the bad luck to stay with his confreres at Saint Firmin, where Louis Joseph François was the superior. Just after Gruyer's arrival, a guard was placed at the door, and no one was allowed to leave again. Gruyer was slaughtered with the others, but no one knows how he died or what happened to his body.

The Church beatified him with 190 other martyrs, whose deaths were clearly carried out in hatred of the faith. The ceremony took place in Rome on 17 October 1926.

A monument and plaque in the church of *Notre Dame* preserve his memory. It reads: "To the pious memory of the Servants of God who died for the faith." The first of many to be listed is Gruyer, J.H., "Lazarist, killed in Paris, 2 [3] September 1792." This plaque was erected 9 October 1917.

## SANCEY-LE-LONG*

Hidden in one of the many valleys of the Jura mountains is Sancey-le-Long, birthplace of **Jeanne Antide Thouret**.

The Sisters of Charity have developed a center for pilgrims and guests around the Thouret home, where the future saint may have been born. This sixteenth-century farm has preserved many of the features she knew as a child and later as a refugee from the Revolution. A large "basilica," completed in 1934, is dedicated to her. The parish church where she was baptized venerates a statue of Mary on the Bouchardon model, before which Jeanne Antide prayed and made her vow of chastity following the death of her father. Several other places in the vicinity are also associated with her, such as the grottoes (La Baume) where she hid priests during the Revolution. The village today has a population of about 400.

Saint Jeanne-Antide Thouret

Eighteenth-century statue, Saint-Saturnin (Puy-de-Dôme)

# Lorraine

For centuries Lorraine was independent of France. This is because in 843, Charlemagne, king of the Franks, divided his empire among his three grandsons. Lothar received the center section, and his name, in many different forms, was attached to the area, Lorraine. This important territory was often fought over. In 1552, Henry II of France occupied the "Three Dioceses," that is the ancient cities of Metz, Toul and Verdun, and from that time on Lorraine gradually became integrated into France. Nancy, by contrast, is younger than Metz, Toul and Verdun, but had a more glorious history as the capital of the dukes of Lorraine.

For Vincentian purposes, Lorraine can be treated as a unit, since all parts of it suffered. Wars and a subsequent plague ravaged Lorraine beginning in 1635. Although he was not present himself, Vincent sent many of his confreres, both priests and brothers, to undertake the relief of Lorraine in those plague years. He wrote in 1639 (Letter 376): "With the help of Our Lord, we have undertaken the assistance of the poor people in Lorraine and have sent Messieurs Bécu and Rondet, and Brothers Guillard, Aulent, Baptiste, and Bourdet there, two to each town: Toul, Metz, Verdun, and Nancy. I hope to provide them with two thousand livres a month." He updated this information the following year. (Letter 433) "Brother Mathieu returned from there [Bar-le-Duc] yesterday evening as well as from Metz, Toul, and Verdun, after having sent Nancy its share of the alms. We are continuing to assist those poor people to the amount of five hundred livres per month in each of the above-mentioned towns. But indeed, Monsieur, I greatly fear that we will not be able to keep it up much longer. It is so hard to find twenty-five hundred livres every month." In general, the relief lasted until 1649, with the Vincentians stationed in temporary centers, such as Saint-Mihiel, Bar-le-Duc and Pont-à-Mousson in addition to larger cities.

His charity and good organization were not restricted solely to the province of Lorraine itself. With the help of many others in Paris, he undertook the care of refugees from Lorraine in the capital. Several monuments in Paris recall this aspect of his work.

## METZ

The ancient city of Metz played an important role in Vincent's various ministries. In its earliest phase (1639-1641), he cared for the poor and refugees from the Thirty Years War. A letter from the town magistrates shows how much they appreciated his aid. *You have placed us under so great an obligation by relieving, as you have, the poverty and extreme need of our poor and our beggars, who are uncomplaining and sick, and especially the poor monasteries of nuns in this city, that we would be ungrateful people were we to remain any longer without expressing to you our sentiments about it.* (Letter 492, October 1640) Vincent's help, as they requested, continued for some time.

Anne of Austria spent some weeks in Metz in 1657 and saw with her own eyes the religious and social disorder that reigned here. One of the causes was that for forty years (1612-1652) the "bishop" of Metz was Henri de Bourbon Verneuil (1601-1682), a layman, and the bastard son of Henry IV. This boy never intended to become a priest, let alone a bishop. He received income from the diocese and committed its governance to his auxiliary bishops. When the queen returned to Paris, she asked Vincent to found a house in Metz, but he could not. She suggested that the members of the Tuesday Conferences undertake a major *mission* there, beginning Ash Wednesday of 1658. Vincent proposed this to the members, and sixteen or seventeen went at first, followed by a larger group later. They stayed for two and a half months. At least one Vincentian priest was among them, and two lay brothers

Church door, Basilique Saint Epvre, Nancy

helped care for the missionaries. The renowned Jacques Benigne Bossuet (1627-1704), then a priest of the diocese of Metz, also preached but mainly took care of the details of lodging the missionaries. His correspondence with Vincent offers insight into their work.

One of the positive results of the Metz mission was that the queen paid for the foundation of a house for Vincentians. They came here to open a mission house and then a *seminary* in 1662, a development Vincent had foreseen. The seminary, named Saint Anne in the queen's honor, continued until the Revolution. Only a few remains from Saint Anne are visible. *(19-21, rue de la Fontaine)*

A new major seminary was built in 1745 and still stands near the railway station, between Rue Jean XXIII and Rue Asfeld. The former Jesuit seminary, Saint Simon, was joined administratively to Saint Anne in 1762, at the time of the Jesuit suppression. Formerly a minor seminary, it continued as a major seminary until the Revolution. This house has been in Vincentian hands since 1921 and is a pilgrimage shrine to Saint Jude, since the two apostles Simon and Jude are the parish patrons. *(6, place de France)*

Daughters of Charity, as well, served in the city of Metz in this period, arriving in 1653 to work in the Holy Cross parish. Vincent sent them off with some pointed remarks about the kind of people they would be serving: *To tell the truth, the people [of Metz] are not bad, but the poor souls have a certain grossness of mind in regard to divine things which they have contracted from associating with the Huguenots and Jews who dwell in that city. You are going, therefore, to make known to all, to Catholics, to heretics, and even to Jews, the goodness of God.* (Conference 101) The Sisters also assumed the care of two hospitals (1687, 1699). The Daughters of Charity returned in 1800 and continue their long service here. The city of Metz today numbers some 120,000 persons.

In the suburbs is the town **Longeville-lès-Metz.** This was the birthplace of the redoubtable Jean Baptiste Étienne (1801-1874), Vincentian superior general and regarded by many as its "second" founder, that is, after the Revolution.

Parish church, Ecrouves

## NANCY

Since Vincentians worked in Nancy only briefly, there is little here of Vincentian importance. One small recollection of Vincent's work for the area is found on the carved church doors of the *Basilique Saint Epvre*. These depict the saint, known earlier as "the refuge of the afflicted poor." (Letter 643) The first Catholic parish here began at the end of eleventh century, and Saint Epvre was the church of the dukes and princes of Lorraine. The present church, however, was finished only in 1871. Perhaps because of its historic importance, several heads of state contributed to the successful achievement of the church: such as the emperor of Austria, Franz Josef,

Ludwig of Bavaria, Napoleon III of France, Pope Pius IX, and Victoria, Queen of England.

Vincentians ran the diocesan seminary from 1779 until their expulsion about 1792. This seminary had been the seminary of the Royal Missions, under the care of the Jesuits. It closed in 1768. The Vincentians then took charge of a new seminary in the old buildings and likewise had charge of the parish of Saint Peter (from 1784). Daughters of Charity came here in 1701 to teach school and continued their works after the Revolution, from about 1803. As in many other cities, there is a Saint Vincent de Paul church with fine stained glass windows, and an adjoining street named after him. Prosperous Nancy is today a city of about 100,000 people.

## TOUL

Vincent sent his confreres to the diocese of Toul in 1635. In coming, they succeeded three members of the Order of the Holy Spirit who had a hospice for orphans and the sick. Vincent sent them to give missions and care for ordinands but, since they were succeeding the pre-

Street sign, Toul

vious occupants, the missionaries had to accept a parish, the first in the history of the Congregation, together with the hospice. They soon realized how time-consuming the hospice service was and engaged others to staff it for them. It was large enough to accommodate some 60 poor and sick soldiers during the wars. Today it is difficult to locate the Vincentian house, the former Hôpital du Saint Esprit, but it could have been on the Rue Saint Amand, in what is now a cultural center. Toul suffered terribly in two world wars. Many old buildings have disappeared, but much of its original defensive walls remain. One of the buildings that disappeared was the parish of *Saint Amand*. Only the street name recalls its presence. Vincent and his confreres had much to suffer from other clergy and their friends in the city administration, but the problems were eventually resolved. Daughters of Charity also worked in Toul, beginning in 1707, and they continue their pastoral work here. Today, Toul is a city of some 17,000 inhabitants.

The Vincentians also had care of the church in **Ecrouves**, a short distance northwest of Toul. This parish, together with Saint Amand in Toul, distracted the priests from their main work. Vincent wrote to the superior: *But, Monsieur, what shall we do about those two parishes that are such a great hindrance to you in your work in the rural areas? Can you not find some good vicars? The one in the town could support its man. For the parish in Ecrouves, I prefer that Saint-Lazare give one hundred livres for a few years rather than see you in your present*

*predicament. Please think it over. Do not fail to go there to preach sermons sometimes and visit the sick.* (Letter 1808, 28 November 1654) This old pilgrimage church dominates the town of about 3800 below. There is no souvenir of Vincent or the Vincentians in the church today.

In the parish church of **Crézilles**, a small town south of Toul, are hung four large paintings, originally from the Toul seminary. These are copies of some of the paintings prepared for Vincent's canonization: Vincent at the deathbed of Louis XIII, Vincent preaching, Vincent with the Tuesday Conferences (not the usual depiction), and Vincent preaching to the Ladies of Charity (modeled on the painting of Vincent with the priests and bishops of the Tuesday Conferences, also not the usual depiction). The originals hung in the old Saint Lazare chapel.

## VERDUN

As with Nancy, Verdun had no Vincentian house from the time of the founder. Daughters of Charity worked here from 1693 to the Revolution and afterwards from 1819. They have continued their pastoral work here. The Congregation of the Mission had charge of the *diocesan seminary* from 1928 to 1970. A nineteenth-century altar in the cathedral recalls Saint Vincent as a great benefactor of Lorraine. The city and the surrounding areas suffered greatly during many wars, especially during the two world wars. Verdun today has a population of about 20,000.

Statue by Cabuchet,
Châtillon-sur-Chalaronne

# Rhône-Alpes

*The beautiful countryside of the Rhône river valley and the foothills of the Alps was the area of several Vincentian works: the first Vincentian seminary (Annecy) and the first Confraternity of Charity (Châtillon). It is also the birthplace of figures important in the Vincentian mission: Sister Rosalie Rendu, and the martyr, Saint Francis Regis Clet. Blessed Frédéric Ozanam spent his early years here.*

## ANNECY*

The main religious interest in Annecy, a city of 50,000 persons, is the presence of Saints Francis de Sales (1567-1622) and Jane Frances de Chantal (1572-1641). The *cathedral of Saint Peter*, built only in 1535, records many of their exploits in this mountainous region with its lakes and rivers. Francis de Sales was ordained here, 18 December 1593, and officiated as bishop from 1602 to 1622. Just in front of the cathedral, is the Hôtel Lambert. *(15, rue Jean Jacques Rousseau)* Francis de Sales resided here from 1602 to 1610. He also lived for a while at 18, rue Sainte Claire. Plaques at both addresses recall these details.

The two saints were buried at the church of *Saint Francis de Sales*. This Baroque church, built in 1618, now serves as a church for Italians. The body of Francis de Sales remained in the church from 1623 until 1793. A plaque marks the site, as well as a green ceremonial bishop's hat, hung after the manner of cardinals' red hats. The hat may have belonged to Francis de Sales. The tomb of Jane Frances de Chantal was also in this church from 1641 to 1793. A gilded wooden statue of her over the spot is one of the few to have escaped the iconoclasm of the revolutionaries.

The founders are both buried now at the prominent chapel of the *Visitation convent* on a hill overlooking the city. It was built after 1911. Their modern shrines are in the main chapel, while earlier effigies, with wax face and hands, are on display in a small museum to the side of the church. Saint Vincent de Paul

Dombes, near Châtillon-sur-Chalaronne

appears in one modern window which depicts the activities of Saint Francis de Sales.

The Congregation of the Mission began its mission in Annecy with a mission house. After some time, the Vincentians began a seminary. The *major seminary* of the diocese was built in the 1680s and served as such (interrupted during the Revolution) until 1970. Francis Regis Clet, the future martyr, was a professor here. The present building now houses a library and the local archives. The disused chapel has been converted into an exhibition hall. A plaque in the main corridor commemorates the presence of the seminary. The earlier seminary, the first one directed by the Congregation of the Mission, began in 1642. It is no longer standing.

In the Place aux Bois is a seated *statue* of Saint Francis de Sales, here remembered for his literary work. It was erected in 1924 and stands just in front of the chapel of the second Visitation monastery, erected in 1636 by Jane Frances, and which continued until the Revolution.

## CHÂTILLON-SUR-CHALARONNE***

The town of Châtillon dates from 1273, but the area was inhabited for centuries before. The name Châtillon, meaning "little castle," refers to the one built on the Roman site called *pagus dumbarum*.

Church door, Châtillon-sur-Chalaronne

The remains of the fourteenth-century castle are still visible on the hill above the town. The name of the town in Vincent's day was Châtillon-les-Dombes, that is, the Châtillon at the Dombes, the Dombes being the small ponds left in the region after the glacial period. Most of these ponds lie south and east of the town. The name of the town today means "Châtillon on the Chalaronne," referring to the small river flowing through the town north to the Saône River. The town numbers about 4000 inhabitants, twice the size it was in his time.

Before the town existed there were two parishes in the region, Fleurieux to the west and Buénans to the east. These gradually lost their importance as Châtillon grew. Although Vincent was pastor of Buénans and Châtillon, which depended on Buénans, and was also prior of Fleurieux, he lived in the "newer" town. The distinction between his two churches had little meaning. The Buénans church disappeared in the eighteenth century, and that of Fleurieux at the time of the Revolution. In Vincent's time in Châtillon, formerly part of Bresse, and French only since 1601, its inhabitants mainly spoke Bressan, a franco-provençal dialect that their pastor had to learn.

The chronology of Vincent's few months in Châtillon is spelled out below. All authors agree that his reasons for leaving the Gondi household to come here are unclear, but they point to Madame de Gondi as one of the reasons. It seems very likely that rich, beautiful, powerful, pious, and emotionally needy as she was, Marguerite came to occupy

Old window cover,
Châtillon-sur-Chalaronne

too much of Vincent's time and emotional energy. In addition, he and his two employers were practically of the same age. He wrote, however: *I used to hold it as a maxim to consider the General in God and God in him, and to obey him as God, and his late wife as the Virgin.* (Letter 244) He also noted that one of the qualities that a chaplain in a noble house should have is that "he should be most chaste." (Conference 14) In this dangerous emotional and spiritual mix, the 36-year old priest undoubtedly had to break free to make his own way. He was still nominally the pastor of Clichy, but he undertook to become the pastor of Châtillon as well. Why he came to Châtillon and not somewhere else is probably a question of circumstance: the town needed a pastor and Vincent was

available. The intermediary for getting this information to him was very likely the Oratorian François Bourgoing, who had preceded Vincent at Clichy.

In Châtillon, Vincent founded the Confraternity of Charity. This, the first of his major works, began as a response to a pressing need. He later recounted for the Daughters of Charity what happened here, but the accounts differ in several details. Abelly, his first biographer, adding some details, made the resulting account less clear but more coherent. In any case, Vincent found it necessary to organize the response of the ladies of the parish to similar needs in the future. Besides the confraternity, he also did much good in strengthening priestly life, religious instruction, the proper celebration of the sacraments and generally gave good example of a Christian life.

The most important Vincentian sites in Châtillon are:

(1) *The church of Saint André.* This building dates from the fifteenth cen-

17th century coat-of-arms, Church of Saint André, Châtillon-sur-Chalaronne

Façade, Church of Saint André,
Châtillon-sur-Chalaronne

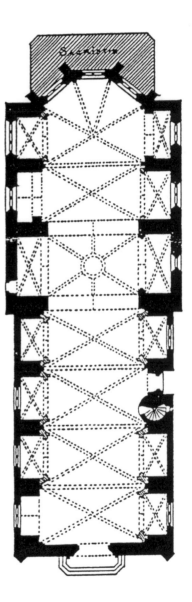

tury but succeeds one or more earlier churches dating from 1272. It is colorful, with its brick façade, clock, rose window, and red tile roof, and it is exceptionally high for a church in this region. A curious octagonal tower (from 1736) encloses the bells.

Inside, it is in Flamboyant Gothic style, but the furnishings (such as the main altar, statues, and organ) represent later styles, after Vincent's time. On either side of the sanctuary and the nave are fourteen chapels, a surprisingly large number, built and decorated by the rich families of the area or by various guilds. Some of

Church floor plan,
Châtillon-sur-Chalaronne

413

Postcard, Chassaigne château,
near Neuville-Les-Dames

these chapels now have other uses, but their existence points to the large number of clergy associated at various times with this church. These clergy were responsible for celebrating weekly or monthly masses for specific intentions, and they lived from the endowments of these chapels. In Vincent's day, about five of these priests lived in Châtillon.

The stained-glass windows in the sanctuary were done in 1890-1892 to commemorate the foundation, in Châtillon, of the first Confraternity of Charity. Other windows recall Vincent's career.

During a renovation of the church undertaken in 1966, some coats-of-arms were brought to light that had not been completely effaced at the time of the Revolution. These show the date 1615, that is, before Vincent's brief pastorate, and designate the La Chassaigne and Bachet de Mizériac families. Collet, Vincent's second biographer, identified Madame de La Chassaigne as the one who urged him to speak about the

needs of the sick poor in his homily. She was one of the first members of the Confraternity of Charity in Châtillon, and her family castle can be seen between Châtillon and the nearby town of *Neuville-Les-Dames*. The present castle, however, dates only from the nineteenth century.

In a space under the roof above the nave, accessible through a stairway opening in the body of the church, is an area used in times past by the many *prêtres sociétaires*. These were the priests whose principal responsibility was to celebrate the canonical hours in church with the pastor, and to say mass occasionally for the departed in one or other of the fourteen side chapels. Mentioned as early as 1433, these clergy were forbidden to exercise certain pastoral min-

Blanchard monument, Church of
Saint André, Châtillon-sur-Chalaronne

istries—those belonged to the official pastor—and they consequently passed their time in some idleness. They used to meet in the upper area, probably for companionship. The windows of this area, however, can be seen from outside the church, on the market side, particularly at night. Tongues wagged in the town, and it was widely, though probably incorrectly, assumed that the priests were engaged in immoral or at least idle pursuits in their upper meeting room, commonly called the Kingdom.

One open question is the use of the rite of Lyons in Châtillon. For centuries, the primatial see of Lyons had its own distinctive usages of the Roman Rite. Whether Vincent followed this usage is unknown. He never referred to it. An old inventory of one of the chapels, however, lists liturgical items proper to this rite, leading to the conclusion that it had been followed here.

(2) *The market.* This seventeenth-century market adjoining the parish church is built mainly of wood. The previous market burned in the town fire of 1670 that also destroyed most of the houses. Its vast roof rests on 32 pillars made from trunks of individual oak trees from a nearby forest. Old houses surround the market-place.

(3) *The former Hospital, with its antique pharmacy.* A hospital (more correctly, a hospice for impoverished pilgrims and beggars) existed here from before 1273. It was restored in 1432, was nearly in ruins in 1614, and was completely rebuilt in 1727. The main stairway is noteworthy. Materials for the rebuilding, including the church bell, were taken from the old church of Buénans, among other places.

Either in the (previous) chapel of this hospital, or in another one, the Chapelle des Pénitents (located just behind the hospital and taken down in 1900), the first Confraternity of Charity was founded on 8 December 1617. Its original membership, in August, consisted of nine women but grew to thirteen by the date of its December founding. Jean Beynier was appointed the treasurer. Besides Vincent, three priests attended, all inhabitants of Châtillon and attached to the parish church. The present chapel was opened in 1732. Inside is a painting of Blessed Vincent de Paul, also dating from 1732. Although not a wonderful work, it testifies to the veneration for him in the town.

Hospital, Châtillon-sur-Chalaronne

Above the main altar is another painting of Vincent bringing the eucharist to a person sick in bed. This rare depiction may have been taken from one of the many copies of the "Lord of Charity," a canvas prepared for the Confraternities of Charity during his lifetime.

The antique pharmacy is maintained as a reminder of how old pharmacies worked. A triptych, painted in 1527, is also on view. It represents, among other things, the burial of Christ, and it was probably in the church in Vincent's day.

A large seated statue of the saint, dating from 1855, is located in the Place St. Vincent de Paul in front of the hospital. The statue, a gift of the Society of Saint Vincent de Paul, bears several inscriptions: "Good people of Châtillon: wherever I go, you will always be present to me before God." "Saint Vincent de Paul, pastor of Châtillon in 1617." "Erected 29 September 185[5]." Inscriptions on the statue itself mention that it was designed by Emilien Cabuchet in 1854; and cast poured by the foundry

Statue by Cabuchet,
Châtillon-sur-Chalaronne

of Eck and Durand in 1855. It was erected with solemn ceremonies 27-29 September 1856. (A marble statue of the same design, dated 1857, is found in the church of Saint Sulpice in Paris.) Behind this square is the former Ursuline convent, founded here in 1639.

(4)  *The home of Vincent de Paul.* By the side of the marketplace stands the house where Vincent lived. This was originally two houses, now joined into one. That on the right was used by the pastor and the *sociétaires*, and that on the left belonged to Jean Beynier, Vincent's host. The priests' residence had been leased to a layman, but Vincent was able to get it back. The effective date of this seems

Home of Vincent de Paul,
Châtillon-sur-Chalaronne

Saint Vincent's staircase,
Châtillon-sur-Chalaronne

Walls of former château,
Châtillon-sur-Chalaronne

to have been 11 November 1617, about a month before he left. His room in Beynier's house has been enlarged and turned into the chapel for the Daughters of Charity. They bought the house and the old adjoining presbytery in 1878 at the urging of the bishop and local pastor. The staircase and certain doors date from Vincent's time. In the chapel are shown facsimiles of the original rule of the Confraternity, signed by him in 1617, and other documents. The large painting on the back wall, completed in 1883, furnished the subject for the main stained glass window in the parish church, depicting the foundation of the Confraternity of Charity. A large painting of the traditional subject of Vincent and the foundlings in the snow, a gift from Napoleon III in 1868, was moved from the church and is now located in the sisters' home. The original of this painting, completed by Nicolas-André Monsiau (1754-1837) about 1817, popularized the pre-revolutionary statue by Stouf and is the source of the common images of Vincent and the children in the snow.

(5) *The castle.* Only the walls and small gates remain of the old brick and stone castle, dating from the 1270s at earliest. Its prominent location above the town looking down onto the valleys of the Relevant and the Chalaronne point to the strategic importance of the town in ages past. Formerly attached to Savoy, this area became part of France in 1601. The castle had been destroyed definitively on 10 May 1595 in the battles leading to a change of government.

Below the castle is an interesting

Priest's residence, Buénans

Historical marker, Buénans

restored building, formerly the old salt stores. It had been a part of the ancient village clustered around the foot of the castle before its charter as a town in 1273.

(6) *The Villars gate*. This ancient gate leads out of the town toward the east and to the city of Villars. Traces of the mechanism for the old draw-bridge are visible. The present gate is the best-preserved piece of military architecture in this region.

(7) *The bridges*. Five small bridges and one covered passageway span the Chalaronne. These have been beauti-fully decorated with flowers in recent summers, and small boats filled with flowers have also been placed in the stream. Châtillon's energies earned it the highest awards in a Europe-wide contest for floral decoration. One new bridge, on the Avenue Clément Desormes, is called the Buénans bridge, inasmuch as it leads to that old settlement.

Doorway, Pérouges

Only a few houses remain in *Buénans*, the principal town where Vincent had been appointed pastor. In his day, the main parish was Saint Martin of Buénans, and its chapel was the Châtillon church. A small plaque on highway D2 recalls Vincent's pastorate, but nothing remains of the church. Its stones were removed in the eighteenth century for other uses. A small farm is confidently pointed out as the residence of their saintly pastor, but no evidence for this exists apart from local tradition. He may have lived here before taking possession of the pastor's house in Châtillon, 11 November 1617. The town of Buénans has ceased to exist.

Eighteenth-century map, Châtillon, Fleurieux and Buenaus

Outside of Châtillon, on D17 to the south, is **Maladières**. In the Middle Ages this was a hospice for lepers, cared for by the Fleurieux parish. It is believed that it was at this small farm that the poor people lived whose sad condition was reported to Vincent. His response, and that of his parishioners, led to the Confraternity of Charity, an organization that still exists in the parish. The present house dates only from the nineteenth century.

Some distance to the east is **Pérouges**, named by Celtic refugees from the Romans homesick for their native Perugia in Italy. In the nineteenth century, the use of home looms declined, the former weavers' houses were unsuitable for farm workers, and the railroads bypassed Pérouges, set on a hill above Meximieux. Consequently, the popula-tion of Pérouges departed, and the town was left as it had been in medieval times. Its rough cobblestone streets and open spaces offered authentic locations for the film *Monsieur Vincent*, for one of the many *Three Musketeers* films, and for others. The Place du Tilleul and the Rue des Rondes in particular are worth visiting. Because of its medieval appearance, the town has decided against allowing many modern elements, such as electric lights and wires, on the fronts of buildings. The parish church of Sainte Marie Madeleine was built at the beginning of the fifteenth century and contains several fine examples of religious sculpture. Despite its museum-like character, Pérouges numbers about 900 people.

Count Balthazar de Rougemont was one of Vincent's notable successes in Châtillon. This aggressive duelist was

## Vincent de Paul in Châtillon

### 1614

*5-7 May: Pastoral visit by the arch-bishop of Lyons, who finds the church and the priests' residences in good repair, although the hospital was in poor condition. There are some 900 parishioners at this time.*

### 1616

*18 October: The archbishop of Lyons writes to Pierre de Bérulle, suggesting that Châtillon be given to the Oratorians. Bérulle, their founder, must have suggested Jean Lourdelot, who became pastor 7 January 1617.*

### 1617

*19 April: Lourdelot resigns his pas-torate of Saint Martin of Buénans and its dependency, Saint André of Châtillon. He does not resign the parish to anyone in particular, but leaves the space blank in the docu-ment for inserting the name of his successor.*

*26 May: Inventory of the furnish-ings of the chapel of the Ladies of the Holy Rosary, perhaps the nucle-us of the Confraternity of Charity. The furnishings of this chapel in the Châtillon church were abundant and in good condition.*

*May-June: The canon-counts of Lyons, temporal lords of Châtillon, again ask the Oratorians to propose a successor. Bérulle suggests Vincent.*

*July: Vincent visits Lyons, asking for information on Châtillon.*

*29 July: Vincent de Paul, "a priest, bachelor in theology, of the diocese of Dax," is named pastor. He remains pastor of Clichy.*

*1 August: Vincent de Paul takes possession of Buénans and Châtillon on a Tuesday afternoon, in the company of two priests asso-ciated with the parish, Jean Besson and Pierre Genoud.*

*August: The town council agrees to pay Vincent and the sociétaires a regular salary.*

*16 August: Louis Giraud (or Girard, his spelling), doctor in the-ology, joins Vincent as his assistant. On the same day, Vincent signs the baptismal register as "curé" for the first time.*

*20 August: Exhortation at Sunday mass in favor of the sick at Maladières. [Probable date]*

*23 August: Charter meeting of the Confraternity of Charity.*

*September: Monsieur de Gondi writes his wife with the news of Vincent's intention not to return to their household.*

*October: Monsieur Du Fresne, sec-retary of Monsieur de Gondi and a friend of Vincent's, comes to ask him to return to Paris. Vincent then goes to Lyons to consult with Monsieur Jean Bence, superior of the Oratorians, as to whether he should leave Châtillon.*

*13 October: Monsieur de Gondi receives a letter from Vincent, written in Lyons, announcing a brief trip to Paris to help him discern his future.*

*24 November: The archbishop of Lyons approves the rules of the Confraternity of Charity (a name taken in imitation of the hospital of Charity in Rome).*

*3 December: Vincent celebrates his last baptism in his parish. (He celebrated only four baptisms during this period; his associate, Girard, did the majority of them.)*

*8 December: Formal establishment of the Confraternity, consisting of twelve noble or bourgeois women, one servant. Election of officers, done in the presence of three priests: Jean Besson, Jean Benonier, and Hugues Rey, sociétaires of the church in Châtillon.*

*12 December: Revision of the rules. Signed: "V. Depaul, curé." Four more members join.*

*15 December: Vincent gives Charlotte de Brie, the treasurer, an account book still in existence. It records the first meeting of the Confraternity.*

*18 December: Vincent leaves the parish to return to Paris.*

*23 December: Vincent reaches Paris, after about five months in Châtillon.*

*1618*
*5 January: Second meeting of the Confraternity of Charity in Châtillon.*

*31 January: Vincent formally resigns as pastor of Châtillon.*

*18 July: Louis Giraud, Vincent's associate, succeeds him as pastor of Buénans and Châtillon.*

converted to religion, lived a very pious life, and sold his Rougemont property for the sake of the poor. He had a castle at *Chandée*, north of **Vandeins**, now a town of 1000 people. Vincent visited him there, where the nobleman recounted the dramatic story of his act of detachment when he smashed his sword against a rock. The ancient castle no longer exists.

East of Vandeins is **Bourg-en-Bresse**, an important city of some 40,000 inhabitants. The Congregation of the Mission had a house here from 1701 to 1791. Its purpose was originally to give retreats for clergy and laity, as well as missions. The founder of the house, a diocesan priest, had been touched by the original inspiration of Vincent, and he sought to bring the advantages of that charism to his region. The house concentrated, in fact, on missions.

Southeast of Châtillon is **Ars-sur-Formans**, the renowned pastorate of Jean Baptiste Marie Vianney (1786-1859), known familiarly as the Curé of

Commemorative painting,
Hôtel de Ville, Châtillon-sur-Chalaronne

Ars. His parish church and residence have been preserved. Although Vincent had nothing to do with Ars, he is venerated here, and Vianney kept engravings of his fellow pastor in his home, where they remain. Today, Ars, like Lourdes, lives off pilgrimages. It has a population of about 900.

## CONFORT, GEX, TOUGIN

Rosalie Rendu (1786-1856) was born at **Confort**, at the time a hamlet in the parish of **Lancrans**. This Daughter of Charity was to have a profound influence on the exercise of charity toward the poor, particularly in relation to Blessed Frédéric Ozanam. Only a single room remains of her family home, now part of the chapel of the retirement home founded under her inspiration in

1860, and which bears her name *(Maison de Retraite Soeur Rosalie)*. During the revolutionary period, her fervent parents risked their lives to shelter priests on the run from the authorities. One of these was the bishop of Annecy who celebrated the eucharist in the basement of a nearby house, at which Rosalie received her first communion. Today, Confort is a hamlet of fewer than 500 people.

Her mother brought her to the hospital of **Gex**, staffed at the time by the Daughters of Charity. Louis XIV founded this hospital for the sick in 1660. The

Baptismal font, Church of
Saint André, Châtillon-sur-Chalaronne

Sketch of Rendu home, Confort

Hospice, Tougin

hospital has since been closed, but its buildings remain. The oldest section was in existence in Rosalie's day.

One of the natives of Gex was Jacques André Emery (1732-1811), superior general of the Society of Saint Sulpice from 1782 until his death. His position helped him to be one of the leaders of French Catholics in the immediate post-Revolutionary period. In Paris, he counseled the young Rosalie in her choice of vocation.

Outside Gex is the hospice of **Tougin**, now a small community hospital. Daughters of Charity worked here in Rosalie's time, continuing a service that began in 1742 or 1743. One of its treasures is a remarkable painting of Saint Vincent. Probably painted before the Revolution, the portrait depicts him grasping the flaming heart of charity—an element borrowed from the iconography associated with Saint Augustine and one of the earliest symbols for Vincent. During the revolution, the sisters put their lives in jeopardy by hiding a priest in their house. He was never discovered. Gex is a small city of about 7000 people,

overlooking Geneva.

Vincentians also served alongside Daughters of Charity in the hospital for the aged in **Musinens** (1869-1903), a hamlet near Confort. The government forced them both out following the anti-clerical laws at the beginning of the century.

## GRENOBLE

This episcopal city of 150,000 was home to *Francis Regis Clet* (1748-1820). He was baptized in the church of *Saint Louis*. This is a building in classical style, built between 1689 and 1701. On the baptistery floor is a memorial plaque: "Here was baptized on 20 August 1748, the Blessed Francis Regis Clet, martyred in China in 1820." His *family home* is still standing. (*Corner of Grande Rue and Rue Diodore Rahout*)

Among many art works in the *cathedral* is a nineteenth-century painting by François Rayneri of Vincent taking the chains of a galley convict. Other saints recalled in the same cathedral are Bruno and the first Carthusian hermits, who received the habit here in 1084, and Jean Baptiste Marie Vianney, ordained at

423

the major seminary in Grenoble, 13 August 1815.

## LYONS**

Lyons, France's second largest city in urban population (420,000), and its third, after Marseilles, in area, has for centuries played a leading role in French life, including its ecclesiastical life. For example, its archbishop, styled the Primate of Gaul, enjoys precedence over all French bishops.

Vincent came here on various occasions. Two certain visits were in July and October 1617, concerning his acceptance and then his resignation of the parish of Châtillon-les-Dombes. He consulted the Oratorian superior. He also certainly passed through Lyons during one or more trips to Marseilles to visit the galleys.

A **Vincentian house**, however, did not exist in Lyons until after Vincent's death, although he had planned to open one. The congregation opened its Lyons foundation in 1668, and it remained until 1791. At approximately the same time as the opening of the house, the province of Lyons began. The Vincentians used the Lyons foundation as a residence for missionaries, a novitiate and scholasticate, as well as for the visitor (provincial superior) of Lyons. Many pre-Revolutionary confreres made their vows here, in particular, Saint Francis Regis Clet, 18 March 1771. He may have celebrated his first mass in the large chapel, but another traditions says it was at Valfleury. At the Revolution, of course, the Vincentians were expelled, and eventually the Brothers of the Christian Schools received the property.

They began their work here in 1839 and remained until their expulsion about 1905. The property, once called the Pensionnat des Frères des Écoles Chrétiennes, keeps its original name on the exterior: Pensionnat des Lazaristes. *(24, montée St. Barthelémy)* Presently, this has become part of the "Centre Scolaire aux Lazaristes," a name which also appears on another part of the institution facing the cathedral. *(3, place Saint Jean)* Regrettably, all references to Saint Vincent de Paul have been removed from the chapel.

One result of the arrival of the Vincentians was that the priests of the diocesan *community of Saint Michael* planned to join the Congregation of the Mission, 12 November 1669. The reason being that both groups were giving missions in the diocese, and it seemed better to unite in a common effort. Ultimately

Church of Saint Louis, Grenoble, nineteenth century engraving

Postcard, "Les Lazaristes," Lyons

Courtyard, "Les Lazaristes," Lyons

only one member, the founder, took vows as a Vincentian. His confreres nevertheless agreed to live as a group among the Vincentians and to follow their rules.

At the *Revolution*, various confreres were executed in Lyons. The city rose against the Convention in Paris and raised a self-defense force of some 20,000. Paris reacted and besieged the doomed city, which fell 9 October 1793. The Paris Committee of Public Safety decreed revenge against Lyons. One among the 2000 citizens killed was Jean Baptiste Nantas, the maternal uncle of Blessed Frédéric Ozanam.

Two Vincentians were also executed here in the aftermath. Louis Guinand, a professor at the Le Mans seminary, was guillotined on 16 January 1794, and Claude Leclerc, age 75, suffered the same fate on 24 February 1794. Other members of the house also suffered for their faith: Louis Verne, Antoine Imbert, Jean Antoine Martin, and André Chambovet. Another figure is the celebrated *Antoine Adrien Lamourette* (1742-1794). He had left the Congregation in 1785 and returned to his diocese. He took the constitutional oath and became the bishop

of Rhône et Loire, that is, of Lyons, in 1791. As the deputy of Lyons, he gave a sensational address to the National Assembly (7 July 1792), in which he tried to reconcile its various factions who should have been united against foreign invaders. They agreed but quickly fell back into factions. Their reconciliation was called a "Lamourette kiss," that is, a hypocritical one. Unwittingly, the Congregation of the Mission has given a by-word to the French language. Lamourette protested against the September massacres, retracted his oath, suffered public humiliation in Lyons, and then was guillotined in Paris, 11

Commemorative plaque,
Church of Saint Nizier, Lyons

Charles Meynier, "Saint Vincent preaching to the Ladies of Charity," cathedral, Lyons

January 1794.

The *cathedral* of Lyons possessed the relic of the heart of Saint Vincent for 155 years. At the time of the Revolution, in 1792, some Vincentians and Daughters of Charity left France for Turin. Among their baggage was a collection of Vincent's correspondence, personal clothing and other relics. Hidden in a cavity in a large volume of the lives of the saints was the reliquary of the saint's heart. The Vincentians in Turin kept this relic until 1805. At that date, Cardinal Joseph Fesch (1763-1839), Napoleon's uncle and archbishop of Lyons, demanded that this relic be returned to France. With great solemnity it was returned that same year, and kept in the Saint Vincent de Paul chapel (now reserved for the Blessed Sacrament). In this chapel, a large painting by Charles Meynier (1768-1832) depicts Saint Vincent preaching to the Ladies of Charity on the care of the orphans. In 1953, Cardinal Gerlier returned the relic to the Daughters of Charity at the Rue du Bac, Paris, where it now remains. The original reliquary, however, is in the treasury of the cathedral. Another item of Vincent's is a set of heavily embroidered vestments, nineteenth century, with embroidery coming from another set that he used. It is occasionally displayed in the treasury.

After the Revolution, another *Vincentian house* began. Although used for some years, it was purchased only in 1873. It principally served as an apostolic school, but other works were carried out as well. This continued until the universal expulsion of congregations in 1903. *(49, montée du Chemin Neuf)* The *Daughters of Charity* began their ministries with works of charity in 1679. Although one sister was imprisoned and others were mistreated during the Revolution, the sisters later returned and opened houses in many of the parishes of the city.

Another Vincentian figure in Lyons is *Blessed Frédéric Ozanam* (1813-1853). Although he was born in Milan, his family brought him back to their native home while he was still a child. At first, they lived in a hotel directly behind the

"Les Lazaristes," Lyons

church of Saint Nizier but, after the death of his sister, the Ozanams moved to the third floor of an apartment building. *(5, rue Pizay)* His parish church, Saint Pierre, is now a part of the Fine Arts museum. *(Place des Terreaux)* He made his First Communion here, and one of his funerals would be held here as well. He received his early education at the Collège Royal, now the Lycée Ampère. *(Rue de la Bourse)* In the church of Saint Bonaventure *(Place des Cordeliers)* at age seventeen, Ozanam consecrated his life to the service of God and others. He often wrote about the old chapel of Notre Dame de Fourvière. Today, a monster church of the same name, begun after the war of 1870, dominates the upper city. Since the seventeenth century both the old and new churches have been a place of pilgrimage and prayer, particularly during various epidemics. In 1836, he was enrolled in the bar at the Palace of Justice, clearly visible from Fourvière. Also visible is the large Hôtel Dieu, the hospital where his father practiced medicine. Both his parents are buried at the cemetery of Loyasse, just west of Fourvière. He married Marie Joséphine Amélie Soulacroix in the church of Saint Nizier, as a commemorative plaque there recalls. He moved to Paris for study and work, and there founded, with several others, the Society of Saint Vincent de Paul. Daughters of Charity taught school in this parish in the nineteenth century.

A person of importance, and close to Ozanam, was *Pauline Marie Jaricot* (1799-1862). This laywoman founded the Society for the Propagation of the Faith, the Living Rosary and many other works. She was also a prime mover in the new Fourvière basilica. She lived between the top of Fourvière and Old Lyons below. *(42, montée Saint Barthelémy)* A small chapel here was founded in 1839. She was buried in the transept of *Saint Nizier* church. Her cause for canonization has been introduced.

## VALFLEURY*

This ancient pilgrimage site at the head of a quiet valley south of Lyons traces its legendary beginnings to about the year 800. According to typical traditions, some children or shepherds discovered a statue of the Virgin Mary and the Child Jesus near a broom shrub *(genêt)* blooming on Christmas Eve. At some point Benedictine monks came here and gave the name Val Fleury ("flowery valley") to this area. They left the statue where it was and built a shrine over a miraculous spring that still runs. The hardwood statue is of Romanesque design, dating to the beginning of the twelfth century. This is a Black Virgin, one of many in France and elsewhere, particularly in Europe. The statue has been cleaned and some of its original polychrome has been discovered.

Notre Dame de Valfleury is first mentioned, however, in 1052, as attached to the monastery of La Chaise Dieu (for *Casa Dei*, "the house of God" in contorted French). Secular clergy replaced the Benedictines in 1485, although they continued to be responsible for pilgrimages until 1687, the date on a plaque in the church.

427

History of Valfleury,
Valfleury

Monument to Jean Baptiste Lugan, Valfleury

Vincentians came here in 1687 to staff the shrine and to give missions in the district. When they were expelled during the Revolution, the statue was hidden. Some of the priests attached to the shrine at that time suffered death for their faith. After 1802 the church was restored to Catholic worship and, through the diligence of Brother Antoine Pierron (1757-1833), the statue was recovered and placed in the church. Brother Pierron was responsible as well for the renewal of the pilgrimage. Only a few carved stones remain from the earlier church. The present church building was begun in 1853 and consecrated in 1866. It was built thanks to the munificence of the Vincentian Jean Baptiste Lugan (1800-1884), pastor from 1840 to 1856, and finished under the pastorate of Father Nicolle (pastor, 1856-1871). Lugan willed his heart to the shrine and this donation has been memorialized in a marble plaque at the Blessed Sacrament altar.

In modern times Our Lady of Valfleury is connected chiefly with the work of the same *Antoine Hippolyte Nicolle* (1817-1890). After his seminary studies and ordination to the diaconate, Nicolle applied to join the Congregation of the Mission. He entered in 1840, was ordained a priest the same year and took his vows in 1842. As part of the devotional life of the time (marked by devotion to the Passion of Jesus expressed in prayerful meditation on his human body, such as the Holy Face, the wounds, the suffering hearts of Jesus and Mary depicted on the Miraculous Medal, and the devotion of the Scapular of the Passion, 1846), Nicolle became attracted to the Holy Agony of Jesus in the garden of Gethsemane. He had been in Tours, and there participated in the nightly adoration of the Blessed Sacrament, something he easily connected with the night vigil of Jesus in Gethsemane.

In his new role he energetically developed the pilgrimages and in 1860 presided over the solemn coronation of the ancient pilgrimage statue. He also encouraged prayers for the Church in its agony at the time (particularly for Pius IX), as well as for the dying. A prayer group was begun, and the devotion to the *Holy Agony* spread rapidly. Nicolle later founded a congregation of sisters of the Holy Agony, now called the Sisters of Christ at Gethsemane. They began officially in 1864 when he clothed the first religious. Their work concentrates on care of the sick and dying. Nicolle remained as their ecclesiastical superior, but the sisters are independent of the Daughters of Charity, the Congregation of the Mission, and the Holy Agony devotion. The central house for the Archconfraternity of the Holy Agony is the Vincentian motherhouse in Paris, and its director is the Vincentian superior general.

Father Nicolle began the new community of sisters in the *crypt chapel* of the shrine. The crypt has various plaques concerning the erection of the Archconfraternity of the Holy Agony and of the sisters. The seventeenth-century statue of Notre Dame de Cry, noted for her black face, has recently been restored and replaced here.

Nicolle built a large *way of the cross* on the property, together with a Calvary grotto. Following the fourteenth station, a chapel memorializes the dead of the two world wars. There are also some curious grotto-like structures flanking the property, probably intended as stopping places for pilgrims. High on a hillside overlooking the valley is another series of structures, the mysteries of the rosary laid out like the way of the cross.

Since Vincentians have been here, with some gaps, since 1687, Valfleury can claim the title of being the oldest Vincentian house in France, although

Vincentian house,
Valfleury

Shrine church,
Valfleury

the buildings are much newer. Daughters of Charity worked in the hospital, still standing, from 1872. The present town numbers about 500 people.

In the nearby city of **Saint-Étienne** Daughters of Charity began multiple works of charity and education in the 1830s. Although there was no Vincentian house, *Jean Félix Cayla de la Garde*, superior general at the time of the Revolution, was forced to hide here. He eventually escaped to the Palatinate and then to Rome, where he died in 1800.

## KINGS, EMPERORS, REPUBLICS, 1589-1940

### BOURBON LINE

| | |
|---|---|
| Henry IV | 1589-1610 |
| Louis XIII | 1610-1643 |
| Louis XIV | 1643-1715 |
| Louis XV | 1715-1774 |
| Louis XVI | 1774-1793 |
| Louis XVIII | 1815-1824 |
| Charles X | 1824-1830 |

### ORLEANS LINE

| | |
|---|---|
| Louis-Philippe | 1830-1848 |

### BONAPARTE EMPERORS

| | |
|---|---|
| Napoleon I | 1804-1815 |
| Napoleon III | 1852-1870 |

### REVOLUTIONARY GOVERNMENTS, REPUBLICS

| | |
|---|---|
| First Republic | 1792-1804 |
| *National Convention* | *1792-1795* |
| *Directory* | *1795-1799* |
| *Consulate* | *1799-1804* |
| Second Republic | 1848-1852 |
| Third Republic | 1870-1940 |

## BISHOPS AND ARCHBISHOPS OF PARIS, 1569-1848

| | |
|---|---|
| Pierre de Gondi, cardinal | 1569-1598 |
| Henri de Gondi, cardinal | 1598-1622 |
| Jean-François de Gondi, first archbishop | 1622-1654 |
| Jean-François Paul de Gondi, cardinal | 1654-1662 |
| Pierre de Marca | 1662 |
| Hardouin de Péréfixe de Beaumont | 1664-1671 |
| François Harlay de Champvallon | 1671-1695 |
| Louis-Antoine de Noailles, cardinal | 1695-1729 |
| Charles Gaspard Guillaume de Vintimille du Luc | 1729-1746 |
| Jacques Bonne Gigault de Bellefonds | 1746 |
| Christophe de Beaumont de Repaire | 1746-1781 |
| Antoine Léonor Leclerc de Juigné | 1781-1801 |
| *Jean-Baptiste Joseph Gobel | 1791-1794 |
| *Jean-Baptiste Royer | 1798-1801 |
| Jean-Baptiste de Belloy, cardinal | 1802-1808 |
| Jean Siffrein Maury | 1810-1817 |
| Alexandre Angélique de Talleyrand-Périgord, cardinal | 1817-1821 |
| Hyacinthe Louis de Quélen | 1821-1839 |
| Denis Auguste Affre | 1840-1848 |

* Constitutional bishops

# SUPERIORS GENERAL AND FRENCH VICARS GENERAL OF THE CONGREGATION OF THE MISSION (1625-1939)

| SUPERIORS GENERAL | 1625-1800 |
|---|---|
| Vincent de Paul | 1625-1660 |
| René Alméras | 1661-1672 |
| Edme Jolly | 1673-1697 |
| Nicolas Pierron | 1697-1703 |
| François Watel | 1703-1710 |
| Jean Bonnet | 1711-1735 |
| Jean Couty | 1736-1746 |
| Louis de Bras | 1747-1761 |
| Antoine Jacquier | 1762-1787 |
| Jean Félix Cayla de la Garde | 1788-1800 |

| FRENCH VICARS GENERAL | 1800-1827 |
|---|---|
| François Brunet | 1800-1806 |
| Claude Joseph Placiard | 1806-1807 |
| Dominique Hanon | 1807-1816 |
| Charles Verbert | 1816-1819 |
| Charles Boujard | 1819-1827 |

| SUPERIORS GENERAL | 1827-1939 |
|---|---|
| Pierre de Wailly | 1827-1828 |
| Dominique Salhorgne | 1829-1835 |
| Jean-Baptiste Nozo | 1835-1842 |
| Jean-Baptiste Etienne | 1843-1874 |
| Eugène Boré | 1874-1878 |
| Antoine Fiat | 1878-1814 |
| Emile Villette | 1914-1916 |
| François Verdier | 1919-1933 |
| Charles-Léon Souvay | 1933-1939 |

## D

## H

**M**

## W

## Z

REV. JOHN E. RYBOLT, C.M., Ph.D., completed his seminary studies at the Vincentian seminary in Perryville, Missouri, and at De Andreis Seminary in Lemont, Illinois. He received a doctorate in biblical studies from Saint Louis University. He has taught in Vincentian seminaries in Saint Louis, Lemont, and Denver. He worked for the provincial of the Midwest Province from 1979 to 1981. He joined the board of trustees of DePaul University in 1981 and is currently a life trustee. He also served as a delegate from the Midwest Province to the international general assemblies of the Congregation in 1980, 1986, 1998 and 2004, and managed the archives of the province from 1980 to 1989. Fr. Rybolt served as the director of the International Formation Center, a program for ongoing Vincentian education and formation in Paris, France, from 1994 to 2003. Currently, he is serving as a Vincentian Scholar in Residence at DePaul University. Since 1979 he has been involved in the Vincentian Studies Institute, which he headed from 1982 to 1991. His publications have covered fields of interest in language, biblical studies and history, particularly Vincentian history.